Dude Ranching

Dude Ranching
A Complete History

Lawrence R. Borne

University of New Mexico Press / Albuquerque

Library of Congress Cataloging in Publication Data

Borne, Lawrence R.
   Dude ranching.

   Bibliography: p.
   Includes index.
   1. Dude ranches—West (U.S.)—History.   2. Dude
ranches—Rocky Mountains Region—History.   I. Title.
GV198.96.W47B67   1983   796.5′6   83-14773
ISBN 0-8263-0684-5

Library of Congress Catalog Card Number 83-14773.
International Standard Book Number 0-8263-0684-5.
Manufactured in the United States of America.
First Edition

Design: B. Jellow

This book is dedicated to my parents,
Harold and Madeline Borne.

Contents

Illustrations

Preface

The story of dude ranching is one that should have been told many years ago. This unique industry has played a significant role in the development of several western states—a role few people have appreciated or even mentioned.

Dude Ranching tells the story of many of the personalities and families who developed dude ranching, the appeal of the West for outsiders, and the relationship that existed between ranchers and their guests. It is also a story of conservation and transportation, for these two subjects were of immense importance to dude ranchers. It is not, however, an economic history; very few ranches have made their records available for research, and detailed statistics were not gathered by governmental units during the peak years of dude ranch activity. Thus, it is not possible to show the exact importance of this industry in the economy, either of the whole United States, or of any specific state. Some figures are available showing the income that ranches generated and the money that guests spent; these dollar amounts are noted in the text as indicators of the significance of dude ranching. The voluminous number of references to dude ranches in the early twentieth century also indicates their importance, but it must be emphasized that no detailed, statistical story will be found here.

While this lack of complete economic data is regrettable, it is perhaps appropriate in one way; dude ranching was always a very individualistic enterprise and it seems apt that we cannot reduce it to charts, facts, and figures. Nevertheless, the author does hope that this book may show ranchers the importance of their records and that additional ranchers will open theirs to researchers.

This study examines the development of dude ranching in the nineteenth century, its great success in the early twentieth century, and its continuing history and problems to the present. The stronghold of this industry has been in the Rocky Mountain states of Wyoming, Montana, Colorado, Arizona, and New Mexico; it has also been of some importance in Idaho, Oregon, Washington, Texas, California, and Nevada. It has had little long-lasting impact in the other western states. Wyoming, Montana, and Colorado were similar to each other because of the large number of stock ranches in these states and also because of their climate. Long winters and heavy snowfall limited most dude ranch activity to a short season from May to September. These three states, therefore, are often grouped together and referred to as the northern dude ranch states. Idaho, Oregon, and Washington resembled them. Arizona and New Mexico became more popular as winter, or year-round, vacation spots because of their warmer climate; they are generally discussed together and called the southern dude ranch states. Texas, California, and Nevada were similar to them.

Of course, it has not been possible to tell the story of, or even to mention, every dude ranch that has existed. Even some of the older ranches that are familiar to people in the industry have received little or no mention here. This has occurred, not only because of space limitations, but also because of a lack of sufficient historical data about them. Many are mentioned only as members of organizations, in lists of dude ranches, or in their own brochures; these scattered references have not been sufficient to trace their history or tell their story.

One important part of this study that requires additional explanation is the relationship between dude ranches and the federal government. Many ranches, especially in the northern states, were established near areas that were, or would become, national forests or national parks. Ranchers and their guests often utilized this federally controlled land and thus there was much contact between them and federal officials. The relationship was generally a cordial one in the early years; however, in the last thirty years this relationship has often been antagonistic, especially between ranchers and the National Park Service. The conflicts that are mentioned are not meant to be criticism of any officials in the National Park Service or the National Forest Service; all officials that the author has contacted have been helpful and cooperative in supplying information. But serious problems do exist; certain policies have caused ranchers great harm. These policies have destroyed numerous ranches and have had negative results for the general public. Thus, while there are no visible villains in this story, there are some identifiable victims.

Finally, I would like to note that, while I have made this story as complete as possible, I am quite aware that this is not the last word on the subject. Even as this book is going to press, the author has learned that two individuals in Wyoming are writing books on dude ranches in their vicinity. One will detail those in the Wind River region (Dubois) and the other will cover those near Sheridan and Buffalo. The latter book will contain an especially important analysis of the significance of dudes who later moved to Wyoming. It will show the hundreds of dudes who returned to the West, their contributions to the area, and the economic impact they had; it will also emphasize the importance of Eatons' Ranch in the Sheridan region. Besides these books, it is possible that more ranch records will be made available and more data may be unearthed by persistent digging in various archives and documents. Dude ranching is a rich field that merits further exploration and investigation.

Acknowledgments

This study of dude ranching has been possible only because of the friendly assistance and cooperation of many people. I wish to thank all of them. I apologize if I have inadvertently omitted anyone. Of course, any errors or interpretations in the book are the sole responsibility of the author.

The idea for a book on the history of dude ranching originated with Dr. Clifford P. Westermeier, now retired from the Department of History at the University of Colorado. Professor Westermeier's extensive research on the American cowboy convinced him that dude ranching was a topic that deserved serious study. I am grateful to him for suggesting the idea and for encouraging my research in this field. I also received early encouragment for this work from Dr. Robert G. Athearn, also of the University of Colorado, and Dr. John Guice, of the University of Southern Mississippi; I thank them for their support and for pointing me in some of the right directions. Dr. H. Lew Wallace, as chairman of the Department of History at Northern Kentucky University, did much to smooth my path as I ventured into an uncharted field; his help is greatly appreciated. I would also like to thank the members of the Academic Affairs Committee and various administrative officials at Northern Kentucky University; the grants that I received through their assistance enabled me to do some of this research.

As far as the gathering of the material, I must pay special tribute to Mary Ellen Rutledge and Mary Kelm, librarians at Northern Kentucky University. They processed an enormous number of interlibrary loan requests and they made special efforts to obtain nearly everything I requested. Their help was indispensable in obtaining articles, books, theses, and other material needed for the completion of this book.

I wish to thank the following people, as well as the members of their staffs, for their assistance while I worked in their collections and/or when I requested additional material from afar:

At the Western History Research Center, University of Wyoming, Director Gene Gressley, and research historians Emmett Chisum, David Crosson, and Charles Roundy; and a special note of thanks to Charles Roundy for gathering a great deal of information about dude ranching. Mrs. Eleanor M. Gehres at the western history department, Denver Public Library; Mrs. Katherine Halverson at the Wyoming State Archives and Historical Department in Cheyenne. Mr. P. W. Stafford, public relations department at the Burlington Northern in St. Paul; he opened the company files to me and generously furnished me with many photographs. Michael Kelly, librarian and archivist at the Buffalo Bill Historical Center in Cody; Lois Olsrud, reference librarian at the University of Arizona, Tucson; Duane Swanson at the Minnesota Historical Society in St. Paul; Mrs. Harriett C. Meloy of the Montana Historical Society in Helena; Mrs. Teri Cestnik at the University of Montana Library in Missoula; the staff at the State Historical Society of Colorado in Denver; the various officials I have contacted in the National Park Service and National Forest Service. My thanks also go to Joe Ruh, who made copies of many of the photographs used in the book, and to Debbie Chism and Ellen Curtin, who typed the bulk of this manuscript.

The nature of this study meant that it was necessary to obtain information directly from ranchers. I wish to thank all of those people who are, or were, in dude ranching for answering my letters, questionnaires, requests for literature, and telephone queries. Even though many of their answers have not been specifically cited, all were read and they helped give me the background data required for the fascinating story of dude ranching. The names of many of these people, or their ranches, are listed in the bibliography. However, I want to emphasize that Mrs. Peggy Schaffer of the Dude Ranchers' Association has regularly aided me over the years; her assistance has been invaluable. I am also especially grateful to those ranch owners who have made their records available through various libraries and archives.

I owe a unique debt to ranchers Jim Murphy, Lynn Gillham, and Johnnie Holzwarth, who hired me to work on their ranches. They helped me learn much about dude ranching that can be discovered only from personal contact with guests and ranch work. And I will always be grateful to Johnnie Holzwarth and Frank Wright for opening up to me the incredible world of high-country horseback riding; there are no words to describe adequately the sights and experiences I have enjoyed because of the opportunities they made available. I shall never regret having taken those opportunities.

And finally, I want to thank my trail partners who shared with me those sights and experiences on our many rides. Some of them were experienced horsemen and others were novices, but all were fine companions as we journeyed over or through sunny meadows, snow banks, dark woods, fields of wildflowers, rainstorms, hailstorms, rock slides, mountain passes, and hard-to-find trails. To Glenn and Vickie, Noelie, Barb, Bo, Bob, and many more, I say simply, may we meet again on the trail.

Abbreviations

The following abbreviations are used in the notes and the text. All brochures that are mentioned in the notes are in the author's possession unless otherwise indicated.

C. C. Moore, DPL   Charles Cornell Moore Memorial Collection, Western History Department, Denver Public Library

CD & GRA   Colorado Dude and Guest Ranch Association

CGR WHRC UW   Charles G. Roundy Collection, Western History Research Center, University of Wyoming, Laramie

DPL   Western History Department, Denver Public Library

DRA   Dude Ranchers' Association

DRA Minutes   Variously titled accounts of annual DRA meetings, found in DPL, WHRC UW, Wyo.S.A., and *The Dude Rancher*

HH RMNP   Holzwarth Homestead Cabins, Rocky Mountain National Park, Colorado

IHL BBHC   Irving H. (Larry) Larom Manuscript Collection, Buffalo Bill Historical Center, Cody, Wyoming

MHS   Minnesota Historical Society, St. Paul, Minnesota

NPRCR   Northern Pacific Railway Company Records

WHRC UW   Western History Research Center, University of Wyoming, Laramie

Wyo.S.A.   Wyoming State Archives and Historical Department, Cheyenne

ONE

The Unknown Pioneer

Although a part of American life for nearly eighty years, the dude
ranch has remained a cultural orphan, neglected by historians and
journalists alike.
                    —Jerome L. Rodnitzky, "Recapturing the West:
                        The Dude Ranch in American Life," 111.

The dude ranch is the single most unique contribution of the Rocky
Mountain West to the ever-growing national vacation industry.
        —Charles G. Roundy, "The Origins and Early Development
                            of Dude Ranching in Wyoming," 5.

The Union Pacific locomotive sped south from the station at Butte, its bright
light cutting through the blackness of the night. Just a mile from the Idaho
border the train slowed and halted at the small station marked "Monida." One
teen-aged passenger emerged, and the porter put his bags on the platform. The
train edged forward, quickly picked up speed, and soon vanished into the Montana night. The young man looked around but saw little. The Monida station
was merely a platform and a small building, dark and locked tight. The only
visible light was about a hundred yards away, across an automobile road; he
picked up his bags, crossed the road, and entered a building that was a small
hotel and bar. Someone from the 7L Ranch was supposed to meet the newcomer,
but the bartender said no one from the ranch had arrived. The young passenger
sat on a bench and waited; ten minutes later a station wagon drove up, and a

1

man wearing cowboy boots, jeans, a western shirt, and a broadbrimmed hat walked in. He introduced himself as Andy Forsythe from the 7L Ranch; after they packed the luggage in the car, the young man slid into the seat, and Mr. Forsythe turned the automobile east toward the ranch.

One more easterner had arrived in the West by train and was about to be introduced to a dude ranch. It was, of course, quite appropriate for this young man to come to Montana via the railroad. The railroads had opened the West to thousands of people; their importance is well known, and numerous historians have told the story of the Union Pacific and other western lines. But the other part of this visitor's introduction, the dude ranch, is less well known; its story has never been told in detail.

The two quotations at the beginning of this chapter summarize the enigma of dude ranching. One of the most important contributors to the vacation industry in the West has been sadly neglected by historians. Of the considerable research on outdoor recreation in America, most has been about government, rather than private, involvement, and much of it has been done by government agencies.[1] Federal, state, and local branches of government have assumed a great deal of responsibility in the field of outdoor recreation, and many studies have naturally focused on their actions. An indication of government dominance is the tremendous amount of federally controlled land—over one-third of all land in the United States, and far larger percentages in the West where dude ranching has been prominent.[2]

And yet private recreation clearly preceded federal programs in the West and dude ranching preceded most federal laws, rules, regulations, and tracts set aside for recreational use. Why then have historians continually neglected this fertile area? One reason is simply the lack of statistical data. The statistics that could have shown the interrelationships and importance of different parts of the economy were not compiled at the end of the nineteenth century and beginning of the twentieth century—the years when dude ranching began, grew, and thrived.[3]

But it is not just lack of detailed statistics on the economy that has proved a major barrier to the study of dude ranches; it is also the scarcity of all types of records. Dude ranchers did not publicize their business much in the early years of their development. Because of the nature of dude ranching as a host-guest relationship, ranchers tended to avoid public scrutiny of their activities even when the business grew more important to them; they preferred the personal contact and exchange of references that suited the concept of having a guest in the rancher's home. Besides this restraint there is also some doubt whether many of the dude ranches even kept detailed records of their operation. Many of those that eventually went out of business apparently destroyed whatever records they had, although some may still be hidden away. Those ranches that have continued to operate have, with very few exceptions, been reluctant to allow researchers access to their records. One can certainly sympathize with the dude rancher who is averse to releasing records that contain the names and addresses of all his guests or who wearies of answering a seemingly endless series of questions from students and other curious people. But the lack of records and data has obscured the importance and significance of dude ranches, and public officials have often slighted them and their interests when formulating public policies that have affected their business. Even when dude ranch records have been in libraries, there have been other problems. Most ranch brochures, whether published by ranches or railroads, have not been dated. Researchers have also been frustrated at times in trying to get permission to use these records. For instance, the family has refused access to a set of papers belonging to a former Montana rancher in the archives of the Montana Historical Society; these include fifteen interesting diaries, many of them illustrated with skillfully drawn sketches of events mentioned in the diaries. And at the University of Wyoming there are recorded interviews of many people connected with dude ranching. But some of these people also refuse to allow this material to be quoted or used.

Thus historians have faced severe difficulties in locating enough data to piece together the interesting and important story of dude ranching. One of the first articles by a historian on the subject was published in 1968, "Recapturing the West: The Dude Ranch in American Life," by Jerome L. Rodnitzky. Another large step forward in this field occurred in 1972 when Charles Roundy of the Western History Research Center at the University of Wyoming became interested in the topic. Asked to deliver a paper at Colorado State University in Fort Collins, he chose dude ranches and began collecting data. His paper was later published in the *Annals of Wyoming;* he also spoke to the annual convention of the Dude Ranchers' Association and urged its members to gather more information and to donate their records to the University of Wyoming. Roundy was successful in bringing many important records to the university. Jerome Rodnitzky and Charles Roundy thus deserve recognition as pioneers in this study.[4] A few other scholars have shown interest in dude ranching, and at least three theses were written in the 1970s that covered some aspect of this topic.[5] Gradually more ranch records are also becoming available.

Difficulties remain, however, and one of the most basic of these is the definition of the dude ranch. Part of this problem is the word *dude.* It has developed a number of strange meanings in modern urban slang, and, before this, it had often had derogatory connotations. To some people it has implied a tenderfoot, a greenhorn, or someone who dressed in outlandish clothing. While some dudes did indeed fit into one or more of these categories, the word meant something far different when used by westerners in this newly developed industry. A dude was simply someone from another area who came to the West and paid for food, lodging, riding, and/or guiding services.[6] This is the meaning used throughout this book, with no derogatory connotation ever implied. The word *dude* is discussed further in Chapter 3.

Given this definition, the phrase *dude ranch* is narrowed down somewhat but not completely. Some people have differentiated between *dude ranch* and *guest ranch* with the latter considered a bit more elaborate than the former.[7] Generally *dude ranch* has been more common in the northern Rockies and *guest ranch* in the Southwest, but both phrases have been used throughout the western states; no distinction is made in this work and both are used interchangeably. The dude ranch was legally defined once; in Wyoming the 1937 legislature exempted certain businesses, including dude ranches, from the unemployment compensation tax. But then it was necessary to define them to prevent resorts, tourist camps, and other places from trying to evade the tax. After much consultation and study the Wyoming officials finally defined a dude ranch as "a ranch offering accommodations, entertainment, and participation in regular ranch activities to guests for a monetary consideration."[8]

The definition is clear but, unfortunately, does not cover enough ground; the obvious problem still is defining what a ranch is. Generally, the word *ranch* has meant a place that raised a large amount of livestock. Most early dude ranches did raise cattle, sheep, or horses, yet some of the very earliest ones had no stock other than the horses that the ranch workers and dudes rode. As they developed, certain characteristics have been considered the most important features of a dude ranch: (1) It was generally the year-round home of the owner where the visitor was considered a guest; (2) it was located in western North America, usually in the United States but occasionally in Canada; (3) it offered food, lodging, and horseback riding, most often at one price (i.e., the American Plan); (4) in location or in its outdoor activities it was remote from crowded areas; (5) its main activities have been horseback riding, fishing, hiking, hunting, sightseeing, and ranch work, although few of these activities were regimented and none mandatory; simple relaxation was always an option for the dude; (6) reservations were required, and transient trade was refused or formed little of the ranch's business; (7) atmosphere was the key ingredient; it was informal in manners and dress, people were on a first-name basis, hospitality was genuine, and guests did things together as part of a ranch family.[9]

Obviously the dude or guest ranch was and is difficult to define; yet the experienced rancher or dude could tell in a short time whether a place was a ranch or a resort. The intangible factors of atmosphere and the personalities of the owners clearly distinguished the ranch. It was a place where the owners were personally interested in the guests' activities and enjoyment. A resort was a place where a person did as he or she chose; a ranch was someone's home where the dude temporarily joined the family and became a part of the ranch. In recent years additional criteria have been added, stating what ranches don't have. Modern dude ranches have no public bar, no sauna, no highway advertising, and generally no swimming pool or tennis court—all of which are common at resorts.

Another distinction must be made for a clear understanding of dude ranching. This is the difference emphasized by Daniel Boorstin between the words *traveler* and *tourist*. As he has pointed out, the character of travel changed in the nineteenth century, and these two words symbolized the change. The traveler was an active man or woman who suffered distress and inconveniences in order to travel; the relationship of *travel* to *travail* emphasizes this concept. Travel required effort; it was difficult and sometimes even dangerous. The tourist, on the other hand, was someone who made a pleasure trip; he was passive, expecting things to happen to him, and wanting no inconveniences or difficulty along the way.[10]

The history and development of dude ranching illustrate these two concepts very well. The early dudes, like Isabella Bird and Theodore Roosevelt, endured considerable inconveniences and tribulations as they worked to enjoy the sights and pleasures of the West. But this work made their enjoyment all the greater. The idea of travel (travail) continued for years in dude ranching; even with improvements in transportation and living facilities, the dude of the early twentieth century resented many improvements or conveniences. Yet along the way the dude did change and became a tourist. So much money was supposed to buy so many days of excitement or adventure or western happenings, and a fake atmosphere was sometimes created to satisfy these expectations. This change clearly occurred, but the guest or dude at a real ranch has always remained, at least partly, a traveler. Dudes have always generated their own entertainment and taken an active part in western activities. It is a matter of some debate whether this role will be retained or whether it must disappear with the relentless advance of "progress."

Besides preserving some part of the original meaning of "travel," dude ranching has been significant in other ways. Probably the most important is the new viewpoint that the dude rancher or dude wrangler brought to the West. Unlike any previous group, the dude rancher saw that the land had value for recreation and especially for its scenic beauty.[11] Mary Roberts Rinehart once stated that there were four great migrations to the West: Indians and buffaloes, pioneers and soldiers, cattle and cowpunchers, and dudes.[12] Many may take issue with her simple categorization of the western movement but there is a great deal of significance and thought in including that fourth category. The dude symbolizes a very important part of western history—the infusion of outside capital to stimulate growth. Outside money, of course, had come to the West from other sources, including mining, the U.S. Army, and the cattle industry. But dude ranching was a significant addition to these, and it brought in needed income at some very crucial times to rejuvenate certain ranches in the West. It also brought in new citizens, for enthusiastic dudes often returned to the West to stay; the presence of these newcomers meant there were more ambitious people in the territory or state who brought in new money to develop productive ranches which then added to the wealth of the area for years. The economic effects of dude ranching percolated through the entire economy as dude ranchers helped make the Rocky Mountain West well known throughout the rest of the country.

It is no exaggeration to say dude ranching was the origin of the vacation industry in some western states, especially in Montana and Wyoming; later it had similar positive and substantial effects in Colorado, Arizona, and New Mexico. While few people realize it, dude ranches can be considered the grandparents of most of the resorts, lodges, and inns throughout the Rockies.[13] Dude ranches sprang from the same origins as outfitters and anyone else who has launched pack trips in the Rockies; dude ranchers and outfitters are at least first cousins and maybe even brothers who just took a different turn on the road decades ago.

While there is no institution in American history quite like the dude ranch, there are some intriguing similarities between the dude ranches of the northern Rockies and some of the vacation developments in Maine. Early Maine farmers took guests into their homes much as ranchers did; the ranchers and the farmers both drew from the same regions of the East, the same social strata, and sometimes even the same people. And, in what seems like a remarkable coincidence, the Rockefeller family bought land in both Wyoming and Maine and turned it over to the federal government so it could create or add to national parks (Grand Teton and Acadia).[14] Whatever future investigations might reveal about farmers and the vacation development in Maine, it is clear that dude ranching was a chief factor in bringing tourists (or travelers) to the West and in initiating a major industry.

Two other aspects of dude ranching also merit special attention. One was the great importance of women in the industry. Both as guests and as managers or owners, women were consistently active in the operation of dude ranches. While men were, not unexpectedly, mentioned more frequently as dude ranchers, there was no doubt in the minds of people familiar with the industry that women were an integral and indispensable part of dude or guest ranch success. And, after dude ranching began to grow, women were just as frequent guests as men on the ranches.[15]

Another part of dude ranchers' activities that merits attention is their constant involvement in conservation activities. Long before the word *ecology* came into popular use, dude ranchers were keenly aware of man's interrelationship with the environment and of the need to protect it. Their love of the land, of the animals, and of the outdoor life was often a key factor in their desire to be ranchers, and they knew that misuse of the land, especially in the West, could mean permanent damage to it.[16]

But the most important thing about dude ranchers is that they were pioneers in the West. Some may object to this designation since they came much later than the mountain men, miners, soldiers, and cattlemen, but they do date back further than most people realize—at least to the 1880s and possibly to the 1870s. Isabella Bird visited Colorado during the panic year of 1873 and climbed Long's Peak just five years after it had first been ascended. The Eaton brothers established their Custer Trail Ranch in Dakota Territory in 1879, just three years after the Battle of the Little Big Horn. Charles Moore grew up at Fort Washakie in Wyoming Territory where he learned to speak the Shoshone and Arapaho languages, and he said he remembered the visit of President Chester Arthur in 1883 on his journey to Yellowstone Park. Dude ranchers introduced both Theodore Roosevelt and Owen Wister to the West before either man was famous. Larry Larom was a neighbor and friend of Buffalo Bill Cody, and dude ranching antedates all the national parks in the West except Yellowstone.

Dude ranchers have thus been around for many decades although they certainly were later than most recognized pioneer groups. But they were still pioneers. They saw the wildness of the West as something beautiful and intriguing that should be preserved. It was valuable for its own sake and it could be enjoyable to others who would travel far to see it. Some people understood this pioneering role and stated it clearly; in 1929 a Wyoming state official, L. L. Newton, told some of the early dude ranchers that the day would come when they could look back on their lives and say:

> Well we pioneered this great work. We were the ones who started
> this thing going. We were the ones who blazed the trail. We
> found the road that leads to a greater development of our splendid
> western country.[17]

And so they did. These ranches grew slowly in the last quarter of the nineteenth century. They became more clearly defined in the first years of the twentieth century as industrialization and urbanization created both a desire in the East to visit the West and also a middle-class group of people who had the time and money for summer vacations.[18] Stimulated by World War I and other factors, dude ranches then entered the boom era of the 1920s; this was a decade of tremendous growth during which their importance was most clearly seen. The Great Depression affected them severely, but many survived and another era of relative prosperity came to them in the late 1930s. Business slowed again during World War II, although many continued to adapt to a fluctuating economy and other changing conditions. After 1945 there was another spurt of growth in some states, but the changes brought by the war gradually shoved dude ranches into the background of the burgeoning vacation and recreation business.[19]

In short, the dude was someone who went to the West and paid for his food, lodging, horse, and guide services. The dude rancher or wrangler was the man who furnished these items, and the dude ranch was his home. The story has no exact date of birth since a variety of factors developed and finally converged to set the stage for something new on the American scene—the dude ranch.

TWO

The True America

The Alps, from the Lombard Plains, are the finest mountain panorama I ever saw, but not equal to this [the Rockies in Colorado];
for not only do five high-peaked giants, each nearly the height of
Mont Blanc, lift their dazzling summits above the lower ranges, but
the expanse of mountains is so vast, and the whole lie in a transparent
medium of the richest blue, not haze—something peculiar to the
region.
> —Isabella Bird, *A Lady's Life in the Rocky Mountains*, 33.

I feel more certainly than ever, that no matter how completely the
East may be the head waters from which the West has flown and is
flowing, it won't be a century before the West is simply the true
America with thought, type, and life of its own kind.
> —Owen Wister's Notebook, July 10, 1885.

Dude ranching did not begin at a specific time and then simply grow into a large
industry. It developed slowly from several divergent sources in different locales
and varying circumstances and then gradually assumed a definite and identifiable
form.

One of these sources is simply the general appeal of the Rocky Mountains and
western plains country. To trace this appeal to an absolute beginning point is,
of course, impossible. One can only surmise how many times the Indians traveled
to a favorite scenic area or climbed a mountain and simply enjoyed the view.
Among Anglo-Americans we can find some early specific examples, although we
are still far from a precise starting spot or time.

After the epic expedition led by Meriwether Lewis and William Clark and a
few less notable treks by other explorers, the mountain men were for years the

most common visitors across the plains and into the Rockies. Many of these bold adventurers kept diaries and noted the people they encountered in this vast area. One, Osborne Russell, met a small party in June 1835 while traveling through the mountains. The group had arrived from Fort Vancouver on the Columbia River under the direction of Francis Ermatinger, an employee of the Hudson's Bay Company. While some in this group were British traders and trappers, one was Captain William George Drummond Stewart, the seventh baronet of Grandtully from Perthshire, Scotland. He was a military officer on half pay who "was on a tour of pleasure in the Rocky Mountains." The captain was one of the early visitors simply out to enjoy the American West.

The mountain men themselves admitted that they were involved in their occupation partly for the thrill of traveling and seeing what was over the next hill or around the next bend of the river; Russell himself admitted spending a very cold night on a mountain above Great Salt Lake just so he could get "a view of the lake when the sun arose in the morning."[1] Rufus Sage, a Connecticut resident, began three years of adventurous travel in the West in 1841. Even though he worked as a trapper and trader, he also journeyed through the Rockies to enjoy the scenery and to gather material for a book. He has been identified as the first true traveler-for-pleasure in the well-known Middle Park area of Colorado in 1842.[2] As the fur trade declined in significance some of the mountain men became guides; while most guided governmental explorations or immigrants, there was at least one example of a tourist guide. Famed mountain man Bill Sublette was engaged in 1844 to take a group of people to Brown's Hole for a "summer outing."[3]

These are merely a few examples of different types of early visitors who had discovered the scenic appeal of the Rockies and other areas long before tourism was important in America west of the Mississippi River. In the 1840s and 1850s the Oregon and California migrants also viewed this area, but they were just passing through and considered the Great American Desert mainly an obstacle to their progress. There were also some visitors then, like the young Francis Parkman, who appreciated the scenery even when the main attractions were seeing Indians and hunting buffalo.

Western hunting was a second source that eventually led to dude ranching. One of the early famous hunters was Sir George Gore, who was guided by Jim Bridger in the mid-1850s on trips in Wyoming and Montana. On one expedition he led a party of about two hundred men, and the large quantity of game they bagged inspired other hunting trips by both foreigners and Americans. Sir John Watts Garland was an English hunter who headed west about 1869; he established camps and built cabins to which he returned regularly every two years or so. In his absence his horses and dogs were cared for by the men he hired. He was especially popular with westerners, for he lived as they did, sleeping in the open, taking his turn at camp duty, and riding his horse in races they staged. Because of the absence of suitable places to stay Garland had even started the trend of private hunting facilities.[4]

While Garland and Gore provided their own facilities and escorts, some hunts were guided and guarded by contingents of the U.S. military. Buffalo Bill Cody helped guide several of these, and he said the best-equipped group he accompanied came from New York to Fort McPherson in 1870. General Philip Sheridan was host to a group that included his father-in-law, General Rucker, his brother Colonel M. V. Sheridan, and numerous other military and civilian guests. Major W. H. Brown of the Fifth Cavalry commanded two companies that escorted the group, which even had its own surgeon. There were nearly three hundred men that started out in September 1871, and they killed over 600 buffalo, 200 elk, and lots of small game. Indians hovered nearby, but the soldiers took extensive care to prevent any trouble. This was a luxurious trip since three of the twenty-five wagons were traveling icehouses used to keep the game and wine cold. Dinner was prepared by French cooks from New York and served by waiters in evening dress. The dining tent was floored and carpeted, and much linen, china, glass, and porcelain were in evidence. Cody was also involved in another large hunt, the one arranged for the Grand Duke Alexis of Russia in 1873. The military escort this time included two companies each of cavalry and infantry. In addition to General Sheridan again, other high-ranking officers were Generals Palmer, Ord, Sandy Forsyth, and George Custer. All the soldiers, teamsters, and cooks added up to almost five hundred men. The grand duke killed eight buffalo and viewed an Indian buffalo hunt staged for his benefit.[5]

Not all hunts featured such elaborate facilities, but they showed the westerner that there were opportunities available in catering to these outsiders. Another of these many hunters was the earl of Dunraven from Ireland, whose actions clearly helped encourage early guest facilities in the West. He came to America in 1869 on his honeymoon; he had always dreamed of going to the western United States because of the exciting tales he had heard. His uncle had known George Gore and told Dunraven of the great hunting available in the West. Illness forced the earl back to England before he saw the West on this first trip, but two years later he returned, this time with the inherited title Lord Dunraven. He brought his own physician, George Henry Kingsley, and the two men hunted elk for a month guided by Bill Cody and Texas Jack Omohondro, a cowboy, scout, and good friend of Cody and Wild Bill Hickok. Dunraven was fascinated with the Rockies and returned for more hunting the next year. While in Colorado he heard for the first time of Estes Park, Long's Peak, Griff Evans's dude ranch, and the mysterious Mountain Jim Nugent. It is worth noting that this reference to a dude ranch in 1872 is one of the earliest made.

In 1873 Dunraven went to the Estes Park area where "the dude ranch at the mouth of Fish Creek was still open. Griff Evans assigned the Dunraven party to the two-room cabin near the little lake." The Irish lord hunted the area and thoroughly enjoyed it before returning home. He sent an Englishman to study U.S. land laws, and in July 1874, Denver newspapers announced that he had developed a grandiose plan to build a hunting lodge north and west of Estes Park. It was to be a summer resort and cattle ranch developed by a stock company. Dunraven bought Griff Evans's squatters' rights and his Fish Creek buildings, and the project was begun.[6] In August of the same year Texas Jack met Dunraven in Denver and guided him on a Wyoming hunting trip that lasted nearly three months. Dunraven's book, *The Great Divide,* was based largely on his hunting experiences in Yellowstone Park on this trip. The journey was also partly exploratory since the area was not well known; Dunraven Pass in the park is named after this Irish lord.[7] When his lodge was completed in 1876, he brought as his guest the famous painter Albert Bierstadt. Dunraven began building a herd of Swiss cattle and acquired thousands of acres of land, but his elaborate scheme was now threatened by various challenges to his land claims. These discouraged him and his visits became briefer and less frequent; he also began to visit incognito. He made his last hunt and visit there in 1880 after numerous lawsuits. Three years later he leased what he had left to Theodore Whyte, who operated a hotel, and in 1907 he sold his property. One of the purchasers was Freelan O. Stanley, who developed a large tourist facility in Estes Park using as one of the attractions the Stanley Steamer he and his brother had invented.[8]

Lord Dunraven's story illustrates several aspects of increasing western travel. It shows that a dude ranch of some sort was already in operation in the early 1870s, but it disappeared in Dunraven's elaborate development scheme. Dunraven stayed at another ranch when he first hunted in the area, the homestead of Abner Sprague along Big Thompson Creek. From this visit Sprague got the idea of hosting visitors and started his own dude ranch. Like other visitors, Dunraven and Dr. Kingsley also spread the word about the Rockies and encouraged travelers to visit this isolated paradise teeming with game. Another famous hunter was William A. Baillie Grohman whose expeditions in the Jackson Hole country encouraged other Europeans to journey to America.[9]

The hunter-tourist became a regular visitor to the trans-Mississippi West as he followed the fur traders, traveled to army posts, and rode the early railroads. Hundreds of Americans and Europeans traveled thousands of miles to hunt and enjoy Western hospitality. They brought some money to the area and undoubtedly stood in awe of the majestic peaks and wilderness, which were unlike anything they had seen before.[10]

Of course, some of the visitors were not interested in hunting at all. One was Isabella Bird, a friend of George Kingsley, Dunraven's physician. She left an extensive record of her journeys, chiefly in Colorado, and it shows the harsh conditions that early travelers had to endure. Once off the main roads and away from large settlements like Denver, she learned there were no hotels or taverns; many settlers, however, did let her stay with them for a small fee. She was glad inns were scarce since she was able to learn more about the lives and homes of the Coloradans by living with them. Her living conditions were far from ideal, however. When she was in Fort Collins in September 1873, she was overwhelmed by bugs and questionable food. She wrote, "The beef was tough and greasy, the butter had turned to oil, and beef and butter were black with living, drowned and half-drowned flies."[11]

Her hosts recommended she board with a nearby settler. Mrs. Bird found there only a wagon, a tent, and a broken-down, one-room cabin. The owners offered to let her stay for five dollars per week if "she would be agreeable." Undaunted by the surroundings, she accepted because she would be closer to the mountains and Estes Park, the spot Dunraven and Kingsley raved about. Rattlesnakes, wasps, grasshoppers, and locusts made her stay miserable, but when she finally got a horse at Longmount and made the difficult ride to Estes Park, she found conditions a bit better and the scenery inspiring at 7,500 feet. She had a small cabin to herself near a lake; it had a stone chimney, a hay bed, a chair with a tin basin on it, a shelf, some pegs, a small window overlooking the picturesque lake, and two doors, neither of which would close. It was not luxurious but surpassed what she had seen before. Her hosts were two ranchers, Welshmen named Edwards and Evans, apparently the same Evans that Dunraven stayed with. They charged her eight dollars per week which also gave her the use of a horse when one could be caught.

Although enjoying the magnificent scenery and activities, this intrepid Englishwoman now decided she should journey farther and climb Long's Peak, a major undertaking since it had first been scaled only five years earlier in 1868. "Rocky Mountain Jim" agreed to guide her and two young men who had ridden over from Longmount. This guide was the same "Mountain Jim Nugent" that Dunraven referred to; he was known as a rough character with a questionable past but, true to western form, he was polite and chivalrous toward women. This quartet of three dudes and one guide baked enough bread for three days, cut a number of steaks, packed tea, sugar, and butter, and began their trek. The trip to and up Long's Peak was a rugged one, and Mrs. Bird was nearly exhausted by the time they approached the summit. Mountain Jim had to drag her over the most difficult spots so she could reach the top. After the trip down, which was simpler, she returned to the ranch and stayed a bit longer, even helping to round up cattle for her hosts in the mountains. She then returned to Longmount and rode horseback alone to Denver. Here she met ex-Governor Alexander Hunt and William Byers, publisher of the *Rocky Mountain News.* They advised her to ride west into the mountains for more scenic adventures; Hunt even drew her a map of the area and gave her a circular letter of introduction to the settlers along the way. This remarkable lady continued her trip until her allotted travel time was gone and she had to board a train and head east. In addition to poor conditions, she also suffered from a lack of cash, for the Panic of 1873 had caused Denver banks to suspend payment of checks. After three months in Colorado, her wardrobe was reduced to one handkerchief, one pair of stockings, a black silk dress, her flannel riding suit, a pair of slippers, and her arctic boots. Mrs. Bird demonstrated that a woman could travel in safety, if not comfort, in the West; her journey, which was described later in a book, mentions some of the western attractions and also points out the need for better facilities for travelers.[12]

Americans were heading to the Rockies also, especially sons of well-to-do families; they journeyed across the plains, not to seek their fortunes or to settle, but to search for adventure. One of these "expensively educated young men" was Owen Wister. An 1882 *summa cum laude* graduate of Harvard, Wister suffered some unknown health problems in 1885, and his doctor, S. Weir Mitchell, urged him to go west.[13] Wister had heard a glowing account of the West from Theodore Roosevelt, and he was soon on the train to Wyoming, where he stayed on a ranch belonging to Major and Mrs. Frank Wolcott, apparently friends of his parents. Major Wolcott was involved in the Johnson County War later, but all was peaceful during Wister's stay. The Wolcotts were delightful hosts, their house was clean and neat, and Wister was enthusiastic about his "discovery" of Wyoming, the fresh air, and his daily bath in nearby Deer Creek.

This visit was not only the beginning of Wister's love affair with the West but also the impetus that made him give up his law profession and become a writer of western fiction. Wyoming remained his favorite spot in the West, but he also traveled to Washington, Oregon, California, Colorado, Arizona, New Mexico, Texas, and British Columbia. He hunted big game, fished mountain streams and lakes, camped in the wilderness, and studied the Indians. He also sought colorful individuals, scenes, and experiences so he could write accurately and effectively about a region that was undergoing rapid change. He journeyed west many times and eventually took his family there on trips, including visits to the JY dude ranch in Jackson Hole.[14] Wister's western heroes, Lin McLean and the Virginian, would present popular images of the westerner and help attract even more visitors to the West.

Most of the factors that were drawing travelers to the West were private activities. But two major events in the late nineteenth century connected with the federal government helped publicize the area in a favorable way. One came in 1872 when thousands of acres of Wyoming Territory were set aside for the formation of Yellowstone National Park. Located in northwestern Wyoming (and including small parts of Idaho and Montana), this area featured geysers, hot springs, magnificent scenery, and outstanding hunting. Yellowstone is generally recognized as the first national park and its designation as a park meant national publicity that would attract more people to the area than ever before.[15]

A second major event that drew attention to the Rocky Mountain West was the trip taken by President Chester Arthur in 1883. He traveled to Fort Washakie, Wyoming, where a large pack train was arranged; then the presidential party journeyed up the Wind River, across Jackson Hole, and through Yellowstone Park. Arthur made the trip to relax, to acquaint himself with the West, and to learn more about the Indians. Of course, the publicity surrounding his visit also made the area better known and encouraged travel there.[16]

Thus publicity, hunting parties, and general scenic appeal helped popularize the West and create a growing demand for places for visitors to stay. One other very important element was necessary, however, for the threads of dude ranching to be tied together. This factor is cattle ranching.

The post–Civil War cattle boom added another dimension to the West when it brought longhorns, cowboys, and ambitious ranchers up the trail. The initial activity was simply a matter of supply, demand, and transportation as Texas cattle were driven to railroads to be hauled east to feed urbanites in the industrializing Northeast and in Europe. The Long Drive and the cowboy became part of American folklore. The cattle industry spread across the West; new grazing areas were found throughout the Great Plains, and new markets developed as miners and soldiers demanded beef while hunting for gold or Indians. The range cattle industry was soon such a huge success that hundreds of easterners and Europeans wanted to get involved in the business and take part in the enormous profits being reported.

The interest in hunting now dovetailed quite readily with raising cattle. Many men who had come west for hunting trips became so fascinated with the country that they remained and bought their own ranches. Sometimes an easterner went into partnership with a guide he had had on a trip, who would select a ranch and/or cattle. Some of the English cattle outfits developed in this fashion.[17]

Because wealthy hunters had their own permanent hunting lodges, they were often the first to become ranchers. Hunting and ranching became inextricably connected. By purchasing a ranch some of these men persuaded themselves that their enjoyment of hunting was a by-product of a sound business investment. The connection between hunting and ranching in the case of Lord Dunraven has already been noted. Another British cattle king, Moreton Frewen, started a ranch along the Powder River, which flows through Wyoming and Montana; he invited dozens of his English friends there in 1879. They received luxurious service and accommodations at the ranch and, for those who arrived in time for fall hunting, there were elaborate facilities on the pack trips. Frewen had a guest book where these visitors recorded not only their names, but also the trophies they collected. Many of his friends, impressed by the cattle and grazing land, invested money in ranches as a result of this visit.[18] Frewen continued to entertain lavishly in the 1880s and thus advertise the West. And for those travelers who stayed at his ranch, living conditions had certainly improved.

In 1882 another prominent Englishman joined the western scene in the person of Sir John Pender. Pender, a London capitalist who had helped finance the laying of one of the Atlantic cables, toured the United States that year and decided to join a syndicate in western cattle ranching. The following year he and the duke of Sutherland financed a man named Gregor Lang to investigate the ranching opportunities more closely. Lang's family left Dublin, Ireland, for Dakota Territory and settled along the Little Missouri River at Yule; soon Lang was looking after a herd of cattle for Pender and the other backers of the enterprise. One year Pender's son, Henry, and three other Englishmen, came to the Badlands to spend the summer on the ranch and to enjoy a real western roundup.[19] As on many other ranches, the living conditions at Pender's were improved to satisfy these visitors.

Those hunters not fortunate enough to know men such as Frewen and Pender still could find places to stay since the western ranchers were quite hospitable. Both foreigners and easterners were delighted by their courteous way of sharing food and shelter at no charge. Ranchers had few close neighbors so they welcomed visitors; some recently transplanted easterners even encouraged their friends from the East to visit, and they in turn, spread the word of the free and easy life of the Plains.[20] Of course, hospitality on every American frontier has become almost legendary. People on the fringe of settlement were isolated, hungry for news and companionship, and eager to meet and talk to outsiders.[21] Ranch hospitality would, however, eventually lead to a new industry and thus it differed a little from earlier forms of hospitality.

Open-handed generosity was common, but some hunters did offset the cost of their stay. Ranchers often made an agreement with a sportsman to furnish board, lodging, and a horse so he could hunt; in return the sportsman furnished fresh game for the ranch. Other westerners even became professional guides; Vic Smith was a well-known hunter in the Badlands country who took out many people, including the controversial marquis de Mores, who lived in the Dakota Territory for several years. Smith charged outsiders $200 for short hunting trips and as much as $1,000 for a lengthy one into Montana. He made a good living from the fine hunting available in the area.[22] Another guide, John Carnes, a former Union soldier, was believed to be the first settler in Jackson Hole, Wyoming. He guided Scottish, English, and German nobles on hunts in that area, housed them in his two-room log cabin and called that his dude ranch.[23]

Another feature of the West that helped tie together the ranch, hunters, and improved living conditions was the remittance man. Simply stated, a remittance man was someone living far from home supported by remittances sent to him. Ranches owned by Europeans or easterners were ideal places to send these individuals. The reasons these men left home varied considerably. Mary Shawver, who helped operate Holm Lodge in Wyoming for many years, explained that a remittance man was

> the embarassment to some family in the east; he may be a real or fancied one. He may have an unquenchable thirst, his mental IQ may at times lean a little toward the minus side; it may be any number of things that Sister may think impedes her progress toward the inner circle of the Astorbilts. Mother may tell Dad that she thinks Son needs a change of climate. Dad, very likely sympathetic with Son, assures Mother she is right and Son is sent west where his monthly remittance makes him independent and popular.[24]

Dude rancher Struthers Burt learned that there were several remittance men near his ranch in western Wyoming. There was, for instance, the handsome son of a well-known New York family sent west as a supposed drunkard; he surprised everyone by developing into a shrewd and sober cattleman. Burt also met the son of an American admiral, an ex-policeman from Pennsylvania who had shot a man there, the illegitimate child of a noted New England family, and the mysterious heir of a South African official who always carried in his pocket the photograph of two beautiful sisters.[25]

These men, whether American or foreign, needed places to stay, and westerners were able to accommodate them. When Abner Sprague, visited by Lord Dunraven, made his ranch available to visitors, his first guests were English and eastern remittance men, and so began his dude ranch along the Big Thompson

River in Colorado.[26] Every remittance man who arrived in the West provided incentive for the local rancher to improve his facilities somewhat. These men were used to comfort and were willing to pay for it. Englishmen made up a significant percentage of this group since they were especially eager to experience western life and ranching activities.[27]

Two enterprising Britons, Neil Egerton Gresley and John George Clinton Robbins, decided to capitalize on this situation and on the British infatuation with stories of western life. They bought a ranch twenty-five miles west of Laramie, Wyoming, and then solicited members from rich families eager to learn the cattle business. The two ranchers called these men "learners" rather than "dudes," but this was an early form of dude ranching. These "learners" paid Gresley and Robbins $500 or more per year and then put in long hours of labor trying to understand the tasks needed for successful ranch management. This unusual ranch thus provided an ideal place for an English family to send a son who needed a change of scene. A similar ranch was begun along the Medicine Bow River by Richard Brackenburg, an Englishman who migrated to Wyoming in 1884. His ranch took young Englishmen who paid a premium as "pupils" or "apprentices" to learn ranching and stock improvement.[28]

One of the first "learners" that Gresley and Robbins had was Clement Stuart Bengough, a remarkable remittance man who was the son of one of the landed English gentry. His parents, John Charles Bengough and Caroline Augusta Cornwall, reared ten children at the palatial family estate, the Ridge, Wotton-under-Edge in Gloucestershire. Reared in a strong Christian home, keenly athletic, and having a sound public-school education, Clement seemed to be set for life in England. He was so shy, however, that even normal social contacts were painful for him. He was comfortable only when in his room or out of doors. Apparently his father gave Bengough a cheque when he turned twenty-five and told him to make his own way in the world. The young man decided to go abroad and left for the United States in late 1886 or early 1887. He went to Wyoming where he had all the open spaces and isolation he wanted and became a "learner" with Gresley and Robbins. Evidently he was a successful student, for he soon acquired some land and raised cattle. After this he lived most of the time as a recluse in a small cabin, content with his fine library and large quantity of mail. He was a colorful addition to the territory in several ways; a Latin scholar, he not only wrote entire letters in Latin to his sisters in England and South Africa, but at least once he also wrote a check in Latin to be cashed locally. He also kept eleven Siberian wolfhounds, so vicious that he was afraid to turn his back on them—a curious thing for a man known for his gentleness. He received regular remittances from home but refused to return there to claim a $300,000 estate left him by an uncle. Bengough spent the rest of his life in Wyoming even though he had contemplated visiting home on two occasions. He died in 1934 leaving a modest estate worth $39,000, most of it cash in a checking account, and a 3½ percent war loan in the Bank of England.[29] Although not a typical remittance man, Bengough was one of the many outsiders who brought substantial amounts of money to the West. This money, badly needed, formed part of the capital necessary for growth in the area.

Unfortunately, the great cattle boom ended after the disastrous winter of 1886–87; blizzards, bitter cold, and constant snowstorms killed thousands of cattle and ended the glory days of the open range industry.[30] The cattle business continued, of course, but it was less spectacular and successful. Profits were sporadic for many years (so capital was scarce) although for some ranches money still flowed in regularly from remittance men and other visitors. A few westerners began to consider other ways to make money. The story must now turn to Howard Eaton and Dick Randall, two men who eventually helped give a form to an emerging and amorphous industry.

Before discussing these two men and their ranches, it is necessary to examine briefly the question of which was "the first dude ranch." A number of claims have been made about which ranch was the first to accept paying guests; it has generally been conceded that Eatons' Ranch was the first dude ranch with respect to the way the industry finally developed. Clearly, however, in the development of early western tourism, the word *first* is difficult to apply. Many people accepted money from visitors at different times and places; dude ranching was not defined or organized for many years, and the word *dude* did not come into common usage until the 1880s. As already noted, Griff Evans and Abner Sprague operated "dude ranches" in the Estes Park area in the 1870s, but the exact nature and extent of their operations are not clear. Although other places and people are vaguely referred to in various states and territories, most of these operations lasted only a short time and left few traces. Realistically, it is neither possible nor essential to state which westerner first accepted money for tourist services from someone from the East.

These various comments are not meant to disparage in any way the claims made about Howard Eaton and Dick Randall. The Eatons and Randalls gave some shape to dude ranching as it developed into a major industry and their ranches endured for many years. Their places as pioneers in the field are secure.

The story of Eatons' Ranch began in Pittsburgh with two men, Howard Eaton and A. C. Huidekoper. Howard, born in 1851, was one of nine children, and at the age of seventeen he went to Omaha to see the West and work there awhile. He returned home the following year, traveled to a variety of places, and spent a few months at sea with his brother Charles. The activities of the Eaton family in Pennsylvania are not detailed, but some sort of financial reverses occurred, and in 1879 Howard returned west, this time to the Dakota Badlands, to make his fortune. After passing through Bismarck he lived with the traders at the infantry post on the west side of the Little Missouri River. With his partner, E. G. Paddock, he made a living hunting buffalo, elk, deer, sheep, bear, and antelope, selling the meat to the men building the Northern Pacific Railway. They also made money by returning lost horses to the railway camps.[31] Howard soon settled near Medora and took over a cabin abandoned by the Bismarck and Fort Keogh Stage Company located on the road used a few years earlier by General Alfred Terry's soldiers on their way through the Badlands. Eaton named his place the Custer Trail Ranch because George Amstrong Custer had served under Terry and had apparently camped nearby. Of course the name Custer was widely known at the time because of the Battle of the Little Big Horn in 1876.

A. C. Huidekoper, meanwhile, had also visited the West; a member of a prominent Dutch family, he was invited to take a trip over the completed part of the Northern Pacific Railway by Congressman S. B. Dick in 1879. Huidekoper enjoyed the trip so much that he returned in 1881, the same year Alden Eaton joined brother Howard in the Dakotas. The Eatons knew Huidekoper from Pennsylvania and invited him and two friends to join them in a buffalo hunt. On the trip the Eaton brothers talked enthusiastically about the Badlands, which were about 150 miles long and 25 miles wide. Timber and coal were abundant, over sixty varieties of grass grew there, and game thrived in the area. Convinced that a cattle ranch could operate successfully there, Howard persuaded Huidekoper to join in such an operation, and they started the Custer Trail Cattle Company in 1882. Huidekoper supplied money to purchase the stock, and the Eatons did the work. The profits were to be split equally. Willis Eaton, who had joined his two brothers this year, helped them build shacks and cabins while Howard purchased a thousand cows in Minnesota. Huidekoper also shipped in a carload of full-blooded Shorthorn bulls and a few full-blooded cows and bought some railroad land.[32] With the ranch in operation, expectations were high for the future.

The Eaton brothers, like other new westerners, raved about their newfound paradise and wrote letters to their eastern friends describing the wonderful country. One of these letters led to the westward migration of the most famous dude of all—Theodore Roosevelt. Howard Eaton's letter to a friend was published in a New York newspaper, Roosevelt read it, and he decided to go west in 1883. He came as a guest to the Lang ranch to hunt buffalo; conditions were primitive but Roosevelt did not complain and enjoyed himself thoroughly. His first love was for the outdoors but he soon became interested in raising cattle. For him, like the hunters mentioned before, ranching was an excuse to do what he enjoyed: riding, hunting, and camping. Within a few months Roosevelt owned the Maltese Cross Ranch near the Custer Trail Ranch and was a frequent visitor at the Eatons'. Other famous Eaton guests were Count Fitz James and the enigmatic Frenchman, the marquis de Mores, both of whom were avid buffalo hunters. When de Mores moved to the area, the town Medora was named after his wife. He, the Eatons, and Roosevelt became pillars of the ranching community in the Badlands.[33]

The Eatons, like most ranchers, were very generous; since de Mores and Roosevelt were often absent, the brothers became the hosts for hundreds of people eager to hunt or experience ranch life.[34] They were pleased to have guests but costs were overwhelming; fortunately, some of their visitors offered to pay enough to cover their extra expenses. Although the practice was contrary to the code of ranching hospitalilty, the Eatons did take their first paying guest in 1882, Bert Rumsey of Buffalo, New York. A guest book was purchased, and Eatons' ranch was accepting dudes; Howard even led the first of his many pack trips to Yellowstone Park the following year.[35]

Most people in the Badlands found the dude ranch idea a bit comical. They said a person could get a laugh about "Eatons' dudes" at "Bill Williams' saloon when nothing else could wake a smile."[36] But hunters and friends continued coming, and the ranch even took a strange turn when some wealthy and distracted parents sent offspring there who were addicted to strong drink.

> Why any parent should send a son to the Bad Lands with the idea of putting him out of reach of temptation is beyond comprehension. Eatons did their part nobly and withheld intoxicating drinks from their guests, but Bill Williams and the dozen or more other saloon-keepers in Medora were under no compulsion to follow their example. The "dudes" regularly came "back from town" with all they could carry without and within; and the cowboys round about swore solemnly that you couldn't put your hand in the crotch of any tree within a hundred yards of the Eatons ranch house without coming upon a bottle concealed by a dude being cured of "the drink."[37]

Howard, Willis, and Alden were learning that dude ranching held some surprises. They were still primarily stockmen, however, and suffered greatly when a fire started by Indians got out of control and destroyed most of their property.[38] They persevered and were soon building up their cattle herds just as hundreds of other ranchers were doing in the 1880s. The harsh winter of 1886–87 hit the

Custer Trail Cattle Company also. At the roundup that year an accurate count was made, and the partners learned they had about the same number of cattle as when they had started the business several years earlier. Deciding that the hard work had been futile, Huidekoper got out of the cattle business. He didn't want to be completely cut off from western life, however, so, when he learned horses had fared much better than cattle in the brutal weather, he began a horse ranch. At this point the Eaton brothers and Huidekoper ended their partnership amicably. The latter's Little Missouri Horse Company grew quickly while the Custer Trail Ranch continued to raise horses and cattle.[39]

Yet they were still concerned about their visitors; although a few people had paid, the Eatons counted 2,200 free meals they had given guests in just one year. They decided to charge ten dollars per week for all guests, but this did not keep people away.[40] Paying guests continued coming through the 1880s and became a regular feature at Eatons' Ranch in 1891; dudes were a permanent factor in their ranch operation from this point on. The brothers had no comprehensive scheme yet but had decided to take advantage of the extraordinary surroundings to found a place where "easterners of the better and more influential classes, more particularly of the younger generation" could build themselves up mentally and physically through association with nature.[41] Their business did not boom immediately, but many guests returned East with glowing accounts of the free, open life, hunting and adventure, and good fellowship.

It was fortunate that easterners were seeking this outdoor life, for economic necessity was making more people look at dude ranching in a different light. The winter of 1886–87 was probably the worst disaster that hit the cattle business, but the Panic of 1893 also hurt westerners and recovery from it was not rapid.

Howard Eaton took charge among the brothers for he enjoyed taking the dudes on hunting and scenic trips. As he did so, he tried to learn what they enjoyed most about the West and what additional things he could do to please them. In 1898 he launched his first large pack trip into Yellowstone Park with forty guests (all men); he took lots of saddle and pack horses, tents, a wagon, a cook, horse wrangler, teamster, guides, and other workers. From this time on the Eatons' ranch had a pack trip to Yellowstone Park every year.

On one of his trips to Yellowstone Howard Eaton met Dick Randall. Howard had never hunted this area before, so Dick Randall took him along on a hunting trip so he could learn more about it.[42] Randall's background was similar to Howard Eaton's but by no means identical to it.

James (Dick) Randall was born in Birmingham, Iowa, in 1866. He ran away from home at age twelve to work in a packing plant at Ottumwa. In 1884 he headed west, apparently following the example of his brother, Billy, who had gone there in 1873 and finally settled at old Junction City, Montana.[43] In Miles City Dick worked for Paul McCormick who managed the 7 Bar 7 Ranch. Randall learned the skills of cowboy work and helped care for the 50,000 cattle that ranged east of Billings down to Junction City. When the cold winter of 1886–87 killed a lot of cattle in Montana, Randall and a friend from 7 Bar 7, June Buzzell, realized that herding for the big outfits was over. A search for a new way to make a living eventually led Randall to dude ranching, although it was a roundabout trip of many years. In the spring of 1887 they bought eighty horses from the Indians and drove them to Yellowstone Park to sell or rent them for pack trips there; they didn't make much money but the trip taught them a lot about Indians and horses. That summer they took care of horses for George Wakefield who ran the stage company in the park. And the following winter they moved in with an old trapper and hunter named Proctor; this was a bonanza for the young men since Proctor explained to them in great detail about hunting and the habits of big game animals and even drew them maps of good hunting sites. Randall and Buzzell put together their own pack outfit and took out a few hunting parties. During the next three summers Randall drove stagecoaches for Wakefield, making contacts with easterners who wanted to go hunting in the fall. He and Buzzell also had some hunters referred to them through a nearby army post as the word spread that Dick and June knew the Wyoming, Montana, and Idaho territories well and could get excellent trophies for their clients.

Randall did other miscellaneous jobs over the next several years, but he had found his primary occupation in taking out dudes on hunting trips. His new work also led him to his wife-to-be, Dora Roseborough. Her family had moved to Montana from Kansas and eventually her father moved close to Yellowstone Park where there were some jobs. Dora and Dick met at Gardiner, on the northern edge of the park in Montana, and they were married in 1892.[44] Dick continued guiding hunters and building up the experience that would make him known as the "father of dude ranching" in Montana within a few years.

Dick Randall and the Eaton brothers, whose stories will be completed later to show their growing influence, were not the only men active in the 1890s in the dude business. The examples of Vic Smith and John Carnes in the Badlands and Jackson Hole have already been noted, as have the earlier activities of Griff Evans and Abner Sprague.

In the Middle Park area of Colorado, a leader in this field was Henry Lehman, an immigrant from Germany. He was born in Bremen and, like Dick Randall, ran away from home when he was young—at the age of fourteen. Soon after arriving in the United States about 1867, he moved to Colorado because easterners had heckled him about his inability to speak English. He met and married a German girl named Amelia at Brighton, Colorado shortly thereafter, and in 1878 or 1880 they moved farther west to the Middle Park region with their three children and eighty head of cattle. Most of the cattle died but the Lehmans hung on like true frontiersmen and developed a conglomeration of enterprises to make a living: hauling freight, cutting timber and operating a sawmill, and selling dairy products.[45] Henry Lehman became popular enough to be chosen county commissioner. Two incidents gave him a reputation as a pretty rugged character: first he won a fight with a bear at his ranch even though he had no gun, and then he shot a man named Samuel Covington who had shot two men, including the marshall, in Central City.[46]

Like other frontier families, the Lehmans were very hospitable and their ranch near Granby was a regular stopping point for travelers caught at nightfall between Georgetown or Empire and Grand Lake. Like Howard Eaton, Dick Randall, and others, Henry Lehman learned he could supplement his slim income by acting as guide for these outsiders. The Grand Lake area was known especially for its excellent fishing so Lehman guided many people on fishing trips although he also took out some hunters. By the 1890s the Lehmans had developed an authentic dude ranch, "known for miles around as 'Lehman's Ranch,' a fisherman's paradise," one of the first in that part of the Rockies.[47]

Although little is known about the Davis Ranch in neighboring Wyoming, it also had become a center of recreation and hunting by the 1890s. Mr. Davis was conducting hunting trips into the Big Horn Mountains as early as 1893.[48]

Another early enterprising westerner was William Wells, born in Chicago in 1862; he came west when he was a teenager, eventually arriving in Colorado where he worked as a cowhand and on the Denver and Rio Grande Railway. He eventually ran his own cattle in Colorado and Wyoming. He began guiding people in the White River country in Colorado and claimed to have started the "first" dude ranch in the Rockies on Marvine Creek a couple of miles below Trapper's Lake; unfortunately, no dates or other information are available about this operation.[49] In 1897, however, it is clear that he built a sportsman's lodge on the Green River, twenty-five miles east of Jackson, Wyoming. The main building was elaborate and comfortable, over eighty feet long with a thirty-foot-square living room, an indoor bathroom, and hot and cold water. For the dudes there were also seven separate sleeping cabins, fifteen by fifteen feet, plus a bunkhouse and buildings for equipment and provisions, all in a long row connected by covered platforms. This was called Gros Ventre Lodge, but the local people called it the Dog Ranch because of the twenty-five to thirty dogs kept there for hunting. Wells eventually had at least one hundred saddle and pack horses in his very substantial dude operation.[50] William Wells may not have had the first dude ranch in the Rockies as he claimed, but he certainly was another early westerner who took advantage of some of the possibilities in the dude business.

A variety of factors had led a number of men to provide services for outsiders visiting the mountain West. Although their ranches and lodges were scattered throughout the Rockies, most of them were in the Dakota Badlands, Montana, Wyoming, and Colorado. Near the turn of the century, the dude business was ready to take shape and emerge as a clear-cut and permanent part of the West.

THREE

Kind and Generous Hosts

Howard Eaton, as kind and generous a host as ever lived.
—A. C. Huidekoper, *My Experience and Investment in the
Bad Lands and Some of the Men I Met There,* 22.

The setting was wild, as Nature had made it, until civilization kind
of moved in on it. It was that wildness that appealed to folks.
—Dick Randall, as quoted in *Music, Saddles and Flapjacks,* 37.

Dude ranching had developed in the late nineteenth century from four major
sources: hunting parties, remittance men, the scenic appeal of the West, and
ranches, which added their own type of appeal and which provided the hospitality
to accommodate visitors. The first two decades of the twentieth century would
see the growth of dude ranching from an occasional experiment to a widespread
institution in the northern Rockies; these years also set the stage for the great
boom and expansive period of the 1920s. Although no single event or date
signaled or started this growth and development, several notable and long-lasting
ranches began in this era or underwent important changes.

Dick Randall, who had already been guiding hunters for a decade, decided in
1898 that he needed a ranch as a base for his activities. He ran across a cabin
on Cedar Creek in southern Montana while riding one day and liked the location,

just twelve miles from the Gardiner entrance to Yellowstone Park. He learned that the two men who occupied it and claimed the site were the pair that had been robbing the Yellowstone Park stagecoaches. The thieves had decided it was time to be "movin' on," so Randall bought their horses, packs, equipment, and cabin. He and his wife now both "proved up" on a half section of land in the area to get a firm legal claim for their property, the basis for the OTO Ranch they would operate for over thirty years.

Randall added a kitchen and two bedrooms onto the cabin; built corrals, a blacksmith shop, a barn, and a root cellar; and plowed some land for a garden. With his ranch started, Dick's skill as a guide continued to bring him numerous hunters, and he continued to enjoy the association with people from other countries and the eastern United States. Some of his hunters were well known or became famous later—Thomas F. Ryan, Owen Wister, Hartley Dodge of Remington Arms, railroad magnate Henry Villard, writer Phillip Ashton Rollins, Theodore Roosevelt, and foreigners such as the German general Paul von Hindenburg, Lord Todd, Lord Kinley, Arthur Paxton from Jamaica, and Alex Mitchell of Scotland.[1] When Randall launched a hunting trip, he usually took three or four men but hunted with only one or two at a time. His increasing knowledge of the game and the country enabled his clients to get trophies of bear, elk, deer, moose, sheep, and antelope, and he once was even able to take Mitchell on a buffalo hunt on the Flathead Indian reservation.

The hunters loved it and often came a week or two early, before the season began, to ride and toughen up a bit. They helped with ranch work and took pot luck at the dining table with the family and crew. They came back year after year and recommended the OTO to their friends. Soon the one-room bunkhouse and spare room in the family house were too small, so the Randalls put up several twelve-by-sixteen-foot wall tents with wooden floors and sides. These still did not suffice, however, since the hunters started bringing their families. Some of the men even sent their children to the ranch in the summer while they and their wives went abroad. Dick and Dora Randall often gave their house to summer visitors and slept in a tent; the guests also were given horses for roaming over the surrounding countryside. In 1910 the Randalls had to buy more horses, build additional cabins, and also raise more beef, chickens, and vegetables to feed these guests, who were still being accommodated free of charge. In 1911 Dick Randall built a hunting lodge on Hell Roaring Creek northeast of Gardiner, and in the following year the Randalls started charging all their guests at the OTO Ranch. From a young boy seeking adventure in the West in 1884, Dick Randall had become a full-fledged dude rancher. The OTO seems to have been the first dude ranch in Montana.[2]

While Randall continued as a hunting guide, the dude ranch business grew quickly, and in 1914 the first large ranch building was started at the OTO. It contained a large lodge room, kitchen, dining room, recreation and trophy room, and ten guest rooms. The Randalls also built a hydroelectric plant, a new saddle room, and corrals. The OTO thrived as Dora Randall proved to be a genial and efficient hostess and manager while Dick continued to be an effective guide and storyteller whose dynamic personality helped enlarge the popularity of the ranch. More ranch workers were hired, and the dudes, both parents and children, enjoyed their visits and participation in ranch activities. The Randalls bought some railroad land, leased some forest land, and were soon managing 5,000 acres. The OTO was busy enough that the U.S. Post Office granted its application for a third-class post office called Dude Ranch, Montana.[3] One way Randall built up his ranch was through an indirect connection with his old acquaintance Howard Eaton, who had a contract to supply milk cows for Yellowstone Park. Eaton bought them in Minnesota and sent them to the park; then, in the fall when the park closed, Randall would buy the cows, thereby building an OTO dairy herd. Randall and Eaton also visited each other over the years and undoubtedly discussed ideas about dude ranching.

Before returning to the Eaton brothers, another early Montana ranch should be mentioned. This one was started by Pete Karst, who settled in the Gallatin Valley in the early 1890s. He established the first stage line in the area to run mail and passengers from a tie camp to Bozeman. The Karst Ranch was homesteaded in the early 1900s; details of its development are lacking, but apparently it too had to accommodate visitors very soon; the first guest cabins were built in 1907. The Karst Ranch is generally thought to be the second dude ranch in the state, preceded only by the Randalls' operation.[4]

Meanwhile the Eaton brothers were also making changes. As noted in the previous chapter, they had made the dude business a regular part of their ranch by 1891; in 1898 Howard took the first of his large, annual pack trips to Yellowstone. In 1899 some of the partners of the giant Carnegie Steel Company took this Yellowstone pack trip, and in 1902 the first women made the trip. As Eatons' Custer Trail Ranch and pack trips were becoming fairly well known, the dude business brought the brothers a certain amount of prosperity.[5]

Besides the growing importance of the dude business, other changes were coming to the Dakotas. Thousands of "dry farmers" were moving to the Badlands, putting pressure on the ranchers to move out. At the same time the dudes were asking for "a more varied scene of vacation activity." Many wanted pack trips to Yellowstone and also to the Big Horn Mountains in Wyoming. Rangeland was disappearing fast in the Badlands; the Eatons were being "pushed" out of North

Dakota and "pulled" farther west as the frontier continued to move west. One day some men offered them cash for the Custer Trail Ranch, so the brothers sold out in 1903 and turned toward Wyoming. Other Badlands ranchers felt it was a calamity when the Eatons moved, for they had been a positive force in the area and were the first of the old-timers to leave. Eventually, the Huidekopers and other horse ranchers were also forced out, so the Eatons apparently made the right choice in leaving when they did.[6]

They were now looking for a new ranch that had several desirable characteristics: good horseback riding, both mountain trails and level country; a high enough altitude for comfortable summer weather but low enough so the winters weren't too miserable; a spot reasonably secluded from towns and the intrusions of passersby but not too far from the railway that brought supplies and guests; abundant natural feed for the horses and an unfailing water supply; some fishing and hunting nearby; and open country for pack trips away from settlements. They found what they wanted at an elevation of 4,500 feet along Wolf Creek in the foothills of the Big Horn Mountains, just eighteen miles from Sheridan.[7] The Eatons' sense of what was needed for a successful dude operation shows how thoroughly they had analyzed their business, and the fact that Eatons' Ranch operated in the same location for nearly eighty years indicates that they chose their site well. In 1904 the three brothers made their move and signed their new guest register—Howard as "Ever Genial" (in the remarks), Willis as "Best Ever" and "Beau Brummel," and Alden as "Cheer Up."[8] They sent out a brochure to "announce to their friends and patrons, and to the public, their change of location from the Bad Lands of North Dakota to the Big Horn Mountain region of Northwestern Wyoming."[9]

They had decided not to take any guests that first year because they did not have the cabins or other buildings ready, but they did not count on the tenacity of the dudes. Seventy of them arrived that first summer of 1904. They slept in tents or on the ground, ate off ironing boards or anything else that would hold a plate, filled kerosene lamps, helped with beds and dishes, cleaned the cabins as soon as the builders finished constructing them—and, of course, paid for the privilege.[10] This dogged loyalty is significant, for it shows how early some easterners had become absolutely dedicated to their ranch vacations and how this dedication could ensure the continuation of some ranches for years or even decades. In 1905 the Eatons began a campaign to get a railway stop called Ranchester at their ranch, and by 1910 the Burlington Railway granted their request. They also succeeded in getting a post office established at the ranch, and Wolf, Wyoming became the official mailing address of the ranch now known simply as Eatons' Ranch.[11]

Here in Wyoming Howard Eaton continued to shape dude ranching in the direction that seemed most appropriate. He was better known than his brothers because he was a great hunter and very interested in animals and conservation. Willis and Alden worked hard and helped the ranch grow, but Howard remained the dominant figure.[12] He realized that the factor bringing people west was not just the climate, the quiet atmosphere, or the activities, but the picturesque, charming, and peculiar life of a ranch. He always kept his place a ranch even when the dude business became the largest part of the operation. One later Wyoming rancher believed that dude ranches would not have developed as they did without Eaton's ideas and perceptiveness; peoples' desire to visit the West would have been inadequately met by summer boardinghouses and hotels.[13] Another important contribution the Eatons made was to open the western vacation to a broader spectrum of people. As noted earlier, private hunting parties had always been available for the rich, but the dude ranch made the West available to the middle class.

Howard Eaton was also an incredibly genial host. He never appeared to be a businessman but always seemed more interested in being with his guests than in making money. He had boundless enthusiasm and patience in showing people the beauties of the West. For him life was "twenty-four hours in the open air,—half of that time in the saddle,—long vistas, the trail of game, the camp-fire at night, and a few hours of quiet sleep under the stars."[14]

Clearly Eaton had found the best of all possible ways of life—he did exactly what he wanted to do and was able to make a living at it. Hundreds of guests journeyed to Wolf, Wyoming, during a season that lasted from June 1 to mid-October, enjoying excellent food, good service, and magnificent scenery.

Howard, Willis, and Alden Eaton's concern about their guests was always appreciated. Of course, another factor that aided Eatons' Ranch was the association of the brothers with Theodore Roosevelt, who was president when they moved to Wyoming and were getting firmly established there. By 1917 Eatons' Ranch comprised over 7,000 acres of land, 500 horses, hundreds of cattle, and accommodations for 125 guests; it was the largest dude ranch in the country.[15]

While Eatons' Ranch and the OTO were growing, other westerners in greater numbers were also turning to the dude business. Not too far from Eatons' was the IXL Ranch near Dayton, Wyoming; it had been settled in 1892 by an Englishman, Captain Grissell, who named the place after his crack cavalry outfit, the Ninth (IX) Lancers (L). By 1912 another Englishman, J. B. Milward, owned and ran it as a dude ranch. Like Eatons', it featured a relaxed, informal atmosphere and offered its guests riding, fishing, hunting, and ranch activities.[16]

West of Sheridan about 110 miles was the Cody region, not even settled much until after 1896. From 1900 to 1903, however, a series of events occurred that made sure it would be a tourist center for the rest of the century. In 1901 the Burlington Railway reached Cody, giving the town ready access to the outside world; in 1903, the road to the east entrance of Yellowstone Park was opened, giving access from Cody to a major scenic attraction; and between 1901 and 1903 the famed William F. Cody opened a chain of lodges from Cody to the park: the Irma Hotel, Wapiti Lodge, and Pahaska Tepee. These lodges, of course, encouraged travelers to visit the area.[17] The region soon became a center of dude ranching, and Holm Lodge was one of the earliest places established on the route between Cody and the park. J. W. (Billy) Howell was the best-known figure involved with it; he was born in 1874 in Indian Territory, moved farther west in 1890, and then became a rancher. He managed the Cody Canal Company for seven years and then took charge of pack outfits through Yellowstone for the Holm Transportation Company.

This company had been using a stagecoach stop established in 1898 for visitors to Yellowstone Park. By 1903 Tex Holm had erected tents and a lodge at the stage stop, and he guided visitors by wagon and buggy through the Rockies. A fire destroyed the main lodge in 1906, but Holm built a new and larger one the following year which continued to serve as an overnight stopping point for passengers traveling through the park.

Holm eventually went broke because park visitors began traveling by automobile. He was unable to pay Billy Howell, so he turned Holm Lodge and all the horses over to Howell, who then operated the lodge as a dude ranch, probably the first ranch entirely dependent on the dude business. Holm Lodge and others in the Cody region are interesting additions to the dude ranching business for several reasons: the growth of dude ranching there was not primarily from stock ranches as in the Sheridan area, but from the significant volume of travelers already numerous early in the twentieth century; also the location emphasizes the importance of Yellowstone Park in the growing popularity of dude ranches. Howell later ran into financial troubles while operating Holm Lodge and in 1930 took in Mary Shawver from Chicago as a partner. They were then able to operate the lodge successfully until 1947, when they sold it to a group of Californians. The name was changed to Crossed Sabres Ranch, in reference to the brand that Billy Howell and Tex Holm had used.[18]

Another very early Wyoming dude ranch was Trapper Lodge, in Shell Canyon, southwest of Sheridan. In an unusual twist the owners moved east to Wyoming from the Pacific Northwest. Two brothers, Gay and Watson Wyman, visited the state in 1906 because their sister had married a Wyoming rancher. The young men liked the Cowboy State so they took $1600 they had saved from miscellaneous work and in 1908 bought a homestead from William Calls. When they started their own cattle ranch, their parents moved from Seattle to join them. Just like the Eatons in the Badlands, the Wymans soon had more guests staying for longer visits than they were prepared for. At the suggestion of their guests, Wymans charged them for food, lodging, laundry, and the use of a saddle horse. They erected twelve-by-fourteen-foot tents on wooden frames and floors for the dudes and even enlarged a cow camp in the Shell Creek Basin at an altitude of 8,000 feet for those who liked the high country. Guests staying there paid nearly double what those at the main lodge paid, but they did get daily guided horseback rides. Besides riding, the dudes enjoyed excellent fishing in Trapper and Shell creeks. Owen Wister and his family, who were guests at Trapper Lodge for several years along with other authors and artists who visited, gave it a reputation as "the intellectual dude ranch" of the West. The Wymans operated it till 1930 when they sold it to Brent Wyeth of Philadelphia. The new owner allowed sheep to graze on the watershed above the lodge, which led to soil erosion and water damage that forced the ranch to close.[19]

Farther south in Wyoming, the Jackson Hole area developed more slowly as a dude ranching center. This region had a rather severe climate with long, cold winters and deep snow. There was abundant water, but the soil seemed suitable only for growing hay or oats or for grazing cattle. The tremendous big game hunting drew outsiders by the hundreds and led ranchers into the guiding business since nonresidents had to have a "qualified guide" according to state law. One resident of the area thought the hunting business was a detriment since people neglected their ranches and cattle to take out hunters.[20] The ranchers, however, believed the dude business was essential since they made little or no money on their cattle. The eastern and foreign hunters gave such glowing accounts of the beauty of Jackson Hole that their families insisted on going there. The story is nearly identical to that of Dick Randall in Montana. These visitors stayed at the cabins of their guides, putting up with many inconveniences until the rancher-guides built cabins for them.[21] Paying visitors were accommodated as early as the 1880s but the first known ranch there was Sheffield's, established in 1903 as a hunting ranch. The first identifiable dude ranch, not dependent strictly on hunting, was the JY begun in 1908 by Lou Joy and Struthers Burt. Owen Wister and his family also visited here, staying at the JY for three months in 1911. The area was still quite remote and difficult to reach; both food and guests had to come 104 miles by wagon from St. Anthony, Idaho.[22]

During the next three decades Struthers Burt proved to be the most important of these pioneer Jackson Hole ranchers. He was born in Baltimore in 1881, graduated from Princeton, and studied at both Oxford University and the University of Munich; he had won early recognition as a poet and author and eventually wrote much about dude ranching to explain and popularize it. After the 1911 season he ended his partnership with Joy, homesteaded some nearby land, and opened the Bar BC Ranch with Dr. Horace Carncross. Burt married a fellow author, Katharine Newlin, in 1913, and operated the dude ranch for many years while continuing his writing career. Burt tried an interesting experiment at the Bar BC, building a separate ranch for children called the Little Outfit. This idea of separating visiting families did not succeed, however, and disappeared.[23] Burt eventually sold this ranch to buy the Three River Ranch, where each party built its own cabin but all used a common dining room and lounge.[24] Remaining in the Jackson Hole country until his death in 1954, Burt was continually involved in publicizing and explaining dude ranching. Other dude ranches were begun in this area following these early examples, but the whole Jackson Hole country was soon embroiled in a seemingly endless fight over a new national park surrounding the Teton Mountains.

Before leaving the Cowboy State temporarily, it is interesting to note the fate of the Gros Ventres Lodge of William Wells, discussed in Chapter 2. He continued to lead numerous hunters on the chase for trophies in the twentieth century. Often his early season hunters were Americans, like Hulbert Taft, editor of the *Cincinnati Times-Star,* and late season ones were English sportsmen. Game, especially elk, was abundant, and Wells reported great success through 1905. But in 1906 Gros Ventres Lodge was declining rapidly. Its main difficulty was the tightening of game laws, especially strict observance of the shortened season. Cutting the hunting season to about two months meant the luxurious lodge could not accommodate enough hunters to continue to operate. Wells was also hurt by competition from local guides who outfitted parties from their ranches without the expense of a big lodge. Wells turned to cattle ranching for a few years, then left for Oregon.[25] The failure of Gros Ventres Lodge shows that growing too fast and becoming too elaborate could be risky; it also indicates the changing nature of the dude business. Most places that succeeded were stock ranches that also took guests, such as those in the Sheridan area; those that depended chiefly on tourists, such as those in the Cody region; and ranchers who used their unpretentious ranch homes as centers for hunting trips.

While Wyoming was leading the way in the growth of dude ranching, and Dick Randall was setting the pattern in Montana, there was also some dude ranch development in Colorado. The early ranches of Griff Evans and Abner Sprague in the Estes Park area have been noted, and some ranches there continued taking guests in the 1890s and early twentieth century.[26] On the western side of the Continental Divide Squeaky Bob Wheeler began another early dude ranch. In 1907 he built a cabin at the end of the road north from Grand Lake. Wheeler, whose nickname came from his peculiar high-pitched voice, had been a cowpuncher and guide before setting up his "Hotel de Hardscrabble," a tent camp for hunters and trout fishermen. He became famous for his good cooking, fanatically spotless housekeeping, and witty, far-fetched stories embroidered with profanity. He claimed to have entertained President Theodore Roosevelt, Supreme Court Justice Charles Evans Hughes, actor Otis Skinner, and other famous travelers. When Wheeler sold his property in 1928, Phantom Valley Ranch developed on the site, alongside Trail Ridge Road, the only paved route through Rocky Mountain National Park.[27] The creation of this park in 1915 indicated that Wheeler had chosen a prime site for scenic enjoyment as well as for fishing and hunting.

Farther south and west in Colorado, but still in the Middle Park region, another ranch began in 1904. Lizzie Sullivan was the first owner of this land along the Colorado River, about one hundred miles west of Denver. She sold it in 1905 to James Ferguson and Edgar Messiter, who called their ranch Buckhorn Lodge. Many friends from "crowded" Denver met there for good fishing and occasional hunting. Like other ranches, it soon had too many guests to handle for no charge, so in 1912 the first paying guests were accommodated in tents along the river.[28] This ranch, now known as the Bar Lazy J, was developed primarily for its fishing, just as the Lehman Ranch had been in the Grand Lake area in the 1880s and 1890s.

Meanwhile, back in Wyoming, two more important ranches were started during these years by Charles C. Moore and Irving H. Larom. Moore is a bit of an exception among dude ranchers since he was reared in the West. His father, J. K. Moore, a Senate page during Lincoln's administration, moved to Montana and then to Wyoming, where he raised cattle and served as post trader at Fort Washakie. Charles, his brother, and two sisters grew up at the fort surrounded by soldiers, Indians, cowboys, cattle men, hunters, trappers, freighters, stagecoach drivers, and outlaws. Charles learned to speak the Shoshone and Arapaho languages and was an ardent hunter and trapper. All the children went to secondary schools in the East; Charles attended Lawrenceville, in New Jersey, returning to Wyoming for summer vacations. He then rode as a cowboy and bronc buster in Buffalo Bill's Wild West Show in Chicago, New York, and other cities before deciding to study law at the University of Michigan. He was successful with his studies but his heart remained in the West. He often brought friends home for camping and hunting trips as early as 1895 while still in prep school.[29] After receiving his LL.B. degree, he practiced law in Cheyenne for a year but decided he wanted to return to a life of outdoor activity. Remembering his classmates' enjoyment of western trips, he decided in 1906 to open a boys' camp to take pack trips, especially through Yellowstone Park. He recruited teenagers in the East, listing as references Owen Wister, Governor Brook of Wyoming, Charles Potter, chief justice of the Wyoming Supreme Court, and several professors at the University of Michigan. The charge for a ten-week session (virtually the entire summer) was $250. The youngsters came to Lander by private railroad car under the direction of a physician; they then went to Moore's ranch near Dubois, where they learned horsemanship; how to set up, pull down, and pack a camp outfit; cooking; and a little geology and botany. Besides being a part of dude ranch development, Moore's camp was somewhat of a forerunner of the survival camps and schools that have grown in recent times.[30]

By means of successful recruiting, he increased the number of campers over the next several years. Eventually he needed three wagons, each pulled by four-horse teams, to carry the necessary supplies on his Yellowstone trips.[31] In the fall, after his teenagers were back in school, he took out hunting trips. Thus Charles Moore found that dudes provided him a way to return to the outdoor life he loved. But, like Howard Eaton, Dick Randall, the Wymans, and others, Moore soon found that the dudes would modify his plans. The boys were so enthusiastic about their trips that their parents, brothers, and sisters also wanted to see the West. They came at the beginning and end of the summer sessions and Moore had to provide living quarters for them. After World War I, he built the C M dude ranch to accommodate them.

North of Dubois, near Cody, another famous ranch was in its formative stage. Jim McLaughlin had a homestead at the head of the south fork of the Shoshone River. In 1910 Irving H. (Larry) Larom, a twenty-one-year-old Princeton College student, visited McLaughlin's homestead; his first view of this part of Wyoming must have been alarming since the railroad simply dumped him off in the dead of night at the foot of a water tank.[32] But Larom liked this wild section of the West and in 1915, he and Winthrop Brooks, a friend from Yale, returned there, bought McLaughlin's homestead, and started the Valley Ranch. Like many other westerners, they found their ranch the destination of many eastern visitors. Larom noted:

> as their [Larom's and Brooks's] revenues were small these visits
> became a hardship. They decided to capitalize on the idea of
> entertaining and the result was that they sought a limited number
> of guests who could pay.[33]

They had only two old shacks and less than seventy-five acres of land, but they gradually increased the number and quality of their buildings and their acreage and were able to accommodate their guests. Like the Eaton brothers in the Badlands, Larom and Brooks had to face the hostility of cattlemen and sheepmen who scorned the idea of a dude ranch. The Valley Ranch (like Charles Moore) soon began to specialize in summer pack trips for boys. Larom became the dominant partner in the ranch and, in the 1920s, emerged as the chief organizer of dude ranching.[34]

Many other dude ranches were begun between 1900 and 1915, primarily in the Sheridan and Cody areas. One interesting trip that a visitor recorded indicates just how widespread dude ranching was by 1915. The dude, Leon Dusseau, journeyed by train to Sheridan where he became acquainted with an artist also anxious to travel through Wyoming. The two men rented an automobile, followed the Big Horn River for hours, then climbed up a canyon to visit a ranch owned by Mr. and Mrs. Hilton of Cincinnati. They enjoyed the Hiltons' hospitality, then got some horses and rode with Mr. Hilton for several days to Bald Mountain, Medicine Mountain, and the Falls of the Porcupine in Devil's Canyon. When Mr. Hilton finally turned back to his ranch, the two travelers continued on to meet Mr. Milward who invited them to his IXL Ranch. After sampling his English hospitality, they rode to Eatons' Ranch for an exploration of the country thereabouts. Then they visited Gabriel's Ranch, Coffeen's Camp, Tepee Lodge, and Hilman's Ranch. They returned to automobile travel briefly to go to Piney Inn, where they resumed their horseback trek, this time to Horton's H F Bar Ranch, to the Paradise Ranch, and on to Alderson's Ranch in southern Montana. On these lengthy trips Dusseau and his artist companion viewed the strange stone formation called the Medicine Wheel, located in the Bighorn National Forest; it was supposedly built by the Indians for religious purposes. They also visited the sites of the Fetterman Massacre near Banner and the Wagon Box Fight near Story, plus numerous scenic canyons, mountains, and other sights that thrilled them both. Their easy traveling was possible, of course, only because dude ranches were scattered throughout this historic and scenic region.[35]

Even in the years before World War I, some characteristics of successful dude ranches were evident. Certain definitions were coming into common usage, and several types of dude ranches were in operation.

One fact that was becoming clear was that the successful ranches generally had a combination of eastern and western influences. A 1913 writer, Jesse Williams, saw this exemplified in the Wyoming partnership of a man from the U.S. Forestry Service with a former member of an English department at an eastern university. The forestry man had tried city life but preferred an outdoor occupation. The land he bought was not suitable for raising cattle, but he met the eastern professor, who was a keen sportsman; a dude ranch was the result of their partnership. The westerner furnished the experience and the easterner the friends who wanted to travel west. A later rancher made the same point in the 1920s.[36] Men from the East knew what other easterners wanted while westerners had the skills needed for finding water supplies, raising horses and cattle, and building log cabins. If a ranch didn't have two people, one from each section of the country, then it needed an easterner with western experience.[37] This concept is evident in the ranches described earlier in this chapter. Howard Eaton, Dick Randall, and Billy Howell were easterners who acquired western experience before accommodating dudes. Struthers Burt teamed up with a westerner before operating on his own; Charles Moore was a westerner who had been educated in the East and who had many friends there; and Larry Larom was an easterner who picked up considerable western experience before having much success with his ranch.

Even in these early days, ranchers and others were conscious of terminology. The word *dude,* the basis of the new terminology, actually became the center of controversy among some ranchers. The topic remained controversial and will also be mentioned in other contexts. The word has acquired so many connotations that few people are aware of its origin and meaning. Various dictionaries agree that it originated as western slang in the 1880s, but they list definitions varying from a dandy to an army recruit, and modern slang has added more. The term's connotation of "tenderfoot" or "someone wearing outlandish clothing" aroused the ire of many.[38] Western ranchers insisted that these uncomplimentary ideas were inappropriate and inconsistent with the original meaning, which was simply "someone not a resident of the northern Rocky Mountains." Rancher Struthers Burt claimed that Howard Eaton invented the term; to Eaton it did not imply ignorance, softness, or any tenderfoot qualities. Rather it meant "someone, usually a person not resident in the country, who hires some one else to guide him or cook for him, or who pays money to stay on a ranch." Dick Randall believed the word originated in Yellowstone Park and was first used by early park guides to mean a visitor from the East.[39] Mary Shawver, of Holm Lodge, said dudes were "guests who pay for accommodations, service and entertainment." Author Jesse Williams said that it was merely a generic term to classify all who came to ranches for a good time and that it had no reference to clothes, riding ability, or skill with rod and gun. Larry Larom accepted the much simpler definition: someone who was not a resident of the Rocky Mountains.[40]

A few variations of the word also appeared: "dudeen" or "dudine," referring to a female dude; "dudette," which sometimes referred to a child and other times to a woman who came west to marry a cowboy; "dudolo," which referred to the rare westerner who sponged off dudes;[41] and "dudelette," which meant someone who knows how to get on or off a horse. Other variations appeared but all except the word *dude* vanished, and no slur of any sort was intended by it. Throughout this text the term is used in this fashion and nothing derogatory is ever implied. A dude is someone who lived elsewhere, usually the Midwest or East, came west, and paid for riding, lodging, meals, and other services.[42]

While the word *dude* became controversial, the phrase *dude ranch* was nearly impossible to define. It would seem simple enough to say it was a ranch where dudes stayed, and this was adequate in the early days when the only places for outside visitors were ranches. But the definition became somewhat complicated when some facilities, like Holm Lodge, were designed just for visitors, and gradually inns, hotels, boardinghouses, and resorts became common in the West and muddled the situation. The key idea at this stage—pre–World War I—was that a dude ranch was the proprietors' home; they accepted dudes as guests to whom they furnished food, lodging, and the use of a saddle horse. Under this general description there were two types of dude ranches; one was the working stock ranch set up to make a profit on the horses or cattle it raised. These ranches were usually large, and their appeal was based on their size and the actual ranch activities. The second type was the mountain ranch, sometimes called a lodge, generally located in some breathtaking scenic area. Snow often covered the pasture for a large part of the year and that fact, or intense cold in the winter, made a year-round stock operation impossible or at least unprofitable.[43]

As dude ranchers developed their operations and made some distinctions about their status, they also had some thoughts about just what activities they should furnish their guests. As noted in Chapter 1, there was a distinction between travelers and tourists. Dude ranches clearly served travelers at first, such as Isabella Bird, Lord Dunraven, and the many early guests that the Eatons and Randalls accommodated. But would the guests be satisfied with normal activities or were staged events necessary? As early as 1913 a few ranches were contriving western pageantry such as daily afternoon cattle roundups.[44] Were dudes becoming tourists instead of travelers?

Ranchers did not worry about these questions yet; they were simply building their own businesses, generally small, without definitions or rigid rules. Besides, a storm was brewing across the Atlantic that was about to change the whole world.

The storm was, of course, "the war to end all wars"; after seven decades its evil effects can still be seen throughout the world. In a curious way, however, the war had a beneficial effect on dude ranching. Because Europe was virtually closed to travel, Americans began exploring their own country for vacation sites and areas of scenic beauty.[45] The U.S. Department of the Interior was also increasing its advertising of U.S. national parks as a virtual "See America First" campaign developed, and this helped draw many Americans westward. Another, smaller benefit also appeared at this time as gasoline tractors became more common, freeing many work horses and mules for pack trips.[46] All these factors, especially the "discovery" of the West by easterners, plus the ranches already in existence, set the stage for the golden decade of dude ranching from 1919 to 1929. During this period many new ranches began, dude ranching spread to other states, existing ranches matured, and there were attempts to organize this new industry.

Setting its own special standards for over fifty years was one of these new ranches, Holzwarth's Neversummer Ranch in Colorado. The Neversummer Ranch story started with John G. Holzwarth, Sr., who migrated from Germany in 1879, and it is tied in with two men who ran earlier ranches in the Middle Park area— Henry Lehman and Squeaky Bob Wheeler. Holzwarth first came to the Middle Park area in 1881, left, came back in 1885, and worked there awhile, part of the time for Henry Lehman.[47] He returned to Denver and in 1894 married a German girl, Sophia. She was a good cook and wanted to run an inn or hotel someday. The Holzwarths remained in Denver and in 1906 bought a saloon-boardinghouse which they built up successfully until Prohibition ruined the saloon business. They then considered a move across the Continental Divide to the Middle Park area, where Holzwarth had worked earlier. One factor that influenced them was that their youngest child, John, Jr. (always referred to as Johnnie), was getting into some trouble with boyish pranks in Denver. In the summer of 1917, John and Sophia staked a homestead claim ten miles north of Grand Lake and west of the north fork of the Grand (Colorado) River. In 1918 they returned to stay, built a cabin and barn, got some cattle, and started to reclaim hay meadows from the numerous beaver ponds; the Holzwarths were going to try ranching in the high altitude (8,900 feet) of Kawuneeche Valley.

Sophia was vivacious and hospitable, just as the Lehmans had been in the 1880s and 1890s; she served every afternoon caller coffee and cookies or cake. As a result, Holzwarth's ranch soon had lots of visitors.[48] In the summer of 1919 a freak accident changed the Holzwarths' lives when a team of runaway horses overturned a wagon on John Holzwarth, Sr. For the rest of his life he had to walk with a cane and could do no heavy work; he learned taxidermy through a mail-order course and used this skill to make money. The accident forced Johnnie, then but seventeen, to assume a great role in running the family homestead. In 1920 Fall River Road was finished nearby, connecting the east and west sides of Rocky Mountain National Park, thus increasing travel to the Grand Lake region.

Some of the new travelers were the Denver friends of John, Sr.; they came to the ranch to visit, fish, and drink, not necessarily in that order.

The Holzwarth hospitality had to be increased as numerous visitors arrived in warm weather. One day the guests, too drunk to fish, persuaded Johnnie to catch them some trout for supper. The Colorado River was teeming with fish so the young man soon caught over a hundred of them, but then the visitors could not decide how to divide the fish. An argument ensued, and Johnnie and Sophia became angry over this latest of many such incidents. They laid down a firm new rule: all guests, whether friends or strangers, had to pay to stay on their ranch. John, Sr., was appalled at first but finally acquiesced, and Holzwarth's Trout Lodge and Ranch was born; the rates were two dollars per day and eleven dollars per week including lodging, meals, and the use of a horse.[49] The first paying guests were some visitors whom Squeaky Bob Wheeler couldn't handle at his Hotel de Hardscrabble farther north along the Fall River Road. Young Johnnie consulted Wheeler and learned several things about how to take care of a large number of dudes.

The Holzwarths housed their guests in tents, but when these ran short guests had to sleep outside on box springs and mattresses. On holidays as many as a hundred people would be sleeping around the cabin and barn. Feeding all these people was a major problem since the valley had a very short growing season and was a long distance from Denver and other supply centers. But Mrs. Holzwarth served tasty meals of trout, dandelion greens, biscuits, and occasionally meat from big game animals Johnnie was able to kill. As busy as the Holzwarths were, however, the dude business was seasonal, coming mostly from June through September. So John, Sr., continued to stuff trophies for hunters while Johnnie put up hay, broke horses, ran a sawmill, and laid trap lines for marten and beaver.

To accommodate their visitors they built two cabins, but these were not sufficient; in 1923 they moved across the Colorado River to be closer to Fall River Road where they could take care of their guests better. The casual visitors became regular guests and gradually a new ranch was erected between the Colorado River and Fall River Road.[50] The new place was called Holzwarth's Neversummer Ranch (after the mountains visible to the west); it was in an ideal location since people who traveled the lengthy, tortuous route through the park were worn out when they reached the west side. A huge, three-story lodge, built of logs from the surrounding area, was begun in 1929 and nearby fields were cleared of willows for pasture and hay fields. The Holzwarths were able to make a decent living from dudes in the summer and on everything from hunting to hauling freight the rest of the year.

Holzwarth's ranch differed somewhat from most dude ranches in its origin and development. It was not established for the dude business and had not been in existence long enough to be a successful stock ranch. It took on dude business almost immediately after starting, and this assuredly helped it last, since most other ranches in the Kawuneeche Valley failed because of the harsh climate that enveloped them most of the year. Holzwarth's was also one of the few dude ranches that depended on local (Colorado) people for much of its early business.

Hundreds of miles north near Big Timber, Montana, the Lazy K Bar Ranch followed a more typical pattern of adding dudes to an existing operation. The Paul Van Cleve family has operated the ranch in the Melville country for four generations. Paul, Sr., came to Montana from Minnesota in 1882, homesteaded a piece of land, and raised sheep and cattle. As the ranch succeeded, Van Cleve eventually built a huge thirty-six-room house, a polo field, and several garages for the automobiles of his many eastern guests. The large house burned, but the ranch continued under Paul, Jr., born in 1889 and known as Scrumper. The many eastern visitors in the late nineteenth and early twentieth centuries did not force the Van Cleves into a dude ranch operation; however, a slump in cattle prices in 1922 convinced them to start taking paying guests. They had only six dudes the first year but built that number into the hundreds as they let their guests take part in regular ranch activities.[51] The dudes also fished, hunted, and rode horseback among "the beauties of snow-capped mountains, forests of pine and spruce, crystal-clear lakes, glaciers, deep ravines and mountain streams of the Crazy Mountains."[52]

The Lazy K Bar also began raising quarter horses and became well known for its dude horses in later years. It is interesting that here, in south-central Montana, the dude business helped preserve a stock ranch that might otherwise have failed.

A few years later a similar story unfolded at the Ox Yoke Ranch near Emigrant, about twenty-five miles north of Yellowstone Park. The Ox Yoke brand was one of the oldest in Montana, having been used by Nelson Story, a pioneer prospector in the 1860s. He used $10,000 of the money he made from his gold strike to buy a thousand head of cattle in Texas; then he put the Ox Yoke brand on them and drove them north to Montana Territory. He increased his herds on a ranch south of Livingston until 1885 when he sold his cattle just before harsh winters hit the open range industry. Years later Nelson's son, T. B. Story, formed a partnership with Charlie Murphy and his wife Peg. In 1919 they bought the Ox Yoke Ranch that contained some of the best grazing land Nelson Story had used. Murphy and Story stocked the 5,000-acre ranch at Emigrant with sheep and cultivated hay for winter feeding. The cold, wet weather caused heavy lamb losses, however, and some late winters in the 1920s increased their feeding costs.

T. B. Story was discouraged, so the Murphys bought out his interest in the ranch. Peg and Charlie Murphy had a great appreciation for natural beauty, and one summer when they were packing salt and supplies to a sheep camp in Big Creek Basin, they got the idea to move the ranch headquarters there from the valley. They decided they could add a few extra log cabins to accommodate paying guests from the city who would enjoy simple western life in a family-style atmosphere. They built these cabins in 1929 and started taking guests; the following year they sold their sheep, put the Ox Yoke brand on some cattle they had bought, and ran a successful cattle and dude ranch for many years.[53]

There were at least six other dude ranches in the mid-1920s in Gallatin County, the most famous being Dick Randall's OTO, the Karst Ranch, and the Miller's Elkhorn Ranch near Bozeman.[54] Farther east was another concentration of ranches between Billings and Sheridan, including Bones Brothers, the Quarter Circle U, and Rosebud ranches. Toward the center of the state, within a triangle formed by Helena, Livingston, and Lewistown, were several ranches like the Lazy K Bar, Alt, and Hart Bar T. Another area of concentration was in the northwestern part of the state near Missoula, Kalispell, and Glacier National Park; here were the Bandman Manor, Fox and Acuff, M Lazy V, Tee Bar ranches, and others. By the late 1920s there were approximately three dozen dude ranches scattered across the Treasure State with the concentrations heaviest south of Billings and in the vicinity of Glacier and Yellowstone parks.[55]

In Wyoming dude ranching also continued to thrive. In Jackson Hole country another durable ranch began in the 1920s. John S. Turner had visited the area on a vacation and bought some land there in 1925. He tried to make a living raising potatoes but the land wasn't suited to farming. Turner then tried cattle but ranching was always precarious in Jackson Hole; he noticed the frequent visits of fishermen and elk hunters to the region so he built some cabins for them while continuing to raise cattle. The Turner Ranch was on a more solid footing now although there were several name and organizational changes before it became known as the Turner Triangle X Ranch and before the business was extensive. Eventually, hunting and dudes became its mainstays.[56]

East of Jackson Hole, near Dubois, Charles Moore continued to conduct his pack trips for boys, but the constant visits of the youngsters' relatives prompted him to buy some land in 1920 and begin the C M Ranch. Here he built cabins and accommodated dudes while continuing his trips for boys. The dude business soon became so important, however, that he abandoned the pack trips for boys; to take care of his dudes, he built a hydroelectric plant and raised dairy cattle, chickens, and vegetables.[57] Moore was able to continue his outdoor activities for the rest of his life because of the success of the C M Ranch.

His "neighbor," Larry Larom, was also successful at his Valley Ranch where the original two shacks and 74½ acres had grown to more than 60 buildings and 8,000 acres that were owned or leased. The ranch southwest of Cody attracted many dudes, but Larom added something unique to the Valley Ranch—a boys' school. In 1922, just about the time Charles Moore was switching from the boys' camp to a full-time dude ranch, Larom and his partners decided to open a college preparatory school. Larom had graduated from Princeton and his partner, Winthrop Brooks, from Yale. Another man associated with their school venture, Julian Bryan, had graduated from Colgate. The three men thus had contacts at several important eastern universities that might prove valuable to graduates of the ranch school. Brooks and Bryan remained in the East but Larom lived on the ranch and became headmaster and director of the school; he hired men from Harvard, Princeton, Penn State, and the University of Illinois to teach English, history, mathematics, physics, Latin, German, and French. The school provided an interesting combination of academic work, discipline, and outdoor activities. Mornings were reserved for classes while afternoon sessions included rifle shooting, polo, horseback riding, trapping, fishing, mountain climbing, football, soccer, and other sports. All-day rides and weekend pack trips to the mountains were common, attendance at nondenominational religious services was required, and the school reserved the right to dismiss any student without stating the cause. The cost for all teaching, housing, food, books, supplies, and use of a horse and saddle was a hefty $1550; students had to furnish their own clothing and a quality .22 caliber rifle. The school caught on quickly and by 1925 was one of three places in the Rocky Mountain country where the College Entrance Examination Boards were given. Students from the Valley School were soon entering Princeton, Yale, Harvard, Dartmouth, and other universities. The school operated from fall to spring, except for a four-week vacation at Christmas, and lasted into the mid-1930s.[58]

While new ranches sprouted throughout the Rockies, two of the earliest ones, Eatons' and Randalls', continued to grow and set a strong pace for others. Dick Randall continued to guide hunters after World War I, but the dude business became dominant in the 1920s. It became so important that Randall began to depend on it; he had to start advertising in order to assure reservations in time to hire workers, and buy provisions and equipment. The ranch kept a herd of beef cattle, some milk cows, and about three hundred horses for the care and feeding of the dudes; the latter liked the animals so much that Randall added some lambs and a pet pig. One year Charlie Herbert, who made full-length films for Fox Movietown News, came to the OTO and filmed some of the animals there for a special feature. This experience inspired the dudes to add to the ranch menagerie, and they trapped porcupine, badgers, coyotes, and even a bear for Herbert to photograph.[59]

The Randalls were helped in operating their ranch by their son, Lesley, and by their daughter and son-in-law, Bess and Clyde Erskine. The rugged road to the ranch was improved over a two-year period since some guests were coming by automobile in the 1920s. Clyde Erskine decided to put baths in two of the cabins although Dick Randall thought it was a needless luxury. The "luxury cabins" proved so popular, however, that the rancher installed two bathrooms in the lodge, set up a shower house and laundry room, and installed a 1,000-gallon hot-water tank. They then built an icehouse and hauled three tons of ice ten miles to fill it. Erskine and Mrs. Randall made several hundred pounds of cheese and butter each year while they purchased about three truckloads of canned goods from Chicago. When some families wanted to send their children alone to the ranch, Dick Randall and Clyde Erskine built a two-story dormitory for eighteen people, with girls on the second floor and boys on the first.

The OTO Ranch thrived as guests enjoyed the ranch activities, good food, horseback riding, and pack trips. Over and above these activities, the personalities of Dick and Dora Randall held the ranch together; he was the hunter, guide, and storyteller, and she was the hostess and manager. The dudes called Dick "the Governor" and Dora "Mother Randall." The dedication and loyalty that the guests showed was significant. One season, early in the summer, a flash flood in Cedar Creek destroyed the bunkhouse and power plant and damaged much of the equipment and buildings. The entire season was ruined by this flood and all the guests had to be hurriedly evacuated, but, as they left, they made their reservations for the following year. The OTO survived this disaster and was ready for them the next season.[60]

A similar dedication and loyalty had been built at Eatons' Ranch near Sheridan. By 1919, the first year after the war, the Eatons had well-established annual pack trips—fifteen days through Glacier Park and twenty days or more in Yellowstone. In that year they also offered a month-long trip to the Grand Canyon and to various Indian villages in New Mexico. The Eatons branched out some distance for a few of their trips, but northern Wyoming was the center of most activities. Even these spectacular trips did not overshadow the personalities of the Eaton brothers, especially Howard. He could take a mixed group of easterners and mold them into a homogeneous whole in a few days. He was able to teach people about riding, camping, and the West without appearing to do so.[61] Always a host and thinking of his guests, he was setting a firm pattern for other ranchers to follow. It was important for a working ranch to remain a ranch and keep that special flavor for the dudes. It had also become customary for dudes and ranchers to have direct personal correspondence; since dudes were truly guests in the rancher's home it was necessary that they be compatible with the ranchers and other guests. This was especially important since long stays of several weeks or months were common. [62]

Howard was also very concerned about wildlife. In the winter of 1922, hearing that the elk in Jackson Hole were starving, Howard (then seventy-one years old) went in to help feed them. He was snowed in for a few days and suffered from hunger and cold himself before getting out. A few days after returning to the ranch, he was seized by an attack of appendicitis. He was brought to Sheridan on March 21 and operated on, but he died on April 5 of peritonitis. [63] People throughout the country mourned the founder and shaper of dude ranching. Mary Roberts Rinehart wrote a tribute to him years later that summarized him well:

> I can see Howard now, erect in his saddle, in the ordinary gray
> suit and big soft hat which were his constant wear. In that same
> type of gray suit . . . he went, complacently to White House or
> mansion, and always he was joyfully received. Dear Howard, with
> his kindness, his eternal patience, his sturdy independence. [64]

But what he had built lived on. Four of his eight brothers and sisters had come to Wyoming and three, Alden, Willis, and Mary Gillespie, worked on the ranch. Willis and Alden took over, and Eatons' continued to attract dudes by the hundreds. Horseback riding remained the chief attraction, with trout fishing a close second. Most of their dudes were relatively unknown, but the ranch could boast of some famous guests: Teddy Roosevelt, Mary Roberts Rinehart, Will Rogers, and Dan Beard. [65]

The success of Eatons' and other early ranches led to a rapid expansion of the industry in Wyoming. The concentration was even more pronounced there than in Montana. Nearly all the dude ranches in the mid-1920s were within fifty miles of Cody, Sheridan, or Jackson with the great majority near the first two cities. Ranches were located around Jackson because of the hunting, the Teton Mountains, and Yellowstone Park; near Cody because of Yellowstone; and near Sheridan because of Eatons' and the Big Horn Mountains. The Eatons' influence is seen, not only in the dozen or more Wyoming ranches near Sheridan, but also in those just across the border in Montana; one of these, Bones' Brothers Ranch, was operated by former Eaton dudes. Some of the others in the vicinity were Jones, Klondike, Lodore, Mountain Home, Red Cliff, Spear, and Staples ranches. Near Cody were the Absaroka and Aldrich lodges, the Double L Bar, Majo, Morris, N.E., P Bar P, Snyder, Sunlight, and Fred J. Richard ranches. [66]

By the mid-1920s there were more than sixty dude ranches in Wyoming and Montana with a smaller number established in Colorado and a few spreading to other states. It was clearly time for this new industry to get organized.

FOUR

The Outdoor Life

The work of the Dude Ranchers' Association in fostering appreciation of the outdoor life and of the unexampled opportunities offered
by our Western country for its fullest enjoyment for purposes of
health, education and recreation deserves the warmest commend-
ation.

> —Letter from President Herbert Hoover, March 3, 1931,
> *Minutes of the Fifth Annual Dude Ranchers' Meeting, 2.*

The growth of dude ranching from 1900 to 1925 was substantial enough to affect
the economic situation in the northern Rockies. Since cattle prices dropped after
1919 and hay prices rose because of a drought, the raising of cattle became a
precarious business and the result was the abandonment of many dry farms and
small ranches. But a number of cattle ranches were saved by the growing dude
business in the West. Dude ranches brought approximately a million dollars in
business to Wyoming and an equal amount to Montana.[1] The merchants of
Gunnison, Colorado estimated that tourists brought in about $60,000 to the
town and a total of $100,000 to the entire county. The businessmen of this city
credited much of this economic activity to dude ranches, and the commercial
club even noted where future dude ranches might be built to increase this business. Throughout Colorado, tourism accounted for approximately $5.5 million

being spent in the state; there are no figures, however, to show how much of that total could be attributed to dude ranches.[2]

The absence of such specific information points out one of the most difficult aspects of studying dude ranching: the lack of statistics to show its exact importance and place in the economy of the western states. In the second half of the twentieth century one can locate recent statistical data on every conceivable subject, but this information was simply not gathered during the late nineteenth and early twentieth centuries when dude ranching grew so rapidly and became the key factor in tourism in the Rocky Mountain West. There is no question, however, of its importance. The scattered figures, such as those mentioned above, are part of the evidence, but there are circumstantial facts that also demonstrate this. The railroads serving the West recognized clearly that much of their passenger business came from dude ranch guests. Local and state governments realized it also; this was especially true in Wyoming, where dude ranch growth and development convinced state officials to look at tourism as an industry of major significance.[3] This early awareness of the importance of dude ranches has remained consistent in state government in Wyoming to the present. Another sign of the preeminence of dude ranching in the western travel industry was the manner of advertising that other tourist attractions adopted. Hotels, inns, and other facilities tried to identify with dude ranches in their appeal, and stories about western attractions often mentioned dude ranches first and then a variety of other types of accommodations.[4]

Journalistic accounts noted the dominance of ranch vacations in western travel and pointed out that these vacations kept American money at home; they gave Americans a local place to spend their vacation dollars and drew more investments to the West.[5] The latter case often occurred when a dude ranch visitor became so enchanted with his western visit that he stayed or invested some money in the West. Thus, F. W. Leach, a New York businessman, came to a Wyoming ranch and liked it so much that he severed his financial ties with the Empire State and invested in his own ranch near Kearney, Wyoming. This was the TAT Ranch where he entertained his own guests—first his friends, then other dudes. The OTO Ranch in Montana entertained a number of foreigners who invested money in that state; Lord Kinley built the Albemarle Hotel in Livingston and Lord Todd the Toddy Building in Great Falls.[6] This type of investment was similar to easterners and foreigners investing in cattle ranches in the late nineteenth century, mentioned in Chapter 2.

While these bits of circumstantial data are not as satisfying as a complete set of statistics would be, there is no doubt that dude ranches were of great importance in the West. This importance was most visible in Wyoming, Montana, and

Colorado, but the idea of ranches accepting guests was spreading in the 1920s to other states. This growth and the realization of the importance of dude ranching led also to the formation of organizations of these ranchers.

The first of these groups was the Dude Ranchers' Association, formed in September 1926. There were at least twenty new ranches started between 1920 and 1926, and some ranchers began to realize that their mutual problems relating to transportation, forestry regulations, game laws, insurance, and other items required an organization. It is difficult to say who had the first idea of forming such a group, but it is clear that railroad officials of the Northern Pacific, as well as dude ranchers, cooperated in getting the formative meeting together. According to several sources, Ernest Miller of the Elkhorn Ranch near Bozeman convinced Max Goodsill, general passenger agent of the Northern Pacific, of the value of some kind of organization. Goodsill passed this idea on to A. B. Smith, the passenger traffic manager.[7] It is certain that Smith then proposed and arranged the meeting at the Bozeman Hotel for September 27 and 28, 1926, and the DRA later acknowledged him as the "Father of the Dude Ranchers' Association." Larry Larom of the Valley Ranch was also a prime mover in getting the organization started; he was elected its first president and was reelected to that position for many years.[8]

The Northern Pacific sponsored this meeting because of the advantage to the railroad of increased passenger service that an organized group could promote. In a newspaper interview Smith emphasized the railway's intentions:

> We Want Young America to . . . know the grandeur of the
> Rockies, the traditions of the old pioneer trails, the fine spirit of
> the great western out-of-doors. We hope to outline a program that
> will bring Montana and Wyoming to the forefront as national
> playgrounds. . . .[9]

He noted that thousands of new prospects would be sold on Montana and Wyoming trips by the introduction of popularly priced vacations from large towns in the central part of the county. Another important participant at this initial meeting was Horace N. Albright, superintendent of Yellowstone National Park; he assured the ranchers of the sympathy and cooperation of the park administration with ranch parties making excursions into the park. This was the era when the federal government was trying to increase usage of the national parks; dude ranchers and their guests were probably the prime users of Yellowstone Park at this time and thus there was a cordial relationship between ranchers and Albright.

The official purposes of the September meeting were five: (1) to establish cooperation and acquaintance among ranchers and railroad officials; (2) to discuss problems of getting and properly caring for guests; (3) to make advertising and publicity plans for 1927; (4) to standardize practices; and (5) to form an efficient sales organization.

Besides railroad and park officials, 70–100 ranchers attended the two-day gathering presided over by A. B. Smith and discussed these ideas and other problems that arose. Among the prominent ranchers taking part were these from Montana: George McCarn, Hunter's Hot Springs; P. F. Karst, Cold Springs Ranch; James W. Parker, Gardiner; G. J. Ikerman, Beartooth Ranch; Paul Van Cleve, Jr., Lazy K Bar Ranch; Dick Randall, OTO Ranch; Ernest Miller, Elkhorn Ranch; A. H. Croonquist, Camp Senia at Red Lodge; from Wyoming came: Fred J. Richard of Cody; I. H. Larom of the Valley Ranch; and representatives from Eatons' Ranch at Wolf.

One of the most significant questions debated was whether to use the terms *dude* and *dude ranch* in the name of the organization. Some people thought the words undignified for a business growing to be an important industry. The word *dude* apparently originated in the northern Rockies and simply referred to an outsider who paid for lodging, riding, hunting, or other services, but it had acquired less complimentary connotations in some places as a tenderfoot or as someone wearing foppish or outlandish clothing. Dick Randall and the Eatons especially emphasized, however, that "dude ranch" had already become a valuable trademark that people liked and recognized. Randall believed that the word *dude* had lost its derisive implications. Horace Albright echoed these views, saying the name was distinctive and well liked. The ranchers were won to this view and unanimously agreed to accept the name "Dude Ranchers' Association."[10]

The plans they outlined were broad but covered several key points: classification of ranches according to accommodations and rates; active support for the protection of game and fish; cooperation with the Northern Pacific officials and sales organization to promote travel to dude ranches; and aggressive advertising plans and personal solicitation of prospective patrons in cities of the East and Midwest. These stated goals generally followed the purposes mentioned by A. B. Smith before the meeting, but it is noteworthy that the ranchers added the idea of support for protecting fish and game; dude ranchers were ardent conservationists, both from personal belief and because of the importance of game and fish to their guests.

The DRA officers elected at this meeting were I. H. (Larry) Larom, president; A. H. Croonquist, vice-president; and Ernest Miller, secretary-treasurer. Seven directors were also chosen to represent the different sections of the dude ranch country and the different types of ranchers: W. A. Binko of Missoula; Dick

Randall, OTO Ranch, Corwin Springs; Mrs. Walter Shaw, Shaw's Camp, Cooke City, Montana; Paul Van Cleve, Lazy K Bar Ranch, Big Timber; Ed Wyman, Trapper's Lodge, Shell, Wyoming; William Eaton, Eatons' Ranch, Wolf; and Dr. Horace Carncross, Bar B C Ranch, Jackson Hole.[11]

Twenty-six ranches were signed up as charter members at this first meeting, and committees were created to deal with writing a constitution, advertising, transportation, and legislation regarding fish and game. The meeting had been an obvious success: the ranchers had organized quickly, and the Northern Pacific immediately began including dude ranch advertising in its 1928 budget.

The list of officers and directors shows clearly that the DRA was a Montana-Wyoming organization, although it later accepted members from other states. A major reason for this was the direction given to the group by officials of the Northern Pacific Railway, who organized and presided over the founding meeting. Although the importance of railroad transportation eventually declined, this direction and emphasis has continued, and the DRA has remained primarily an organization for the northern Rockies—Wyoming, Montana, and a few ranches in Idaho and other states.

There were three types of facilities included in the DRA in these early days. The first was the working stock ranch, located in the plains or foothills country; riding, fishing, and visits to scenic sites were the primary activities on these ranches. The second was the mountain ranch or lodge that emphasized fishing and trips on foot or horseback. A third type was the hot springs resort with the springs and bathing pools the chief attractions. This last group eventually disappeared from the DRA; their inclusion shows, however, the rather wide nature of the organization at its beginning. It again emphasizes the pioneering nature of the dude ranches in the western tourist industry.

The DRA grew quickly, with forty-seven ranch owners signed up at the second annual meeting in 1927; its importance was emphasized by the attendance at the convention of the governors of both Wyoming and Montana; they saw clearly the value of the million dollars or more spent by dudes on their western vacations.[12] The organization got a big boost in 1928 when Larry Larom (who continued as president for eighteen years) and Max Goodsill of the Northern Pacific persuaded T. Joe Cahill to become the group's executive secretary. This newly created position was arranged by a cooperative agreement between the railroad and the Dude Ranchers' Association; the Northern Pacific gave Cahill inter-railroad passes for his extensive travel and paid part of his expenses while the DRA paid his salary and the rest of his expenses. He was a very forceful organizer and served as executive secretary for four years. He helped publish "Annual Books" for the association in 1929, 1930, and 1931 containing data on the value of the ranches, the land they controlled, money spent by the dudes, and the numbers of horses, cattle, and sheep the ranches owned. These books also included reports on committees and legislation that interested ranchers. Cahill helped get newspaper and magazine publicity, showed movies of ranches, and even sponsored a dude ranch contest. The executive secretary thus gave a big boost to the fledgling organization and helped it get off to a flying start.[13] In 1928 the DRA also began to solicit associate memberships in the organization. These were open to anyone who wished to help support the DRA with annual dues of five dollars; many stores, hotels, and other small businesses in Montana and Wyoming soon joined in this new category.[14]

Even as the DRA organized and cooperated with the Northern Pacific and Burlington railways, dude ranching was spreading from the northern Rockies to other western states. Besides Wyoming, Montana, Colorado, and Idaho, there were some early dude ranches in New Mexico and Arizona. Little information is available on most of the New Mexico ranches, but at least five of them were operating in 1926, the year the DRA was organized. The Santa Fe Railway served these five ranches: El Rito and San Gabriel, both in Rio Arriba County, Los Alamos near East Las Vegas, the Mountain View Ranch in San Miguel County, and the Valley Ranch. The San Gabriel Ranch, at Alcalde near San Juan Pueblo, was built into a thriving operation by an interesting combination of eastern influence and western skill. A young girl from Boston visited New Mexico where she met and married a Texas cowboy; he had the knowledge to run a ranch, and she had the social connections in the East to attract guests. The result was the successful operation of the San Gabriel for about a decade. A number of other ranches, probably two dozen, operated in New Mexico for the next few years.[15]

One of the most unusual of these was the elaborate facility known as Vermejo Park Ranch in the northern part of the state. It began when a wealthy Chicago grain dealer, W. H. Bartlett, visited the area around the turn of the century because of poor health. His health improved considerably in the high, dry country, so he stayed and, in 1901, developed a huge estate and game preserve of 300,000 acres; it extended from the Sangre de Cristo mountains eastward for forty miles with the main ranch located at an altitude of 7,000 feet. He stocked the streams with trout and a lake with bass, then administered his own game laws under a park license. Like the Eatons, Randalls, and other northern ranchers, Bartlett developed a working operation but also provided facilities for guests; he did it, however, on a much grander scale than these other men and women. Besides guest houses for his wealthy friends, he built hunting lodges on different parts of the property and kept a string of saddle horses with guides and wranglers available for hunting trips. It was a commercial cattle ranch, running 10,000–

15,000 head of Herefords; more than 2,000 acres were irrigated and produced thousands of tons of alfalfa, timothy, and blue-stem vega hay. An additional 3,000 acres were devoted to barley, Mexican beans, and forage crops without irrigation. The ranch was relatively self-sufficient with its own electricity, heating facilities, telephone lines, reservoirs, pumping plants, machine shops, greenhouses, a commissary, and a fish hatchery. Bartlett spent about three million dollars developing this ranch so he could enjoy good health and the western outdoor life. His actions were very similar to what Theodore Roosevelt, Moreton Frewen, and other men had done years earlier in the Dakotas, Montana, and Wyoming; they loved the western life and built ranches in the west so they could enjoy it and have a commercial operation to justify the expense.

When Bartlett died in 1918 after seventeen years of this idyllic existence, his heirs decided to dispose of the property. In 1926 Harry Chandler, publisher of the *Los Angeles Times*, purchased it for an undisclosed sum and made it into a recreation retreat for the well-to-do. Chandler formed the Vermejo Club, set a quota of 150 members, and sold life memberships for $5,000. These members then had the privilege of riding, fishing, hunting, hiking, or merely relaxing along with their families. The quota of memberships was sold quickly and Vermejo Ranch set the tone for a new style of luxurious dude ranches in the Southwest.[16]

In neighboring Arizona there was an even larger growth of guest ranches; the pattern of this development was similar to that of states farther north. Hunters, campers, and other sportsmen traveled to Arizona seeking outdoor recreation; many made their headquarters at cattle ranches and worked out an arrangement to pay for food, shelter, a guide, and the use of horses. The ranch atmosphere added to their enjoyment and the appeal of ranch life attracted many more people. Soon a number of stock ranches were regularly accepting guests or dudes.[17]

Pinpointing which Arizona ranch first accepted guests is just as difficult as identifying the first dude ranch in the country. One of the earliest ones was the Brill Ranch, a 960-acre cattle operation near Wickenburg. In 1912 or 1913 it was renamed the Garden of Allah Resort; horseback riding was provided while homegrown fruits and vegetables, fresh milk, butter, and cream guaranteed appealing meals for the guests. This early ranch was later operated under the name of the Circle Flying W Ranch.[18]

Another early guest ranch was Faraway Ranch, located in the southeastern part of the state. It was begun as a cattle ranch in the 1880s by Neil Erickson, a former soldier in the U.S. Army. His father had migrated to the United States from Sweden and was killed by Indians in the Dakotas. Neil joined the army, seeking revenge against the Indians, and was sent to Arizona where the army was still fighting the Apaches. Erickson soon decided that the Indians deserved more sympathy than vengeance as he campaigned against Apaches led by Loco and Geronimo. He left the army after attaining the rank of sergeant and married Emma Peterson; they decided to remain in Arizona and homesteaded in the area east of Tucson. This land, in Bonita Canyon, was known as the Wonderland of Rocks because of the unusual rock formations there. (It was later made into the Chiricahua National Monument.) Years later the Ericksons' two daughters, Lillian and Hildegarde, opened the ranch to guests; the principal attraction for visitors was the view of the rocks that covered the landscape. In 1923 Lillian married Ed Riggs, who had explored the Wonderland of Rocks territory extensively, and they operated Faraway as a cattle and dude ranch for several decades. They drew up detailed plans to develop it into an outstanding guest ranch, but they had to halt these plans because Lillian's eyesight began to deteriorate from injuries she had suffered in a fall from a horse. Faraway continued to accept guests, but it never became a large operation like some others in the Southwest.[19]

Several other Arizona ranches decided to enter the dude business in the 1920s. Cattle prices declined significantly just as they had in Wyoming and Montana after the prosperous years of 1914–18. The cattle business declined so much that some of the ranches had to start accepting guests to avert bankruptcy. Many cowboys could not find jobs herding cattle, so they went to Oracle, Wickenburg, or Castle Hot Springs (northwest of Phoenix) to get jobs wrangling dudes on the newly formed or recently converted guest ranches.[20]

Among these early dude ranches were Donnee's Dude Ranch, the Triangle L Ranch, and Rancho Linda Vista, all near Oracle (north of Tucson), and Bishopp's C-4 Ranch and the Remuda Ranch (near Wickenburg). Beaver Creek Ranch was another early dude ranch, located about fifty miles from Flagstaff near the town of Rimrock. Set in a wide canyon with sheer cliffs on both sides, this guest ranch featured stone cottages, electric heaters, and refrigerators for its visitors as early as 1929. It offered swimming, hunting for a wide variety of game, and visits to an Apache village as special attractions.[21]

Another ranch with a long history of operation and with an indirect tie to Wyoming was La Cebadilla Ranch near Tucson; Jim Converse bought it in 1928 and changed its name to Tanque Verde Ranch. He had read about Eatons' Ranch in Wyoming and decided to imitate it by accepting guests. He was mostly interested in riding and hunting, so his wife, Billie, took charge of the dudes and built Tanque Verde into a successful guest ranch. Farther south, near Patagonia, a similar story unfolded at the Circle Z Ranch. It was a cattle ranch until the 1920s when the Zinsmeister brothers, Carl and Lee, purchased it. They began accepting guests while retaining the cattle operation; the dudes joined in with the ranch work when they were not enjoying the excellent big game hunting and fishing that were available. Like Tanque Verde, the Circle Z has continued its activities to the present. Another of the old and famous Arizona guest ranches was the Y-Lightning near Hereford in the southeastern part of the state. It was owned and operated by F. B. Moson, who had come to Arizona Territory in 1884. Comprising 25,000 acres, it continued its cattle raising in the 1920s while the owners added a wide variety of activities such as hiking, mountain climbing, polo, and pack trips.[22]

A very famous spot in Arizona that was known for a time as a dude ranch was Phantom Ranch near Bright Angel Creek in the Grand Canyon. The cottonwood grove where it was located had appealed to visitors for years; as early as 1903 Dave Rust of Kanab, Utah, established a tent camp there as a stopping place for hikers, horse or mule riders, and perhaps an occasional daring river runner. After Theodore Roosevelt visited there in 1913, it was called Camp Roosevelt for a while. It was neglected during the war years; then in 1921 the Santa Fe Railway and Fred Harvey interests obtained the site and built Phantom Ranch. Eventually, it became quite well known as an overnight stop for the many hikers and mule riders journeying into the canyon.[23]

A few northern dude ranchers operated Arizona ranches for several years so they could offer year-round vacations to their guests. The Eaton family, whose main ranch was near Sheridan, Wyoming, also owned Rimrock Ranch near the town of the same name in Arizona. The Miller family operated the Elkhorn Ranch south of Bozeman, Montana, and also ran a ranch with the same name south of Tucson. And the Van Cleves operated the Lazy K Bar near Big Timber, Montana, and one with the identical name in the mountains near Tucson.

These various Arizona ranches appealed to people for many of the same reasons that those farther north did. Horseback riding was the central attraction while roundups and rodeos were not far behind. But Arizona guest ranches also differed in certain ways from those farther north; bright sunshine and warm weather throughout the year added a new dimension to the appeal of the Grand Canyon State. From the first this meant Arizona ranches would have a large following among winter travelers, and they offered a wider variety of activities for their guests. Tennis courts, swimming pools, and golf courses were common attractions in Arizona that were seldom, if ever, available on ranches in Colorado, Wyoming, or Montana.[24]

Like the railroads that served the northern Rockies, railroads serving the Southwest featured guest ranches in various brochures.[25] The Southern Pacific and Santa Fe lines, however, never became as deeply involved with dude and guest ranches as did the Northern Pacific, Burlington, and Union Pacific railroads. Ranchers in Arizona also decided to organize in the late 1920s; their first group was the Arizona Dude and Guest Ranch Association, which for a while had an official publication, *Hoofs and Horns* magazine. This organization lasted only a few years, so in the 1930s another was formed: The Arizona Hotel and Dude Ranch Association. This group faded away after a brief existence, and the Southern Arizona Guest Ranch Association appeared in the mid-1940s. It too disappeared, and several more dude or guest ranch groups have been launched since the late 1940s. None of these Arizona organizations attained the importance or permanency of the Dude Ranchers' Association or the group that would appear in Colorado in the early 1930s.[26]

During these same years one of the most peculiar developments in dude ranching was occurring in Nevada. The key to it was the passage of an easy divorce law there in the early 1920s; it permitted a divorce for someone who had been a resident only six months. This lenient residency requirement drew many people to Nevada. It was changed to three months in 1929 and later reduced to six weeks.[27] The stage was set, but the actual beginning of dude ranching was initiated, ironically, by a minister, the Reverend Brewster Adams. In 1929 he returned home to Nevada after a visit to Eatons' Ranch in Wyoming. He believed Nevada should have a dude ranch similar to Eatons' and suggested this to an acquaintance, Neill West. West was a cattleman, operating the T-H Ranch above Pyramid Lake just north of Reno; he took the advice of Brewster Adams and built ten small wooden cabins on the ranch. He charged guests thirty-five dollars per week for these quarters, two meals a day, and the use of a horse.

The T-H Ranch and others grew, partly because of the appeal of scenery and ranch life, but more because of the easy divorce law. There were few good hotels in Reno, so these dude ranches became popular; the rich and famous who journeyed to Nevada liked the privacy and isolation of dude ranches, where they could be shielded from newspapermen and photographers. In addition there was a provision in the divorce law that an applicant had to be able to prove that she (generally women were the ones seeking these divorces) had not been out of the state for more than twenty-four hours during the required residency. Dude ranch owners and managers could and did verify this in court when divorce cases were heard.

On Nevada ranches the talents required for operating successfully were similar to those on other dude ranches: the men had to know horses, horsemen, and sometimes cattle, while the women had to manage food, entertainment, and other details. But an additional burden that the hostesses had to shoulder was the need to be a sort of a mother confessor to women with shattered marriages and broken lives.[28]

Cornelius Vanderbilt, Jr., eventually bought the T-H Ranch and also the Lazy

M Ranch, south of Reno. Vanderbilt advertised in only two publications, *Town Topics* (New York) and *The Beverly Hills Script*, both of which catered to wealthy people and were strong on snob appeal. These advertisements brought some people to the ranches, but Vanderbilt learned the value of a different kind of publicity when Amelia Earhart stayed at the Lazy M Ranch. This led him to invite Hollywood stars such as Douglas Fairbanks, Jr., Charlie Chaplin, Will Rogers, Tom Mix, Gary Cooper, and Clark Gable for visits; the ranch gave them free accommodations for a week in the hope that their presence would draw more guests. This plan worked for a while, but, after the appeal of the famous declined, Vanderbilt offered a package ranch divorce; for $795 he furnished room and board for six weeks (the residency requirement after 1931), a horse to ride, two trips to Reno each week, a free pack of cigarettes each day, and a free bottle of liquor once a week. News of this offer brought the ranch a flood of reservations, so the owners quickly enlarged their facilities to accommodate fifty to sixty guests. The ranch also did a big business with lawyers handling these easy divorce cases.[29]

In Nevada, Arizona, and New Mexico, cattle ranches had helped spawn dude ranches, although other factors were also involved as noted above; ironically there was much less development in nearby Texas, the home ground of the western cattle industry. There was some dude ranching, however, in the hill country near Bandera. Rancher Ebenezer Buck invited some friends from Houston to his ranch in 1921; they enjoyed the good food and ranch life for only ten dollars a week, so they returned for later visits. Within a few years his ranch was booked solid with guests; one of Buck's neighbors summed up this new business well when he noted, "You can run more dudes to the acre in these hills than you can cattle."[30] Bandera eventually became the center for a half-dozen ranches or so. Probably the most famous dude ranch in Texas in the early part of the twentieth century was the Gallagher Ranch near San Antonio, a cattle ranch of 10,000 acres. It began accepting guests and was accepted as a member of the Dude Ranchers' Association.[31] These few guest ranches in the Lone Star State did not increase significantly in number, however, and Texas never became an important dude ranch state.

A few dude ranches also developed in California, with a small center for winter vacationers in the Palm Springs area and another for summer guests in the foothills of the Sierras. Numerous other types of vacation facilities developed in California, however, and dude ranching never achieved a great deal of prominence there. There were also a few dude ranches in Oregon, Washington, Utah, and other states west of the Mississippi River,[32] but dude ranching did not attain great importance in any of them. There were a few dude ranches in Canada with at least three in operation in Alberta by 1926: the Buffalo Head Ranch, the

Kananaskis Dude Ranch, and the T.S. Ranch. Another early one was the S Half
Diamond Ranch in British Columbia which was a member of the Dude Ranchers'
Association.[33]

There is also an intriguing reference to a dude ranch in Hawaii, run by two
sisters, Armine and Lorna Von Tempsky. The girls' mother had died when they
were young and their father, Louis, had reared them like boys. He managed the
Haleakala Ranch on the island of Maui for the Baldwin family. Since the sisters
lived on the ranch, they worked with cattle and horses, camped in the hills,
and were familiar with the wild game of the area. They read about dude ranches
in Wyoming and figured they could make money doing the same thing in Hawaii.
They had twenty saddle horses to use, a large house, and easy access to Mount
Haleakala, the largest dormant volcanic crater in the world. In 1923 they wrote
to the tourist bureau in Honolulu and to various hotels that they were in the
business of guiding and dude wrangling. Their first guests were a professor and
his wife from Boston who arrived unannounced. More customers came, and
Lorna led them on camping trips through the huge crater and on hunting trips
in the fall. The sisters were moderately successful until Armine gave up the
business for a writing career. Gordon Von Tempsky, a second cousin of Armine
and Lorna who currently lives and works on Maui, does not believe they ever
had a real dude ranch even though they did take people on horseback rides and
overnight trips in Haleakala Crater. He is probably correct, but it is significant
that the sisters publicized their activities as a dude operation. They played on
the popularity of the well-established phrase *dude ranch* and tried to imitate the
dude ranches of Wyoming.[34]

With the addition of ranches in these different states there was some confusion
about just what constituted a dude ranch. Some facilities in the Southwest
particularly clouded the issue, since many resembled elaborate resorts that just
happened to be in the West, rather than true western ranches. There were some
clearly discernible differences between ranches in the northern and southern
states. Those in the north had a higher percentage of younger people and there
was generally a lot of horseback riding, helping with ranch work, fishing, and
big-game hunting in season. Southern ranches had a higher percentage of older
people on them, and, while riding was also popular, there was more emphasis
on rest and relaxation. The seasons varied also, as the northern ranches operated
primarily in June, July, August, and September with hunting later in the fall.
The southern ranches either operated throughout the year or from approximately
October to May.

Dude ranchers also emphasized that their ranches were family-owned homes where dudes came as guests of the family. As such, many ranchers demanded an exchange of references and advance reservations for a minimum stay. The length of the stay varied with each ranch but generally was for at least two weeks. Many ranchers began to emphasize these advance reservations and their refusal to take off-the-road traffic in contrast to the resorts. The phrase *dude ranch* was, however, commonly used for many types of guest facilities in both the northern and southern Rocky Mountains.

Thus, by the late 1920s, dude ranching had the appearance of a new, rapidly expanding industry. In a quarter century it had grown from an informal, relatively undeveloped tourist activity to over one hundred ranches in Wyoming and Montana. The three-year-old Dude Ranchers' Association had expanded from its original twenty-six members to ninety-one at the end of the 1929 season, with a vigorous executive secretary working effectively with railroad officials to improve the business even more. But this growth and optimism soon met a check in the economic troubles that began in 1929.[35] The economic slowdown that began that summer, and was then underscored by the stock market collapse in October, led to a rapid deterioration of many businesses across the country. Dude ranches were not immune to these difficulties, and one of the casualties was the San Gabriel Ranch of New Mexico mentioned earlier; the depression kept away its guests, so it had no income. It did have huge debts, however, and went bankrupt. Ranches in the Kawuneeche Valley in Colorado were also injured; mortgage and tax delinquencies forced a number of them out of business.[36] Even at Eatons' the effects were felt as the number of guests dropped below one hundred for the first time in many years. The Great Depression did not end quickly, of course, and conditions continued to deteriorate for years. Max Goodsill, still general passenger agent for the Northern Pacific, noted that 1932 was a very bad year for both the railroads and ranches; this was not the fault of poor publicity or service but came rather from the large number of business failures in the spring of that year just at the time when people normally made their vacation plans.[37]

However, despite the glum news, dude ranching was not destroyed by these problems; many ranches survived, and there was even some growth during the 1930s. In certain areas dude ranching proved to be the salvation of cattle ranching, a situation remarkably similar to what had occurred in the early 1890s and 1920s.[38] When cattle prices dropped drastically in the 1930s a number of stock ranches started accepting dudes to offset these losses. One couple, Mr. and Mrs. Deane Glessner, began the Drowsy Water Ranch in Colorado after the crash of 1929 as a safety measure. During their second summer, friends began to "drop in" on them and within a few years they began charging their guests for lodging, food, and entertainment; Drowsy Water Ranch still operates in the 1980s as a dude ranch. Many established ranches in the 1930s also cut their rates to keep or get business just as other businesses did during a depression.[39]

During this decade a second major ranch organization started with the beginning of the Colorado Dude and Guest Ranch Association. Details are somewhat sketchy, but it appears that officials of the Union Pacific Railroad got a few ranchers together in 1931 to plan such a group, and they formed the organization in 1933 with the continued help of the Union Pacific and Burlington Railway officials. These ranchers worked on mutual problems and getting more guests, but the CD & GRA was not very active till 1945.[40]

The Dude Ranchers' Association remained busy in the 1930s. Executive Secretary Joe Cahill reported in 1932 that he had traveled over 30,000 miles that year, contacting 193 outfits to get acquainted with ranchers and their problems. The organization had 87 active members and 343 associate members; the latter were friends, guests, and advertisers who helped finance the DRA, but they had no votes in its business operation. Cahill defined the first group as those actively engaged in operating ranches, camps, lodges, or pack outfits and accepting advance reservations for a definite period of time. He also mentioned an affiliated membership open to resorts, lodges, camps, and hot springs "of the first class" catering to "high grade" transient business who were interested in the creation of travel west and the development of the recreation business. Cahill's definitions are instructive for two reasons. First, they show the growing emphasis that dude ranches could be distinguished from other recreational facilities by their demand for advance reservations for definite time periods. Second, the affiliated membership category, and the types of facilities it contained, demonstrate the success that ranchers achieved in making the name *dude ranch* well known. These other tourist operations wanted to identify with dude ranches because they were symbolic of western travel and were highly respected.[41]

The DRA also had a completed constitution by 1931. The purposes were to put the dude ranching business on an organized basis with a view to show the public the advantages of a western vacation, to interchange ideas in order to better business, to cooperate with officials of national parks and forests for conservation and preservation of game and the land, and to obtain cooperation from the railroads to produce and improve travel to the Northwest. The DRA also took on a political function as its members actively lobbied both on the state and federal level on certain important issues. Of the active members listed at this time there was one each in Texas, Colorado, Idaho, Arizona, and California; all others were in Wyoming and Montana.[42]

An unusual problem that the DRA faced in the 1930s was the formation of alleged dude ranches in the eastern United States. One had been started in Florida in 1928 under the supervision of a former western rancher when a herd of cattle and seventy-five horses were sent there from Wyoming.[43] But President Larom of the DRA was most concerned with a number of places claiming to be ranches in New York and New Jersey. While imitation is supposed to be the sincerest form of flattery, the dude ranchers certainly did not feel that way about this problem. Larom believed it was unfair and a "dirty trick" for these eastern resorts to copy the names of western ranches and "trade on our good names and publicity of years past." This problem accentuates again the success of westerners in getting the phrase *dude ranch* well publicized and respected; these eastern resorts certainly would not have borrowed the term unless it was well known among easterners. While western ranchers did not condemn or criticize the use of the phrase in Canada, they were insistent that all dude ranches were in the West and that no such thing existed east of the Mississippi River. But *dude ranch* was not a copyrighted phrase, and there was little the DRA could do beyond emphasizing that real ranches were to be found only in the West.[44]

Despite this particular difficulty and other problems, there were a number of factors that boded well for the industry. The DRA sent questionnaires to its active members and in 1934 could report some interesting statistics to bolster the ranchers' claims that they were of substantial importance to the economy. The estimated value of all money spent in Wyoming from efforts of the dude ranchers (on accommodations, travel, hunting, and so forth) was $12 million. The ranches covered in the survey were worth over $6 million and could accommodate 10,000 people per season. Ranchers also noted that 214 former dudes had settled in Wyoming and Montana and their property was valued at more than $4.3 million. Without question dude ranching was a large business, well known throughout the country.[45]

No organization included all these ranches, and there never was a complete list made of them. The closest thing to such a list was compiled by Lawrence Smith as an appendix to his book, *Dude Ranches and Ponies,* published in 1936. He simply printed lists put out by the DRA and various railroads. The elimination of duplicates on different lists gives a total of 356; by far the greatest number were in Montana (114) and Wyoming (95). The third largest number were in Arizona (65), with substantial numbers in New Mexico (26) and Colorado (25). These five states thus accounted for over 90 percent of the dude ranches; the remainder were in Idaho, California, Nevada, Texas, Oregon, and Canada. While this list is not definitive, it gives a reasonably good count of the widespread range of such ranches in the 1930s. Many of the places are listed as camps or lodges, and one DRA member is simply identified as a big-game hunter.[46] Dude ranches were clearly the leaders in tourist activity in the Rocky Mountain West, and people throughout the country easily identified them as the leaders in western vacations; other vacation or tourist facilities obviously found it advantageous to be listed with them.

All this activity and interest finally brought dude ranching to the college campus. Beginning with the 1934–35 academic year the University of Wyoming offered a bachelor of science degree in recreational ranching through its College of Agriculture. Frederick S. Hultz, head of the Animal Production Department, took charge of the new program. Dr. Hultz explained that eastern visitors to the West were not content with just going through the states; dude ranches were able to satisfy their desires for a better understanding of, and feel for, the country through horseback riding, fishing, hiking, swimming, and exploring. He noted that the summer season was so short that it was not practical to construct elaborate facilities in remote areas to entertain guests. But ranches were already available, and it was natural to adapt them to entertainment in the summer. Ranches were based on livestock, since the dude season provided too brief a usage of their valuable property. In addition to understanding his animals, the dude rancher had to be an accomplished host, offer entertainment, and provide good food. The rapid growth of dude ranching led to a shortage of people with the necessary skills, and that is why the University of Wyoming launched the four-year program as part of its regular curriculum.[47]

Essentially, this was a creative interdisciplinary approach that utilized numerous existing courses. The program was centered on basic ranch topics like cultivation of field crops; handling farm machinery; and the breeding, feeding, and management of livestock. But it also included the study of food purchasing and human nutrition, institutional cooking, bookkeeping, journalistic writing, and public speaking. The young men and women also studied western animal and bird life, psychology, political economy, botany, geology, and legal problems. They could even take "suitable courses in equitation" if necessary. The whole schedule included 189 hours of course work; it was an innovative approach to provide trained people for a clearly identified and growing industry. The curriculum was endorsed by the Dude Ranchers' Association, and the university received inquiries from individuals in twenty-eight states by the fall of 1936.[48] Seven students joined the program in the 1935–36 academic year, and a Dude Ranchers Club was formed on campus in 1936. The records do not indicate how many people followed this curriculum, but the program lasted nearly a decade.

While ranching expanded geographically, numerically, and into college, most of the older ranches survived the Depression. James Ferguson and Edgar Messiter had made Buckhorn Lodge near Parshall, Colorado, a dude ranch about 1912;

Ferguson died in 1917, Messiter married his widow, Florence, and they continued operating the lodge until 1945. It remained primarily a fishing ranch as it had been since 1904.[49] North and east of Buckhorn Lodge was the Middle Park area where some of the ranches continued to develop. By 1932 the Fall River Road through Rocky Mountain National Park was realigned and named Trail Ridge Road. This improved access to the area and ranches continued to cater to travelers. In 1928 Squeaky Bob Wheeler had sold his place to the Phantom Valley Ranch. This was just one-half mile from the road and it featured fishing, horseback riding, and breathtaking scenery. Just two miles down the road lay Holzwarth's Neversummer Ranch. The Holzwarths had begun construction of their three-story main lodge in 1929 near the main road, so they continued to garner business from the people driving through the park. Fishing was especially attractive here through the 1920s; for years the limit on trout was twenty pounds, and since trout weighed but a few ounces each, guests at Holzwarth's often took home fifty to sixty fish. Johnnie (John, Jr.) built a smokehouse so the guests could smoke their trout and take them home more easily. He was also gradually clearing the willow trees off the land and breaking up beaver dams so the fields could be used for grazing and raising hay. In 1930 the Holzwarths sent out their first guest ranch brochure to draw more business; they also continued to sell cattle and run a sawmill, thus keeping a varied operation going. In 1931 Johnnie married Caroline Pratt at her parents' summer cottage at Grand Lake. After John Holzwarth, Sr., died in 1932, Johnnie and Caroline, his sister Sophia, and their mother were able to keep the ranch running for many years and gradually to expand its business.[50]

While the Holzwarths, Messiters, and other ranchers continued with a certain amount of success in Colorado, dude ranching was faring even better farther north. Near Dubois, Wyoming, Charles Moore had successfully made the transition from leading pack trips for boys to heading his family-oriented C-M dude ranch. Although the boys' pack trips had continued for a while in the 1920s, they were soon dropped completely. Moore undoubtedly missed some of the humorous incidents that occurred during the Yellowstone trips. One little boy visiting the park had noticed Moore's chaps and, after carefully walking around him, observed sagely that "his pants haven't any seat in them." And some girls observed him, his clothing, and his demeanor for several minutes before daring to come forward and ask if he were "real or imitation."[51] Times had certainly changed since Moore's youth at Fort Washakie.

Charles Moore became one of the most active of the Wyoming dude ranchers; he was eventually elected vice-president and president of the DRA and, in 1931, he was elected to the Wyoming legislature. Here he often joined battles relating to game and fish laws or other items that affected dude ranchers and their guests.[52] And, like many others in western Wyoming, he had strong feelings and opinions about the creation of Teton National Park. Taking a strong position in favor of the park, he lectured Robert Carey, U.S. senator from Wyoming, on the impact of dude ranches on the state's economy. Moore emphasized that Carey ignored the

> great amount of money that the dude ranches have brought into the country, the large number of people who have bought ranches in the State, after spending a Summer on a ranch, the number of financially responsible people who have become permanent residents of the State, the great number of residents who have been given profitable employment by dude ranchers, the great amount of supplies and produce that the dude ranches buy and consume.[53]

The propriety or wisdom of establishing Teton Park was certainly a debatable and highly emotional issue, but Moore made a strong case for the value of dude ranching in Wyoming.

An even stronger and more vigorous advocate was Larry Larom, owner of the Valley Ranch a few miles from Cody. Larom, who had married Irma Elizabeth Dew in 1920, had bought out his partner, Winthrop Brooks, in 1926. The Laroms expanded the Valley Ranch by adding to it the A 2 Z Ranch as well as others owned by Mary Brown Thomas and Juanita Lens. The Valley Ranch launched large saddle trips for children through the Yellowstone and Jackson Hole country with as many as sixty boys or girls on them; to accommodate such a group, it took a staff of counselors, a crew of eighteen men, thirty teams of horses for the cook, supply, and provision wagons, and over a hundred saddle horses. Special thirty-day pack trips were also conducted by "Pokey" Kaufman, a member of the faculty at a school for girls in Farmington, Connecticut; they went to the Thorofare country and Bridger Lake, south of Yellowstone Park.[54] These various trips were in addition to the family groups that met and vacationed at the ranch. Like many early dude ranches, the Valley was relatively self-sufficient with eighty dairy cattle, a two-acre vegetable garden, and other facilities for feeding the many guests.

Larom was probably the most active of all dude ranchers in the 1920s and 1930s. He remained president of the DRA for eighteen years and spent a great deal of his time studying the National Forest Service, national parks, the federal and state game and fish departments, and other matters relating to conservation. He incorporated and directed for six years the Cody Stampede and was active in forming and developing the American Forestry Association. As noted in

Chapter 3, he initiated a college preparatory school at the ranch in 1922; a victim of the Great Depression, it ceased operation in 1934. The depression also brought an end to a unique method the Laroms had organized for their guests to get to the ranch. They had arranged for special Pullman cars and a diner to be attached to the train in New York City; these cars then were pulled all the way to Cody, where guests were met by people from the Valley Ranch.[55]

Meanwhile, west of Cody, the famous Holm Lodge continued to operate under the direction of Billy Howell and Mary Shawver, both of whom were active in the DRA. Miss Shawver dealt with ranch management programs whle Howell was an active director and was especially involved in game and fish activities.[56]

In the Jackson Hole country the Turner family was becoming more involved with dude ranching. John S. Turner operated the Turpin Meadows Ranch while his son, John C., leased back the old Turner Ranch, which had been sold to the Rockefeller family, and made it into a boys' ranch in the 1930s. Like Charles Moore, however, Turner found that the parents of the boys wanted to come west also so he had to modify the Turner Triangle X to a family operation. Like most ranches Turner's grew its own vegetables, raised beef and dairy cattle, and made ice for ranch use; it was a bit more modernized than some, however, since it had a swimming pool and was equipped with electricity by the mid-1930s.[57]

Not all the old ranches survived under the same management, however. In 1930 the Wymans sold Trapper Lodge in Shell Canyon to Brent Wyeth of Wyeth Pharmaceutical Company in Philadelphia.[58] At nearby Wolf, Wyoming, Eatons' Ranch continued despite several serious problems. After the death of Howard in 1922, Willis had taken charge of the guests while brother Alden assumed management of the other facets of the ranch operation. In 1927 a fire caused an estimated loss of $50,000 when it destroyed the kitchen, laundry, dining room, and main building. Eatons' Ranch was solid and prosperous enough to rebuild, however, and continued its season without interruption. In 1929 death claimed the second of the Eaton brothers. Willis had left the ranch in February for his annual trip to Pittsburgh (Eatons' original home); he stopped on his return trip to visit friends in Louisville, Kentucky, and suffered a heart attack. Brother Alden left Wyoming and went there to help, but Willis's condition worsened and he died in May.[59]

Alden and his son, Bill, continued to operate the ranch at Wolf as well as the Bar Eleven Ranch, a place near Echeta, Wyoming, that they had purchased to supply good grazing country for their horses. In 1928 the Eatons also acquired the Rimrock Ranch in Arizona, east of Prescott and south of Flagstaff. They saw the growing interest in the Southwest and bought this ranch so they could offer ranch vacations to their guests throughout the year; Bill Eaton managed Rimrock

Ranch which they kept until 1939. The family then sold it since it proved too much trouble to operate two ranches so far apart. Bill and his wife Patty were also tired of running a dude ranch twelve months of the year and wanted some time to themselves. Alden Eaton, the last of the brothers who had come west to "make their fortune," died at the ranch at Wolf in 1937. The three men, known for decades as Uncle Howard, Uncle Will, and Uncle Alden, were all gone, but Alden's son, generally referred to as "Big Bill," took over and the ranch stayed in the family.[60]

Eatons' was, of course, more than just another ranch. It has generally been regarded as the first real dude ranch, and its operation led directly to the development of several other ranches. One of these was the famous Bones Brothers Ranch in southern Montana; two of the four owners, the Alderson brothers, worked at Eatons' before starting their own ranch.[61] And a number of other dude ranches were begun in the Sheridan area as people clustered around Eatons' and their "Ranchester" train station. As previously noted the Tanque Verde Ranch in Arizona and the T-H Ranch in Nevada were also started in direct imitation of Eatons' operation by people who had heard of their success. Undoubtedly numerous others owed their beginning, at least indirectly, to Eatons' because of its success and the publicity it generated.

In Montana the story was similar to that in Wyoming, as many ranches continued while others fell by the wayside. One of the successes was the Lazy K Bar in the Melville country. As noted in the previous chapter, dropping cattle prices in the 1920s encouraged the Van Cleve family to take a few guests. They offered good scenery and fishing, but more than most ranches, they also offered a lot of actual ranch work on horseback. The ranch comprised over 40,000 acres where they raised horses and cattle; it included several large streams, three lakes, and an entire mountain over 11,000 feet in elevation. Paul Van Cleve II (Scrumper) noted later that the ranch didn't really need the mountain, but he got tired of the federal government telling him where to camp so he bought the area.[62]

Similar success, but on a smaller scale, came to the Murphys' Ox Yoke Ranch south of Livingston. Charles and Peg Murphy, along with their son Jack, were able to combine the raising of cattle and herding of dudes throughout the 1930s. Scenic horseback trips, fishing, and some ranch work were the main activities here in the mountains west of the small town of Emigrant.[63]

Not far from Emigrant was the OTO Ranch run by Dick and Dora Randall. They had added substantial improvements in the 1920s to accommodate their guests; in an unexpected way Dick was able to locate new visitors for the ranch. He bought eighty acres of land from an ex-Florida real estate man; when he journeyed to Miami to inspect the property, he learned that his land was under water. But the old hunter-rancher saw some prospective dudes in Florida; the millionaire playboys and retired businessmen who vacationed year round had traveled nearly everywhere. But they had not visited a dude ranch, so Dick, in his natural and friendly way, found it easy to interest some of them in trying this "new" form of vacation. The OTO offered fishing and extensive horseback riding, especially pack trips; another feature of the ranch was simply sitting in the lodge in front of the big fireplace listening to Dick's stories of hunting, Old West characters, and famous guests. In 1930 the Randalls received another boost of visitors when the American Boy Expedition was started in Boston. Parents had "discovered that this dude ranch [OTO] was an ideal, safe, and wondrous place for their sons. . . ." The program was developed to bring hundreds of teenage boys to the ranch in southern Montana.

Dick Randall was active in other areas beyond his own ranch; he was a charter member of the Dude Ranchers' Association and was especially interested in conservation activities. For years he supplied, at no charge, the lion's share of saddle stock and bucking horses for the Livingston rodeo; he realized that well-run rodeos were a perfect match for ranch life and activities.[64]

But the depression greatly injured the OTO and bookings dropped drastically in 1931. The Randalls' daughter and son-in-law, Bess and Clyde Erskine, moved to Yellowstone Park to manage Old Faithful Inn while their son, Lesley, ran the OTO. Soon one of the ranch guests, Chan Libby from Boston, offered to buy the ranch. Dick and Dora sold out in 1934; the OTO then comprised 5,000 acres, had 300 horses, and could accommodate 100 guests. Dick was finished as an active dude rancher, but he remained a lifetime director of the Dude Ranchers' Association. After a brief fling at city life, he bought a 12,000-acre cattle ranch in Paradise Valley, south of Livingston.[65] Chan Libby continued the operation of the OTO as a cattle and dude ranch for a number of years.

Even as these problems occurred, however, an elaborate plan was being developed for a series of ranches in Montana. Originator of the scheme was Judge Charles Cooper, who owned a cattle ranch approximately forty-six miles north of Helena along the route of the Great Northern Railway. The plan was to build a series of ranches between Yellowstone and Glacier parks—anywhere from three to six ranches according to different stories. The key to promoting these ranches was the Judge's son Gary, who was being featured by Paramount-Famous-Lasky Corporation in moving pictures. Judge Cooper and other business partners approached the Milwaukee Railroad for financial assistance, but A. B. Smith, the Northern Pacific official who had helped organize the DRA, advised them to seek help from the Northern Pacific and Great Northern.

Judge Cooper wrote Charles Donnelly, president of the Northern Pacific, and explained that Paramount was considering a film about Montana starring Gary; the judge suggested the Lewis and Clark expedition as the best subject for the movie. Plans to film on the sites for the proposed ranches would be a big boost for them; one of the Lewis and Clark campsites was on one of these ranches, and filming at that spot was to add an air of authenticity to the whole project. Railway officials investigated the request to help finance the movie as planning extended over several years. They finally decided, however, that producing a movie was too foreign to their railroad organization. They offered assistance but no direct financial aid. The movie idea faded away, but plans for the dude ranches went forward anyway.[66] The first was planned on the old Nine Quarter Circle Ranch of 7,000 acres along Taylor's Fork of the Gallatin River. A crew of twenty-five men worked through early 1928 building or improving twenty-two log cabins, an electrical plant, and a water system. The plans were pretentious, with a polo field, golf course, archery range, and private landing field in the works. The ranch not only would be luxurious but would also serve as headquarters for prominent movie stars several months of the year; their presence, of course, would generate publicity and, therefore, more guests. The initial building was finished in 1929, the name was changed to Gary Cooper Ranch, and the managers prepared to receive guests in 1930.[67] Hartley Bell was named general manager of this complex, and it was financed chiefly by Carl Hansen, president of the International Re-Insurance Corporation of Los Angeles.

The ranch owners requested that the Great Northern officials change the name of the local railway stop from Sunnyside to Gary and that they install a siding at the ranch for unloading freight and for private Pullman cars. The railroad officials acceded to the name change but did not believe there was enough business to justify installation of the siding. The ranch finally opened and featured fishing, hiking, trail trips, rodeos, and ranch activities. But apparently no movie stars, other than Gary Cooper himself, came to the ranch—the railway officials had judged correctly the small amount of business the ranch would generate. The grand plan of ranches never materialized, and no dude ranch chain was forged to join the two great national parks of Glacier and Yellowstone. Gary Cooper Ranch did not endure through the 1930s.[68]

While this scheme was failing in Montana, a similar grandiose plan was under way in New Mexico and Arizona on the Vermejo Ranch. As mentioned earlier in this chapter, Harry Chandler had bought this fabulous private ranch from the estate of W. H. Bartlett in 1926. Chandler's idea of a luxurious resort for the wealthy started well but faltered in the crash of 1929 and had disintegrated by 1932. Jack Hauskins, a cowman and later ranch manager in Colorado, had visited Vermejo Park Ranch in 1924 and expressed an interest in it; so, in 1933, Mr.

Chandler sold him a twenty-five-year lease on the Vermejo Club and property together with an option to buy it for $1 million; this was considerably less than the previously appraised value of $5.5 million, so the effects of the depression are clear. Hauskins promised the club members good service and decided to make the ranch business a year-round one. Vermejo Park operated only from May 1 to November 1, so Hauskins also secured an option to purchase Rancho Esplendor at Nogales, Arizona, as winter quarters. This included 1,045 acres and an incredible seventy-seven-room guest house; plans were also made to establish an outpost on the Gulf of California, 125 miles away in Mexico. This would add deep-sea fishing to horseback riding, golf, tennis, and other sports for the winter vacationist. Hauskins certainly thought big, as he determined to provide year-round service at the "world's best located, best equipped, best managed, and most unique guest ranch in existence" with both western and five-gaited saddle horses, quiet surroundings, and exclusiveness. He emphasized that the managers would "welcome and provide for all members of a guest family, including nurses and chauffeurs" and noted that this included excellent food served any time day or night without extra cost. This combination of ranches and extraordinary service was renamed All-Year Guest Ranches, Inc., and accommodations were offered on the American Plan at a cost of only nine to fifteen dollars per person per day. As might be expected, this elaborate scheme did not last through the troubled times of the 1930s; after the Vermejo Park Club disbanded during the continuing depression, the land was leased out for raising cattle.[69]

The failures of All-Year Guest Ranches, the Gary Cooper Ranches, and others should not obscure the general success and endurance of dude ranching. Indeed the failures emphasize how success was achieved. Dude ranching worked when year-round local residents accepted guests. The ranches grew at a reasonable pace as the owners developed new skills and learned to balance the demands of the guests with the ability of the land to meet these demands. When ranches were sold to outsiders who did not understand this balance or the peculiar skills required in dude ranching, the ranches often failed. And trying to increase quickly the size and grandeur of a ranch seldom led to success. Those dude ranches that did become large, such as Eatons' and Randalls', grew gradually and established a solid business foundation and reputation before such growth materialized.

Dude ranching thus survived the Great Depression even though the nation's economic troubles lasted an unprecedented length of time, from 1929 till approximately 1938. Even though some ranches disappeared during the thirties, others were started and many of the older ones emerged intact. But another catastrophe was about to hit the United States—World War II—with profound effects on the nation and on dude ranching.

FIVE

Ride in the Rocky Mountains

If you are normal and philosophical; if you love your country; if you like bacon, or will eat it anyhow; if you are willing to learn how little you count in the eternal scheme of things; if you are prepared, for the first day or two, to be able to locate every muscle in your body and a few extra ones that have crept in and are crowding, go ride in the Rocky Mountains and save your soul.
　　　—Mary Roberts Rinehart, *Through Glacier Park*, 3–4.

The growth and development of dude ranching were gradual at first, then rather rapid for several years. As the industry grew and as its importance became more obvious, ranchers had to become more concerned with the amount of dude business they had and learn about techniques of advertising. Dude ranchers eventually relied on some unusual methods for advertising in addition to some common ones.

The history of dude ranching is important for an understanding of dude ranch advertising. As noted in previous chapters, this was not a planned industry in the beginning. No one set out in the 1800s to start a guest ranch in the West. It was a matter of people coming and accepting hospitality; finally, of course, it was as a matter of survival that ranchers began charging their guests money for food, lodging, and the use of horses. Thus the earliest advertising was simply people telling their friends about their enjoyable visits to a ranch. By personal contact, word spread about ranch trips, and the number of dudes grew over the decades. This simple method is a very important factor in dude ranch growth; it not only drew more guests at the time but also shaped ranchers' ideas about advertising in general. Well-known visitors to the ranches also drew attention to them. The most famous was, of course, Theodore Roosevelt, who journeyed to Dakota Territory after reading a letter by Howard Eaton. His visits later prompted Owen Wister's western travels, which inspired his famous fictional writing. While these men were not famous at the time of their first visits, both became well known between 1895 and 1905, when dude ranching began to grow. These two men exemplify the many people, known in their own areas, who went west in the late nineteenth and early twentieth centuries. Over the years the presence of famous visitors continued to attract guests; as noted in the previous chapter, a visit by Amelia Earhart prompted Nevada ranchers to invite other famous people to their ranches, and the plans for the string of Montana ranches linking Glacier and Yellowstone parks was based not only on the name of Gary Cooper, but also on the hope that numerous movie stars would spend vacations there.

Although prominent visitors were well publicized, reliance on famous guests was never the chief thrust of the dude ranch appeal or advertising. Personal contact was. And, since people tended to go where their friends, relatives, and acquaintances went, often a large percentage of a ranch's guests were from the same city for many years or even decades. Thus Eaton's Ranch tended to get many guests from Pittsburgh, hometown of Howard, Willis, and Alden Eaton; Horton's H F Bar Ranch got many of its early guests from Chicago; Siggins Triangle X from New England, home of Mrs. Donald Siggins; the Dead Indian Ranch from Washington, D.C., where their first large group of dudes came from; and so on for different ranches, depending on the hometown of the owners or of their first guests. The strongholds of dude ranch visitors were New York, Boston, Philadelphia, and Chicago.[1]

As dude ranchers became more dependent on guests for a substantial part of their business success, they began to accentuate and develop the personal contact that had won their first successes. They decided to supplement the natural and informal contacts between friends and family members with personal visits to the East to meet potential prospects and sell the western way of life. Because one of the Eaton brothers returned to Pittsburgh every year, the ranch continued to draw a substantial number of visitors, first to North Dakota, later to Wolf, Wyoming. They were obviously quite successful; by 1915 they were accommodating over seventy people throughout the summer season. Guests at the OTO

Ranch virtually demanded that the Randalls and Erskines come east for visits and then introduced them to more people interested in Montana. Dick Randall was such an engaging entertainer and storyteller that people booked him to speak before Rotary clubs, chamber of commerce luncheons and various men's clubs. As mentioned in Chapter 4 Randall even used a personal trip to Florida to line up some dudes from the South.[2]

Other ranchers also took eastern trips and soon a regular pattern emerged. Sometime in late winter or early spring the rancher would communicate with various guests and arrange a visit. The former ranch guests would invite their friends for a party where the ranchers, often husband and wife, would talk about their ranch and its attractions. These visits became annual affairs that served as reunions between old friends and opportunities to make new ones. Ranchers sometimes went from city to city for a number of party-visits in order to line up enough business for the entire summer. Some ranchers enlarged upon this basic idea by having an agent in the East arrange a party where rancher and prospective guests could meet. And sometimes groups of dude ranchers went together for these parties in midwestern or eastern cities.[3] Larry Larom of the Valley Ranch had an even more substantial eastern contact with a permanent office in New York City. He and his early partner, Win Brooks, set up offices in the Brooks Brothers Building. The ranch could always get mail there, and Larom spent several weeks in New York in the spring. Of course, nearby guests or prospective ones had a close and convenient contact when they wished to make inquiries or reservations.[4]

The great value of this type of business arrangement was the personal contact that it permitted. Ranchers felt they were inviting friends into their homes, and they wanted to get to know these people before doing so. This situation was obviously far different from other types of tourist facilities that catered to anyone stopping by. In addition ranch vacations tended to be rather extensive; it was quite common for families or individuals to remain three weeks to an entire summer on a ranch. Obviously such a lengthy stay could become quite trying if there were significant personality clashes or if there were misunderstandings about what ranch life was like. A rather dramatic example of the success of this approach was revealed at the fall 1930 meeting of the Dude Ranchers' Association. The 1930 season was generally below normal because of the difficult economic times. One member reported a rather drastic decline but admitted he had not gone out after business since he just took it for granted that people would come to him. Another member then pointed out that he had gone east and, in two weeks, booked all the business he could handle; he had had but one cancellation during the season. There was obviously nothing better than personal contact in this business where the personality of the ranch owners was so much a part of the whole undertaking. For those ranchers who could not take an eastern trip, there was direct correspondence between rancher and prospective guest who had been put in contact with the rancher by a friend or relative. References were often exchanged and mutual contacts sought so both parties felt they would be comfortable with the arrangements for the summer.[5]

Another aspect of this personal contact was the publication at the end of the season of a list of guests who had been at the ranch that year. This list was often appended to a ranch publication sent to all visitors during the winter or to new prospects. This publication or ranch news would, it was hoped, rekindle the warm memories of summer activities and stimulate people to begin making vacation plans. Ranchers also sent Christmas cards and letters to keep in touch with friends from previous seasons. All these items were geared toward the personal contact of friends rather than the impersonal business arrangements of many tourist facilities.

There were a few exceptions to this at ranches such as the Bar Lazy J and Holzwarth's Neversummer Ranch in Colorado. These ranches were heavily dependent on local visitors and thus were not too concerned with eastern business in the early days of their operation. Holzwarth's started taking guests in 1919 but did not send out its first brochure until 1930. This situation was the exception, however, and it existed only because there was a large urban area (Denver) close to the fishing and scenic attractions of the Grand Lake–Granby area.[6]

Far more common were the ranches dependent on eastern business. And success was clearly tied to getting compatible people on the ranch, keeping them content, and sending them home happy and satisfied. People returned to a particular ranch partly because they liked the scenery, the horseback riding or the fishing but primarily because they formed personal friendships with the rancher and his whole "family"—meaning the ranch workers too. Larry Larom noted at the first meeting of the Dude Ranchers' Association that one dude family going home satisfied after a pleasant vacation was worth $1,000 in magazine advertising.[7] Many ranchers obviously did well in this regard; as one railroad official noted, "Dude Ranches occupy a very high status in the public mind; they have won and have held a certain recognition as being the cream of the vacation business. . . ."[8] Repeat business was the mainstay of most dude ranches, and many reported that 50 percent or more of their business came from former guests or their friends.[9]

To keep their business and to get more, the ranchers also relied on other types of advertising. Their single most valuable source of assistance was undoubtedly the railroads. The western railways were, of course, always seeking new passengers for their western routes and publicized many features of the country to achieve this. These railroads advertised in general ways just to make the public aware of the West and in specific ways to focus precisely on getting passenger business. At the founding meeting of the Dude Ranchers' Association, A. B. Smith, general passenger agent for the Northern Pacific, estimated that the NP spent $1 million in advertising to publicize the Pacific Northwest. He heartily supported this to aid the general upbuilding of agriculture and industry in the area. This long-range planning would eventually benefit the railroad. But railroad officials were also quite aware of the short-term benefits of selling tickets to people who wanted to visit the scenic areas featured by this publicity. These officials noted that the Northern Pacific and Burlington lines sold 5,500 tickets at an average cost of $20 per ticket to dude ranches during the 1927 season, a fact that made them much more interested in promoting ranch vacations. They looked forward to increasing that $110,000 substantially in the following season.[10] These two lines were clearly the leaders in this type of advertising that benefited dude ranches; other railroads soon joined in with similar programs.

Although the methods they used varied, there was a substantial amount of advertising in newspapers and magazines. They took out ads worth thousands of dollars, beginning about 1925 and continuing for many years. By 1930 the Northern Pacific advertising manager reported that they used forty-six magazines with a combined circulation of twenty million people. These ads appeared on a regular basis in late winter and spring, trying to attract people at that time of year when they were making summer vacation plans. When the *New York World* put out a special dude ranch supplement in May 1929 the Northern Pacific and Burlington put in a substantial half-page ad emphasizing horseback riding, hiking in flower-filled valleys, fishing, sleeping in log cabins, and being with cowboys on vacation. In the following year an intense heat wave and drought in the East led the NP to place ads noting how much more comfortable summer weather was on a western ranch. The magazines the railroads chose were quite varied, including the sophisticated ones such as *Country Life, Town and Country, Vogue, The New Yorker, Cosmopolitan,* and *Red Book* as well as *Sportsman's Magazine, Sports and Field Magazine, Spur, Polo, Time, Photoplay,* and a couple characterized as comic publications. Their range and coverage was certainly broad enough to reach many different people.[11]

In addition the railroad men developed special programs, spending eight to ten thousand dollars on display materials and putting together moving pictures of western scenes and ranch life. The NP had 172 reels of film in its library which they showed regularly or lent to interested people. There was some radio publicity also, as well as posters and window arrangements in department stores.

Some of the ads with caricatures of horses and riders were designed to startle the readers and get their attention. Such displays were also tied in with plans to show that "the dude ranch is the smart place to go." All these activities make it clear that railroads were trying to make the nation dude ranch conscious.[12]

Of all the advertising they did, however, the publication of dude ranch booklets was among the most effective and long lasting. Beginning probably in the 1920s, these booklets or brochures varied in size and quality but showed a dude ranch vacation at its best. One of the earliest (ca. 1927) was a brochure of forty-eight pages put out by the Burlington Route. Titled "Ranch Life in the Buffalo Bill Country," it contained a general description of dude ranching and specific details of ranches in Wyoming. A center map showed the ranches in Wyoming east of Yellowstone Park, and an end map showed the railroad routes.[13] Other booklets were similar, listing the locations of ranches, the types of accommodations available, the activities offered, and often the rates. They advised interested parties to write directly to the ranches for more details and reservations. Some of these booklets became quite elaborate, featuring gorgeous color photographs of scenery, fishing, horseback riding, or corral activity. With titles such as "Dude Ranches," "Western Dude Ranch Vacations," and "Dude Ranches Out West," they played a large part in making people keenly interested in ranch vacations. The railroads of the West clearly acted as sources of general information to midwesterners and easterners; they hoped to make ranch life so attractive that people would sign up for vacations and, of course, make reservations on the railroad that supplied them the original information about the ranches.

These attempts to sell the West as a vacation site used a variety of tactics. The publicizing of the West was based on changing eastern perceptions of the Rocky Mountain country. Throughout the nineteenth century the West had been viewed as wild and woolly, and that image of a rugged and dangerous land was strongly embedded in the minds of outsiders. Early attempts at selling the West as a vacation area had to tone down this rough image. Westerners pointed out that life was safe and modern comforts were available, from steam heat and adequate bathing facilities, to varied and tasty meals. But later in the twentieth century, a new problem emerged: a rural and western spirit was developing to which westerners had to appeal. They were forced to emphasize the West was still wild, rough, and adventurous—in short, just as western as it had ever been. In some cases the two ideas were mixed to convince people that ruggedness and comfort could be found in the same spot. An ad for Bones Brothers Ranch near Birney, Montana, for instance, pointed out that guests should not expect to find an eastern resort hotel. They would see the Old West of the cattle days with wholesome meals and every attention and courtesy. But, on the same page, there was a photograph of a ranch house interior with the caption: "Just to correct any mistaken idea you might have about these ranch homes being sod-houses, or dugouts with dirt floors."[14] Since the early twentieth century, advertising has been faced with this dilemma of trying to emphasize comfort and yet show that the real West was still alive and available.

The appeals made by dude ranch advertising have been varied in other ways also. The mild summer climate at northern ranches has been a constant selling point for ranch trips as has the wholesome food from the ranches' own gardens, flocks, and herds. Another source of appeal was the simplicity of life, the lack of pretentiousness on a ranch. People would be able to merge easily into the informal, comfortable atmosphere. The harried urban dwellers would find a new calm as they traded offices, subways, and traffic for saddles and mountains. Ranches were portrayed as refuges where ragged, exhausted people could recover their health and vigor; then, rejuvenated, they could go back to their life's work.[15] One rancher even noted that his best prospects were physicians, families on the verge of a breakup, or ones that had already been broken up by divorce. The calm life was viewed as a chance to recuperate. During the 1930s this point was especially emphasized as an aid to businessmen and their families who had been through economic turmoil, and indeed, this simplicity and naturalness were enjoyed by the easterners. Tied to this recuperative quality was the carefree nature of a dude ranch vacation. It was a complete experience; once the guest stepped off the train, he was with friends and did not need to worry about planning other activities for the rest of his stay.[16]

Of course, more specific details were mentioned as appealing aspects of the vacation. Many of these were based on the heritage of the West—the Lewis and Clark Trail, rivers and mountains famous in western literature, old stage and pony express stations, sites of range wars, and so on. And tourists could visit important historic sites such as forts, battlefields, and mining towns. The color and pageantry of Indian activities were recognized as drawing cards for visitors, so ranchers specified which Indian reservations were near their ranches. Indian troupes were even available to present tribal songs and dances.[17] The ranchers noted these features, not merely to be observed casually but rather as interesting parts of American heritage to be studied and understood. People remaining at one ranch for several weeks or months could indeed get some feel for, and understanding of, the land, its background and character.[18]

Ranches also offered vigorous endeavors for their active guests; a ranch vacation was certainly not designed to be a passive one. Especially emphasized were hunting, fishing, and pack trips. Ranches in the Sheridan area also publicized polo matches while those in western Wyoming, Montana, and Colorado often emphasized visits to nearby national parks.[19]

Dude ranches also benefited from, and took advantage of, advertising campaigns that they could link with ranch vacations. There was, for instance, a substantial effort undertaken in the decade of 1910–20 to get Americans to "see America first." This movement argued that America had as much or more to offer than Europe. Some observers noted that Americans spent millions of dollars on European vacations; it was a job of the dude ranchers to hold a substantial portion of that money in the United States. Tied in with this was an intense effort to publicize the national parks. In his 1919 publication, *The Book of the National Parks,* Robert S. Yard argued persuasively that American parks outshone other, more celebrated vacation spots. The Swiss Alps, he stated, were excelled by several U.S. parks in beauty, sublimity, and variety. Glacier Park matched the Canadian Rockies; Yellowstone outranked any similar volcanic area and was one of the most heavily populated wild animal sanctuaries in the world. Furthermore, Mt. Rainier had a single peak glacier not equaled anywhere; Crater Lake was the deepest and bluest accessible lake in the world; Sequoia contained an immense forest of giant trees, some of which were the oldest and largest living things in the world; and the Grand Canyon was the noblest example of erosion in the world. The superlatives went on but the point was certainly clear—see America and quit spending vacation dollars elsewhere.[20] Dude ranchers were able to take advantage of these campaigns, especially since many were close to the national parks.

They also had their own organized advertising efforts. As noted in the previous chapter, the earliest one was the Dude Ranchers' Association organized in 1926. At the third annual convention in 1928 the board of directors was authorized to hire an executive secretary to carry out publicity to help further the dude ranch industry; the board hired T. Joe Cahill for this job. An aggressive and energetic man, he soon developed a number of ideas to push the dude ranch message into many areas. In 1929 the DRA decided to launch a program of national advertising with Cahill in the forefront. One of their plans was to sponsor a dude ranch contest for children. In conjunction with the magazines *The American Boy* and *Youth's Companion,* the DRA asked for essays on the subject "Why I Desire To Spend My Vacation On A Dude Ranch." The magazines, which had wide circulation, printed the details and promised to publish the winning essay. The DRA joined with the Northern Pacific and Burlington railways to offer substantial prizes to the winners: a four-week vacation on a ranch to the first-place winner, a three-week trip for second place, and a two-week stay for third. The railroads furnished transportation, Pullman accommodations, and meals en route; in addition manufacturers of saddles, bridles, and clothing contributed various items to make a complete western outfit for the top prize winner. And various western books, paintings, and other items were donated for other high finishers. Lots were drawn from DRA members to determine which ranches served as hosts for the three lucky winners. The contest drew a great deal of attention with 7,255 requests for details from all parts of the United States and Canada plus inquiries from Cuba, Bermuda, Alaska, Honolulu, Puerto Rico, and the Philippine Islands; the judges received 5,308 essays. First prize was awarded to Archibald T. Gardner, Jr. of New York City; second prize went to Ralph Allen of the same city; and third prize to Kenneth Lovell of Hutchinson, Kansas. [21]

Besides working on details of this contest Cahill spent several weeks in the East in 1929, primarily in New York City, where he worked on a variety of types of publicity. He was able to get a dude ranch exhibit placed at the Colony Theatre, helped convince all the large department stores in the city to feature western apparel in their window displays and newspaper advertising in May and June, and then had window displays put in stores in Philadelphia, Chicago, and Detroit. Spending a lot of time with the officers of the Associated Press, Cahill finally convinced them that dude ranch stories were news items rather than advertising, so the AP soon carried various information about dude ranches. He had similar success with the International News and United Press. Cahill worked on getting articles in specific magazines also; some of these publications were the same as those the railroads used, but Cahill was successful in getting stories in more varied ones such as *Outing, Park Central Views, Primary Education, Popular Education, Nomad, Doherty News, Outdoor America, Independent Woman, College Humor, Two Gun Stories,* and numerous others. One of the most noticed features was a four-page special supplement published by the *New York World* including articles about dude ranching as well as ads taken out by individual ranches. One of these articles even listed some books that prospective dudes might read to learn about the ranch country before their vacations: *Roughing It* by Mark Twain, *History of the American Fur Trade* by Hiram Chittenden, *The Vigilantes of Montana* by Thomas J. Dimsdale, *Indian Fights and Fighters* by Cyrus Brady, *The Journals of Lewis and Clark,* and Owen Wister's *Lin McLean* and *The Virginian*. [22] This list of informative books fit in well with the dude ranchers' belief that learning about the West was part of a pleasant vacation.

Joe Cahill also noted that interest in dude ranches was so keen in the East that some businesses were considering the adoption of special dude ranch trademarks; these included Knox Hat Company and the American Tobacco Company as well as the Buick and Ford motor companies. This interest also prompted some schemes by sharp and shady operators to exploit dude ranching, but Cahill did all he could to nip these fraudulent plans in the bud.[23] Cahill reported that he traveled over 34,000 miles for the association in 1929, visiting twenty-two states and seventy-nine cities and towns, answering 3,618 letters, and calling on 202 newspapers and magazines. In all these endeavors he acted for dude ranching in general, not for any special ranch and not in the actual signing up of guests. Pointing out that people he called on wanted more than just a list of members, Cahill urged the DRA to publish a booklet or brochure listing ranches and some details of their operation. The DRA board of directors also noted that Cahill might spend some time in the area from St. Louis south. This section of the country had not been exploited much since the bulk of ranchers' efforts had been in the northeast and upper Midwest; the South had a certain amount of potential however. School terms often started later there so families might take vacations later in the season than northerners would. The oppressive summer weather there might also push people to a western vacation in September, the very time when ranchers needed more guests. Cahill also took charge of a plan to publish the minutes of the fourth annual (1929) meeting. Ranchers sold ads to companies that handled dude ranch supplies, and these advertisements paid the cost of printing the minutes. Hundreds of copies of the Minute Book were sold; the whole endeavor was so successful that Minute Books were published for two more years.[24]

In 1929 and 1930 the ranchers also began exploiting rodeos for more publicity. The Midland Empire Fair at Billings set aside a special Dude Ranch Day, and ranchers and their guests turned out for the festivities; their participation added to the pageantry of the fair and brought attention to the ranches. Cahill helped publicize the Madison Square Garden World Series of Rodeo when he was in New York in 1930. He got the names of many dudes in New York City and persuaded fifty of them to ride in the Grand Entry. Ranchers thus saw clearly that it was helpful to tie rodeos in with dude ranches whenever possible. From this point on rodeos were publicized by the ranchers; those in the East helped keep western ideas and trips on people's minds while those in the West were magnets that helped draw people in the summer months.

In 1930 Cahill again reported on numerous activities in the East as part of his continuing promotions. Dude ranchers enjoyed a banner year in 1929—some later called it the Golden Year—and hoped for more in 1930; this season was a big disappointment, however, because of the depression. It might have been an even worse season without Cahill's constant efforts. He got the Grantland Rice Film Company of New York to take pictures of the Cody Stampede and dude ranches nearby; these films, circulated throughout the country, were highlights of the 1930 campaign. He continued to broaden the number and type of magazines that carried dude ranch information adding *Woodmen of the World, Pacific Laundry Journal, Townfolk, World Traveller, Discus, Wingedfoot, Western Advertising and Western Business,* and others. In the summer of 1930 the oppressive heat and drought in the East led to a campaign to boost ranch business. Larry Larom, president of the DRA, and Cahill planned it in August in conjunction with plans of the railroads to emphasize the more pleasant western weather. Cahill made a hurried trip east to ten cities promoting late season ranch trips. This did prolong the season for some ranches by bringing a few more people west but an unusual cool wave spread over the East about the same time as Cahill's visit, blunting much of the impact of the campaign. Cahill also reported on the directive given to him at the previous convention to copyright the name *Dude Ranchers' Association;* he learned that this could not be done because of the nature of the copyright laws.

Cahill did make strong points on two particular issues. He stated again that people constantly asked him for a complete list of ranches, their nearest railroad point, the number of people they could accommodate, and their rates. Nearly every railway office he visited insisted that such a list was essential to be able to talk intelligently to prospective ranch vacationists. Some ranchers didn't want their rates published, but many easterners demanded this information at their initial inquiry and refused to wait for it. Cahill's second point was that the key to success depended on ranchers treating their guests well. His theme was "send your Dudes and Dudettes home satisfied. . . . Treat them right, feed them well and go out of your way at all times, if necessary, to please them. . . ."

Cahill and other DRA officers also noted that members should fill out questionnaires that the organization prepared. It was important to get accurate statistics on the amounts their guests spent in the West, the amount of insurance the ranches carried and other data so the significance of ranch vacations to the economy could be documented; officers and ranchers could then give specific facts to banks, clubs, businesses, state agencies, and other interested parties. One-third of the DRA members had not sent in this information for 1929 so only partial figures had been available. Ranchers were urged to cooperate with each other in this and other projects since they really were not competitors; they were instead competing with Europe, Canada, Hawaii, and possibly even California and Florida.[25]

In 1931 Cahill embarked on his last year of activity for the association since the deepening depression finally would force it to curtail expenditures. He again worked on getting articles in various nationwide publications and spent several weeks in New York City on a variety of publicity projects. While advertising was the key item discussed for many years, the DRA itself had been changing somewhat during these years. Until 1930 any ranch asking to join it had been accepted without question; at that meeting, however, the members decided that future applicants would have to be inspected by the DRA director who lived in the region where the ranch was.[26] This was done mainly to see that prospective members were advertising their ranches honestly. The original membership was composed of those present at the founding meeting in 1926, and all others had to be approved. Three classes of membership were clearly defined: active members—those actively engaged in operating dude ranches, resorts, and pack outfits in the northern Rockies; associate members—individuals, companies, or officers of companies who were interested in the development of the business; and honorary members—men in public or private life who would be interested in furthering the objectives of the DRA. In this last category were the governors of Wyoming and Montana, the director of the National Park Service, supervisors of national forests, railroad officers, various game wardens and protectors, and western writers. The DRA also divided Wyoming and Montana into twelve districts with a director for each district.[27]

At the 1931 meeting, however, a more serious organizational problem had to be faced—inadequate financing. The most immediate and pressing question was whether to retain an executive secretary. Mr. Cahill's work had been very satisfactory, but it was doubtful that the organization could continue to pay his salary. The members decided to retain the position but to curtail his activities since the DRA could no longer afford to send a man on any eastern trips. In the future he was directed to work mostly in the West, visiting ranches and working on game and fish matters. Cahill had to move his family to California for personal reasons, so he would no longer be associated with the organization; when he made his farewell speech in 1931, he was heartily applauded for his hard work. He had traveled tens of thousands of miles and made hundreds of contacts, laying the base for many years of successful relationships between ranchers and people throughout the country. The DRA then chose as the new executive secretary, A. H. Croonquist of Camp Senia, Red Lodge, Montana, who had served for several years as vice-president of the organization.[28]

A second question was a new method of financing the DRA; previously funds had been received from a flat rate of ten-dollar dues per member plus an assessment based on the value of different ranches. Some of the smaller ranchers seemed to think the big outfits had been reaping the benefits of DRA activity, but this apparently was not the case. Max Goodsill of the Northern Pacific pointed out that three big ranches in Wyoming had actually paid over half the organization's expenses in the first few years. And the small ranches received publicity and exposure they could not otherwise afford. The three principal officers for the first five years—I. H. Larom, A. H. Croonquist, and Ernest Miller—had done a tremendous amount of work and spent much of their own money to push the organization's objectives.[29] The assessment procedure had caused some difficulties in estimating ranch values and in bookkeeping so a new financial plan was now developed. Under it each outfit in the organization would have one vote for each ten dollars in dues it paid. The dues schedule was then based on the capacity of each ranch or lodge: ten dollars for every ten people accommodated, up to fifty dollars. This proposal was unanimously adopted and added to the DRA constitution.[30]

Dude ranching continued to get good press coverage in spite of the great difficulties of the depression years. The *Sheridan Post Enterprise* published a special sixteen-page supplement on dude ranching in May 1930 containing numerous photographs of ranch activities and scenery. The publisher, Charles W. Barton, took a business trip to the Midwest and East and became a volunteer salesman for the dude ranch country as he took pictures, literature, and stories to the people he met. Mr. Yates of the *Sheridan Press* volunteered a dude ranch column in his paper as the voice of the DRA; he also gave association members a half-price rate on newspaper subscriptions. Another offer came from Mr. C. E. Piersall, editor of *The Voice of the Sportsman;* this publication of the Wyoming division of the Izaak Walton League offered to publish any stories the dude ranchers sent. In 1934 *Sports Afield* published a special dude ranch and western issue, and in 1939 *Horse and Horseman* magazine included a dude ranch directory, an article on the industry, and a map of the ranch country.[31]

Cahill had certainly done sound work; his recommendation of a brochure apparently helped convince the DRA to publish a complete list of member ranches with data about accommodations, activities, and other pertinent details. This list eventually became a major method of publicity for the ranches and the organization. The last Minute Book was published in 1931, but in 1932 the DRA brought out the first issue of its magazine, *The Dude Rancher*. This was then published three or more times per year and served several functions. It replaced the Minute Book as a source of data from the annual meetings and other official business; it also contained advertisements from stores and manufacturers and listed the names of associate members whose dues helped the organization financially. But the magazine became more than a replacement for the Minute Book as it added other features over the years and became popular with the dudes. There was a president's page to relay messages to the members or guests;

a page for women members that went under different names—"Home Management" and "Mrs. Dude Rancher"; articles on different ranches and ranchers; and features on dude ranch horses, people wanting to buy ranches, and other stories.[32]

Besides the DRA there was also some activity in the 1930s by the Colorado Dude and Guest Ranch Association. The Union Pacific officials were mainly responsible for getting it started and helping publicize Colorado ranches in dude ranch booklets just as the Northern Pacific and Burlington lines had done for the Wyoming and Montana ranches.[33]

Dude ranches also benefited from some state programs, especially in Montana and Wyoming. Mr. W. W. Moses, publicity director of the Montana Department of Agriculture, spoke before the fifth annual meeting (1930) of the DRA. He reported that the Montana Development Congress had been held the previous winter at Helena and DRA President Larry Larom was one of the few people invited to give an address. Larom's talk proved to be a revelation to businessmen at the conference. Apparently they were quite surprised at how much business dude ranching accounted for in the state. It was clear that the ranchers had to sell some local people on their industry as well as people out of state. The governor of Montana noted that dude ranches were doing more than get business for themselves; they were making friends for "the great Northwest." Moses encouraged ranchers to urge state legislators to appropriate money for publicity funds since any publicity would benefit the entire economy. Moses also initiated a plan of sending telegrams of welcome in the governor's name to prominent people who came to the state as an extra touch of courtesy. He asked ranchers to join in this campaign by advising him when they had notable guests on their ranches; he promised to have telegrams sent to them also.[34] The president of the Montana State Hotel Men's Association, William T. Cruse, also urged cooperation between his group and dude ranchers, noting that hotels weren't really competitors with ranches since they catered to a different type of tourist.[35]

There were similar contacts between ranchers and various government and private groups in Wyoming. Mr. L. L. Newton of the State Board of Commerce and Industry worked closely with the DRA and attended some of their meetings. He urged the members to respond to questionnaires about their operation so state officials could help boost dude ranching. This board worked with ranchers to set up a miniature dude ranch exhibit that was displayed in Sacramento at a Pacific Coast exhibition in August and September of 1929 and later at Omaha, Chicago, and Kansas City. Newton made a point similar to that of Montana officials when he noted that dude ranchers were not just promoting their business but were building an industry that benefited the entire economy. Grocers, merchants, and every other imaginable business grew with its success. He emphasized that when they spoke of dude ranch business, they were talking about outside money, which Wyoming needed badly.

State officials at Cheyenne got inquiries about ranch vacations and urged the DRA to publish a complete brochure so they could send out quick and direct answers to these requests. Wyoming officials also entertained some three hundred newspapermen of the National Editorial Association at Cheyenne. These men were then taken on a ten-day tour of the state that included stops at two of the leading dude ranches. As a result dude ranching in general received untold publicity through the columns of numerous reporters.[36]

There were also many links between dude ranches and nearby cities. One of the most active city groups was the Cody Commercial Club; its members assisted in building roads, constructing telephone lines, and stocking fish. Each of these endeavors aided the ranches in some way, and the Cody merchants benefited in return. Ranchers recommended that their guests wait till they arrived to buy boots, hats, and other articles of clothing for their ranch vacation. Sometimes a rancher even rounded up all the dudes and brought them to town at the beginning of the Cody Stampede to make their purchases. Such cooperation meant thousands of dollars of business for the local stores. Other city groups and individuals cooperated with the ranchers also, and cities vied with each other to be the site of the annual DRA meeting. The one chosen, of course, got the added benefit of convention dollars. Billings and Sheridan got the bulk of this early business since five of the first six conventions were in those two cities. But meetings were then rotated to other locales: Livingston, Cody, Missoula, Bozeman, Cheyenne, Sun Valley, Coeur d'Alene, Jackson Hole, and others. Because there were many benefits for both ranchers and local stores, cooperation was the order of the day. Many hotels, clothing stores, and other merchants became associate members of the DRA to boost it, and dude ranchers were urged to patronize these members' establishments when they bought supplies, ate a meal, or stayed overnight in town.[37]

Dude ranchers also received inquiries from other sources such as the Outlook Travel Bureau in New York, the American Travel Service in California, the camp bureau of *Parents' Magazine,* the American Forestry Association, and various schools and tour groups from different cities. And different ranches advertised on their own in whatever ways seemed suitable.[38]

Of all these sources of advertising and support, the railroad activities were unquestionably the most effective and useful. Probably the second greatest benefit came from the free publicity in articles and books about the West in general and dude ranches in particular. These stories were not just those placed by the DRA officials nor the ads and special supplements mentioned, but were often the work of people eager to share their experiences of life on a ranch.

One of the earliest of these, written by Jesse Williams, appeared in 1913 in *Collier's* magazine. In it Williams explained a bit of the background of dude ranches but mainly emphasized the plain, uncomplicated life on a ranch and the pleasant, engaging attitude of westerners. He noted that the atmosphere was relaxed so anyone could enjoy it whether or not he had been on a ranch or horse before. He also pointed out that accommodations were comfortable and the food was varied—the approach noted earlier to assure easterners that the West wasn't as wild or dangerous as they had been led to believe by some of the popular writers of fiction. "The most significant thing of all," wrote Williams, "is the inherent gentility of strong men who have got beyond the immediate influence of the funny little ideals of our permeating pecuniary culture. It is so different from artificial gentility."[39]

This emphasis on the character of westerners was common in many articles. Another early paean of praise to the West and dude ranches appeared in 1915. The author, Leon Dusseau, discussed his trip through northern Wyoming and southern Montana. He emphasized the historical and archaeological sites and the incredible scenery that greeted him and his companion wherever they rode— the climb up Bald Mountain, the Falls of the Porcupine, Castle Rock, and more. And the dude ranches that accommodated the two men made their trip pleasant and easy.[40]

In a 1920 article, "Dude Wranglers," Hal Evarts used the visit of a successful businessman to the West as an outline to explain ranch life. He emphasized the egalitarian attitude that prevailed when dudes from all walks of life and ranch workers mingled together; Evarts also pointed out that exercise, a quiet atmosphere, and good food could ease the nerves of even the most harried businessman. The dude ranch was clearly a place where one's status or job elsewhere was unimportant.[41]

A different theme was sounded in some articles, such as "A Lady on A Dude Ranch"; here the point, obvious in the title, was that women made just as worthy dudes as men and could feel comfortable about going to a ranch for a vacation.[42] A variety of articles appeared during the 1920s and 1930s to help popularize the ranch vacation; most were straightforward personal stories, a few were fictionalized, but all were great free publicity for ranches.

Writing about ranches also extended to books, both fictional and factual. Several of the fictional accounts are discussed in Chapter 7, some containing a range of events and scenes that can be described only as highly imaginative.

One of the funniest was Ross Santee's account of an enormous Arizona ranch that was turned into the world's largest golf course—for dudes; on it the shortest hole was fifteen miles long and had a par 300. Each dude-golfer was accompanied by a cowboy, and there was a campsite with cook and wrangler at the end of each hole. While this book mostly pokes fun at golf and golfers, it contains a few observations about dudes and dude work.[43]

Surprisingly, one of the best books about dude ranching is a work of fiction—a Dodd Mead "career book," *Dude Rancher: A Story of Modern Ranching.* In this novel the central figure is Philip Marshall, an easterner who goes west to find a life that suited him, fulfilling his liking for outdoor life, farming, working with people, traveling, and selling. Through Marshall the author explains quite realistically how a dude ranch should develop slowly, the types of skills required to run one, and even the methods of advertising. It included what is probably the most complete description of the eastern trips that ranchers made to line up summer business.[44]

Most of the factual books were personal accounts by guests or ranch owners. But there were two that were types of guidebooks for prospective dudes.[45] In *Dude Ranches and Ponies* Lawrence Smith mostly explained horses, their background, origin, and training in America but also included some practical advice for people going to dude ranches. In *Hi, Stranger!* Arthur Carhart discussed in great detail the types of horses, bridles, saddles, and clothes a dude might see and use; he also explained what he or she should expect on a hunting, pack, or fishing trip from a ranch. Among other things the appearance of these books shows the widespread popularity of the dude ranch vacation.

Probably the earliest book coming from a rancher was *The Diary of a Dude-Wrangler;* written by Struthers Burt, already a published author, it combined the practical experience of a rancher with the skill of a storyteller. The result was an enjoyable book with some practical ideas about dude ranches and a number of interesting and colorful stories. Other books by ranch owners and operators came too late to be prime factors in publicizing dude ranches. However, books about Theodore Roosevelt's western adventures probably boosted ranches, since he had been a guest and friend of the Eaton brothers at their early ranch in North Dakota.[46]

Books written by former ranch guests were also powerful boosts for the ranches. The ranchers realized their value, and the executive secretary of the DRA noted the publication of such books at the organization's annual meeting. One of these was *French Heels to Spurs* by Loraine Fielding; it was a straightforward account of the author's summer vacation at Bones' Brothers Ranch in southern Montana, detailing the various activities of a dude ranch and the friendly atmosphere she found there. The association valued writing about any aspect of the West and, in appreciation for it, gave honorary memberships to a number of western writers— Owen Wister, Arthur Chapman, Courtney Ryley Cooper, Struthers Burt, Will James, and Mary Robert Rinehart.[47]

The last-named author stood head and shoulders above all others in the amount of publicity she gave to dude ranching; her work even rivaled the importance of railroad publicity since some of it predated their activities. Many people who know of Mary Roberts Rinehart are aware of her mystery stories. But she was a woman of much broader background and depth than some of these stories might indicate. She was a nurse, a war correspondent during World War I, and a very active outdoorswoman, and she was certainly an excellent writer. She noted the motivation for her outdoor endeavors in one of her books:

> Led by the exigencies of my profession, by feminine curiosity, or
> merely by the determination not to be left at home, I have been
> shaken, thrown, bitten, sunburned, rained on, shot at, stone
> bruised, frozen, broiled and scared with monotonous regularity.[48]

She paid for her curiosity and enthusiasm with blisters and scratches, uncomfortable beds, and numerous stings, aches, and pains; to ease these she had "bathed in a glacial lake and sat in the mud of a hot spring, in a hole in the ground in a Mexican Canyon, to get the soreness out of my aching bones."[49]

With a husband and three sons, Mrs. Rinehart had to work hard sometimes not to be left behind as she journeyed through the West and Mexico. And, although she disclaimed any attitude of being an outdoorswoman, she clearly enjoyed her treks, and she rates as a true traveler, not a mere tourist. In many articles and several books she broadcast her message to thousands of readers in the period from 1916 through 1931. Mrs. Rinehart first became interested in the western United States about 1915. She had met many Europeans who knew more about America than she did, and she was rather ashamed of her ignorance of her own land. She visited some of the national parks, stayed on a dude ranch, and was hooked for life. Her earliest book, *Through Glacier Park,* was a relatively brief account of a three-hundred-mile trip through the Rocky Mountains; in it she particularly praised Howard Eaton who had led over forty people on this enjoyable vacation trek. Two years later she combined some stories she had published in *Cosmopolitan* into *Tenting To-Night,* the tale of two rather rugged pack trips in northwestern Montana and northern Washington. In 1921, after a serious operation, she went to Eatons' in Wyoming to recover. While there she thought seriously about her life and decided she had worked too vigorously at her profession and had neglected herself and her family. She gave up some of her work to slow down. What that really meant was that she and her family worked in the winter and traveled in the summer. By her own definition rest and vacation meant change of occupation, not idleness. And she certainly practiced what she wrote.[50]

She followed her early books about the West with *The Out Trail* (1923), *Nomad's Land* (1926), and *My Story* (1931). None was exclusively about the West but all contained some accounts of ranch life or trips. And her articles appeared throughout the 1920s, mainly in *Cosmopolitan*, *Saturday Evening Post*, *Harper's Bazaar*, and the *Ladies' Home Journal*.[51] Implicit in all these articles was the obvious concept that women could and should visit the West, but they contained far more than that idea. She emphasized that the wilderness of America would not survive long, and people who wanted to see the West should do so soon. If they did, they would see cowboys breaking horses and handling cattle as they had done in the old days. She also wrote regularly about the relaxing atmosphere of the West, noting that guests left their worn clothing at Eatons' when they departed in the summer or fall; when they returned the following year, they put these old clothes on and stepped back into their relaxing life, literally as well as figuratively.[52] She described in picturesque detail the main activities of her ranch trip—some of her hilarious escapades while fly fishing, joining a grueling cattle roundup with the Bones brothers in southern Montana, and helping the Eatons bring in the horses for the season. "To Wyoming" presented her firsthand view of the fiftieth reunion of both Indians and troopers who had participated in the Indian War of 1876; as if to dramatize the encroachment of civilization on the wild West, the tourists overwhelmed Indians and soldiers as they attempted to carry out the ceremony that had been planned.[53]

Mrs. Rinehart also used her writing to educate. "The Sleeping Giant," for example, explained the beauty of the national parks and warned that private interests threatened to despoil them with dams for electric power. She urged readers to oppose this destruction by putting pressure on congressmen to prevent it. She received numerous queries in the 1920s about this new form of vacation on a ranch that she was publicizing and she used a 1927 article to answer many of these inquiries.[54] But above all Mary Roberts Rinehart extolled dude ranches and Howard Eaton.

Her clear message was the same as that spread by the railroads, state officials, and others: see the Old West before it is gone; enjoy the relaxation and hospitality of ranch life; refresh and renew yourselves in the beauty of the mountains; ride, fish, hunt, and hike. Above all, come to the West.

SIX

Wranglin' the Dudes

What impresses one most on a "dude" ranch is what a good time anyone can have whether he has ever been on a ranch or a horse before in his life. He may not ride very well nor know a cantle from a pommel but what of it? The object is to have a good time, not to illustrate a rule.

—Jesse Williams, "Joy-Ranching and Dude-Wrangling," 23.

The appeal of dude ranches has centered on the chance for the visitor to get outdoors and to live closer to nature.[1] It was also important for the guest to be able to do these things in a physical environment different from his home territory in the East or Midwest.

The special attractions of the West included mountains, the plains country, isolation, clear water and air, wild animals, different weather, and rugged but friendly people. Easterners were certainly familiar with mountains—the Adirondacks, Smokies, Alleghenies, and others—but the Rockies were spectacularly different from the mountains they knew. Not only are they much higher—approximately an 8,000-foot difference in the highest peaks—but they present a totally different image. The Appalachian Mountains are heavily forested and give the impression of closeness. The Rockies, often bare, present awesome

91

spectacles of grandeur. The trees that do grow are different—generally aspen, willow, pine, spruce, and fir. Above timberline, there are unusual wildflowers and even tundra plants in some places, and many craggy prominences support no vegetation at all. The plains country was another unusual phenomenon for the dude, giving him long vistas of horses, cattle, or grasses waving in the breeze— all set in the midst of a huge landscape. Isolation was a welcome change to those accustomed to urban crowds. To the easterner, lakes and streams in the West seemed pure enough to drink from, and the air was not only free of pollution but had the peculiar clarity that exists at higher elevations. Wild animals in their natural surroundings (rather than in zoos) were an attraction, too, and eastern visitors enjoyed seeing western animals—moose, elk, bears, deer, coyotes, antelope, and birds peculiar to the West. The dude certainly welcomed western weather, as the heat and humidity of an eastern summer gave way to the cool, dry climate of the Rockies; anyone who has endured a sweltering summer in the Midwest or East can imagine the relief that the mountain air brought to early visitors and the longing they felt at home as the heat and humidity increased in June, July, and August. Unusual weather phenomena, such as occasional hail-storms in July and August and snow that remained year-round, also delighted easterners. Overall, the attractiveness of dude ranches was to a big land, often accessible only by horseback.[2]

One of the most easily overlooked and least understood attractions of dude ranch life has been its simplicity. One might assume that this particular appeal is a phenomenon recently discovered by psychologists or other analysts with a late-twentieth-century outlook. This aspect of ranches, however, was one of their major attractions during the height of dude ranching.

In this early era only the wealthy could afford vacations of any length, and the informality of dude ranch life was a welcome relief to people whose lives had become dominated by upper-class social mores, political involvement, and family traditions.[3]

It is difficult to appreciate how many restrictions on social activities existed at the beginning of this century. The Victorian attitude was that the sexes had totally separate spheres of activity; this separation extended far beyond the idea that men worked and women stayed home. It covered recreation, especially summertime activity and even the types of hotels available. There were generally two kinds: commercial hotels for men and vacation hotels for women, and each sex felt out of place in the other's domain.

During the summer self-sacrificing husbands and fathers remained in hot cities while their wives and children escaped to breezy, pleasant hotels to relax or play. Even at the resort hotel, however, a rigid routine existed, especially for women.

For them conversation on the veranda was mandatory and monotonous; daughters and sons had to be introduced to socially acceptable people, and women had to have an extensive wardrobe in order to change costumes frequently, at least for each meal. While children could play at various sports, mealtimes were formal affairs for everyone. When the hard-working husband and father was able to leave the city and visit his family at the resort, he felt out of place; in his city attire at mealtime, he was a drab spectator in a strange environment.

By 1900, this rigid formality was breaking down significantly. Women sought a more active public life and many people discussed the advantages of the "companionate" family. Husbands, wives, and children should be friends and companions; they should play together instead of being artificially divided and separated. Many people hailed this way of life as a return to an earlier era when families cooperated in all their activities on isolated American farms. The dress codes, which were common in all hotels, were also beginning to seem artificial and anachronistic; on vacations, at least, Victorian Americans were trying to escape conventions.[4]

The dude ranch was ideally suited to these new concepts. Western ranches were generally organized and run as family endeavors, and most dude ranches were developed for family vacations. Later in the twentieth century, the *Social Register* and its attendant customs became less important to many people, but the tensions and pressures of urban life continued and even intensified. Dude ranches gave people a chance to lead a simpler, more primitive life as they escaped from the complexities that surrounded them.

The hectic urban pace became so intense that dudes needed a considerable length of time to "unwind" and adapt to ranch life; rancher Dick Randall estimated it took a full month for a true adjustment to ranch life, although other westerners had lower estimates. Whatever the actual adjustment period was, early ranchers insisted on a minimum stay of several weeks so that guests could truly appreciate their experience and enjoy their new way of life.

Mary Robert Rinehart noted that many other vacations for the well-to-do were boring compromises. Trips were often arranged to try to please family members with divergent interests. Dude ranches appealed to these travelers because they offered new and varied experiences and allowed people to do what they wanted. Guests could rest and contemplate, read a book, take a vigorous role in the various physical activities, enjoy the serene atmosphere and hearty food, or combine parts of any of these offerings.[5] There was little regimentation at most ranches as each family, or each person in the family, made his or her own choices. Family members could thus vacation together and yet make individual choices in their day-to-day activities.

One facet of dude ranch informality was the egalitarian attitude prevalent in the West. Some visitors, especially in the early days of dude ranching, did not appreciate this characteristic; some of them wore fancy eastern clothes, brought along champagne, and stayed apart from the westerners whenever possible. But this attitude faded quickly, and the trend was clearly toward an atmosphere where dudes, ranchers, and ranch workers could mingle as equals in a pleasant companionship.[6]

Dudes were soon buying and wearing typical western clothes and priding themselves on being accepted as equals by the westerners. As early as 1913, western writers made it clear that on a dude ranch everyone adopted the habits and clothing of the country; they noted that the broad-brimmed hat, silk bandana, and vest were practical pieces of clothing. *Vogue* magazine also emphasized that the "good dude" should dress like the local cowboys and even listed the essentials for a ranch vacation: jeans, flannel or woolen shirts, leather jacket, practical underwear, lisle or wool socks long enough to come above boot tops, silk neckerchiefs, riding gloves, boots, and a Stetson hat. The author urged visitors to buy their boots and hats after they arrived in the West. He also listed some stores in New York City that sold the appropriate clothing and a store in Sheridan, Wyoming, that stocked quality leather goods of all types.[7]

Some dudes allowed their imaginations to run wild and bought some rather flashy western attire as evidenced by a description of two of them by a ranch worker:

> One wore lavender angora chaps, the other bright orange, and
> each sported a tremendous beaver sombrero and wore a gaudy scarf
> knotted jauntily about his throat.

Such a guest could be identified "as far as you can see him on the sky line."[8] One part of Wyoming, where tourism was the chief industry for many years, was known for its ornamental dress—gaudy handkerchiefs, flaring silver-studded chaps, and buckskin shirts.[9] Regrettably many people remembered only those dudes who were gaudily attired, and they sometimes used the word *dude* in an uncomplimentary sense of "fop" or "dandy."

Despite a few flashy dudes, the general trend was toward simplicity in dress and manners. This simplicity fit with the attempt of the ranchers to offer their guests the pleasure of peace and quiet with only the noises of nature to intrude on their days of respite. The informality, equality, quiet, and individuality combined to form the simpler life that drew thousands of people westward and kept drawing them back every year.[10]

While the above attractions may seem a little vague and difficult to pinpoint, there are others that are much more specific. One of these appeals can be summarized in a single word: horses. Dude ranches and horses have been inseparable, and no definition of a dude ranch is complete without horses. Even on ranches where other activities were more important, horses and riding were available.

In the early days of dude ranching, horses, of course, played a very different role in American life from their present status. They had been the chief mode of transportation in the East as well as in the West for many years, except for long journeys. Thus when ranch guests were met at the train station by a wagon or stagecoach to transport them to the ranch, they were not especially surprised. Even so, these early visitors liked the idea of horse-powered transportation as a symbol of their temporary return to the simple, rural life that was fast disappearing in the urban East. Many were especially glad that their children could sample this form of transportation. In this way the appeal of horses was part of the appeal of the simplicity of life mentioned before.

Once on the ranch, however, horseback riding became even more important; here it was a practical part of ranch work and a way to get to good places for fishing and hunting, or to remote scenic areas.

The details varied from ranch to ranch, but generally ranch prices included the use of a horse for the entire stay. Each guest would be assigned a horse the first full day of his vacation and would often keep the same animal throughout his visit, whether it was for a week or an entire summer. There were a few factors that could alter this plan; one would be if the horse and dude didn't "fit together."[11] This could relate to a variety of situations; one is simply that the horse was too small or too large for the guest. Since the rancher or wrangler usually sized up guests fairly accurately, this was not a frequent problem. More serious was a guest who could not control his or her steed. The guest's experience and skill might have been overestimated or the horse's cantankerous nature underestimated. In either case a quick switch would be necessary for the sake of safety. Another, less tangible reason for a change would be that the personalities of rider and horse clashed; to a nonrider, this may seem a strange comment, but ranchers learned that such clashes did occur and could lead to a very unhappy guest. A final factor leading to a change of mounts would be the improving skill of the rider. When the dude stayed several weeks or months on a ranch, it was possible for him to show a vast improvement in riding ability. Ranchers were quite happy to give such a horseman a "better" animal, both to keep the rider happy and to free a gentler, less spirited horse for a less experienced rider.

The riding skill of dudes varied considerably, ranging from the absolute beginner to a few who thought they knew everything about riding. To the former

the rancher gave some basic instructions, and, within a few weeks, many begin-
ners became reasonably competent riders. From the latter, ranchers sometimes
had to endure some boasting; if this became too intense, ranchers might saddle
up a bronco and give the braggart a chance to show off or eat dirt and a little
humble pie.[12] Most riders were somewhere in between these extremes, skilled
but not given to braggadocio; many of them were even very nervous about their
western mounts at first. One difficulty the eastern rider faced was the switch
from using an English saddle to the standard western stock saddle; a second one
was the change from manipulating double reins on a bridle with a snaffle bit to
handling a single set of split reins that were attached to a curb bit. These were
handled with but one hand since western horses were trained to respond to
pressure on their necks rather than to the direct reining common in the East.

In order to make these changes easier, the knowledgeable and sympathetic
ranch owner might point out the value of "neck reining," the historical background of the western seat, and the hang of the stirrups; he could trace the rich
heritage of the western style through Mexico, Spain, and the Saracens. The
western saddle was, and is, a very practical working rig whose utility could be
explained to ease the fears of eastern riders. Unfortunately, many westerners did
not know this background or did not bother to explain it to the guests. Some
were even too ready to ridicule the "postage-stamp" English saddle without understanding it or realizing that a great deal of skill was needed to ride such a
saddle, which was practical for its own uses.[13]

Problems often occurred when rich people who had spoiled horses came to
ranches. While these guests had some riding skills, they were used to their own
animals, which were often pampered by grooms and had developed bad habits
that the owners did not correct. Struthers Burt, a Wyoming dude rancher, made
a point of trying to protect his horses from these guests, who could easily abuse
or injure their mounts. Some of his cowboy-wranglers were too polite to tell the
dudes what to do or to tell them to alter certain habits they had developed. Like
many horsemen, Burt remembered a particular "horror" story about his animals.
He once saw a 225-pound football player panic while riding a narrow trail; he
jumped off the horse on the wrong side and managed to shove the animal down
a precipice. Fortunately, the horse was uninjured; it is interesting that Burt
insisted he would always worry about protecting a horse first if he had to choose
between the horse and the dude. Burt distinguished between a horseman and a
rider; the former tried to know the animal, and the perfect ride came when man
and horse rode together as one. The true horseman was generally modest and
unassuming, knowing he could learn more. The rider merely sat on the horse
and, in effect, left the animal in control of the situation.[14]

Similar problems have been discussed by horseman Frank Wright, who has long supplied horses for dudes in Colorado. Since he has operated extensively in the high country of the Centennial State, he and his wranglers have to watch especially for guests riding their horses too hard, which not only tires the animal but can rupture a lung. Like Burt, one of Wright's wranglers remembers a specific unpleasant incident illustrating the problems of dealing with inexperienced people. One spring some riders were in the mountains and crossed a creek still covered with ice; the horses broke through the ice so the riders just dismounted, abandoned the animals, and walked back to the stables.[15]

Thoughtless actions such as these could sour anyone on inexperienced dudes. These and similar stories certainly gave some westerners a poor image of the eastern rider. But there is another side to the picture that these tales tend to obscure. Spike Van Cleve, Montana dude rancher, has analyzed this subject:

> For some reason that completely eludes me, most westerners have the idea that a dude can't ride. We've run a dude ranch for better than fifty years right along with our cow and horse outfit, and by and large I have developed a hell of a lot of respect for eastern riders. Perhaps I should say horsemen, or better yet, horsemanship. Over the years I have seen a lot of guests at the ranch who will stack up right along with any horse hands in the west.[16]

Van Cleve did note that easterners and westerners sometimes handled horses differently, and he had some minor differences of opinion with the former about riding. Nevertheless he was pleased to put dudes who knew horses on the best ones that he had, because he knew the animals would be ridden well.

On some dude ranches, riders played polo. A number of ranches in the 1900–1930 era organized teams for their guests and invited neighbors to the matches. Several Wyoming ranches were devoted to the breeding and training of polo ponies, "fleet, iron winded little animals" that were much in demand in the East as well as in England.[17] Needless to say, few people capable of riding well in a polo match would be considered poor riders, although Spike Van Cleve thought they were inferior to those who frequently rode on fox hunts.

Even where polo was not featured, there was evidence of competent horsemanship. All ranchers were aware of guests' skills, and some even had special rides reserved as rewards for people who showed sufficient equestrian skill. At one ranch, Devil's Thumb, near Fraser, Colorado, competent horsemen were allowed to take the twenty-eight-mile trip along the crest of the Continental Divide past the rocky spire known as Devil's Thumb. Author Rochelle Klein described how she and her daughter rose regularly at the H Ranch in Montana at 6:00 A.M. to ride before breakfast; they soon demonstrated their interest and proficiency enough to be invited on after-supper rides on a very steep trail—an honor extended only to the best riders.[18] At the Holzwarth Ranch in Colorado, guests who knew the trails and the horses were allowed to ride all day without ranch guides in the Neversummer Mountains and in Rocky Mountain National Park. A similar situation prevailed for many years at the Arapaho Valley Ranch, where riders roamed freely through the Indian Peaks country.

It should be noted that the skill required of these riders was not the ability to ride a bucking horse. Rather one had to be able to ride long distances without undue hardship, to ride daily without developing bruises and blisters, and to possess common sense (perhaps horse sense in this case). This meant being familar enough with horses to expect the unexpected and being capable of coping with problems. The rider also needed the skill to sit to a horse's trot and gallop; sitting to the trot of a western horse was probably the most difficult thing that an eastern rider had to learn. It was especially important on those ranches with a lot of level ground where the trot was used frequently to cover great distances. In mountainous territory, learning to sit to a trot or gallop was of less significance since riding in this country was usually not at a fast pace. Actually, on rugged mountain trails the competent rider had to keep his horse at a walk.

Overall, while the riding skill of dudes varied considerably and led to both humorous and dangerous incidents, most guests gained confidence in their mounts and many became very attached to them by the end of their stay on the ranch.[19]

A typical routine of riding on dude ranches would be a two-to-four-hour ride in the morning and a one-to-three-hour one in the afternoon, with an all-day ride occasionally. For the competent riders the all-day rides were the most popular since some of the more remote scenic areas could be reached only by four-to-eight-hour trips. On days when such rides were scheduled, ranches were the scene of even more activity than normal. In the kitchen food would be packed in individual sacks or in bulk for large groups while wranglers put saddlebags on the horses and dudes packed cameras and binoculars and filled their canteens.

Holzwarth's Neversummer Ranch was one of the best-known of the dude ranches that featured frequent all-day rides. Throughout the summer three such rides were scheduled every week; this was unusual since many ranches featured but one per week and some had them less frequently. Describing one of Holzwarth's rides, therefore, may be the best way to explain the appeal of this dude ranch feature. Since the ranch emphasized these rides, there were many riders, and the food was often packed in bulk. Soup, coffee, powdered drinks, bread, meat, cold fried chicken, and fresh fruit were frequently on the menu. While the kitchen help assembled the food and cooking equipment, the dudes gathered at the corral with their gear. They also added full-length slickers on every trip since the Neversummer country received frequent, heavy storms. One of the most common and perhaps most spectacular rides was called Around the Horn, a seventeen-to-eighteen-mile trek through the Neversummer range.[20]

After all this gear was assembled, the riders left the main ranch, which was at an elevation of 8,900 feet, and rode slowly for an hour through hay fields and a campground, then along a stream and past some beaver dams until they joined an old mining road that snaked its way up Bowen Gulch. Then the riders started to climb westward and got tantalizing glimpses of snow-clad mountains as they wound their way through the evergreen forest. They passed various relics of nineteenth-century mining and saw more sparkling streams as they rode rocky switchbacks or soft, carpeted forest trails in an endless rise higher into the Neversummers. After about three hours of this scenery, they reached the lunch stop, a huge open valley near the timberline. The abandoned Ruby mine was nearby as well as a fallen mine shack and one of the most beautiful mountain lakes imaginable—the incredibly blue Ruby Lake. The horses were let loose to graze while guests helped prepare a hearty lunch. Wood was gathered for a fire, and someone scooped up clear mountain water to make soup, coffee, and other drinks. Soon everyone was wolfing down a large meal while admiring the scenery that surrounded this idyllic site.

After about an hour the horses were gathered, saddles retightened, and gear packed for the long afternoon ride. Now all climbed high above the timberline to Bowen Pass, where the vista opened up even more; another hour's ride led across a huge valley and toward Parika Pass. On this stretch the group reached the high point on the trail, a spot over 12,000 feet high; at the pass the riders were awed by the scene that had unfolded in front of them. To the east was the familiar square shape of Long's Peak and the rest of Rocky Mountain National Park; to the south were Grand Lake, Shadow Mountain Reservoir, and Granby Reservoir; to the west, seven ranges of hills and mountains; to the north, the immense valley called North Park and some of the mountains in Wyoming—overall a spectacular and awesome panorama. One view justified the hours of difficult riding. After drinking in as much of this sight as they could, the riders had to cross the pass and begin their descent. Usually this was a simple matter of following a narrow trail, but early in the season a snow bank often extended across the path; in this case the dudes joined in the unique experience of pushing and pulling horses over a mass of snow ten to fifteen feet out from the side of the mountain and thirty feet or more from top to bottom. It looked impossible, but many horses got used to it and some even jumped over the edge on their own. Once this obstacle was surmounted the trail led down rapidly as the beautiful scenery continued. The riders dropped into a bowl-shaped area, past Parika Lake, through one of those peculiar boggy areas common in the Rockies, all the while trying to spot elk sleeping in the shadows. Finally, they passed the Big Ditch that carried sparkling water across the Continental Divide to Fort Collins, and then descended quickly into rugged Baker Gulch, through aspen and conifers, past beaver dams, and at last back into the Kawuneeche Valley where they had begun.

Lest any flatland rider be inclined to scoff at a mere seventeen-to-eighteen-mile horseback ride at a walk, it must be emphasized that the Around the Horn trip was a difficult one. Most of the riding was rugged, occasionally over treacherous mountain terrain, tiring for both horse and rider. Sore knees (and other parts of the anatomy) were common, but the view made it worthwhile. No words can adequately describe such an experience; the ride alone would bring guests back annually to the same ranch.

Such rides were popular, but many ranchers believed the ultimate activity for the horseman was the pack trip. This combined several of the appealing aspects of ranch life to produce an experience that was seldom equaled and hardly ever surpassed on a western vacation.[21]

The chief objective of most pack trips was simple: to get to otherwise inaccessible scenic areas. There were, of course, few automobiles or auto roads through the Rockies. Trains connected the populous cities but had lines to only a few of the best-known tourist sites. Travel by foot was possible but certainly not feasible for most guests; long treks with heavy packs in the mountains were only for a few hardy vacationers. Even with modern, lightweight backpacking equipment, the great percentage of travelers simply cannot carry food and gear any appreciable distance at elevations that are as much as 10,000 feet higher than where they live. Obviously the dudes of the 1880–1930 era who wanted to see remote areas had to plan a pack trip.

The enjoyable trek included several aspects of the simpler life sought by travelers. Not only did the pack trip participant leave the East and/or city behind, he now abandoned the ranch and its comforts. Getting a lot closer to nature than most people ever expected, those on pack trips sacrificed comfortable, dry beds, indoor plumbing, frequent changes of clothing, and various other conveniences. The necessities of life and a few comforts had to be packed on horses or mules, often including a cook tent and sheet-steel stove plus smaller tents for sleeping, bedrolls, food, and clothing. In these earlier days equipment was heavy, and many pack animals were needed. Guests were usually limited to one "war bag" apiece for all their personal gear, and they often had to make difficult decisions about what items were truly essential for their trek into the wilderness.[22]

But the men and women who took such trips had their rewards in the opportunity to see little-known lakes, streams, and canyons; the majority of Americans never even suspected that such beauties of nature existed. They also had better chances to see wild game such as moose, sheep, elk, deer, and bear. They came in closer contact with the dude wranglers and developed a camaraderie with them and with other guests that would seldom be achieved in any other fashion.

Dude ranchers noted that businessmen who went on pack trips were particularly interesting to watch; they often wanted to return to their boyhood or young manhood and to work with their hands. They enjoyed these outings because they liked to share in the camp activities and they often did a large amount of the work on the pack trips. But women were often better campers than men; they were more eager and helpful, did not pretend to know everything, and were also more self-disciplined.[23] Of course, early western travelers could, and did, take pack trips on their own. Owen Wister, for instance, did so several times, but he and his friends often spent considerable time trying to hire guides and collect the horses, saddles, and other necessary equipment. The dude ranches eliminated this wasted time and effort by having the animals and equipment ready and by knowing where the trails were and which areas were most desirable to visit. Wister himself eventually stayed at the JY Ranch in Jackson Hole and let others take care of details.[24]

Particularly appealing were trips to areas that became national parks—especially Yellowstone in Wyoming. Howard Eaton and Dick Randall, two of the ranchers discussed earlier, concentrated on Yellowstone pack trips. These were extended and necessarily well-planned expeditions. Randall's Ranch, the OTO near Gardiner, Montana, may have handled the largest trip of any ranch when it arranged a pack trip in 1926 for 368 people from the Sierra Club of San Francisco. The Sierra Club took care of the food and brought its own cook, Judge Tappan of Los Angeles; twenty Sierra Club members acted as his assistants. Randall's son-in-law, Clyde Erskine, handled the rest of the details. He hired 23 men and made them sign contracts to stay for the entire trip; he had 80 pack horses, 10 mules for the kitchen equipment and supplies, 18 saddle horses for those who wanted to ride, and additional horses for the crew. There was a total of 126 animals and 392 people. Erskine met the Sierrans at Old Faithful Inn inside Yellowstone and guided them through the park for slightly over two weeks. He divided his crew and animals into companies like those in a military unit, and the trip went smoothly. There were no accidents, and no horses or equipment were lost. Mr. Colby, head of the Sierra Club, later wrote that this was the best, most pleasant trip they had ever taken.[25]

Howard Eaton apparently took no trips with a group this large, but he led dozens of pack trips over the years; his first to Yellowstone was in 1883. These annual Yellowstone treks, generally about three weeks long, developed as one of the special features of Eatons' Ranch in Wyoming. They eventually became luxury trips for those early days since Eaton brought along more than the average number of workers from the ranch. Girls made the guests' beds and served them food while wranglers took care of the horses and set up the equipment. In honor of these early Eaton trips a special trail was built in Yellowstone Park, and in 1923 it was dedicated to Howard Eaton. Over 150 miles long, it was marked by about 200 signs and a biographical tablet about Howard Eaton.[26]

Eaton also led one of the earliest pack trips into Glacier Park in 1915, although this was far less luxurious than his Yellowstone trips. Forty-two riders participated, including cowboy artist Charley Russell and author Mary Roberts Rinehart. They rode the better-known trails and viewed the more remote west side of the park from a distance. Interest in this western area was so great that in 1916 Howard Eaton scheduled a truly rugged trip through the western part of Glacier Park and into the Cascade Mountains. His crew even carried two boats on a wagon to the Canadian boundary of Montana, and the group, which included Mrs. Rinehart and her family, ran approximately a hundred miles of the Flathead River (including rapids) on a stretch where few, if any, white man's boats had been before. The Rineharts then crossed the Cascades with another pack outfit over a route never before used; this group consisted of thirty-one horses and nineteen people. These hardy travelers suffered from a scarcity of supplies, and extremely dangerous "trails" that were nearly impassable; one of the Rinehart boys suffered an infected knee, a potentially dangerous problem so far from civilization, so it was fortunate that his father, a doctor, was on the trip too.[27] All survived and the expedition whetted the appetite of the Rinehart family for more trips west for years to come. Considering this and other difficult western trips that Mrs. Rinehart made, it is not surprising to learn that she was one of the first American newspaper correspondents in Europe during the Great War.

Despite some rough trips, Eatons' dudes generally fared well. Rising at 5:00 A.M. each day, they ate enormous quantities of food—flapjacks, molasses, and bacon for breakfast, sandwiches at noon, and fried beef and potatoes at supper, with plenty of strong black coffee every day.[28]

Other ranches conducted numerous pack trips although few, if any, matched the size of the one Clyde Erskine handled, and seldom were any as adventurous as Eaton's early Glacier trips. For twenty years Holzwarth's Ranch in Colorado scheduled an annual pack trip from the vicinity of Grand Lake, across the Continental Divide and into Central City for a night at the opera. The trip lasted two and one-half to three and one-half days, depending on the exact starting point; after that long on the trail, the unshaven and unwashed outfit created quite a stir wending its way to one of the city's hotels. After cleaning off the trail dust, the transformed dudes were entertained by presentations such as *Falstaff* or *The Marriage of Figaro*.[29] The famous Valley Ranch in Wyoming commonly conducted trips up to forty-five days long in the 1920s.[30] Many other ranches took guests to and through every conceivable scenic spot in the Rockies.

In recent years, pack trips on dude ranches have grown somewhat less common. The very long trips became too expensive and disappeared during the Great Depression. More significant was the fact that extensive development of national park areas have made many places accessible to automobiles, thus eliminating the need for some of the trips. But pack trips have never vanished completely and probably will not do so as long as there are beautiful areas of wilderness left.

Since horseback riding was such an important part of the dude ranch, the ranchers eventually had to pay particular attention to the dudes' horses. In the early days they simply used cow ponies, Indian horses, and extra ranch horses; for a time "dude horse" conjured up images of the leftovers—nags that were swaybacked, heavy-footed, coarse, and hard-mouthed. This reliance on whatever horses that were available could create dangerous situations. Arthur Pack, who ran the Ghost Ranch near Tucson, remembered that some of their animals, just off the range, were really wild. One tried to kill the foreman and had to be shot.[31] Many of these wild horses or broomtails made decent saddle animals once they were broken, but, as dude ranching developed into a substantial business in the twentieth century, it was important to pay more attention to horses and to work to improve them. The rancher had to be able to mount a wide variety of guests—old, middle-aged, and young; male and female; timid and bold; expert and beginner—and under widely varying conditions. When acquiring horses it was necessary to search for good disposition, conformation, and a free-moving gait. A horse with a good disposition was safe to ride, and guests could feel free to mount and dismount it from either side and to tie onto their saddles elk antlers, cameras, shovels, and other paraphernalia. The rancher sought not only a sound horse, but also one with a short back and good withers while avoiding animals that were too big, too wide, or too round. A free-moving gait would include a quick walk, comfortable trot, and smooth gallop or lope. Obviously, not every horse had all these good traits but ranchers soon learned what type of animal they needed. Eventually the dude horse became a specialized animal and was valued accordingly.[32]

In order to get these qualities ranchers scoured the West searching for the proper horses; many ranches started their operations slowly and gradually added good horses when they could find them. Unfortunately, in the early twentieth century, there was a scarcity of good riding stock for several reasons. Just before 1900 many draft horses, brought west for farming activities, were crossed with the saddle stock. The quality of horses deteriorated, with most of them unfit for riding, especially on dude ranches. In addition, large numbers of horses were sold to the government for use in World War I; since many dude ranches started just before 1920, desirable riding horses were scarce. After the war August Belmont and other men interested in horses donated several thoroughbred stallions to the U.S. government to establish a Remount Service. Within a few years over 800 stallions were acquired and used to breed better western riding stock. Dude ranchers were greatly indebted to the Remount Service for improving the quality of horses available to them.[33]

Besides thoroughbreds, other horses have been tried for dude ranch use depending on the particular type of riding to be done, the layout of the land, and the personal preferences of the ranchers. Struthers Burt preferred Morgans, especially in rough, mountainous country, but he always wanted some "cold blood" in his animals and believed the best horses were produced from a pure-bred sire and range mares. Johnnie Holzwarth bred a Hackney stud to his range mares for about ten years to get horses for his high-altitude riding in Colorado. He chose a Hackney because of its stylishness and fiery disposition. Holzwarth also liked thoroughbreds because of their adaptibility, but he did not like quarter horses since their gait seemed too choppy for mountain riding.[34]

In Montana the Van Cleves originally bought their dude horses but found that these went bad too often so they decided to breed their own. They used both quarter and thoroughbred mares and bred them to quarter horse stallions; they have produced hundreds of dude horses in the last fifty years and have developed their own extensive breaking and training program to produce the best animals for their dude string. Frank Wright prefers to use Appaloosas in his Colorado operation; he has found that they have fewer back problems and foot trouble. "They make terrific mountain horses," Wright says, "and they are easy keepers."[35]

Many other ranches buy or even lease their own horses. The variety of combinations of different breeds is, of course, nearly endless. Some ranches have concentrated on acquiring colorful horses such as pintos or palominos. But even on these ranches the key traits mentioned before are essential; a showy horse that breaks down is of little value to the dude or the rancher. Building a solid string of capable horses was obviously essential to meet the ranch guests' needs, and it sometimes took years to acquire the correct combination of animals.

In addition to pack trips and scenic rides, horses were also used for hunting and fishing trips—two outdoor activities that have long served as drawing cards for dude ranches.

Hunting trips preceded and helped create dude ranches in many areas. Dick Randall, pioneer Montana dude rancher, believed that hunting parties were the forerunners of all dude ranches in the southern part of that state. Sportsmen lingered at camps after their hunts to see the West and some people eventually came just for sightseeing.[36] This same situation prevailed farther south in the Jackson Hole country, considered a hunter's paradise. The tales the hunters told in the East prompted their families and friends to insist on seeing the area. Nonhunting visitors soon became so numerous that the guides built cabins just for them. As noted in Chapter 3, this was the way the Turner Triangle X Ranch developed.[37]

When state fish and game departments began setting specific hunting and fishing seasons, hunting began to be combined with dude ranching. The seasons for hunting were usually short and in the autumn whereas the ideal time for ranch guests in the northern dude ranch states was generally limited to June, July, and August when children were out of school and family vacations were possible. Also warm weather usually prevailed during these three months. By offering both sightseeing and hunting, the rancher-guide was able to extend his season of business operation.[38] Hunting trips were similar to pack trips in their organization although they required more equipment and planning since most occurred when harsh weather was a constant threat. Also skilled guides were needed, and the ratio of guides to hunters was higher than that required on a regular pack trip for scenic enjoyment. On the latter there might be one wrangler for eight or ten people, while hunting trips often required one guide for every two hunters.

The lure of fishing, especially for mountain trout, has also been an important factor in the popularity of dude ranches. Fishing trips required a lot less planning and were less complex than hunting expeditions for several reasons. One is simply that fishing was usually available throughout the summer, the regular ranch season; thus it was easily a part of other ranch activities. Pack trips and daily rides often included plans for fishing in fast-flowing streams or high mountain lakes. Many ranches, such as the Flying V in Wyoming, the Snowshoe in Colorado, and the Ox Yoke in Montana, were located on trout streams, so fishermen could simply walk to their favorite fishing sites from the ranch house.[39]

A few dude operations were founded primarily as fishing ranches. One is the Bar Lazy J (also known as Buckhorn Lodge), established in 1904 along the

Colorado River with fishing as the main attraction. Several others, mentioned earlier, were in the Grand Lake area of Colorado.[40]

Fishing received a big boost when state fish and game departments launched extensive stocking programs. Ironically, people seeking a simple vacation in isolated areas have been supported by complex and expensive methods of stocking trout in mountain lakes and streams.

Besides hunting, fishing, and horseback riding, a number of other factors drew vacationers to dude ranches. One was the desire to take part in ranch work, and many ranch brochures specifically mentioned this as a feature of their vacations. Working ranches that accepted guests were very common in the earlier days; many still exist. On these ranches guests could help in the roundups of horses or cattle, branding the stock, checking the fences for repairs, and various other activities essential to ranch operation.[41] Short and long horseback rides, as described earlier in this chapter, were often combined with these routine ranch chores.

On the Lazy K Bar Ranch in Montana, dudes were pushed to hard labor on roundups until the owners realized they were insisting on too much work from paying guests. The issue came into focus one hot summer day when the cattle were sullen and all hands were needed to keep them moving in the proper direction. Ranch owner Paul Van Cleve noticed one of the guests stretched out on the ground resting in the shadow cast by his horse. He hurried over at a run, pulled his horse up beside the boy, and asked:

> "Why in hell aren't you helping hold these cattle?" The youngster grinned and replied perfectly truthfully, "But, Uncle Paul, I didn't come out here to work."[42]

Van Cleve appreciated the point and let the young man enjoy his rest. From that point on guests at the Lazy K Bar worked when they wanted to and rested without being harassed.

Dudes on the Quarter Circle U Ranch in Montana were given three horses each in order to help actively on a cattle roundup; this, of course, was similar to the way cowboys functioned with their own strings of horses on the roundups and long drives of the post–Civil War era.[43] Guests actually did a significant amount of work on many early ranches, but the trend has been toward letting them feel they are a part of the work without pushing them to do it.

The Ox Yoke Ranch in Montana and the Neversummer in Colorado were among many that let guests "jingle" the horses—that is, chase them to the corrals in the morning. Rising at 5:30 or 6:00 A.M. for this job was considered a chore by the wranglers, but paying guests thought it a privilege.[44] The Alisal Ranch in California held a steer-roping event each Sunday for local cowboys; while guests seldom took part in the roping, the better riders were allowed to chase the hapless steers in from the hills each Sunday morning for their ordeal in the arena. These are but a few examples of the many things ranchers let the dudes do to take part in ranch work. Ranches that had no real ranch chores for guests held occasional amateur rodeos or gymkhanas, which consisted mainly of games on horseback.

Another appeal of the ranches has been the chance for visitors to learn about the animals, plants, and history of the West. Guests expected the rancher or wrangler to identify the flowers and trees of the Rocky Mountains and to point out the different animals and their habitat. Whether it was a Stellar's jay, marmot, moose, or elk, someone was sure to be interested in how and where it lived. One dude in Colorado spent eleven years of his vacations studying wildflowers and then wrote an excellent book on the subject. Guests also enjoyed hearing about pony express and stagecoach stations in the vicinity, sites of military trails or Indian battles, nearby forts and mining camps, and range wars or local feuds. Even a little western exaggeration in telling these stories was acceptable if kept within bounds. All this information helped give the dude a feeling of learning and belonging to the West.[45]

Another factor leading people to dude ranches has been what they could offer children and teenagers. Each activity previously mentioned, except hunting, played a role in the appeal ranch life had for youngsters, although horses and cowboys were probably the most popular features for them. As horses became less common in the East these animals held special fascination for children who came to ranches.

Additional inducements specifically caused some parents to seek dude ranches for their children. Many parents discovered that western living could instill such values as independence and self-reliance in their children. Some youngsters who had been to Europe and had gone to camps in the eastern United States learned quickly at western ranches that money and prestige meant nothing in the wilderness; many returned from ranch trips, especially those including pack trips, with a new outlook and a change in values.[46]

Some parents also looked upon ranches as good places to get sons and daughters away from problems such as drugs and alcohol. As noted in Chapter 2, the Eaton brothers faced this situation in the Badlands as far back as the 1880s. Using dude ranches for this purpose became more popular in the twentieth century. William and Barbara Hooton, who operated a dude ranch in New Mexico, reported one interesting case when they had as a guest the son of a wealthy lawyer. He was an alcoholic sent there to be cured, and he was accompanied by a hospital orderly disguised as a valet. He got whiskey secretly from a ranch worker, however, and, while under the influence, drove his car into the swimming pool. After that incident, the Hootons sent him home.[47] In the 1930s writer Dorothea Park-Lewis urged parents of adolescents between fifteen and twenty-two to consider dude ranch vacations. She argued that the young people would not be exposed to late parties, dancing, and drinking; besides, they would be too busy and too tired to think of such things. One veteran dude, however, warned people not to ship adolescent boys alone to ranches since "a dude ranch is not a nursery, nor is it a cure-all for the vicious or weakling." And it certainly should not be an excuse for parents to shift their own responsibilities.[48] Nonetheless, many parents were convinced that the western life had certain values, and sometimes a ranch vacation did help children with problems.

No dude ranch had all the features or attractions that have been discussed. Each one had its own appeal and specialty, whether it was horseback riding, pack trips, superior fishing, excellent hunting, square dancing, ranch work, or good food. In a sense, each ranch had a personality reflecting its owners; the dudes became very attached to particular ranches that suited them and often referred to their favorite as "our ranch." This attitude represented the height of success for the rancher, for it fit exactly with his desire to make the guests feel comfortable and, literally, at home.[49] Dude ranches were different from any other form of western accommodations because even though some grew large and dude ranching became a thriving industry, a dude ranch remained some family's home, a place where people lived year-round and where they invited friends to share their western way of life.[50]

SEVEN

Cowboys and Cooks

No one sees human nature in queerer aspects than the guide or tourist-man. In the end these two fortunate unfortunate classes realize that there is nothing too grotesque, or fantastic, or out of the way to be beyond the reach of human intention.
—Struthers Burt, *The Diary of a Dude-Wrangler*, 25.

Operating a dude ranch required many talents and meant paying attention to numerous details; an obvious necessity for ranchers was to know what factors drew people to their ranches and to improve or modify these whenever possible. One constant factor was the use of horses, since horseback riding was the key activity on most ranches; therefore, the rancher needed cowboys to take care of the horses and the riding. Any good dude ranch needed

> men who will ride twenty-four hours straight and think nothing of it, who can tough it out for a week hunting horses, with no bedding and little grub, who can handle animals and, if need be, people, through every accident of rain and storm and sand. A world of hard work lies behind the smooth running that brings your saddled horse to you every morning.[1]

The situation was simple: no cowboys, no horseback riding; and no horseback riding meant no dude ranch. The cowboy's importance, however, went far beyond that of an ordinary ranch worker. As the cowboy was becoming an American folk hero at the turn of the century, many people were lamenting his passing and the change in the Old West. In the public mind the cowboy lived a free and simple life, was heroic and adventurous, and possessed unusual skills unique to his trade. Cowboys became part of the rural American myth and were soon a principal attraction of dude ranches. Owen Wister probably did as much as anyone else in the early twentieth century to create this heroic image in his famous novel, *The Virginian,* as well as in his other stories. It is interesting to note, therefore, that Wister was one of the most famous dudes in the nineteenth century. His works were an idealization of an era already gone—the golden age of the western cattle industry. In his writing he created as much as he observed and recorded; while the nameless hero of his most famous novel did little actual cowboy work, Wister was trying to create the ideal Wyoming cowboy.[2]

Most dudes had absorbed the fascination for cowboys or at least had a curiosity about them and expected to see these bold riders on their ranch trips. Some of the women who went west were enthralled with cowboys and brought a huge dose of romantic fantasy with them. Sometimes when an enthralled female met the irresistible cowboy, marriage was the result. It is a little difficult to envision a rich, "proper" girl from the East marrying a rough, footloose cowhand, but many people mentioned such matches. Some of these couples returned to the East; others remained in the West. There were many cases of young girls who tired of the formality and restrictions of their eastern lives, journeyed to ranches, married cowboys, and settled down to become ranch wives in Wyoming and Montana.[3] Mary Roberts Rinehart used this theme for one of her novels, *Lost Ecstasy.* Similar matches occurred on some of the southwestern ranches; just after World War I, for example, one young girl from Boston traveled to New Mexico, where she met and married a Texas cowboy. They not only stayed in New Mexico but built a famous dude ranch near San Juan Pueblo. She had the social connections in the East to attract guests; he had the knowledge to run the ranch.[4] Many such marriages, however, foundered when harsh reality collided with romantic fantasy; the myth of "living happily ever after" was not always the end of the story.

But fantasy was enhanced when dude ranch cowboys entered the world of fiction and acquired their own mythic qualities. Jim Dawson, the hero of several novels by Gene Hoopes, was the most spectacular of these characters. Dawson had been a cowboy on the Flying X Ranch in Montana, served as an army scout, met Teddy Roosevelt, and joined the Rough Riders—all before working on the

Lazy R Ranch, the Cross Triangle Ranch, and the Rainbow Guest Ranch in the Southwest. He was an expert horseman, cook, guitar player, singer, and story-teller; he possessed excellent health, loved wide open spaces and disliked cities, was a crack shot with a pistol, and, of course, was exceedingly attractive to women. He generally spurned the idea of matrimony but finally succumbed to the charms of the owner of the Rainbow Guest Ranch, Gipsy Lynn, and proposed in the following epic words: "Listen, Chiquito. Seein' as neither o' us is headin' for any place in partcular [sic], what's to hinder us from goin' together?"[5]

Caroline Lockhart presented a similar image in Wallie Macpherson, an east-erner who headed to the range to "prove" himself in a book titled *The Dude Wrangler*. He became a cowboy and bought 160 acres of dry plains land with the wages he had saved. In order to make more money he turned his quarter section of land into a dude ranch. Macpherson was not as colorful in background or characteristics as Jim Dawson, but he did perform a few daring deeds to dem-onstrate his grit and determination. He became a cowboy in order to learn to "ride and shoot and handle a rope with the best of them" before becoming a dude wrangler. Of course, he won the heart of the girl who was the object of all this frenetic activity.[6]

These images of the twentieth-century dude wrangler thus differed little from those of the nineteenth-century cowboy.

Regardless of whatever image or mythical qualities easterners expected of wranglers, the rancher was faced with the reality of hiring men to handle horses and riders. On some of the early dude ranches the owners were able to hire men who were fairly well known in the West at the time, some having been bronc fighters, marshals, trappers, prospectors, champion bulldoggers, and ropers. Be-fore working on a dude ranch, Earl Crouch had been a top hand with many large cow outfits in the Northwest and had toured foreign countries as a bronc fighter in a Wild West show. Fred Richard, another dude ranch cowboy, had guided the Prince of Monaco on one of the last of Buffalo Bill Cody's hunting trips. Others locally known for their exploits in the late 1800s and early 1900s included Johnny Goff, Hardy Shull, Bill Howell, and Hurricane Bill Herrick. All these men had varied experiences worth recounting, and the dudes who met them reaped the benefits.[7]

Hiring cowboys for dude ranches seems not to have been a major problem at first; as noted earlier, dude ranches started slowly and guests simply took part in normal ranch activities. There was little additional work except possibly catching a few extra horses in the morning and answering a few questions about the West and the ranch. Besides, men who had been in the limelight, such as Crouch and Richard, probably found dude work compatible with their previous showy activities. This situation changed somewhat, however, as the economic significance of dude ranching grew and ranchers paid more attention to the guests. Cowboys were eventually referred to more frequently as wranglers, as they had to devote more of their time and effort to the dudes. There was still plenty of ranch work to be done, but some activities were carried out primarily for the amusement of the dudes. Clothing worn by the cowboy-wrangler was occasionally more "picturesque" than before, and some westerners chided the man wearing such attire as a "diamond-pointed" or drugstore cowboy.[8] But wearing a bit of flashy clothing was not the worst thing that might happen to a dude ranch cowboy, according to a Wyoming newspaper.

> Did you ever see a cowboy that could be induced to go near a
> milk cow in the old days? Go to the dude ranch now and watch
> him in his high heeled boots and wide brimmed hat, a milk
> bucket on his arm going jauntily down the path to the corral
> where the gentle "moo" of the Jersey greets him. All this change
> so that the comfort of the dudes may be insured.[9]

This was a notable change for the former "prince of the rangeland. His was a wild, free life with none of the luxuries of civilization. Beans, sourdough bread and meat were his lot cooked in the old dutch oven."[10] But now, to satisfy the dudes, the cowboy had to milk the cows.

Some cowboys were not interested in these new, rather uncomfortable aspects of dude ranching and preferred to remain "real" cowboys. After all, animals were easier to handle than people; animals didn't talk back or play politics, were not consciously unkind, and could be herded.[11]

There was obviously a significant distinction in some westerners' minds between being a cowboy and a dude wrangler, and the latter had to endure some ridicule. The comments were pointed at times, such as the remarks that wranglers were just cowboys who had "gone soft."[12] But humor also entered the picture. The wide variety of duties for the cowboy-turned-wrangler prompted an anonymous author to pen "The Wrangler's Lament" as an introduction to Nevada dude ranches. After discussing his switch from cutting hay to breaking horses to taking care of guests, the imaginary cowhand described his trials and tribulations with dudes; he finally summarized his experiences:

> Ten days I spent a-herdin' them green gals and greener men.
> An' I shore lost my religion 'fore we hit th' ranch again.
> I'm a tough, hard-boiled old cow-hand with a weatherbeaten hide,
> But herdin' cows is nuthin' to teachin' dudes to ride.
> I can stand their hitoned langwidge an' their hifalutin' foods—
> But you bet your bottom dollar I'm fed up on wranglin' dudes![13]

An even better commentary on this attitude toward dude work came from Gail Gardner, a cattleman in Arizona from 1916 to 1928. In the 1920s hard times hit the cowmen there, and they couldn't afford to hire any cowboys. So the cowboys went to Castle Hot Springs and Wickenburg to wrangle dudes on the ranches. One of Gardner's "cowboy friends got sorta ruined," so Gardner, who had already written a few cowboy songs, penned "The Dude Wrangler" and sang it, with some trepidation, to the cowboys he knew at Castle Hot Springs:[14]

I'll tell you of a sad, sad story,
Of how a cowboy fell from grace,
Now really this is something awful,
There never was so sad a case.

One time I had myself a pardner,
I never knowed one half so good;
We throwed our outfits in together,
And lived the way that cowboys should.

He savvied all about wild cattle,
And he was handy with a rope,
For a gentle-well reined pony,
Just give me one that he had broke.

He never owned no clothes but Levis,
He wore them until they was slick,
And he never wore no great big Stetson,
'Cause where we rode the brush was thick.

He never had no time for women,
So bashful and so shy was he,
Besides he knowed that they was poison,
And so he always let them be.

Well he went to work on distant ranges;
I did not see him for a year.
But then I had no cause to worry,
For I knowed that some day he'd appear.

One day I rode in from the mountains,
A-feelin' good and steppin' light,
For I had just sold all my yearlin's,
And the price was out of sight.

But soon I seen a sight so awful,
It caused my joy to fade away,
It filled my very soul with sorrow
I never will forgit that day.

For down the street there come a-walkin'
My oldtime pardner as of yore,
Although I know you will not believe me,
Let me tell you what he wore.

He had his boots outside his britches;
They was made of leather green and red,
His shirt was of a dozen colors,
Loud enough to wake the dead.

Around his neck he had a 'kerchief,
Knotted through a silver ring;
I swear to Gawd he had a wrist-watch,
Who ever heard of such a thing.

Sez I "Old scout now what's the trouble?
"You must have et some loco weed,
"If you will tell me how to help you,
"I'll git you anything you need."

Well he looked at me for half a minute,
And then he begin to bawl;
He sez, "Bear with me while I tell you
What made me take this awful fall."

"It was a woman from Chicago,
"Who put the Injun sign on me;
"She told me that I was romantic,
"And just as handsome as could be."

Sez he, "I'm 'fraid that there ain't nothin'
"That you can do to save my hide,
"I'm wranglin' dudes instead of cattle,
"I'm what they call a first-class guide."

"Oh I saddle up their pump-tailed ponies,
"I fix their stirrups for them too,
"I boost them up into their saddles,
"They give me tips when I am through."

"It's just like horses eatin' loco,
"You can not quit it if you try,
"I'll go on wranglin' dudes forever,
"Until the day that I shall die."

So I drawed my gun and throwed it on him,
I had to turn my face away.
I shot him squarely through the middle,
And where he fell I left him lay.

I shorely hated for to do it,
For things that's done you cain't recall,
But when a cowboy turns dude wrangler,
He ain't no good no more at all.[15]

These and other examples show how the seriousness of the cowboy-wrangler conflict was alleviated with humor.[16] Conflict or not, wranglers were found. Some cowboys were more or less forced into wrangling jobs by economic necessity, such as those Gail Gardner referred to in Arizona. Others began listening to more favorable comments about wranglers. In Wyoming, rancher Struthers Burt defended wranglers and denied that keeping up the western tradition meant retaining a myth. He told his hands that they were still cowpunchers and led the same life their fathers and grandfathers had. Their practical and picturesque clothes would help them make money since people would travel a long way to see them. Other writers also emphasized that a few pieces of colorful clothing had not changed things; cowboys were "still the same raw-boned, hard riding, kind-hearted lads. . . ."[17]

Dude ranchers in the Sheridan, Wyoming area had little difficulty with prejudice against dude wranglers. These ranchers, such as the Eatons, Bones brothers, and the Hortons, were often better working cowboys than the men they hired; they competed in rodeos with the local cowboys and did very well. Thus, no stigma was attached to dude wrangling in this particular area. Sometimes cowboys were even attracted to dude wrangling because regular ranch work often meant lonely weeks riding fence and attending to other chores. Some cowboys alternated between the two types of jobs, finding cattle work restful after dude wrangling and finding people a relief from pushing animals around.[18] Because of the unusual relationship between wranglers and guests, some cowboys could make this transition easily. An anecdote told by a Wyoming dude illustrates this relationship. The dude noticed that his fellow guests always disappeared after supper; after several days he learned that they always adjourned to the bunkhouse after eating, where they listened to the wranglers discuss a variety of subjects, mundane to the westerner, but fascinating to the dudes. He finally observed that:

this was the only resort he had ever seen where the guests
deliberately sought the servants' quarters for recreation. And there
was a reason for this: The dude wrangler does not consider himself
an underling in any sense whatsoever. He has his full quota of
self-respect, feels that he meets his dudes on a footing of equality
and does his best to show them a good time.[19]

The order of things was even further reversed on a dude ranch; the wrangler was, to a certain extent, the boss of the dudes because they were in a strange environment and he knew how to help them adapt to and enjoy it. To many dudes this was "a new sensation, which they really enjoy and to which they submit for the sheer novelty of it."[20]

In this situation the cowboy could overlook some problems and retain his self-respect and independence; making the transition to wrangler was thus more palatable. As the West changed and became more mechanized, the cowboy, at times, even grew envious of the wrangler. The cowhand often drove a tractor, sprayed insecticide on crops, harvested hay, and did a lot of jobs normally associated with the farmhand. Meanwhile the wrangler at the nearest dude ranch wore colorful but traditional cowboy clothes, carried a rope while taking people for rides, sang songs, and was paid more money.[21]

The skills required of a wrangler varied considerably, depending on the type of ranch he was on and the era when he worked. Some, especially on the plush resort-type ranches in the Southwest, bore little resemblance to cowboys; they were merely handsome young men who liked to guide attractive women on horseback rides. But most wranglers were not "drugstore cowboys" as some people mistakenly assumed; they were real cowboys who could rope, brand, and do the other practical work needed on a cow ranch. Many competed in various rodeo events; others developed additional skills. Some were passable musicians; the guitar-strumming cowhand may seem to be a mythical figure, but on a dude ranch he was often a reality. Other wranglers acquired a practical knowledge of such diverse topics as geology, botany, zoology, wildlife management, and forest conservation and were able to answer at least some of the questions that the guests asked.[22] This constant questioning highlights the peculiar relationship between wranglers and guests that was previously noted. The latter simply assumed that ranchers and wranglers were interested in, and knowledgeable about, wild game, plants, trees, all kinds of animals, and various conservation practices. They expected answers to their queries, and astute ranch owners supplied them whenever possible, either from their own knowledge or through knowledgeable wranglers. Besides these various skills, the wranglers still had to be capable riders; know how to care for horses, especially on pack trips; and be able to make a comfortable camp in fair weather, rain, or snow.

Deciding what type of person to pick for a wrangler was a major task for ranch owners, and their choices varied. Some picked men skilled in rodeo events; they knew they could handle horses and assumed their rodeo competence would impress the dudes. The Van Cleves in Montana hired old-timers from the hills— prospectors, trappers, moonshiners, sawyers, and old stove-up cowboys. These men were pleasant but pretty raspy characters, and their talk was often very crude.[23] The owners of the OTO Ranch tried several methods to find the best wranglers for their operation. One of their first ideas was to hire college boys during summer vacations, but this group did not fare well. Then the ranch hired Mr. and Mrs. Bloodworth; he had been the champion cowboy at Madison Square Garden one year and she was a saddle-horse trick rider. These two guided the guests on rides, entertained them with riding and roping exhibitions, and, at least once a week, helped put on a rodeo for the dudes. The Bloodworths also led the dudes in riding in local parades; an appearance in these parades was exciting for the guest and good advertising for the OTO. Eventually, however, the ranch's owners decided that former guests were the best people to hire; the owners knew what ability these ex-dudes had for handling both horses and people. They knew the country well from previous visits and understood what guests wanted.[24]

Larry Larom of the famous Valley Ranch had some difficulty in finding enough wranglers, so he experimented with working dudes. These young men worked for their keep and mingled with the guests but rode for pleasure in their spare time only if horses were available. The White Grass Ranch in Wyoming even developed a formal working dude program to train wranglers. Usually high-school-age boys, the working dudes paid lower fees than regular guests and assisted the wranglers; they then were given first consideration when the ranch hired its crew in subsequent years.[25]

Out of this diversity a new breed emerged: the professional wrangler—a personable and talented individual who saw dude work as one type of cowboy work. Wranglers were actually more versatile than cowboys since they had to socialize with the guests and have a genuine liking for people. They could even be drifters in their work, just as cowboys had been, since they headed north in the summer to work on the mountain ranches and then turned to the Southwest to work where there were winter vacation sites. Knowledgeable ranch owners sought such men because they learned that the personal popularity of their wranglers was a valuable asset and sometimes the key factor in the success of a ranch.[26]

Both dude wranglers and rodeo riders present the image of the cowboy to the American public. Rodeo cowboys travel widely, compete in violent and dangerous sports, and maintain a high degree of independence, and rodeo promoters have certainly pictured them as the true heirs of the American folk hero.[27] While dude wranglers will probably not supplant these ropers and riders as the accepted successor to the "old-time cowboy," they have presented the cowboy image to ten of thousands of western visitors throughout the twentieth century. Their jobs are not as dramatic as riding a wild Brahma bull for eight seconds, but then, seldom were the cowboy's daily activities either. Dude wrangling is not a pathway to riches or fame, but neither was riding fence or trailing Longhorns.

A typical example of the new type of wrangler is Dennis White, who learned how to ride on a small Michigan farm. A vacation in Colorado convinced him to move west, and he chose a dude ranch over a cattle ranch because it was more glamorous and he enjoyed being around people. For years he worked from mid-May till mid-September on the Arapaho Valley Ranch near Granby, Colorado, and from October through the end of April on the White Stallion Ranch near Tucson. This switching of locales kept him away from most snow and cold weather and furnished him with a comfortable living. The wrangler's life may be glamorous in a sense but his hours are long—from 6:00 A.M. to 6:00 P.M. seven days a week with only an occasional weekend off. White resents insinuations that a dude wrangler is not much of a cowboy; he has been a bareback bronc rider in rodeos, shoes horses regularly, and insists he can do any of the things a cowboy can.[28]

This conflict over the cowboy-wrangler echoes many charges and complaints since the 1880s that the real West and the true cowboys are disappearing or no longer exist. The emergence of the dude wrangler, in fact, can be seen as evidence of the adaptability westerners have shown ever since there was a "West" in America.

Many different types of people still become wranglers as college students, ex-dudes, "old cowboys," and others have shown up on various ranches. If many of these are easterners, that merely repeats a trend, for many cowboys came from the East in the 1870s and 1880s. There is no point in trying to claim too much for the dude wrangler; the simple fact is that he has been around for many decades and is a true part of western heritage. As one guest ranch manager commented: "Joke if you will, but there is a real future here for a cowhand who can ride, play the guitar, and still smell nice."[29]

One might assume that if a ranch owner could hire a sufficient number of competent wranglers, most of his difficulties would be solved and his dude operation would be successful. However, the owners faced an increasing array of problems as their businesses became more complex. Of course, this complexity applied only to a large ranch when dude ranching became popular; as noted previously, when a ranch first began accepting guests, they caused little additional work. It was estimated that a ranch could accommodate up to five guests with little or no extra help and make a decent profit. With dozens of guests every week, however, many details had to be attended to and more employees were essential.

As ranches grew, some ranchers believed that there was an employee even more important than the cowboy-wrangler in keeping the dudes contented—the cook. The cook, unlike the wrangler, worked behind the scenes. Wranglers were supposed to be prominent, even a little flamboyant, while catching horses, saddling them, taking guests on rides, and telling stories. The cooks were quiet, usually unseen, and nearly anonymous. But they were important, since guests just assumed that meals would be varied, well prepared, and ready whenever wanted.[30]

Traditionally, hiring and keeping competent cooks has been a major problem on dude ranches. Of course, some ranches, such as Buckhorn Lodge, had reliable, excellent ones who returned every year and caused no problems. The cook at Buckhorn worked at an eastern college most of the year and spent her summers on the ranch in Colorado. She not only cooked the standard fare but also baked all the bread and rolls needed on the ranch.[31] But her case is a rarity; more common are tales of eccentric characters with a reputation for losing their tempers and walking out on the job just when the season was in high gear and they were needed the most. Nearly all books written by ranchers about their operation contain stories of problems with cooks. The job of preparing food for large numbers of people is never simple, of course, but dude ranches presented special problems because of their peculiar situation. Food supplies generally had to be hauled a considerable distance and could not be replenished easily; the isolation of most ranches also meant the cooks usually were not able to get away frequently and had to spend weeks in what could be a monotonous situation for them. Also the dudes had to be more catered to than restaurant diners or other customers since they were like guests in the rancher's home, and a variety of different menus was desirable since dudes might be at a ranch for a month or more. Cooks were professionals, however, and if they were dissatisfied or felt abused, an emotional explosion sometimes occurred.[32]

Dick and Dora Randall owned the OTO Ranch in Montana, and their experiences with culinary eccentrics illustrate the problems. Dora, or her daughter Bess Erskine, often had to take over kitchen duties when the cook decided to leave or go on a spree. One of their cooks was Chinese; he was a good chef but insisted on cooking lettuce instead of using it for salads. Twice a day he selected the choice heads and boiled them vigorously; Dora Randall's attempts to hide them were in vain, and she finally had to fire him. Another cook she had to contend with was a sullen, mean-looking character whose watery mashed potatoes were inedible. When Mrs. Randall tried, tactfully, to get him to change, he quit; there were seventy-five guests at the ranch at the time so she once again had to take charge of the kitchen. A Japanese cook who had worked for moviemaker Cecil B. DeMille came to OTO one summer and wanted to prepare only the choicest cuts of beef and throw all the rest away; fortunately, he learned to change his ways and endured as chief chef. Another Japanese cook presented a totally different problem: he and the rest of the crew decided to use the ranch's rice to make saki. When the Randalls dumped the potent brew down the drain, the whole crew nearly quit. A woman cook they once had was very competent but she was so fond of beer that sometimes she couldn't cook. One evening, instead of starting dinner, she spent her time frantically searching for a mouse that she had seen go into the woodpile. Between the beer and the mouse, the Randalls had to let her go, and Dora became Chef Randall again. After one of these frequent escapades, the Randalls were saved by a guest, Colonel Knox of Corpus Christi, Texas. He had brought with him an army quartermaster, an excellent chef who had graduated from a cooking school. When this man took over in the ranch kitchen Dick Randall was so grateful for the help that he named a mountain in the Absaroka range after him.[33]

But the Randalls were not unique in the problems they had. William and Barbara Hooton, who left New York to operate Rancho Del Monte in New Mexico, had similar problems with emotional outbursts, departing cooks, and rapid turnover in the kitchen. At the Flying V Ranch in Wyoming, marriage claimed a cook in midseason so the owner's wife had to don the chef's apron until she got her mother to journey west from Michigan to take charge.[34]

These and other tales make clear the problems associated with cooks. They were frequent and frustrating, and generally humorous only in retrospect. Suggestions for ways to retain competent chefs and reduce these problems began making the rounds among the dude ranchers. Mary Frost, wife of one of the early famous dude ranchers, noted that the cook should have a room to herself near the kitchen; she should have a chore boy to give her whatever help she needed promptly. Charles Moore thought that cooks should have private baths, an unusual privilege for anyone on most ranches. John Holzwarth believed that cooks should be treated as professionals and generally left on their own; given a menu and a budget, most would accept the challenge and do a favorable job.[35]

If a rancher could locate and retain a cook and find competent wranglers, the rest of his crew was not as critical. While the other jobs to be performed were important, none was as uniquely professional as that of the cook nor as clearly necessary as that of the wranglers. Depending on the size of his operation, the rancher would need several waitresses, cabin girls, and a handyman or two; larger ranches might require a secretary, bookkeeper, and manager.[36]

There were problems in locating workers for these various duties. As the population of the West increased, a larger number of people were available who knew the area and could get to the ranches quickly. Many were hired and some performed well; somewhat surprisingly, however, many ranchers learned that hiring easterners eventually led to better results than getting local people. Local boys, especially, wanted to run off to rodeos instead of sticking with the job; also local workers were more interested just in making money and were sometimes dissatisfied with the isolation of ranches and the somewhat low pay. On the other hand, many youngsters from the East applied for jobs with a romanticized view of the situation. They had little work experience and few qualifications but had an image of a pleasant summer outdoors with lots of horseback riding. This was an unrealistic picture, since ranch chores required hard work; easterners who were ready to do their jobs, however, often succeeded in adapting. They were often pleased with the unique opportunity to work on a ranch in spite of the difficulties.

They did get to enjoy themselves, too. On the Dead Indian Ranch these workers got off in the afternoon every third day and could become dudes for a while. Most other ranches allowed their workers some time off and let them ride when extra horses were available.[37] As noted previously, former dudes sometimes returned as wranglers; some were hired full-time while others were given only room and board and received no pay. Many ranchers decided that their best bet was to hire college kids who had job experience and were willing to work. The long distance of the ranch from their homes and the unusual working situation often helped to make them reliable laborers.[38]

On small ranches the members of the family were able to do nearly all the work; children reared in this fashion learned about dude ranch problems thoroughly in preparation for their own adult lives in the same occupation. Thus dude ranching was generally a family operation.[39] It differed from those western activities that were male-dominated, such as fur trapping, mining, and military camps. It was much more like the frontier farm run by a husband, wife, and children, although there were some famous exceptions such as Eatons', where three brothers operated the ranch. Even here, however, one of the brothers married and his descendants eventually took over the ranch. The well-known Holm Lodge was operated for thirty-five years by Mary Shawver and J. W. Howell; even at Holm, however, it was clear that smooth operation required more than one person and a division of work. Miss Shawver was a charming hostess and handled reservations, while Howell took care of the horses and riding.[40]

On most ranches women, as business partners with their husbands, often made the difference between success and failure. They greeted the guests, substituted for the cook, planted gardens, and helped entertain the dudes. They were also responsible for keeping the workers well housed and happy; the major problems with workers involved dissatisfaction with jobs, fights among the girls, and drinking among the boys.[41]

The DRA magazine, *The Dude Rancher*, published several articles giving suggestions to prospective ranch owners. One of these was a warning that ranching was a joint enterprise; husband and wife had to work together closely and both had to like it. Another point made in one of these articles was very pertinent to the naive easterner contemplating a dude ranch career; the land purchased must have adequate grazing for the stock, not just beautiful scenery. Most successful dude ranches had to grow slowly, gradually adding facilities for guests as the enterprise proved feasible. Some newcomers, however, were impatient and desired a substantial facility at once. This attitude was a typical characteristic of the urban scene where everything had to be done NOW![42]

Newcomer and old-timer eventually learned that, while each ranch was distinct, all had some common features. An unfailing water supply was, of course, an absolute necessity. When buildings were planned, a prime feature was a central lodge; it should have one or more fireplaces and porches. No ranch was complete without its roaring fire, and the porches emphasized the relaxation and slower pace where guests sometimes just sat around watching the ranch operate. The lodge needed three or four large rooms for lounging, square dancing, other recreation, and eating, unless a separate building housed the dining room. The kitchen had to be adjacent to the dining area as did rooms for food storage and refrigeration. Some lodges had living quarters in them while other ranches had one-, two-, or three-room cabins nearby for the guests. Other buildings would provide quarters for the foreman, preferably a separate house, and for the cook, cabin girls and waitresses, and wranglers. An additional building was often available to store linens, blankets, mattresses, and other household supplies, and storage was needed for tools and equipment. Of course barns and corrals were needed for the horses. It was desirable that the central buildings be of log construction because of the appeal of log cabins; another important factor was that the buildings be spaced far enough apart to eliminate hazard if one caught fire, and yet close enough for ease in getting around the ranch. A good view of the surrounding countryside was very helpful, and the astute rancher also arranged it so the horses and corral activities were in sight of the guests' cabins or lodge rooms. Some ranchers even drove the horses past the cabins when bringing them in from pasture in the morning; these last items simply reemphasize the appeal of horses and wranglers to the dudes. A good road to town was desirable but was almost never present in the early days of dude ranching; it became important later when most guests drove to the ranches.[43]

The number of horses needed was almost twice the number of guests expected, allowing for injuries, rest for the animals, and a wide range of different sizes and temperaments to please the guests. Even if the ranch didn't run cattle for profit, a few cattle should be purchased to provide meat for the outfit and be a colorful adjunct. None of these features had to be elaborate, since simplicity was desired, but the ranch had to be well planned, clean, and comfortable. In 1924 *The Cattleman* magazine estimated that someone could start such a ranch to accommodate twenty guests for approximately $20,000 to $40,000.[44]

This extensive advice about physical facilities did not obscure the overriding importance of the personality of the owners. Western hospitality and a spirit of friendliness were essential; most people also learned that having an easterner involved in decisions about the ranch helped significantly. The easterner often became the best booster for the West because of his fresh view of the area; he realized far better than most westerners what a dude would want on a ranch and why he would want it. He would have social contacts in the East that would be helpful in attracting visitors.[45]

The rancher had to please his guests and still preserve the unique image of the dude ranch. This was difficult because the ranch was not a summer hotel or boardinghouse even though it might seem like one or the other to the casual observer. Physically, it needed more buildings than either hotel or boardinghouse, and these had to be spread out to avoid the impression of crowding; it was essential to try to preserve the image of wilderness and isolation.

In his contacts with the guests the rancher also had to avoid crossing the fine line between being an innkeeper and a dude wrangler. While a hotel owner had to be impersonal, the rancher was required to be personal. His was a delicate job requiring a talent for psychology, tact, and taste since he had a social responsibility unlike that of the hotelkeeper. He had a number of people in an environment that was often strange and bewildering to them. It was not sufficient simply to provide the guests with rooms and baths and then turn them loose. He had to teach them to ride and help them find entertainment. At times the rancher had to "herd" them without letting them know they were being directed.[46] Another problem was that guests wanted ranch life but with comforts not normally found on a ranch. The rancher's task was seemingly contradictory—preserving the ranch in its physical makeup while pleasing the guests whose desires sometimes included things foreign to most ranches. The guests wanted to "rough it" but with a certain degree of comfort. Trying to combine the two ideas created some difficulties; it was not easy to decide if a change would be accepted by guests as a true improvement or seen as an unwanted concession to encroaching modernization. One rancher summarized the problem as "give people home-made bedsteads but forty-pound mattresses."[47]

New ranch owners learned that the key element in dude ranching was: "Treat the customers just as though they are guests in our own house." This was the first rule William and Barbara Hooton learned in their initiation as New Mexico ranchers. They also added a second rule: don't kowtow or toady to the guests because it would make them uncomfortable and the owners miserable. The Hootons also realized that children should be welcome but had to behave lest they ruin the vacation of other guests.[48] Obviously any person who has had houseguests could formulate these and some other rules that had to prevail; the difficulty was that the dude rancher had a continual stream of paying visitors and had to be sure they enjoyed their stay without forcing them to do anything.

Whether they learned these rules and guidelines by trial and error or through imitation, the dude ranchers who followed them were successful and their ranches grew in popularity and size. Some ranches were limited in their growth by physical restrictions, such as good pasture for their horses or land necessary for additional cabins. But those with adequate grazing land and building space anticipated significant expansion. These ranchers then faced a new question: how many visitors could a dude ranch handle and still retain its character? As noted previously, a working ranch could accommodate up to five guests with no appreciable change in its operation. Beyond five, more workers were needed and more emphasis had to be placed on the entertainment of the dudes. Once they had made these adjustments, ranchers learned they could handle fifteen or twenty people as easily as ten. Eventually, however, an upper limit of fifty seemed to be the maximum; they could handle that many just as easily as thirty or thirty-five. Once they got beyond fifty, however, ranches seemed to lose the campfire attitude and personal contact so necessary for the feel of a dude ranch vacation. Thus dude ranching tended to develop as a large number of small and medium-sized ranches rather than as a few very large ones.[49] Of course, fifty is not an absolute upper limit, merely an approximation. There were ranches that handled more people—some even over a hundred—and they were successful for many years. But fifty was a reasonable figure to consider when ranchers contemplated growth.

Obviously it took quite a personality to handle such a complex job successfully. In the words of Kipling, the model dude rancher had to be "a man of infinite resource and sagacity." In their own magazine the dude ranchers laughed at themselves a little as they listed the necessary characteristics. The ideal dude rancher should be a man of charm, warmth, and agility. He had to be a man's man, a ladies' man, a prince of a good fellow, and an authority on women, weather, wildlife, game, fish, horses, cows, dogs, sheep, and wildflowers. He also had to be an entertaining conversationalist, a convincing correspondent, a diplomat, a pal of the village banker and town marshal, and a cordial check cashier. His wife, meanwhile, had to be tolerant and sweet, with the tact of Priscilla and the tranquillity of Socrates. She had to be a good rider, housekeeper, and cook; must love children, the help, the guests, and the neighbors; and had to be a gracious hostess and clever entertainer. She was supposed to an authority on men, fashions, babies, Levis, help, popular songs, and home finance.[50]

The comments were lengthy, humorous, and somewhat exaggerated but each item on the list was based on some real quality that was needed. These men and women had to be real ranchers and also possess the qualities that guests assumed all westerners had. Dude ranchers had to be versatile, possessing a peculiar combination of physical skills, sociability, and financial acumen.

The finances of dude ranching are very difficult to analyze. Because few ranches kept extensive records, there has been some question of whether they were even profitable. Certainly some were not and failed, while others obviously did make money. But on working dude ranches it was sometimes unclear which aspect of the ranch made profits. The key problem for those that failed was the short season. For those in the northern Rockies it was often impossible to make enough money in the usual three-month season to operate year-round. Also the very isolation sought by ranches added to expenses because of the cost of bringing supplies long distances.[51]

Finding money to finance a ranch was another problem; many banks had no knowledge of how dude ranches operated and, in the first half of the twentieth century, generally adhered to an old adage that loans should not be given for the purpose of providing amusement. Even a well-informed banker would have difficulty judging a worthwhile application since personality played such an important role in this business. Sometimes the tangible assets of a ranch could not justify the loan desired, but a competent owner might make the granting of the loan a sound idea. Of course, the opposite situation could exist too; a rancher without the proper personality or skills could not make a ranch develop properly.[52]

Some people involved in dude ranching were convinced it produced a good living, but others have emphasized that other satisfactions kept people in the business and that ranchers could never get rich. To some it was like farming; once it got in a person's blood, he didn't want to give it up. Running a dude ranch was suited to friendly, extroverted people who did not want another type of life.[53] Of course, some ranches were profitable and also satisfying; these are the ones that not only survived but thrived throughout the twentieth century.

Whatever the goals or aspirations of the rancher and his family, he could never afford to stray far from an awareness of his guests and their desires. He was offering them a different way of life for a few weeks, life at a slower pace that required the guest to relax; he could not force the dudes into this, but he encouraged it by requiring advance reservations and a minimum stay. There were some visitors who could not unwind; they did not belong on a ranch, never enjoyed it, and seldom remained long.[54] Those who did stay often became enthusiastic, especially those who had traveled widely. They thought they had discovered something new; instead of engaging in an endless series of guided tours in a foreign country or urban scene, they now explored a fresh outdoor setting as equals with a rancher or wrangler. The dude was a strange mixture of tourist and traveler.[55] He wanted to acquire so many days of adventure (like a tourist), and the rancher tried to accommodate him. Yet (like the traveler) the dude on most ranches still had to join in, saddle up, and work to get what he wanted.

Howard Eaton riding "Danger," Yellowstone Park, 1911. Howard Eaton is generally considered the founder of dude ranching. (Biographical photo file, Howard Eaton, Western History Research Center, University of Wyoming.)

Children and horses were a natural combination on dude ranches.
(Buffalo Bill Historical Center, Cody, Wyoming.)

Willis, Howard, and Alden Eaton, Wyoming, ca. 1920. (Western History Research File, University of Wyoming.)

Frank Wright, 1949. An accomplished country-western musician, Frank Wright also became a very successful wrangler and guide in Colorado. (Courtesy of Frank Wright. Print by Joe Ruh.)

Custer Trail Ranch House, Dakota Territory. The Eatons first accepted paying guests at this ranch near Medora, North Dakota.
(State Historical Society of North Dakota.)

Rodeo at Remuda Ranch, Wickenburg, Arizona. (Courtesy of Mrs. Sophie Burden.)

Guests relax at the White Stallion Ranch near Tucson, Arizona. (White Stallion Ranch.)

Patio of San Gabriel Ranch, Alcalde, New Mexico, ca. 1925. (Photo
by Edward Kemp. Courtesy of the Museum of New Mexico.)

Mary Roberts Rinehart at Eatons' Ranch, Wolf, Wyoming. (Burlington Northern.)

Johnnie Holzwarth at Holzwarth's Neversummer Ranch, ca. 1966.
Johnnie Holzwarth and his wife, Caroline, built their ranch into
one of the finest horseback operations in the Rocky Mountains. It
operated from 1919 through 1973. (Courtesy of Fran Needham,
daughter of Johnnie and Caroline Holzwarth.)

Dick Randall, a pioneer dude rancher in Montana. He worked as a cowboy, big-game hunter, and guide before starting the OTO Ranch near Gardiner. He was a charter member of the Dude Ranchers' Association and an ardent conservationist. (Burlington Northern.)

Jim Murphy, Ox Yoke Ranch, Emigrant, Montana. (Burlington Northern.)

Larry Larom, 1910. He became the leading spokesman for dude ranching in the 1920s, helped organize the Dude Ranchers' Association in 1926, and served as its president from that date until 1945. (Buffalo Bill Historical Center, Cody, Wyoming.)

Marion and Charles C. Moore at the C M Ranch near Dubois,
Wyoming. Charles Moore was elected to the Wyoming legislature,
served as president of the Dude Ranchers' Association, and was one
of the most ardent conservationists of all dude ranchers. (Courtesy
Mrs. C. W. Hayes, daughter of Charles Moore.)

Five dudines. These guests at the Valley Ranch show off the varied styles of clothing that ranch guests wore. (Buffalo Bill Historical Center, Cody, Wyoming.)

Spike Van Cleve, Lazy K Bar Ranch, Big Timber, Montana. The Lazy K Bar was one of the charter members of the Dude Ranchers' Association. Spike Van Cleve served as president of the D.R.A., contributed regularly to its magazine, and was the author of *Forty Years' Gatherins'*. (Dude Ranchers' Association.)

Horses and riding were the center of activity on most dude ranches.
(Burlington Northern.)

In the early days of dude ranching, Indians attracted the interest of many western visitors. Many Indians lived near the ranches and visited them each summer. Here a small group sits in a coach at the Valley Ranch. (Buffalo Bill Historical Center, Cody, Wyoming.)

A fishing trip, Canjilon Camp, New Mexico, ca. 1927. (Photo by Edward Kemp. Courtesy of the Museum of New Mexico.)

A lone horseman, viewing the Rockies in Colorado, typifies the appeal of dude ranch vacations. (Courtesy of Fran Needham.)

EIGHT

A Good Memorial

I really feel, in addressing you, that I am addressing a convention
of conservationists; because I believe that you realize the importance
of our wardship and the wild life of our district.
      —J. T. Scott, chairman, Wyoming State Game Commission,
      Minutes of the Fourth Annual Dude Ranchers' Meeting, 93–98.

I wish I could be present at your dedication of the Howard Eaton
Trail July 19th. This will be a good memorial to that good man. No
one loved the Yellowstone Park more than he, and no one knew it
better or has contributed more to its welfare.
      —George Bird Grinnell to Horace M. Albright,
            July 17, 1923, Eaton Ranch Collection.

Dude ranchers had wide interests and needed a variety of skills to succeed in
their occupation. Other than the direct operation of their ranches, they were
probably more concerned with conservation than any other topic. To the dude
rancher conservation meant preservation of the land, controlled hunting and
fishing, and protection of wild animals and fish.[1]

Of course, any conservation activities by dude ranchers contained an element
of self-interest. They wanted adequate game so they could take people on successful hunts or fishing trips; game and fish were attractions even for those guests
who didn't hunt or fish themselves since they enjoyed seeing the animals in their
natural habitat. But the ranchers' continual efforts went beyond the expectation
of economic benefits. Love of the land and animals was a chief factor in drawing

people to the ranch life. It was quite natural that they try to preserve both land and animals in whatever ways they could.

As already noted, much of the initial interest in the West and in dude ranches came from hunting trips, and both hunting and fishing have remained among the chief appeals of dude ranches throughout their history. It is not surprising to learn that sport hunters often became ardent conservationists. John F. Reiger, in his notable book *American Sportsmen and the Origins of Conservation,* has made a strong case for sportsmen in general being the originators of the conservation movement in the United States; dude ranchers and their guests clearly fit this pattern and reinforce Reiger's argument. Of course many people who hear the word *conservation* think immediately of Theodore Roosevelt; when he became president, Roosevelt was an active supporter of reclamation projects, signed the Newlands Act, and withdrew millions of acres of land for various forest reserves. It is pertinent to recall that a letter written by Howard Eaton was the impetus for Roosevelt's first trip west to the Dakotas where he took up both hunting and ranching and formed some of his ideas about the land and game animals.

Howard Eaton was also learning a great deal in the Badlands early in the twentieth century. He was a very active and successful hunter and led many guests on hunting trips; later in his life, he wrote four articles describing his extensive hunting there. This early hunting seems to have been a prime factor in establishing his interest in guiding visitors on enjoyable trips and in making him the best known of the three Eaton brothers in North Dakota.[2] Howard also learned that uncontrolled and unwise activity could damage the environment. The Badlands of the western Dakotas, sometimes known as the northern or Little Missouri Badlands, were approximately 225 miles long and 50 miles wide. It was an eroded, contoured, broken land of great natural beauty. Numerous beaver dams retained the precious water in pools, supporting an abundance of grasses and game. The early ranchers watched in dismay, however, as overgrazing, unrestricted hunting, and farming stripped the land, allowed the water to run off, and turned it into an arid and desolate area.[3] Howard Eaton's concern with this destruction was one reason why he and his brothers moved to Wyoming.

Long before that, as early as 1882, he was involved with plans to try to save the buffalo (bison) from extinction; he worked with Michael Pablo, Charles Allard, and Buffalo Jones to preserve these once-numerous animals. By 1883 Howard had forty buffalo and sold some of them to zoological parks. Eventually, he sold all he had to Pablo, who was able to turn over a herd of five hundred to the Canadian government. Over the years Eaton remained in contact with Theodore Roosevelt, who later appointed him to the National Park Commission to prevent the extinction of the buffalo.[4] Eaton made regular trips to capture game animals and then shipped them to zoos and parks; he sent as many as fifty elk east at a time and sometimes rode along in the freight cars to see that the animals arrived uninjured. Besides buffalo, elk, and deer, he even captured mountain lion and bear, and the deliveries of these animals were duly noted in the records of Eatons' Ranch.[5] Of course, part of the reason for some shipments was to make money, but Howard's interest went far beyond that motive as he developed a keen interest in, and concern for, all wild animals. Among his many friends was George Bird Grinnell, one of the most respected conservationists of the late nineteenth century and a man who also influenced Theodore Roosevelt; Eaton and Grinnell undoubtedly shared ideas about game preservation and habitat.[6] Howard Eaton's concern for animals continued when he moved to Wyoming; at age seventy-one he undertook a winter trek to feed starving elk, a rescue mission that undermined his health.[7]

On one of his trips to the Yellowstone area to get animals to ship east, Howard Eaton had met Dick Randall. Randall was also well known as an ardent and successful hunter, and his dude ranch grew out of his hunting camp. His constant outdoor activity near thousands of deer, elk, bighorn sheep, and black, brown, and grizzly bears made him another enthusiastic advocate of conservation. He was a lifelong fighter for preservation of wildlife, wilderness, and unspoiled natural recreation. Like Eaton, Randall guided Theodore Roosevelt on some hunting trips, and, when the president laid the cornerstone of the north entrance to Yellowstone Park in 1903, Dick Randall was on the platform with him.[8]

In the late nineteenth and early twentieth centuries there was certainly a need for someone to protest the wanton slaughter of animals. One particularly wasteful and appalling situation was the killing of elk for the two special tusks of the bulls; these were ambercolored and marked in the center with what looked like a moccasin track. Used in watch charms, cuff links, and other forms of jewelry by members of Elk Lodges across the country, these tusks sold for five to twenty dollars per pair, and a great slaughter of elk occurred from 1910 to 1920 to supply the demand. Protestors against this destruction (often dude ranchers in the Jackson Hole country) finally convinced the Elk Lodges to discourage the use of these teeth for decorations, thus reducing the demand. Growing emphasis on proper game management also spared the elk.[9]

Of course, there were many more battles to be fought and problems to be solved. Dick Randall was especially convinced that great harm was caused by farming some western land and that even more damage resulted from the grazing of domestic sheep, which ate the feed that wild game depended on. They also ate the underbrush that normally helped hold the snow; without it the snow melted too quickly and brought silt to the streams, which not only stripped the land but also injured or killed the fish. Randall believed the erosion of the land also contributed to the increase of forest fires. He insisted that these problems did not occur when hunting was the major human activity in an area since the sport hunter killed only what he needed. Randall believed that some western areas were better utilized for hunting and recreation than for farming and grazing.[10]

Another rancher deeply involved in the field of conservation was Charles Moore who built the C M Ranch near Dubois. Moore was a native of Wyoming and grew up when wild game was abundant. He became "a militant conservationist. He knew the basic problems of the land and all living things on it."[11] Moore was a teacher about the outdoors too; his pack trips for boys (which led to his dude ranch) were more than pleasant outings. He taught these youngsters about the wilderness and how to get along with it. Later, as a state legislator, he devoted his attention to game bills and other conservation items; when he became president of the Dude Ranchers' Association, he continued his avid support of the preservation of fish, game, and natural resources. He warned that national parks, monuments, and other public lands were in constant danger of being destroyed by pressure groups and selfish individuals. He urged his fellow ranchers to continue fighting to save these lands for the public as a whole. He was especially disturbed by the presence of oil-drilling rigs in the national forests.[12]

Larry Larom, unlike Moore, was a transplanted westerner, but his interest in conservation was no less intense. As early as 1916, shortly after he started the Valley Ranch, he was concerned about the preservation of big game animals; this interest was undoubtedly reinforced by his friendship with William F. Cody, a neighbor. Larom devoted much of his attention over the years to the study of the National Forest Service, national parks, federal and state game and fish departments, and reclamation projects. He even spent some of his winters in New York where he could keep in touch with conservation groups and other people involved with matters of importance to the West. His papers included files of correspondence with the Forest Service plus reports, clippings, and minutes of meetings on numerous conservation questions.[13] He was appointed to the Wyoming Fish and Game Commission, and was offered the position of director of the National Park Service during Franklin Roosevelt's administration. Larom was very much a teacher about the outdoor life also. The boys' school that he operated at the Valley Ranch included shooting, horseback riding, trapping, and fishing.[14]

Billy Howell of the famous Holm Lodge near Cody was another well-known rancher who took an active role in game management. He was an avid hunter and served for years on the Game and Fish Committee of the Dude Ranchers'

Association.[15] In a sense all dude ranchers became teachers to their guests, explaining game and fish problems, land management, and related matters.

As noted in Chapter 5 Mary Roberts Rinehart was very active in publicizing dude ranching. She was equally concerned with trying to generate support for various conservation measures. Her article "The Sleeping Giant" was aimed primarily at explaining the national parks and garnering support for them; in addition nearly everything she wrote (except her fiction) supported preservation of parts of the West so that future generations could enjoy it. And, like dude ranchers, Mrs. Rinehart advocated hunting as an integral and humane part of an effective game program. To answer protests against hunting she noted that most easterners had no concept of the rigors of western mountain winters, the depth of the snow, or the hardships that a late spring could mean for wild animals. Effective game management included hunting; as a lover of wildlife, she saw the advantage of a quick bullet in a vital spot as opposed to the slow anguish of starvation that was often the fate of game animals.[16]

Another noted writer who combined hunting and conservation was Arthur Carhart. He worked for the Forest Service in the 1920s and began a long friendship with Charles Moore at that time. He turned to free-lance writing in the 1930s. Between 1938 and 1943 he headed the wildlife restoration program in Colorado, and after that he returned to writing; his books included *Hunting North American Deer, Fishing in the West, Fresh Water Fishing, Conservation, Please!, Water—or Your Life,* and *Crisis Spots in Conservation.* Carhart also wrote a book on dude ranching, recognizing the industry as one clearly supportive of conservation. His friendship with Charles Moore was partially responsible for the fact that Moore's papers and records were placed in the Denver Public Library, just one floor away from that facility's Conservation Library.[17]

Another clear and constant support of conservation came from the activities of the Dude Ranchers' Association. The close connection was emphasized by a number of different events. At the founding meeting of the DRA in 1926 Horace Albright, then superintendent of Yellowstone Park, was an active participant, and he retained his ties with the organization for years. One of the committees created at that first meeting was set up to deal with legislation regarding fish and game matters. This type of involvement was emphasized in the DRA constitution; one of the four stated purposes in founding the organization was to cooperate with officials of the national parks and forests for conservation and preservation of game and the land.[18] Later, when the organization began to grant honorary memberships, many were given to men connected with conservation: the director of the National Park Service, supervisors of various national forests, game wardens and protectors, and members of state fish and game commissions. Many of these people were prominent speakers at the DRA conventions also as they explained their particular functions, praised the dude ranchers' activities, and promised cooperation with them.[19]

So interested were the ranchers in these activities that, at the sixth meeting of the DRA, President I. H. Larom stated that the first step in their program was accomplished—the recognition of the dude ranch as a valuable factor in the development of the western states; dude ranchers, therefore, could now turn to conservation:

> Our present efforts are being directed towards the building up of a
> closer understanding of the problems in our districts, with
> particular reference to the restocking of streams and proper
> conservation of our game and fish resources.[20]

To these ends the DRA was openly involved in political matters. It passed resolutions urging action by the U.S. Congress to appropriate specific sums of money for definite and precise purposes in preservation projects. President Larom visited Washington, D.C., to keep in contact with state delegations as well as the Forest Service and Park Service. In the late 1930s the DRA opposed a reorganization bill relating to the Forest Service, fearing that this group would not be able to function as well as it had before—which meant along lines of conservation, multiple use of the land, and cooperation with dude ranchers. The group also opposed the extension of Yellowstone Park south to include Bridger Lake and the Thoroughfare country. This would have eliminated some of the best available hunting and pack-trip areas in Wyoming.[21] In the 1940s President Charles Moore specifically protested a proposal to turn federal lands over to the states for fear it would eventually mean that a few rich people would own all of Wyoming; the DRA then went on record opposing the removal of any part of the national parks or forests from federal ownerships. In 1947 testimony before the House of Representatives Subcommittee on Public Lands, Moore stated that the DRA was founded on conservation, and ranchers were primarily interested in the protection and preservation of natural resources so they could be enjoyed by present and future generations.[22]

As already noted, the DRA was also involved in state politics, primarily in Wyoming and Montana. The group was sometimes represented on state game commissions, and several of its members, such as Charles Moore and Frank Horton, were state legislators. Indeed, a reading of the organization's minutes shows page after page of meetings and discussions of fish and game matters. The DRA urged cooperation with stockmen, sheepman, and others who wished to use the same areas of federally controlled land.[23]

Dude ranchers were not just involved in passing resolutions or giving testimony relating to what they wanted from government officials. They were men of action willing to work positively for preservation. In the severe winter of 1909–10 local ranchers led the way in feeding 30,000 elk in Jackson Hole even though they had to skimp on feed for their own stock. Thirteen years later, Howard Eaton repeated the effort, and ten years after that Larry Larom worked with Wyoming game officials on the same project.[24]

In the early twentieth century, when some of the critical decisions about game management were made, dude ranchers were in the forefront of conservation measures. They encouraged hunting and fishing but strictly within legal limits, in contrast to the earlier days of unrestricted destruction of game and fish. Ranchers often acted as deputy fish and game wardens to assist the still-slim ranks of state and federal game officials. The ranchers also helped stock lakes and streams and, on at least one occasion, joined the railroad in a particularly large project. The Burlington Railway shipped in a carload of fish with no freight charged, and ranchers hauled them out to the countryside and then helped officials stock the streams.[25] The ranchers were in an ideal position to explain the need for conservation to their guests, who trusted and respected the ranchers and were often eager to learn how they could help in land or game preservation.

In 1931 dude ranchers played a special role fighting a series of destructive fires. The chief ranger of Yellowstone Park noted that it was the most disastrous fire year since 1910; the park had thirty-one fires and at one time was using 120 horses from Jackson Hole dude ranches to pack supplies to the fire camps. He gave high praise to the ranchers for their cooperation. Officials of the Forest Service were equally grateful and noted especially the aid received from Charles Moore in averting what forester John Spencer called a "national catastrophe." One terrible fire burned in the region south of Yellowstone for weeks; thanks to Moore's help, Forest Service firefighters were able to halt it at the crest of the Warm Springs divide. Had they not done so, Spencer said it would have gone north to Yellowstone and become the worst fire in Wyoming history. To get their job done, the Forest Service admitted, it "practically wrecked" Moore's ranch, using all of his pack outfits, his hands, and everything else. Moore

> practically turned the place over to us. We packed in fire fighting apparatus and supplies and one thing and another for about two weeks there, and fortunately we managed to hold the fire . . . the only reason we were able to get supplies up there was through Mr. Moore.[26]

Was this self-interest? Certainly, but it was far more than that as Moore and others constantly worked for preservation of game and fish and also for keeping the land available to the general public. The federal government, of course, later became more deeply involved in land management programs. The Great Depression did not halt this involvement since conservation agencies offered opportunities for many recovery and relief programs, and these agencies received more money and manpower than before. Several parks even expanded noticeably in the 1930s as they received added funds. This decade also spawned a back-to-the-soil movement that led to more camping, hiking, and other outdoor activities. This continuing growth also raised questions and led to conflicts over just what federal policies were. John W. Spencer of the U.S. Forest Service explained to dude ranchers that the primary purposes of his agency were to ensure a perpetual supply of timber and to protect watersheds. But it was clear that there were other interests to be considered, especially livestock grazing and various forms of recreational use that were quite legitimate and required cooperative endeavor.[27] Many times cooperation between federal officials and ranchers was clear-cut and successful; there was an interesting case in the 1920s when a major effort to dam Jenny and Leigh lakes in the Jackson Hole area halted because of the combined interest of the National Park Service and the dude ranchers. A victory for leaving nature alone was won and ranchers could rejoice at the outcome.[28]

But conflicts of various sorts with federal officials continued to develop and eventually these seemed more common than mutual interests. That dude ranchers should eventually be involved in disagreements over federal land policies is not surprising since federal officials themselves were in conflict. The Park Service and Forest Service became virtual enemies as they contended for control of federal recreation areas. In a sense the federal conservation movement was not really conservation oriented; rather it was a move to have government officials, rather than state or private interests, manage the land. Gifford Pinchot, probably the most famous conservationist in the late nineteenth and early twentieth centuries, and others were actually utilitarians who wanted to use scientific management of public land to the best advantage. They scorned the so-called aesthetic conservationists—those who wanted to preserve beautiful areas—as muddleheaded and impractical.

More than a dozen national parks had been created by 1916, but they were run without much planning or coordination. The Department of the Interior had legal jurisdiction over all of them, but the War Department actually controlled Yellowstone, Sequoia, General Grant, and Yosemite parks, and some others received little more than custodial care.[29] In 1916, however, Congress created the National Park Service in the Department of the Interior to "promote and regulate" the parks, monuments, and reservations; the purpose was

> to conserve the scenery and the natural and historic objects and
> the wild life therein and to provide for the enjoyment of the same
> in such manner and by such means as will leave them unimpaired
> for the enjoyment of future generations.[30]

The purpose of the National Park Service seems clear enough but the problem was that promoting the parks might impair them for future generations. This cannot be overemphasized; it would generate conflicts for decades. Steven Mather and Horace Albright were two very avid supporters of the national parks in the early twentieth century; Mather was appointed as first director of the National Park Service and Albright, assistant director; later Albright also became director of the Park Service. They had toured the parks in 1915 and were convinced they needed development, which meant roads and tourist facilities. So the Park Service embarked enthusiastically on development projects including the construction of new roads, the rebuilding of old ones, and the creation of franchises or regulated monopolies to provide facilities in the parks. As the projects proceeded successfully, the Park Service has continually faced the dilemma of trying to achieve two fundamentally incompatible objectives—maintain areas unimpaired and make the parks easily accessible to tourists. Mather and Albright were really utilitarians who emphasized tourist development but primarily the type that would increase tourist use of the parks.[31] Dude ranchers generally opposed the building of dams in scenic areas but they were often torn between conflicting desires: increase the number of visitors or keep areas in a true wilderness condition. Ranchers often reopened and/or maintained old trails so visitors could view scenic areas and were convinced that a true wilderness experience precluded driving a car or flying to remote areas. Some government officials agreed and congratulated ranchers on their work to keep sections of the West in a pristine state. But dude ranchers also wanted more guests, and they learned that selling scenery or promoting the wilderness tended to destroy it.[32]

Steven Mather launched the "See America First" campaign in 1915 and in the same year hired Robert S. Yard as publicity director for the parks. Yard had worked for two New York newspapers and on *The Century* magazine. Later he helped organize the Wilderness Society, served as its president and permanent secretary, and edited its magazine, *The Living Wilderness,* for ten years. One of his endeavors was the publication of *The Book of the National Parks.* Mather himself had been a top-notch salesman for Twenty Mule Team Borax, and he used his skills to sell the parks. He made friends with many newspaper and magazine editors and soon many writers were publishing enthusiastic articles about the parks.[33]

One of these promoters was George Lorimer, editor of *The Saturday Evening*

Post. He pointed out one of the chief dilemmas of the national parks in an editorial in 1919:

> Selling scenery is dangerous business. To popularize our national
> parks without destroying the very thing that we are trying to save,
> to sell them to the public without claptrap commercialism is a job
> that calls for unusual qualities.[34]

He advocated adequate roads into and through the parks but not too many of them; these should be trunk roads for access and also "to give those who are unable to do it right a chance to glimpse their glories from a motor." Once there, however, the visitors should go on foot or horseback to live a simple, clean, close-to-the-ground life. Lorimer argued against dance halls, picture shows, funiculars, and cabins as alien to the whole concept of the parks. Yet he saw that already there were three classes of people visiting national parks: those who were in the wrong place because they wanted all the conveniences and comfort of staying in the cities; motor and wagon campers who wanted to do something different and who were often careless and untidy; and the true lovers of the outdoors who left the trail just as beautiful and unspoiled as they found it.

Despite the problems, the Park Service continued its promotion; by getting many visitors to the parks, officials believed they were guaranteeing future support for the park system. One man who disagreed with their approach was Emerson Hough, who wrote numerous books with a western theme. Hough had explored Yellowstone Park on skis in the winter of 1895, and this trip was a prime factor in getting Congress to pass legislation to protect the buffalo in Yellowstone Park. Hough stayed with the Albrights in Yellowstone one season and stated his conviction that it was a great mistake to measure success by an increase in visitors.[35] But quantity was the goal and the number of tourists in Yellowstone more than doubled from 1919 to 1923. By 1929 all the national parks accommodated over 2.6 million visitors, over 3 million in the 1930s, 50 million by the 1950s, and 130 million (and rising) by the Park Service's fiftieth anniversary in 1966.

Some of the promotional methods park officials used were a bit surprising; besides building roads and allowing franchisers to offer services, Horace Albright built a corral in Yellowstone Park and put in it buffalo, deer, elk, coyotes, bears, porcupines, and badgers in cages for tourists to see. He also expanded the bear pits, where people gathered every evening to watch the bears eat garbage. Obviously these tactics emphasized the conflict between preserving nature unspoiled and making the parks quickly attractive for visitors. Although park officials later ordered the removal of the bear pits and corral, the conflict was obvious. Park officials welcomed dude ranchers and their parties, especially at Yellowstone, which had been so widely publicized and whose unusual sights were eagerly anticipated by ranch guests. Even as hard-surfaced roads were constructed, park officials emphasized that this was done to help wagons pulled by teams of horses or mules get into the park easily; ranchers often used these wagons to haul in supplies for their pack trips. In 1929 Park Superintendent Roger Toll noted that one of the best and most legitimate uses of Yellowstone was the visit of pack outfits that stayed two to six weeks.[36]

But the more the parks were successfully "sold" to the public, the more questionable it became which group would be favored in the event of conflicts or who would decide how the public would be served best. One of the wildest and most bitter battles came with the proposal that the federal government control the land south of Yellowstone Park. The land in question included the Teton Mountains and Jackson Hole. As noted previously, this section of Wyoming had a rugged climate, and early ranchers had started accepting guests in order to survive economically. Hunting guides and dude ranchers, therefore, were the real pioneers of Jackson Hole and they were the ones who had chased the elk poachers out of the area; naturally they would be concerned about this new proposal.[37] In 1919 Horace Albright attended a meeting in Jackson Hole to discuss the extension of federal control from Yellowstone Park south. There was a great deal of opposition from local citizens to the idea. Cattle ranchers wanted to use the land for grazing; hunters knew a national park would prohibit hunting; and dude ranchers feared the extension would bring paved roads, hotels, and hordes of tourists who would detract from the wilderness atmosphere and thus destroy their business. In late 1919 a drought injured the cattle business and some cattlemen who were in debt changed their minds; extension of the park now looked better since they would have the possibility of selling their ranches to the federal government. In addition Horace Albright convinced Struthers Burt and Dr. Horace Carncross, two of the earliest dude ranchers in that country, that the park plans would not bring in unlimited roads and tourists and that the Park Service could preserve Jackson Hole from commercial intrusion. Not all dude ranchers agreed with Burt and Carncross in their change of heart on this issue but the opposition did decline.[38] In 1929 Senator John Kendrick of Wyoming introduced a bill creating Grand Teton National Park and it was approved by Congress. This did not, however, include all the area some people wanted in the park so the controversy continued.

In the mid-1920s John D. Rockefeller, Jr., had entered the picture. He took a trip with Horace Albright in Jackson Hole in 1926 and disliked the commecialism he saw there; when he asked for a map showing the "offending" properties, Albright was glad to oblige him. The following winter Albright visited Rockefeller, who said he was willing to spend over a million dollars for property in the area. Rockefeller arranged the organization of the Snake River Land Company in Utah in order to keep his name out of the picture; through this group he gradually purchased several thousand acres of land so he could add it to Grand Teton Park. As he did this, it became clear that Rockefeller favored dude ranching only on a limited scale—an ominous sign for the future.[39]

The controvery over what should be done with the Jackson Hole country continued during the 1930s and into the 1940s, affecting Wyoming politics at all levels. Dude rancher Charles Moore seemed convinced that making the area a national park would be beneficial but there certainly was no unanimity among dude ranchers on this topic.[40] Rockefeller had offered to turn over the land he had bought as a gift to the federal government, but nothing was done for years about his offer; he became disturbed at this lack of action and wrote Secretary of the Interior Harold Ickes in 1942, threatening to sell the land if the government refused to take it. Ickes then persuaded President Franklin Roosevelt to sign an executive order in March 1943, establishing Jackson Hole National Monument adjacent to Grand Teton Park. It included about 100,000 acres of the Teton National Forest, 40,000 acres of withdrawn public land, 32,000 acres donated by the Snake River Land Company, and 18,000 acres of other privately owned land. Congress protested this executive action and tried to void the creation of the monument, obviously just a subterfuge to create a national park in everything but name. Roosevelt vetoed a bill trying to reverse his action, and Rockefeller interests halted similar attempts of the Eightieth Congress (1947–48). Increased tourism in the 1940s finally softened Wyoming opposition and a compromise was arranged. Approximately 9,000 acres went from the monument to the National Elk Refuge and Teton Forest. The balance was then added to Grand Teton Park, the federal government granted tax reimbursements on a descending scale for twenty-five years to local government, and the Wyoming Game and Fish Commission administered the elk herd. The new, enlarged park was created by a bill that Congress approved in September 1950.[41] This long, bitter fight had ended, but it highlights a major conflict that still continues between public and private recreation. The results have generally been consistent—private recreation loses.

When this enlarged park was created, dude ranches were listed as historic enterprises that should be retained. The park bought many ranches and gave the owner or head of the household a lifetime lease; this was attractive to some ranchers, for they paid no local taxes once the park owned their land. But this type of lease was not renewable, and inevitably the number of dude ranches began to shrink as the owners died. A great deal of hostility developed as the

Park Service moved to establish its power in the area. Promises to let ranches continue to operate were not kept. The Half Moon and Bear Paw ranches were purchased and then destroyed; Elbo Ranch was moved to the other side of the valley, and the owner leased land from the park while the old buildings were used by park officials; part of the old Bar B C Ranch still exists but it is on a lifetime lease; the White Grass Ranch sold all but five acres to the park and operates on a lease as does the R Lazy S Ranch; and the Double Diamond Boys Ranch was sold completely. The same thing happened to others, and the Park Service even tried to condemn land to get it; however, it couldn't take private deeded land within park boundaries unless it was offered for sale, in which case it had first choice if it could meet the price the owner asked. A few ranches, such as Turner's Triangle X, operate on a renewable concession basis, and these concessions could be terminated whenever they run out.[42]

Thus Grand Teton Park has destroyed many of the Jackson Hole dude ranches, and it can control the activities of most of those that are left. The only exceptions are those few that are completely on private land. The original fears of the dude ranchers were correct; the extension of the park and improved roads led to the building of many motels in the Jackson Hole area, and dude ranching, which really pioneered the recreational development there, declined drastically. Interestingly, the Rockefellers, who had much to do with closing the area to ranchers and their guests, retained the old J Y Ranch, probably the first dude ranch in Jackson Hole; it is their private resort, open only to friends. By 1972, owing to constant government expansion, only 3 percent of Teton County was private, deeded land; all the rest was owned by the government. Intense commercialism hit the area as originally feared and in spite of the government's assurances that it could prevent such a development. Indeed much of it has occurred because of federal involvement in the area. Private ranchers could not have developed or promoted the vicinity as intensely as the government has done. Instead of the old, rather balanced economy based on cattle raising and catering to a relatively few guests, there developed an intense three-month pursuit of money during the tourist season.[43] Eventually ski resorts were built, spreading the tourist season over a longer period, but these resorts have marred the landscape and further diminished the area's isolation.[44]

An area rather similar to Jackson Hole was the Kawuneeche Valley in Colorado; it extended north of Grand Lake between Rocky Mountain National Park and the Neversummer Mountains. Here too the harsh winter climate had prevented the development of many successful stock ranches, but the trout fishing was good and the scenery spectacular. Therefore, some of the settlers accepted guests for a fee and provided them with lodging, a horse for riding, and access for fishing. A few ranches were able to survive and endure by a combination of catering to visitors, raising cattle or hay, cutting timber, trapping, and/or hunting.

Rocky Mountain National Park eventually expanded farther into and down the valley and gradually began to acquire these ranches. The first tourist facility was probably the Hotel de Hardscrabble started by Squeaky Bob Wheeler. He had been gone for years but the Phantom Valley Ranch was established on his old site in 1928; this dude ranch was ideally located, about twelve miles north of the city of Grand Lake and one-half mile from the road.[45] The owners and wranglers developed eight different half-day rides and about twenty-one all-day rides from this site. The ranch operated for over thirty years and took out thousands of guests, but personal troubles finally led the owners to sell. Rocky Mountain National Park bought the ranch about 1960; the cabins and lodge were then torn down to make a parking lot for a trailhead. Former guests at Phantom Valley Ranch were "totally perplexed at the Government and Park Service's concept of 'progress.'"[46] Of course, the disappearance of this ranch meant that its guests (the public) no longer had the same choice of riding into the surrounding countryside. They did have, for a while, the alternative of going to nearby dude ranches so they could see approximately the same areas as before. But the same fate—purchase by the Park Service and subsequent destruction—eliminated the other ranches along Trail Ridge Road in the valley.[47] The disappearance of most of the ranches in this area has made it nearly impossible for the public to get to the nearby scenic spots of Rocky Mountain National Park and Routt and Arapaho national forests since these ranches provided the only practical access for horseback riding there. Ironically, these dude ranches opened the area to the public and helped popularize the beautiful sites such as Timber Lake, Julian Lake, Blue Lake, Lake of the Clouds, Skeleton Gulch, the Mica Mine, and Parika Lake.

There is a special relationship, too, between dude ranching and game preservation. Ranchers in the Kawuneeche Valley had to clear out beaver dams and willow thickets to make grazing areas and hay meadows for their horses and cattle. Once cleared and developed, however, these fields also provided feed for elk that came out of the parks or national forest.[48] With the disappearance of these ranches, the pastures and meadows will probably revert to heavy tree growth; if this occurs, feed for the elk will diminish, and the herds will probably decline. Such a sequence of events provides a rather clear example of how ranching benefited game animals and helped them increase, and how the disappearance of these ranches may lead to the decline of game.

National park expansion as a threat to dude ranching was and is based on two simple facts: many dude ranches have been located near national parks; and the Park Service has long had a policy of eliminating private land near national parks.

The lists in the appendix show this concentration of dude ranches to be most pronounced in Montana, Wyoming, and Colorado. Of the 114 ranches listed in Montana, 25 were in the area around Glacier National Park, and 40 more were close to the entrances of Yellowstone National Park. Of the 95 in Wyoming, 46 were grouped near Cody or Jackson, the entrances to Yellowstone, and Grand Teton national parks. In Colorado 25 ranches were listed, with 10 in the Estes Park or Granby–Grand Lake areas, the entrances to Rocky Mountain National Park. As noted in the appendix, these lists are not definitive but they are representative of the concentration of dude ranches in the most scenic areas.[49] The reason for this concentration was simple: ranchers saw the appeal of scenery, fishing, and/or hunting and chose the best sites. It is important to note that, with the exception of Yellowstone, dude ranches preceded the publicizing of most of these areas by the government, and they were established on private land outside park boundaries. What happened then was that the national parks grew in popularity, partly because of dude ranchers' use of them, and the Park Service decided to acquire more desirable land and took over the ranches.

In May 1918 the National Park Service announced that its administrative policy was to purchase all private holdings in the national parks. Of course, what that really meant was that far-seeing people had purchased desirable land and then were surrounded by the creation of a national park. Thus the effect of park policy was to eliminate the property owners who most appreciated the beauty and/or isolation of different areas. The directive read:

> All of them should be eliminated either through congressional
> appropriations or by acceptance of donations of these lands.
> Isolated tracts in important scenic areas should be given first
> consideration, of course, in the purchase of private property.[50]

Besides such appropriations and donations, a third method was also used to acquire land, at least on an interim basis—private financing. The actions of John D. Rockefeller, Jr., have already been noted in relation to the Jackson Hole area. A similar technique was used to acquire land at the northern edge of Yellowstone Park. Congress appropriated $150,000 on the condition that this sum be matched by private funds, and wealthy easterners supplied the additional $150,000. In more recent years, the Nature Conservancy has purchased property and held it until the Park Service has had the funds to buy the desired land. The Department of Interior Appropriations Act of 1930 also empowered the

National Park Service to use condemnation proceedings to step up its drive to eliminate private holdings, and it is clear that there was a rapid acceleration of land acquisitions after 1930.[51] This policy has continued over the decades, and the 1975 Management Policies of the National Park System state that the "National Park Service will acquire all lands and waters within authorized park boundaries," unless of course the lands are being used as the Park Service wants them utilized.[52] It should be emphasized that park boundaries have been enlarged so that ranches not originally surrounded by a park soon found themselves in a different position. Also much of the revenue collected at park entrance stations is deposited in a fund which is then used to purchase more land by the federal government. The very popularity of the national parks thus tends to allow them to grow without limit.[53]

Indeed a 1981 printout of land acquisition by the National Park Service shows an interesting story. The four key national parks that related to dude ranches have been Glacier, Grand Teton, Yellowstone, and Rocky Mountain. The figures for Glacier Park require twenty pages of computer printout and indicate acquisition of over one million acres; those for Grand Teton Park require eleven pages of details for acquisition of over 300,000 acres; for Rocky Mountain Park, thirteen pages for over 260,000 acres; for Yellowstone, two and one-half pages for over 2.2 million acres. The listings for Yellowstone contain many transfers from the public domain while those for the other three contain only a few such listings. It is worth noting also that, of these four parks, only Grand Teton has any sort of acreage limitation. This was imposed by a Congressional Act of September 1950; congressional approval is required for any extension of the park boundary.[54]

Thus the growth of the parks cannot yet be considered complete even at their present, huge size. The point that must be emphasized again is that the dude ranchers and others who chose the scenic and desirable spots were those to be pushed out. These people often understood and appreciated the land and demands of the environment better than anyone else, yet they were removed, sometimes to make way for parking lots. As noted earlier in relation to Phantom Valley Ranch, it has sometimes been difficult to understand the definition of progress or conservation that the NPS uses. By building and improving roads and by constant successful publicizing, the NPS has indeed helped to destroy the very thing it has promoted; this has occurred just as George Lorimer in 1919 and Mary Roberts Rinehart in 1921 foresaw. At the same time, it has eliminated the ranches that were striving to give guests the natural, unspoiled experience that all conservationists supposedly preferred.[55]

The methods that the NPS used to acquire land varied; some was simply taken. Some people sold because they couldn't resist the seemingly endless supply of federal money; some were harassed or pressured to the point that they gave up and sold for peace and quiet; and some wanted their land to go to the park in hopes that the scenic beauty of an area would not be marred.

Despite these and other conflicts between the National Park Service concept of conservation and that of the dude ranchers, the latter retain their interest in conservation at all levels. The tradition of working to preserve the land and animals held by earlier ranchers, such as Billy Howell, Dick Randall, Howard Eaton, Larry Larom, and Charles Moore, has continued through modern-day dude ranchers such as Stanley and Don Siggins of Siggins Triangle X Ranch, Ike Fordyce of Teepee Lodge, and Frank Wright, who has served guests throughout Colorado, and down to the Faraway Ranch in Arizona whose owners did their best to prevent the Wonderland of Rocks from becoming a neon-sign disaster.[56]

Dude ranchers generally have had and still possess great respect for the land and animals. They were interested in preserving wilderness areas long before the conservation movement of the last fifteen years. It is regrettable that their concern has not been recognized more widely and even more unfortunate that many have actually been removed from the areas they helped to develop. Both land preservation and game management may well suffer from their disappearance.

NINE

You Can Count on the Railroads

You can count on the railroads for cooperation at all times.
—M. M. Goodsill, *Minutes of the Fourth Annual
Dude Ranchers' Meeting,* 75.

The key to the growth of dude ranches, their success, and many of their problems has been transportation. Since the ranches were in the Rocky Mountains and most early guests came from the upper Midwest and Northeast, it is clear that the method of getting to the ranches would be important. But there is a far deeper relationship between transportation and dude ranching.

To understand and appreciate this relationship it is necessary to retrace briefly the early period of dude ranching and the travel conditions of the time. By the 1870s and 1880s, when dude ranching was beginning, several railroads were being built across the country, but travel was still arduous and time-consuming. A traveler had to plan on spending a week or more getting to the Rockies from the East, and, of course, far more time was required for visitors from Europe. Connections were uncertain and difficult at times, and travel could even be dangerous as the daring dude went farther west. Travel to the West was also expensive, sometimes more expensive for someone from the eastern United States than a trip to Europe. Even when the western visitor successfully negotiated the railroad schedules and difficulties, it was still some distance to many ranches and scenic spots.[1] When Isabella Bird journeyed about Colorado in 1873 she had to borrow a horse at Longmont and ride to Estes Park, a full day's trip that can now be negotiated in less than an hour. When Owen Wister went to Jackson Hole ranches, he had a wagon ride of 104 miles from the railroad stop at St. Anthony, Idaho.[2] This was an extreme case because of the early inaccessibility of Jackson Hole, but most ranches were relatively isolated; this isolation was part of their attractiveness, however, and dudes gloried in "getting away from it all" in a rather literal fashion.

Once in the West the visitor of the late nineteenth or early twentieth century found a world dependent on the horse for transportation. This was not totally new to them since horses were still much in use in the East, but western towns and ranches were so much farther apart than cities in the East that the dependence on horses was greater and more important. Many guests got their introduction to their horses at the railroad station as they mounted up to ride to the ranch while their baggage was carried on pack mules. In some places wagons or stage-coaches were sent to fetch the guests. The OTO Ranch sent a four-horse, nine-passenger coach to the Northern Pacific station at Corwin Springs; while more colorful and probably more comfortable than a wagon, the stage ride was still rough. The journey, which included a ride over two miles of private road, was a mixture of thrill and fright that was a good introduction to ranch life.[3] These early western roads were extremely rough—washed out, narrow, and full of rocks that jolted the riders' teeth. The roads hung over the edge of precipices, and were so steep that a wagon passenger almost fell backward out of a wagon going uphill and practically rode on the horses' rumps going downhill.[4]

Of course, long journeys to ranches by rugged roads meant that bringing in supplies was a problem. Most ranches, therefore, raised as much of their food as they could; dairy and beef cattle and large gardens were common. Ranchers made their own butter and cheese and some hauled tons of ice from creeks in the winter. But some supplies had to be purchased, and it was difficult and time-consuming to get them.[5] At Holm Lodge, for example, it took one day to get to Cody in a wagon and two days to return with a heavy load on the upgrade. Ranches were generally from ten to one hundred miles from a substantial supply center even in this century, and they would have to feed dozens, or in some cases hundreds, of guests all summer plus the wranglers, cooks, and other workers. Conveniences, by modern standards, were rare; some ranches had icehouses where they stored ice cut in the winter while many relied on the cold mountain streams for what little cooling was available for milk and vegetables.[6] Only a few had running water, and kerosene or gasoline lamps were the rule well into the twentieth century at many ranches. When guest went on pack trips in the early days from ranches, their living conditions did not change too drastically; this lack of significant changes helps explain why pack trips were more common before 1940. These large pack trips emphasize the significant supply problems that ranchers faced. When the OTO Ranch took the huge group from the Sierra Club through Yellowstone Park, they used eighty pack horses and sixteen packers with an additional ten mules and two men for the kitchen equipment. The crew was organized like a military unit. While Clyde Erskine rode at the head of the group, the chief packer rode continually up and down the long line checking animals and packs. Charles Moore often used wagons on his early pack trips, and he sometimes needed twelve horses to pull each wagon up the steep inclines along the Continental Divide.[7]

These various conditions meant, of course, that both ranchers and guests were exceedingly dependent on whatever transportation was available. Ranch vacations were rather long because of this; since it often took a week or more to get to a dude ranch, the visitor stayed for weeks or months. On ranches in the northern Rockies, it was not unusual for families to remain in the West for the entire summer; in Arizona some people stayed for six months.[8] Once people arrived, they tended to remain at the ranch. There were numerous short trips to other ranches, rodeos, national parks, and so on, but all activity centered on the ranch.

Early dude ranches depended almost totally on the railroads for long-distance transportation. The earliest well-known men in dude ranching, like Howard Eaton, Theodore Roosevelt, and Owen Wister, came west by rail, and the Northern Pacific even carried the first guests to Eaton's Custer Trail Ranch in North Dakota. Thus, from the beginning, people used the trains to get to the ranches. When the Eatons moved to Wyoming, the guests simply took a longer train trip, and they even used the railroad for some pack trips. When Howard Eaton scheduled one to Glacier or Yellowstone Park, he and the guests rode the train to the park while the horses were hauled there in freight cars. Then the riding part of the expedition began.[9] As dude ranching grew in importance, this dependence on railroads continued, but the railroad officials did not realize the potential of this new business. They were more concerned with visitors to the national parks and actually did the bulk of the advertising for them prior to 1915. They had not shown much interest in the dude ranch business until the early 1920s, when a sudden growth of automobile travel and a reduction in railroad passenger business seemed to shock the railroad officials into an awareness of the importance and growing potential of the guests going west.[10]

This realization reversed their attitude as officials of the Northern Pacific and Burlington railways initiated a cooperation with ranchers that would last for decades. As noted in Chapter 4, railroad officials A. B. Smith and Max Goodsill were the prime movers in getting the ranchers together in Bozeman in 1926 to begin the Dude Ranchers' Association. It was ironic and perhaps fitting that Larry Larom (who had been dumped off the train in the dark at the foot of a water tank on his first visit to Wyoming) was chosen as the first president of the DRA. He remained in that position for eighteen years working closely with the railroads.[11] From this point railroad officials and ranchers worked together on the same goal of getting dudes to take the train west to the ranches. Midwesterners and easterners were exposed to a growing number of advertisements from the railways, in magazines and in other places, that spoke glowingly of the pleasant climate, relaxed living, and intriguing heritage of the ranch country. As noted in Chapter 5, one of the most effective and long-lasting techniques of advertising was the publication of pamphlets or booklets touting the glories of the ranch vacation. These did more than "sell" the railroad and highlight specific ranches; they also explained the background of dude ranching and assured the readers that the word *dude* was not derogatory but "a legitimate hundred percent American term" that meant a visitor from outside the Rocky Mountains.[12] Ranchers soon learned the value of being listed in these books and some credited over 90 percent of their business to such listings.[13]

Some ranchers even arranged special trains for their guests. The Valley Ranch had Pullman cars and a diner put on the train in New York City; its many guests boarded there and the cars were then switched from one railway to another till they reached Cody. Teton Valley Ranch got its youngsters all together in the East on the same train and then shepherded them westward.[14] Most ranches did not have enough guests coming from any one city at the same time to justify such special arrangements but they did point out the ease of rail travel, and the western railways made every effort to give prompt and courteous service to these ranch guests.

The Northern Pacific and Burlington involvement went far beyond simple advertising, however, as officials kept in constant touch with ranchers and attended many of the DRA meetings over the years. A. B. Smith and Max Goodsill were the best known and most active of these visitors, but others also came; as many as four officials from the Northern Pacific attended some DRA meetings. Their presence encouraged numerous discussions about rates, times, routes, and other matters affecting people coming to the ranches. These men were very conscious that there were twenty million automobiles taking people somewhere every day. Seeing each auto passenger as potential lost railroad revenue, they intensified their efforts with dude ranches in order to get as much cross-country business as possible.[15]

Indeed the DRA meetings became virtual workshops as interested railroad men gave ranchers advice and suggestions on how to draw more visitors. Max Goodsill, the general passenger agent, was the most active one doing this work; he was in an advantageous position to help since he received complaints and suggestions from various dudes through different railroad agents. Even after the dude ranchers' most successful year in 1929, Goodsill pointed out some areas for improvement. He noted that, while most reports about dude ranch vacations were favorable, he had heard more complaints than ever that season. The most common complaint was that the guests had expected real cream and home-grown foods but instead got canned milk and vegetables. The solution to that problem was simple: give guests fresh vegetables, milk, and ranch beef whenever possible. Goodsill also noted some of the little things that impressed the dudes: planting flowers in front of the lodge, putting flowers on the table, or placing a piece of ranch equipment in the front yard. Since horses and riding were important to guests, they appreciated it when the boss or wranglers took the trouble to explain bridles and saddles to them, showed them how to judge the age of horses, or let them pick out their own horses. Tied in with these sentiments was the guests' desire to take part in ranch activities. Kids especially liked to help get the cows in, join in the branding of cattle, and take part in any ranch activity. What Goodsill emphasized most, however, was keeping the ranch real—a genuinely western spot. Dudes lived in a land of unreality in the East, surrounded by gilded palaces; when they went on vacation, they wanted to come down to earth and leave artificiality behind them.[16] This astute railroad agent pinpointed some of the errors ranches made by having buildings or decorations that didn't even look western. Some ranches had stucco or tile fireplaces instead of native stone; one had wallboard brought in from New Orleans instead of using native materials. Goodsill noted the superior decorating ability of Mrs. Paul Van Cleve, Mrs. Gay Wyman, and Mrs. Ernest Miller; he urged women who did not possess this ability to ask others for suggestions about furniture and furnishings and praised those at Eatons' Ranch, Norris Ranch, and Elephant Head Lodge. The western ranches had to be truly western and different to satisfy these visitors. Goodsill even wondered if the ranches should emphasize the DRA too much in the East. Because easterners had so many business organizations, they sometimes viewed any such group as a ploy to increase prices. Even though the DRA had no control over or effect on prices, it might be well to avoid even a hint of suspicion in this regard.

He concluded his comments with several specific suggestions. Make a permanent friend of each guest, he urged. "Be sure that you give him enough attention, or her enough attention, so that upon returning home they will swear by you personally and your place."[17] A second suggestion was to go east if possible to see old customers and get new ones; another was to use care and consideration in correspondence. He told a story of one dude who went to Laird's Lodge near Missoula simply because Captain Laird sent a thoughtful letter and a picture of himself. Max Goodsill concluded his suggestions by assuring the ranchers that they could count on the cooperation of the railroads at all times.[18]

After the Great Depression began, ranchers were even more anxious to hear what might be done to regain lost business. A. B. Smith urged ranchers to make trips east if at all possible so they could present a clear and enthusiastic idea of what it meant to be in, and enjoy, the open spaces of the West. The advertising manager for the Burlington Route, H. F. McLaury, was convinced that ranchers did not emphasize their heritage enough. He urged each rancher to capitalize on the history, legends, tradition, and romance of the frontier days associated with the area of his own ranch. Max Goodsill suggested the possibilities of contests in cooperation with theaters and radio stations in the East and of offering a free vacation to one child in a family of newcomers to the ranch. He did not urge a reduction in general rates but thought reductions for lengthy stays or large families might be beneficial. He was generally optimistic since he believed many Americans had the travel habit and would budget money for vacations even in difficult times. But ranchers had to work at getting guests, especially by personal contact.[19]

All of this activity and involvement by the Northern Pacific and Burlington lines seemed to generate interest on the part of other railroads. Soon the giant Union Pacific took an interest in dude ranches. It had been publishing a booklet "Dude Ranches Out West" for several years, and in 1931 the UP sent one of its representatives to the DRA meeting for the first time. Mr. Engleston noted that his line didn't serve many of the ranches that were members of the DRA but did traverse areas where there were some dude ranches: Medicine Bow, Snowy Range, and Jackson Hole country. He correctly predicted that adequate transportation would make Jackson Hole one of the outstanding dude ranch areas in the West.[20] The Union Pacific, possibly from its observation of the success of the DRA, began to work on organizing a ranch group in Colorado, a state that it served extensively. By 1933 it had helped form the Colorado Dude and Guest

Ranch Association.[21] The booklet "Dude Ranches Out West" was continued for years, enlarged to fifty pages or more, and developed into one of the most attractive and comprehensive brochures ever published about ranches. It gave general descriptions of dude ranching, listed which ranches belonged to the DRA and CD & GRA, and then listed and described ranches the UP served in Colorado, Oregon, Montana, Idaho, Washington, Nevada, California, and the different sections of Wyoming.[22]

Another railroad that sent a representative to the DRA meeting for the first time in 1931 was the Chicago, Milwaukee, St. Paul & Pacific Railroad which served Gallatin Gateway, Montana. Mr. Dodge of that line visited Bones Brothers' and Brewster's dude ranches in the summer of 1931 and was very impressed with their hospitality. He admitted at the DRA Convention that the Milwaukee line was the underdog in carrying dude ranch guests but they intended to use their access to Gallatin Gateway to serve those ranches near the northern entrance to Yellowstone Park. This proved so successful that years later the Milwaukee Line even appointed a passenger agent at Butte to call on dude ranchers. Still a third railroad, the Great Northern Railway, sent a representative to the DRA convention for the first time in 1931. Mr. Bates noted that his line was some distance from most member ranches of the DRA, but its access to northern Montana led the Great Northern to take a deeper interest in dude ranching.[23] Because of this the Great Northern too was soon publishing a circular on dude ranches in Montana, Idaho, Washington, Oregon, Alberta, and British Columbia, and the railroad later opened a dude ranch headquarters in New York City. By the mid-1930s brochures, pamphlets, or booklets listing dude ranches for vacation sites were published by the Northern Pacific, Chicago, Burlington & Quincy, Union Pacific, Great Northern, Santa Fe, Southern Pacific, Rock Island, and the Chicago, Milwaukee, St. Paul & Pacific. A few years later they were joined by the Chicago & North Western Line.[24] Not to be outdone, several eastern railroads began to feature dude ranch scenes and advertising; they could not take guests all the way to the ranches, of course, but they hoped to generate business to get people to the connections with the western railways and to garner some of the dude ranch trade that already existed. The Pennsylvania and Baltimore & Ohio issued menu cards featuring ranch vacations, and the B & O did some display advertising about them. The Illinois Central devoted a department in their regular magazine to dude ranching and other western vacations; this went to many parts of the South, an area not very well tapped by the ranchers. The New York Central joined in much of this advertising and even issued its own dude ranch book, "Westward Ho."[25]

The Northern Pacific and Burlington did not cease their involvement as these new lines became active. The NP even provided an office for the DRA executive secretary in the Northern Hotel at Billings and sent out its own photographer, Mr. Brown, to visit as many of the ranches as possible.[26] He took numerous scenic shots, which were used in all sorts of advertising. This photographic collection comprises what is probably the finest pictorial record of dude ranching that exists anywhere. In Chicago and Philadelphia the western railroads also sponsored a travel show for ranches, and their officials joined in western parades and other festivities to keep their name before the public. Like the ranches, they insisted that they were one of the pioneering institutions of the West.[27]

The railroads had to keep active in soliciting passenger business, for they were being pursued and would soon be overtaken by the private automobile. The dude ranchers at first welcomed the automobile as another helpful improvement in transportation but soon came to realize it was also a threat to them because eventually the visitor had too much mobility. For a while, however, ranchers were favorably inclined toward this new mode of travel.

At first the automobile seemed to pose no threat to anyone in the West. The first transcontinental auto trip was made in 1903 by Dr. H. Nelson Jackson of Vermont; it cost $8,000 and took him nine weeks, during which the intrepid doctor lost twenty pounds. Within sixteen years a transcontinental trip was reduced to fifty days with a cost under $1,000, although the automobile had to journey by railroad across one stretch of desert country. Automobiles were obviously improving rapidly and, with passage of the Federal Highway Act of 1916, roads were being improved also. As trips increased in numbers and distance, enterprising people began to build auto camps to accommodate them. A major rival to the dude ranches had come upon the scene.[28]

An even more ominous threat than early transcontinental trips was the entrance of automobiles into Yellowstone Park. One of the first in the area was driven by Jack Scarlett, uncle of Spike Van Cleve. When he journeyed to Yellowstone about 1905, the authorities made him leave his vehicle a few miles inside the boundary at Mammoth Hot Springs because it caused too many problems with the horses pulling stages and wagons. In retrospect, the dude ranchers and railroads would probably both wish that every automobile would have been halted in the same place. For years there were few that came since the authorities prohibited their entry into the park. But on August 1, 1915, private autos were legally admitted and, within two years, Yellowstone was completely motorized as far as transportation and freighting were concerned.[29] The first car was a Ford loaded with tenting and cooking utensils. Robert Sterling Yard, the enthusiastic publicist of the National Parks, praised it: "Those who laughed and those who groaned at sight of it, and there were both, were no seers; for that minute Yellowstone entered upon her destiny."[30]

Yard undoubtedly did not realize the full impact of what he said. While park officials gloried in the increased visitation that the automobiles made possible at Yellowstone and other parks, they could not foresee that the increase would eventually become an avalanche that threatened to inundate the parks.

But the automobile was a fact of life and many westerners saw advantages in it. The Wyoming highway system, begun in 1917, included over 3,000 miles of roads completed by 1931, with nearly half of them gravel, more than the combined totals of unimproved and graded earth roads. There were 341 miles of paved and oiled roads, as those that turned to bottomless gumbo after each rain were being replaced as rapidly as possible. These same officials were convinced that road building would help the ranches by making them more accessible to visitors; it was certainly clear that more people were driving through the Rocky Mountains each year.[31] In Colorado one of the most notable improvements was the completion of the Fall River Road in 1920, linking the east and west sides of Rocky Mountain National Park. By 1932 it was realigned and renamed Trail Ridge Road. Both events increased automotive traffic, bringing hundreds of additional people to this growing tourist locale.[32] Taxpayers in Montana approved a gasoline tax to pay for road construction and, as already noted, civic groups like the Cody Commercial Club worked energetically to improve nearby roads. Ranchers improved their own private access roads so they wouldn't lose the business brought by the auto. At the OTO Ranch the two-mile mountain road was just too steep, narrow, and crooked to be negotiated by a horseless carriage, so a new road was built. It took two years of back-breaking toil, blasting away steep cliff walls to complete it as it crossed the mountain stream thirteen times over log bridges.[33]

In a 1926 article about dude ranches the author boasted about the heritage of the country now crossed by the Rocky Mountain Highway going west from Lander, Wyoming. The historic path of the Shoshones, Arapahoes, fur trappers, and other pioneers was now traversed by a broad, smooth, and well-kept road, wide and safe and thoroughly guarded against the dangers of mountain motoring. She noted that at many spots along the way side roads led to the "innumerable 'dude' ranches" that existed; thus the improved roads there and elsewhere seemed a boon to more business.[34]

A new opportunity for advertising opened up also as automobile clubs developed to dispense information to the motoring public. There was some advertising through the growing American Automobile Association, but the most active of these groups in the dude ranch field seemed to be the Conoco Travel Bureau. As early as 1930 it was including dude ranch advertising with its material, and by 1934 its free trip-planning aids were instrumental in bringing the following number of motor parties to dude ranches, resorts, lodges, and camps: 2,291 to Colorado, 925 to Montana, 669 to New Mexico, 544 to Wyoming, 513 to California, 434 to Arizona, and 109 to Idaho. Less than two years later it was also distributing literature from the Colorado Dude and Guest Ranch Association.[35]

Already, however, some voices warned of the dangers of automobile traffic, which presented three distinct threats to the dude rancher. The first was the growth of many more lodges, cabins, camps, and motels to accommodate auto travelers. The same 1926 article that boasted of the Rocky Mountain Highway noted that "rustic inns . . . came into existence simultaneously with the construction of the highway."[36] Gradually, the number and variety of these facilities increased and offered the tourist new places to stay other than dude ranches. A second and even more threatening problem was the potential destruction of wilderness areas by the constant demand for more roads. John Spencer, assistant regional forester for the Denver District, noted that the Forest Service was besieged by requests to build roads through the national forests. He admitted that arterial highways were needed to connect various communities, and some would have to cross forest land. In addition some secondary roads were needed in the national forests to get out timber and to fight fires. But he realized there was a danger of carrying this building too far; whenever a road was constructed, people flocked in to use it and soon besieged the Forest Service for applications for summer homes and resorts, gasoline stations, coffee shops, and "who knows what else." Some people wanted to start poorly planned developments along these roads with no regard for the damage they did to the scenic aspect of the area. In land usage the Forest Service was much more favorable to the way the dude ranchers operated. They lived in these wild areas year-round, understood the environment, and strove mightily to preserve the unspoiled, natural vacation sites that were at the heart of the appeal of the West. A few years later Spencer noted that the Forest Service had established new primitive areas and barred all auto highways from them, realizing the automobile road was the greatest enemy to the preservation of the wilderness areas.[37] Considering this tremendous impact of roads on the wilderness, it is not surprising that Larry Larom, who spent so much time studying conservation matters, added the study of secondary roads to his interest in national forests and parks.[38]

A third significant problem that the automobile brought to dude ranches was that motorists had an irresistible urge to be moving, even on vacation. It seemed almost as though the pleasure for an auto traveler was in going somewhere rather than ever arriving. This hurt dude ranches in two distinct ways. Some people who wanted a western vacation decided to drive and stay along the way; since the national parks were becoming easily accessible to autos, many of these people saw no reason to go to a ranch. With their own car they could see the beautiful sights and then move on to something else. A second effect of this irresistible urge to move was that guests who did go to ranches stayed a much shorter time. Guests who came by train usually had a specific length of stay in mind, generally three weeks or more, and stuck to their schedule. But motorists often left sooner than planned. They had itchy feet and wanted to use their marvelous new autos to get there, anywhere, as long as it was somewhere else.[39] The dude ranchers, of course, were appalled at this rushing about. They liked

> families who would make long stays, and get their enjoyment out
> of knowing a smaller area intimately and the type of activity well
> rather than short stays which made ranch life chopping instead of
> restful, educational and fun.[40]

It is no surprise that at the Dude Ranchers' Association convention in 1931 one rancher noted that what they wanted was not concrete highways into the ranches,

> rather we want to destroy some of the good roads we have in
> advertising our ranches and make them a sort of wilderness and
> keep them in a natural state. What the easterner wants, I
> presume, is more of the natural life; he sees enough artificial life
> as it is, in fact, he sees too much of it.[41]

Four years later Charles Moore proposed special rates on railroads for families in order to eliminate auto travel. Struthers Burt, who was regarded as one of the old-time dude ranchers by the 1930s, worked with the American Automobile Association on their Committee for Roadside Development, and he attacked one aspect of auto travel in another way. He agreed with the AAA opposition to indiscriminate highway advertising and unplanned building along the highways. This opposition was based on two points: the signs and buildings caused accidents that killed people, and they lessened the value of communities and the countryside by destroying scenic appeal.[42] One has to note that these criticisms and suggestions come from the 1930s and predate by thirty years or more the various "Beautify America" or "Back to Nature" campaigns of the past two decades. This concern also helps explain why dude ranchers have avoided highway advertising and even ostentatious signs indicating the locations of their ranches.

This opposition to automobile travel raises the same question as that posed in Chapter 8 about conservation. Was it merely self-interest that generated this hostility to autos? The answer is the same: of course it was self-interest—partially. The presence of automobiles meant fewer people came to ranches, and those who did come left sooner. But there was more to this opposition that that. Ranchers realized that the hurried and harried visitors needed time to stop and look. It took days or even weeks for someone who jumped out of the hustle and bustle of urban life to get a proper feel for the West and to relax. This was not some idle guess or selfish idea that ranchers had suddenly created. They had seen it in action in their guests for years, and those people who had been publicizing the West had emphasized it constantly for several decades.

The automobile was not the only competitor of the railroads. Another was travel by bus; the Trailways and Greyhound lines became interested in dude ranches and distributed some of their literature.[43] But buses never became a major factor in the dude ranch business except for short-distance trips. Far more of a threat to the railroads were the airlines.

Even in the 1920s airlines were attempting to make a dent in railroad passenger business to the West, but the more serious competition came in the 1930s. In 1931, the same year that three of the railroads first sent representatives to the DRA convention, a local carrier, Wyoming Air Service, sent a Mr. Baldwin to talk to the DRA meeting. He pointed out that Wyoming Air made direct connections with both Boeing Air Transport and Western Air Express at Cheyenne and Denver. Boeing even had a Dude Ranch Special that left New York City at 4:00 P.M. and stopped at Cleveland and Chicago; it left the Windy City at noon and arrived at Cheyenne at 8:56 A.M. Wyoming Air Service made connections from Denver and Cheyenne to Casper and then on to Sheridan and Billings, two major dude ranch centers; the entire plane fare from New York was under $130.00. Baldwin urged the ranchers to use the slogan "Travel by Air" and pointed out that they and his company were working for the same thing—increasing their business.[44] He must have felt a bit uncomfortable at this railroad-dominated conference, for he hastened to explain that the airlines were not trying to compete with the railroads but worked to help them. Baldwin made a valid point when he said the airlines could help the ranches, but it is difficult to see how airline growth could be any help to railroads.

United Airlines became the most active air service in this area as its officials began distributing dude ranch literature in 1932 and put out a folder "Fly to the Dude Ranches." Their people emphasized that some travelers would not or could not take the time to ride trains west. In addition guests who flew to the West could spent more of their vacation time at the ranch, an obvious appeal to all dude ranchers. Besides working with the DRA, United also cooperated with the CD & GRA and began including information on Colorado ranches. United emphasized that it was creating new business for the ranches since most of their passengers were newcomers to the West.[45]

Airline travel was beginning to cut into railroad business somewhat although it was not yet overwhelming. The dude ranchers certainly felt a strong attachment and loyalty to the railroads because of their frequent and continued assistance, but they were not as hostile to the airlines as they were to automobiles. Air passengers and rail passengers tended to be similar. Both had a specific stay in mind and usually had a ticket purchased for the return trip. Of course this was quite different from the automobilists who could pick up and leave whenever the mood struck them. Obviously someone who arrived by plane or train could leave sooner than planned if there were some drastic problem at the ranch or emergency at home, but this was not a common occurrence.

Plane transportation, therefore, was a growing aid to dude ranchers even as it was a threat to the railroads. The great leap in airplane travel, however, would not come till after World War II. Before that situation developed, the war itself brought an entirely new set of difficulties to dude ranches, railroads, and airlines.

When World War II began in Europe in 1939, it was not an immediate problem for dude ranches; in certain ways it probably even helped them. The economy of the United States was gradually improving because of the growing sale of arms to other countries and the nation's own rearmament program; this economic activity certainly made it possible for many people to plan vacations that might otherwise have been deferred. And the trouble across the Atlantic again forced Americans to turn to their own country for vacation opportunities.

But this initial boost was soon offset by difficulties; even in 1940 there was a great deal of uncertainty among Americans as the United States became more involved in the war both in the Atlantic and Pacific theaters. The United States was already supplying aid to Great Britain, while relations with Japan grew continually more strained. Worry about the 1940 presidential election even caused hesitation among people planning vacations, as did concern about business activity. Above all, of course, was the gnawing concern that the United States might get fully involved in the war.[46] These tensions accelerated in 1941, and dude ranchers, like many others, simply didn't know how to plan for the future. One idea, already under way, was to try to entice more people from California to choose ranch vacations instead of relying on the Midwest and East for most visitors. Ranches in California, Nevada, and Arizona had been doing this for years, but now those in other dude ranch states tried it.[47]

The general feeling at the fall 1941 DRA meeting was that business that year had been fairly good, although there was some skepticism about what would come in 1942 because of taxes, economic conditions, and unrest. Max Goodsill of the Northern Pacific thought the cost of living and the European war would alter vacation travel, but he optimistically stated that business would probably be about the same in 1942.[48] Of course, he did not foresee what was about to happen.

In the last month of 1941 the waiting ended. After the attack on Pearl Harbor, the United States made the decision to enter the war both in Europe and Asia. After several years of confusion and uncertainty, the United States became a strongly united country where people boasted loudly of their willingness to sacrifice to win this Great Crusade.

But where would dude ranching fit in this picture? In general it would suffer because of the emphasis on the war and war production. To control and regulate the economy, the federal government soon created another level of bureaucracy that would rival the World War I agencies in size and scope. Especially significant to dude ranching was the rationing of automobile tires and gasoline.[49] Whether ranchers liked it or not, automobile travel was the mode of transportation that many people were using, and now it would be limited. There were also restrictions on train travel, meaning a severe limitation on the method of transportation that ranchers preferred.

The first year of the war was a poor one for the ranchers, and the 1942 DRA meeting was one of intense uncertainty and pessimism. The railroads couldn't get any clear answers from Washington, D.C., about handling tourist travel, although it was obvious that they couldn't operate any additional trains for civilian travel. The airlines had similar problems as the government restricted them also and even took some of their planes. Combined, the restrictions on autos, planes, and trains would make it very difficult for would-be travelers to get to the Rocky Mountain West. President Larom of the DRA urged ranchers to gather data on their food production; he wanted to be able to show that dude ranches were important to the war effort and deserved consideration from the government. Larom was obviously concerned because of the large drop-off in business; he even questioned whether the DRA could continue to operate under the trying wartime conditions. The members were convinced it could and voted unanimously to keep the organization functioning.[50]

In addition to the travel restrictions, the Office of Price Administration and other agencies laid numerous rules and regulations on ranches; because of these, the whole Kawuneeche Valley in Colorado suffered tremendously and the Holzwarth family almost lost its ranch.

Another big difficulty ranchers faced was a shortage of ranch workers, especially wranglers, since the young cowboys joined the military in droves, either as volunteers or draftees. Ranchers fought the problem of insufficient workers in some imaginative ways. In Colorado a number of ranchers simply put the dudes to work; a ranch vacation became a working contribution to the economy and the war effort.[51] While this might sound strange at first, it was not really too unusual. Dude ranchers had seen for years that some guests from the cities considered it relaxing and a change of pace to engage in physical activity on their vacations. The tensions of urban desk jobs in wartime apparently created the same attitude; in addition the patriotic feelings of the wartime emergency encouraged people to do many things differently, if necessary. The Two Bars Seven Ranch, which spread across northern Colorado and southern Wyoming, first began taking guests in the early war years, mainly business executives who needed relaxation from the pressure they were under.[52]

In Wyoming, Larry Larom's Valley and A2Z ranches published a special brochure, "Summer Suggestions." One plan, started in 1943, was called the "Victory Vacation"; organized for youngsters, it provided for a six-to-eight-week stay on the ranch, including a seven-day pack trip at a cost much lower than the regular rate. This was contingent on the willingness of the young people

> to cooperate with the Ranch in its effort to increase war
> production, by devoting several hours each day to helping in the
> vegetable gardens, potato patches, hay fields, corrals, etc., and
> caring for their own cabins.[53]

In Montana ranch hands were equally difficult to find, so Spike Van Cleve hired some Mexican workers for the Lazy K Bar Ranch; they spoke no English but were hard workers and Van Cleve got along well with them.[54]

Besides a shortage of workers, travel restrictions, government rules and regulations, dude ranchers faced another interesting situation—the rise in the price of cattle. Here they had the exact opposite development of what had occurred during the early 1920s and the Depression when cattle prices dropped drastically. Then ranches were encouraged, even forced, to accept guests; now dude ranches were pressured to turn to raising more cattle. The president of the Colorado Dude and Guest Ranch Association, Ralph Salisbury, even predicted that the only ranches that would survive the war years would be those equipped to run cattle or sheep.[55] This significant turn of events in approximately one decade showed the versatility of the working ranch that accepted dudes. Regardless of the twists in the economy many were able to adjust and survive.

During 1943 these adjustments and adaptations made it possible for the ranches to have a fairly successful business year. Guests understood the problems of the shortages of food and help and cheerfully joined in to do the work and enjoy their vacations.[56]

Of course, some of the ranches still suffered; Eatons' Ranch endured a noticeable decline in business primarily because of lack of adequate transportation for the guests. Their decline, however, was not as serious as what they had suffered during the worst days of the Depression. Holzwarth's Neversummer Ranch closed its regular guest operation one year, but they still welcomed anyone who stopped at the ranch; these guests, however, had to eat with the family and join in regular ranch work.[57] In effect, the Holzwarths went back fifty years to the way the first dude ranches had started, providing accommodations for travelers who sought a ranch as the most convenient or interesting place to stay.

Some ranches couldn't adjust or adapt enough and simply closed, like the Ghost Ranch in New Mexico where nearly all the staff quit when the war began.[58] Dude ranch difficulties were also reflected in the special curriculum developed at the University of Wyoming. Lack of sufficient participants led to the cancellation of the special Recreational Ranching program after the 1942–43 school year.

But many ranches and the industry in general continued to fight the various problems brought on by the war. *The Dude Rancher* featured a two-page spread formulated by the Wyoming Department of Commerce and Industry. Titled "The Dude Ranch in War Time," it emphasized the contributions made by dude ranches to the war effort. They supplied beef and other food and offered recreation for soldiers and business executives. Other ranch publicity also emphasized their contributions to the cause, noting that even President Franklin Roosevelt had stated that it was proper for people to engage in recreational activities when possible. Therefore, guests should not feel guilty about going to ranches; they should realize, however, that workers were difficult to find, so they should be considerate and not expect extra service at the ranches.[59] Government officials even made a special effort to see that camps and ranches catering to children got as many ration points or books as necessary to buy food and other supplies and keep operating.[60]

Railroad officials expressed their desire to continue handling vacation travelers in keeping with the expressed desires of government leaders to maintain a proper balance between work and recreation. But there was no mistake about priorities when the president of the Northern Pacific wrote to the president of the Dude Ranchers' Association: "Nothing will be done, however, which will interfere with meeting the needs for the transportation of our fighting forces and the things they must do to win the fight."[61]

The transportation difficulties, which remained a serious problem, occasionally worked for the dude rancher. If guests once got to a ranch, they were likely to stay longer than in previous years simply because it was so difficult to go anywhere else. In addition western ranches played host to more local people than before; native westerners had not been a factor at most ranches before this, but now they too began to see the attraction of a trip to the mountains as a break from the strains and pressure of war work. There were also more local people to draw on since there were many war workers, military personnel, and relatives of military men in the mountain West during the early 1940s. An analysis of military personnel throughout the country showed that in 1943 they made up 14.9 percent of the total 1940 employment figures; in the mountain West the percentage was substantially higher than that national average—33.9 percent. In Arizona it was an incredible 95.9 percent, and three of the other four principal dude ranch states showed similar high figures: New Mexico—32.1 percent; Colorado—29.4 percent; Wyoming—26.6 percent. Thus, with the exception of Montana (5.4 percent), there were considerably more people close to the dude ranches than ever before.[62] Toward the end of the war the government even developed a program to send some soldiers on free vacations to dude ranches for an unusual rest and recuperation trip.[63]

Thus dude ranches again survived a serious disruption and adapted to a totally new, but temporary, situation. They stood in good stead as one part of the giant effort that gripped Americans totally from 1941 to 1945. Now the ranchers would have to face a nation with changed attitudes, values, and expectations.

TEN

Hopes and Realities

The Western Ranch by its very nature cannot let anything change it. If it does, at that very moment it will cease to be a Western ranch.

—*Boston Post,* April 1, 1934.

Although regarded as an historical curiosity by many in the modern world, the dude ranch has played a significant role in the evolution of American society. . . . As a living embodiment of the past, it was an oasis where the Western mystique ever grew afresh.

—Jerome L. Rodnitzky, "Recapturing the West:
The Dude Ranch in American Life," 126.

There is no doubt that World War II injured the natural growth and development of dude ranching. This interruption was particularly discouraging because it came just as the ranches were recovering from the devastating effects of the Great Depression. As noted in the previous chapter, ranchers showed their adaptability by offering various plans to alleviate the wartime problems of shortages and restrictions and by reemphasizing the raising of cattle and sheep in their operations.

Despite these measures they looked forward to a return to normal conditions when the war ended in 1945. The ranchers eagerly awaited the resumption of adequate plane flights and train arrivals to bring guests in great numbers.[1] To an extent, they were not disappointed, as business clearly picked up when the 1946 season began. Recovery was not total, since there were still some shortages in food and manpower, but there was no doubt that change was under way and times were improving.[2]

The recovery, however, did not necessarily mean a return to the life of the prewar years. The postwar United States would be different in many ways, and these differences would be very noticeable in dude ranching. The most immediate and obvious change in the West was growth. The war had brought many people to the West, and the impact on individuals and on the country was significant. Many easterners were impressed with the uncrowded western states; they enjoyed the pleasant climate and general atmosphere of the friendly and relatively un-settled wide-open spaces, especially in the Rocky Mountains. Fields and open areas soon filled up with villages and housing developments. A boom that affected the entire country was especially noticeable in the West as climate and scenic attractions became major factors in people's decisions about where to live as well as in the burgeoning recreation industry. Employment in service industries grew dramatically in the western states; between 1940 and 1960 it increased five times as fast as the national average. In addition to its appeal for those who had seen it during the war, the West also received substantial sums of federal money that boosted its growth.[3]

Many people who didn't move to the Rockies visited dude ranches to get a taste of the area they wished to see, while the new citizens there increased the potential number of local visitors to dude ranches. Three women who had served in the Women's Army Corps in the West carried their dream farther than most by operating their own dude ranch after the war—the Lucky GJ Ranch near Gypsum, Colorado.[4]

A general feeling of improvement and growth was tempered by less desirable changes in the American life-style. The end of travel restrictions seemed to release an overwhelming desire for Americans to travel constantly by automobile. The trend to personal mobility which was clearly growing in the 1920s and 1930s became much more pronounced after 1945. A figurative love affair between Americans and their automobiles became evident as people made up for lost time; the previous years of onerous travel restrictions were forgotten as they hurried to see the U.S.A. Gasoline was cheap, the economy boomed, and the auto and petroleum companies urged people to travel. It may, at times, have seemed like a race as Americans were intent on seeing as much as possible on their vacations in the West. This was, of course, an acceleration of a trend from the 1930s, but the boom this time would be longer and the effects on the West more profound.

The combination of more people in the West with these changed attitudes had varied effects on dude ranching in different states. The ranches so affected can be grouped in four areas: Colorado, Wyoming and Montana, Arizona and New Mexico, and the balance of the western states.

In general, dude ranching in Colorado benefited from postwar change. Tourism in the Centennial State, increasing before the war, continued to grow after the conflict.[5] The appeal of Colorado was partly due to the mountains there; the Rockies spread across the United States from the Canadian to the Mexican border, but they attain their most imposing mass in Colorado. There are more than 50 peaks over 14,000 feet and over 350 above 11,000 feet; since mountain scenery was always one of the chief attractions for easterners, it was natural for Colorado to become a major tourist state. It also had millions of acres of national forests, several national monuments, state forests, and two national parks. The state also had a major metropolitan center—Denver—which became a central point for transportation in the West. Soon Colorado was easily accessible by air and by road as well as by train; in the years after World War II millions of tourists were arriving and spending several billion dollars annually. Tourism was clearly to be a major factor in Colorado from this point on.[6]

Dude ranches were a substantial part of the travel picture; there were at least thirty of them by 1947 and four more were started during the rest of that decade: Tumbling River Ranch, C Lazy U Ranch, Lost Valley Ranch, and the Don K Ranch, the first dude ranch in the Pueblo area. In the 1950s at least six more were started: Rawah Ranch, Deer Valley Ranch, Peaceful Valley Lodge and Guest Ranch, Lake Mancos Ranch, Idlewild Guest Ranch, and Amani Mgeni Uwanda; the last name was Swahili for Harmony Guest Ranch. It was built by Mr. and Mrs. Scott Hayes; Mr. Hayes adopted the unusual name because of his hunting trips to Africa.[7] These new Colorado ranches, like the older ones, were scattered throughout the state with a substantial concentration around Rocky Mountain and Mesa Verde national parks. One noticeable fact about these new ranches, and most others begun after the war, is that few of them raised cattle or sheep; they were developed for recreational use, and were not the direct outgrowth of stock ranches.[8] The pioneering phase of dude ranching was over; it was no longer the primary recreational industry drawing people west. Many ranches were now the beneficiaries of westward drives launched by state tourist or development bureaus or of impulses developed by easterners on their own.

Another clear sign of the growth of Colorado ranches was the formal organization of the Colorado Dude and Guest Ranch Association. The ranchers had done some publicizing before but, in early 1945, they gathered to begin more intense work.[9] The CD & GRA soon became a very businesslike and aggressive organization; it held workshops on dude ranch problems as the many new owners joined the "old-timers" in discussing mutual difficulties and in seeking solutions to them. Colorado state officials began attending these conventions as they realized that dude ranches were an integral part of the state's burgeoning tourist industry.[10]

While there was a clear surge in dude ranching in Colorado after the war, there was no similar dramatic increase in Wyoming or Montana in the postwar years. This did not mean there was a drastic decline in these two states; many ranches actually went back to a nearly peak season in 1946.[11] But this was mostly a return to fairly good business rather than a long new boom. Far fewer new dude ranches were begun in these two northern states in the decade after the war than in Colorado. Most of the ranches that had been operating immediately before the war did continue. The Dude Ranchers' Association remained the major spokesman for ranches in these two states as well as for a few in other states that joined it. The DRA members were very conscious of their unique background and character and paid special attention to the way they functioned. They were especially concerned about not taking transient trade; such a move might cause government officials to classify them as public places. This could subject ranches to various hotel laws and force them to accept anyone who wished to stay; numerous ranchers, especially those who had operated for many years, also disliked this possibility since they still regarded the dudes as personal guests in their homes and wanted to be able to choose these visitors.[12]

Among the older ranches that continued to prosper in Montana was Elkhorn Ranch near Gallatin Gateway. In the 1940s owner Ernest Miller went on a hunting trip to Arizona and discovered a ranch near Robles that he liked. He purchased it, named it Elkhorn also, and it became the winter version of the family's Montana ranch.[13] The Millers were thus able to combine the best of both the northern and southern Rockies in offering ranch vacations to guests.

Other ranches in Arizona, as well as those in New Mexico, were undergoing a boom similar to the one in Colorado. These two southwestern states had developed rather slowly, not attaining statehood until 1912. In the period since World War II, however, both have experienced rapid growth. Most southwestern dude ranches had begun as cattle ranches just as had those in Colorado, Montana, and Wyoming, but the factors that later drew people to Arizona and New Mexico differed significantly from those drawing visitors to the northern states. The Southwest was interesting for its winter sunshine and dry, pollution-free climate rather than for snow-clad mountains or large herds of big game animals. Southwestern dude ranches had gradually become famous for emphasizing relaxation rather than vigorous outdoor activities, and these differences were accentuated after 1945. Instead of treks through pine forests or over mountains that held snow all year long, these ranches featured desert rides or hikes past cactus and other "exotic" plants; desert picnics were common, and most ranches built swimming pools and other sports facilities.[14] Informal, friendly, and comfortable, many of the postwar ranches were strictly for guests, although some remained working ranches. Most also began using the phrase *guest ranch* instead of *dude ranch;* there is no clear explanation why this distinction was made in these states except for the fact that some visitors disliked the word *dude.*[15]

New Mexico ranches were spread over the state, but most were concentrated in the northern, mountainous section around Taos and Santa Fe. One of the oldest of these was Vermejo Park Ranch, which was discussed earlier; the Vermejo Park Club had been disbanded during the Great Depression and the land was leased for raising cattle. In the 1940s and 1950s, W. J. Gourley, a businessman from Fort Worth, began buying the Vermejo land and surrounding areas till he owned 480,000 acres. He brought in more wild game, especially elk, turkey, and buffalo, improved the lakes, and, in 1952, reopened a guest operation, which continued for eighteen years till Gourley's death in 1970; in 1973 his estate sold the ranch to the Vermejo Park Corporation. This group returned the ranch to what it had been when Mr. Bartlett had developed it between 1901 and 1917— a very luxurious ranch resort featuring fishing, hunting, and horseback riding. It includes three separate lodges, each equipped with a dining room and fully staffed with cooks, waitresses, and maids. A number of other huge, resort-type ranches developed in New Mexico, some of them located on Indian reservations. With tracts of land from 10,000 to 750,000 acres, many have offered substantial isolation to visitors to the Land of Enchantment.[16]

Arizona ranches, more numerous than those in New Mexico, were mostly concentrated around Tucson and Wickenburg. Many new ones opened after 1945, although several older ones still functioned: Faraway Ranch near Douglas, Circle Z Ranch at Patagonia, Kay El Bar Guest Ranch at Wickenburg, Tanque Verde Ranch near Tucson, and Rancho de la Osa at Sasabe. While most Arizona guest ranches were started later than those in the northern Rockies, they had somewhat the same effect of drawing people to the state and thus boosting the economy and the population. Most Arizona ranches, like those in New Mexico, became much more elaborate than the northern ones. Tanque Verde featured tennis, indoor and outdoor swimming pools, volleyball, basketball, and visits to nearby racetracks in addition to horseback riding, hiking, and rodeos. It boasted that it was one of only twenty-two places in the United States (and only two in Arizona) that was listed in the *300 Best Hotels in the World.*[17] Many southwest ranches became indistinguishable from resorts and, with the growth of the area, the trend to resorts accelerated. More and more of them emphasized tennis, swimming, room service, and dressing in coat and tie for dinner; those that remained ranches maintained horseback riding, cookouts, and an informal atmosphere as the key attractions.[18]

While dude ranches have tended to grow more elaborate everywhere, the trend is most noticeable in Arizona and New Mexico. One of the reasons for this is the phenomenal urban growth, especially near Tucson. Spots chosen as guest ranch sites were remote from that city when it was relatively small, but many of them were eventually surrounded by the rapidly growing town. Once an area became crowded, subdivided, and incorporated, horseback riding and other ranch activities became nearly impossible, so the ranch would become a resort. A count of the number of guest ranches near Tucson at twenty-year intervals shows this change dramatically. At the beginning of World War II there were probably just ten ranches close to the city; by 1960 the number had mushroomed to an estimated seventy-five as the area became well known. Then urban growth and other factors began reducing these until there were only ten by 1980.[19] This change accentuated another difference between southern and northern dude ranches; those in the north were generally working ranches on land far from urban centers and frequently adjacent to national forests or parks. These federal lands became protective devices against overcrowding and loss of outdoor recreation sites. In addition working ranches had to own hundreds or thousands of acres to be economically viable; their size guaranteed that they would have substantial areas where access to open country would be maintained. After World War II many Arizona ranches were developed just for recreation, and few owned large tracts of land that could serve as buffers against unwanted crowding. Those that have endured, such as White Stallion and Tanque Verde, own hundreds of acres of land that have protected them from being swallowed by the city.

Urban sprawl is not the sole factor, however, that has led to the metamorphosis from ranch to resort. The attractions that drew people to Arizona ranches were also significant contributors to this change. The long season of sunshine meant that those ranches would draw "sun seekers"—golfers, swimmers, tennis players, and those who just wanted to escape foul weather. Some families came to Arizona for months during the winter, so ranches there emphasized their proximity to quality schools as a drawing card; Monk's Guest Ranch even advertised that it was within walking distance of a modern public school.[20] Obviously ranch owners who tried to locate their ranches for the convenience of school children could not choose remote, wilderness locations.[21]

People seeking places to swim, play tennis, or enjoy warm winter weather increased significantly in the postwar years; these visitors differed from early dudes in both the southern and northern Rockies. Early dudes sought quiet, isolated havens accessible to the wilderness; hospitality and scenic beauty were their objectives. The continual popularity of Arizona ranches and the growth of the surrounding areas led to crowded swimming pools and busy tennis courts, heavy traffic that created pollution, formal meals, and even room service at some places. As these characteristics were hardly conducive to isolation or scenic beauty, many guest or dude ranches had to change and become resorts.

The continuing growth in the number of ranches in Arizona led to the development of several organizations. The Arizona Dude and Guest Ranchers' Association, formed in the late 1920s, lasted only a few years. In the next decade the Arizona Hotel and Dude Ranch Association included eight Arizona ranches as well as one in California.[22] In the 1940s the Southern Arizona Guest Ranch Association was formed and in the mid-1960s was replaced by the Southern Arizona Dude and Guest Ranch Association. In about 1965 this group merged with some of the resort hotels and changed its name to the Tucson Innkeepers, Ranch and Resort Association. Also in the 1960s ranchers near Wickenburg formed the Desert Sun Ranchers. These last two organizations still exist, but most of the members of the Tucson group are motels and hotels, not ranches.[23] These numerous Arizona groups and the organizational change to the Tucson Innkeepers symbolize the growth and rapid alteration that has occurred in Arizona guest ranching.

Besides the guest and dude ranches in Wyoming, Montana, Colorado, Arizona, and New Mexico, there have been others scattered over a number of other western states. Approximately a dozen have been listed in Texas since World War II, with the majority centered around Bandera, about forty-five miles northwest of San Antonio. These Texas ranches have been similar in style to those of Arizona and New Mexico, with rather elaborate facilities. The Flying L Ranch has its own golf course, water skiing, sailing, and motorboating; Mayan Dude Ranch features an underwater-lighted swimming pool, a Hawaiian luau, breakfast brought to guest cottages by chuck wagon, and a driving range.[24]

As noted in Chapter 4, several Nevada dude ranches were originally successful in the 1920s and 1930s because of that state's divorce law; there was even a Nevada Dude Ranch Association with a few members in the 1930s. The use of dude ranches as pleasant places to fulfull residency requirements for divorce continued for many years. Women from the eastern states and California often went to Glenbrook or Donner Trail Ranches for six weeks. When one of them finally went to court for the divorce decree, she had to have a witness who could swear that he or she had seen the woman in the state every day of the six weeks, and a dude ranch owner or manager often served as this witness. Some Nevada ranches were of the more traditional type, featuring riding and ranch life. Ten guest ranches of the various types have remained into the 1970s.[25] California has had a dozen or so ranches listed over the years, with a few of them belonging to the Dude Ranchers' Association. Pierson Dude Ranch was a working cattle and horse outfit that dated back to the 1880s; located east of Fresno, it was a member of the DRA for many years. Hunewill Circle "H" Ranch is a cattle ranch in eastern California that currently belongs to the DRA; comprising nearly 5,000 acres and accepting but forty guests, the operation seems very much like the early dude ranches of the northern Rockies.[26]

Idaho, like California, had about a dozen dude ranches listed at various times over the years; they seem to have been similar to those in Montana and Wyoming. They were located in the northern panhandle area, around Sun Valley, or near the western entrance to Yellowstone Park. Both Oregon and Washington have ranch country in the eastern parts of the states, and dude ranching gained footholds there. In the late 1930s, DRA executive secretary Walter Nye met with some Oregon ranchers in Pendleton to form a state dude ranch organization, which functioned as an affiliate of the DRA.[27] After the war, dude ranching picked up a little with eight ranches in Oregon and eleven in Washington. Dude ranching never became a strong factor in either state, however, and only a few ranches continued through the 1970s. Those that did exist there were in the central or eastern portions of the two states.[28]

Since World War II there have been a few scattered ranches that accepted guests in Utah, Kansas, Nebraska, and North and South Dakota. Arkansas had one, Scott Valley, admitted to the Dude Rancher's Association in 1967.[29]

As mentioned earlier, some eastern facilities were advertised as dude ranches in obvious imitation of those in the West. Beginning in the mid-1930s, they offered a much closer and cheaper vacation to those in the large eastern population centers. Westerners always maintained that dude ranches existed only west of the Mississippi River, but surprisingly the Dude Ranchers' Association accepted as a member the Indian River Ranch Company of New Smyrna, Florida.[30] Most eastern ranches were in the mountains: the Berkshires of Massachusetts, Poconos of Pennsylvania, Kittatinies of New Jersey, and the Adirondacks and Catskills of New York. In 1943 several of these ranches even established the Eastern Dude Ranches Association, which set up standards regarding food and accommodations and required its members to have at least twenty-five horses. These eastern ranches were quite popular during World War II, when travel restrictions and wartime jobs made long vacations impossible. But whether they were true ranches or not, they were not passing fads; many have remained through the decades after the war.[31]

Most were in New York, and that state even published a pamphlet on its dude ranches. It listed twenty of them in the Hudson Valley, the Catskills, Long

Island, and the Adirondack-Champlain area. New York claims a heritage of cowboys older than that of the trans-Mississippi West to justify using the term *ranches*. It is true that there were references to "cowboys" in New York during the American War for Independence. In a neutral area of that state, guerrilla war was waged by irregular bands from both sides. Those from the British side were called "cowboys" and those from the American side "skinners."[32] New Yorkers even go back a century earlier than this for their cowboy heritage; mounted men herded cattle on Long Island in 1661. These two examples seem to offer a pretty slim basis for the use of the phrase *dude ranch,* but the whole sequence of events reemphasizes what has been stated before: enterprising people saw that it was a clever idea to play on the popularity of a phrase that westerners had developed. That New York state would have a large number of these "ranches" is quite logical since New York City was one of the prime areas where western ranches advertised for guests. But New York was not the only dude ranch locale; an estimated one hundred ranches were scattered over New York, Pennsylvania, Virginia, North Carolina, Maine, Massachusetts, Illinois, Wisconsin, and Michigan.[33] In the 1970s country singer Loretta Lynn even advertised her vacation facility at Hurricane Mills, Tennessee, as a dude ranch. And singer Rosemary Clooney had an "Aqua-Slim Health Farm" forty miles from Cincinnati that was advertised as a vacation resort, health spa, and dude ranch.[34]

The enthusiasm for dude ranches even spread beyond the borders of the United States. Several operated in Canada, and there was one in Mexico—Meling Ranch, a working cattle outfit southeast of Ensenada. Dude ranching also became a vacation vogue in France; several were developed near Paris while others were located in the Camargue. This area of land near the Rhône River north of Marseilles closely resembles the American West, and here was located the Domaine de Mejanes, a working ranch that raised horses, beef cattle, and fighting bulls. Here tourists could ride horses, buy western jeans and cowboy hats, and sleep in small bunkhouses. One ranch offered the tourist a branding ceremony and celebration called a *ferrade;* it started at 10:00 A.M. and lasted most of the day.[35]

Obviously the phrases *dude ranch* and *guest ranch* have been broadly used to include a wide variety of vacation facilities that bear little resemblance to ranches. The ranches in Canada and probably the one in Mexico were legitimate dude ranches, but the others have simply appropriated a term that does not really apply to their vacation resorts.

Advertising for western dude ranches after World War II has followed the patterns used before the war. The colorful practice of going east to sign up guests continued for years. Members of the Colorado Dude and Guest Ranch Association used to go to Chicago en masse; they shipped their horses back by train, held a big parade, and drew a lot of attention to themselves and ranch vacations. Larry Larom and other ranchers continued to make personal eastern contacts even into the 1960s.[36] By 1980, however, few ranchers took trips to the East to sign up guests, and this practice had become rare.

Another major method of publicity was, of course, reliance on railroads and airlines, and all ranches had to publish quality brochures. The photographs and wording of the brochures were often the only way prospective guests could judge a ranch, so these were often professionally produced and quite attractive. Ranches tended to rely to some degree on city or state chambers of commerce or tourist bureaus, but these organizations were effective only in those few states where there were substantial numbers of ranches, primarily Wyoming, Colorado, Montana, Arizona, and New Mexico. Dude ranches also relied on their two major organizations for publicity: the Dude Ranchers' Association and the Colorado Dude and Guest Ranch Association. The former has lost members since World War II, but it has enlarged its scope by accepting ranches from many states west of the Mississippi. The concentration of membership, however, has always remained in Wyoming and Montana. The CD & GRA has been a bit more aggressive in its advertising but not as restrictive in its membership policies, allowing more facilities of the resort type to join.

Dude ranches also benefited from more books about specific ranches. As can be seen from the bibliography, a few of these were published in the 1950s and more than a dozen in the 1960s and 1970s. And, just as in the 1920s and 1930s, articles have continued to appear in popular periodicals. These books and articles have a special appeal for those who know the area or ranch being described. The books, written by ranch owners and guests, emphasize the ranchers' hospitality as well as enjoyable and humorous incidents that have occurred on the ranch. The articles tend to be short, bright vignettes of ranch life that may tempt the reader to sample a ranch vacation.

Few of these books or articles have dealt with the rather serious problems that dude ranches had to face after the war. These problems led eventually to the disappearance of many ranches, and to substantial changes in others. Some of the difficulties, and their results, are the same ones any business must face. Any industry that booms, as dude ranching did in the 1920s and in some places in the 1940s and 1950s, attracts new entries into the field. Some of these postwar newcomers did not understand ranching and its demands, some people were not talented enough or otherwise suited to the business, and some chose poor locations. Even when these difficulties were not present, there was the basic problem of supply and demand. The boom brought an oversupply of ranches, and, as demand slackened, some ranches inevitably failed. Added to this was an essential problem of northern dude ranching, the short season of three to four months; it sometimes wasn't sufficiently long for the rancher to earn enough income to cover annual expenses.[37] The working dude ranch generally had an advantage here.

Many dude ranchers also failed to develop adequate advertising. They had come to rely too much on word-of-mouth and personal contacts in the early days and neglected to broaden their approach as times changed. In most states they even failed to demonstrate how much business they brought to the area; ranchers were frequently urged to supply statistics so they could impress their significance on state officials, but many were reluctant to do so and many apparently did not keep detailed records to draw from.[38]

Of course, many ranches did handle these normal problems as well as some extraordinary ones. During the Korean War they again had to cope with a manpower shortage, although it never became as severe as it had been in World War II.[39] They had to deal with occasional complaints about poor service and with the problem of heavy rain or other inclement weather that reduced the number of customers. There was even the humorous report that the CD & GRA had to expel a ranch near Kremmling because it operated a sunbathing complex for nudes![40]

But other changes after the war were more baffling to confront. The attitudes of many people had changed significantly, especially in demanding modern comforts. While guests of the 1920s often resented any changes at their favorite ranch that smacked of modernism, those of the 1950s and later demanded private baths, wall-to-wall carpeting, swimming pools, and other conveniences. Some dude ranches refused to accede to all these demands and insisted on basing the ranch vacation on outdoor activities, simple food, and western informality. Some of these failed; even those that survived acceded to many of the conveniences, such as electricity and private baths for each guest or family.[41] Some ranches, especially after 1960, gave in even more as they saw roadside lodges and motels taking much of their business. This applied especially to ranches close to major highways; people were drawn to places with cocktail lounges, swimming pools, and restaurants so many of the ranches adopted these "nonranch" facilities and became more like resorts or lodges. This is very evident in New Mexico, Texas, and Arizona as well as in certain parts of Colorado. Another aspect of this "softness" in dudes was that many just weren't as rugged as the visitors of early decades. Short horseback rides were all they wanted; they weren't up to rides of twenty to thirty miles in a day, or they were unwilling to try them. This trend seems to reflect a general change throughout America; people wanted to be entertained more than they wanted to participate in vigorous activities—an attitude that marks a clear example of the distinction between a traveler and a tourist when applied to vacations. The advent of television is an aspect and symbol of this; as people became accustomed to getting anything at the push of a button, even spectator sports did not require a person to leave his own home.

With this changing attitude, the form of horseback riding began to replace its substance and purpose. People were satisfied with rides of an hour or two or even a ride in the corral or arena on a ranch. After all, they could see the mountains or forests or deserts; why did they have to go out into them? Of course, most of these people did not even realize what they were missing or what they were deciding when they chose short rides. They simply had no concept of being in the forest or desert instead of looking at them. Even those who opted for pack trips tended to choose short ones of one night so they wouldn't be too inconvenienced. After all, one couldn't ride in the rain, or be uncomfortable![42] It became easier to play at the western life and boast of a ranch vacation rather than really work (as early ranch visitors had) at the exciting and unpredictable reality of life in the wilderness. Some ranches accommodated every demand and desire of the comfort-seeking, pleasure-dominated tourists and became elaborate resorts. Some people even began to associate "dude ranch" with "posh resort," not realizing that the latter were descendants of the real dude ranch.[43] Those people seeking a true outdoor vacation then turned away from dude ranches because they assumed this resort image applied to all ranch vacations. Dude ranches were well suited for those interested in ecology, but the environmentalists and backpackers did not seem to realize the dude ranches had been offering the outdoor, back-to-nature vacation for over half a century. The modern nature seekers do not have to depend on a ranch for a base of operations into the wilderness; a camper parked along the road or a car in a government campground apparently serves the same purpose that an old-time ranch did in the 1880s or 1920s.[44] The modern backpackers assume they are getting back to nature with their aluminum pack frames, heavy boots, and freeze-dried foods, but a pack train of horses or mules winding its way into the forest or mountains is actually the more natural and historic way of seeing the wilderness. It is also less dependent on modern technology than the methods symbolized by a camper along the road or a light-weight butane stove.

Tied in with these changes of attitude, of course, are the transportation changes already mentioned. The easy availability of automobiles and constant improvements of roads created the tourist business that demanded the motels and tourist lodges.[45] The West was actually becoming too accessible to retain the appeal it once had. People could drive for miles and see mountains all along the way;

what need was there to see more? One mountain looked like any other mountain when seen from a paved road. It was quite different when one struggled on horseback up a rough mountain trail. The horseman seldom forgot the difficulties of surmounting a steep or treacherous climb, the loose rock or jumbled boulders of a mountain slide, or the drenching rain that struck unexpectedly. But he or she also never forgot the sights, the smells, and the silence that rewarded the horseback *traveler*.

As noted earlier, ranch stays declined in length as auto transportation increased. Ranchers simply had to accept the fact that most people wanted only short vacation stops, although some insisted on a minimum stay for which they would accept reservations. The average ranch vacation became one to two weeks instead of the one-to-three-month visits of earlier decades. One "ranch" in Wyoming even tried to meet the objections of visitors who didn't like long visits or the need for making reservations. The owners created the Dude-for-a-day Ranch near Jackson, Wyoming in 1956. For ten dollars the rapidly moving tourist could get a horse and two cook-out meals while being shepherded by a guide on one of several available rides near the Gros Ventre River.[46]

What might have looked like a fad for speed in the 1930s became a mania in the 1950s and later. People had to drive their autos everywhere; for a while this meant a loss of potential vacation time since these tourists spent seven to ten days on the road. Good highways and larger, more powerful automobiles reduced travel time significantly but didn't alter the incessant desire to move about. In a sense the public was being logical in traveling by automobile; travel by private car was cheaper, and people wanted to see as much as possible in as short a time as they could. Many more people were enjoying vacations as the automobile enabled families of different economic groups to take vacations to distant spots.[47] The masses were on the road and naturally their demands were met. Dude ranches were rapidly losing their ascendancy in their western strongholds.

The railroads fought the threat posed by auto travel. They continued to cooperate with dude ranchers by providing good service and advertising, sending out photographers, and even helping new ranches get started.[48] The Chicago, Burlington & Quincy Railroad officials estimated in 1950 that they spent $50,000 on summer tourist advertising, and 20 percent of that was on dude ranch advertising. Ranchers made special efforts to get people to travel by train or plane; they continued to meet guests at depots, airports, or bus stations and even emphasized that people could rent cars in the West if they wanted to go somewhere after their ranch vacation. The change in transportation was inevitable, however, and nothing was to stop it. Even people who saw railroad advertisements for ranches often traveled by automobile to go West. Ranchers had once met the same train or plane to welcome the same guests every year, but they had to face the reality that the whole world was now open to the vacationist. The Dude Ranchers' Association tacitly admitted the change in a new constitution in 1950; previous constitutions mentioned cooperation with railroads but this one stated the ranchers would seek cooperation with airlines, railroads, and other transportation agencies.[49]

The railroads continued publishing their fine brochures with maps, descriptions, and beautiful photographs to the end of the 1950s. But the decline was too sharp and obvious; railroad passenger business was in a permanent decline and railroad officials less frequently visited conventions of the dude ranch organizations.[50] Some ranchers didn't compensate for the gradual but significant loss of the primary form of published advertising, and these ranches declined also. There was a burst of hope when Amtrak began its operation, but its passenger business was often poor; service declined, connections were not convenient, and rail travel for long distances never regained its earlier popularity.[51]

Airlines picked up part of the slack left by the railroads. They kept pushing their logical theme that the vacationist could save time by flying and use that time for a longer trip. In the late 1950s Northwest Orient Airlines joined with the Montana Highway Commission to produce a twenty-two-minute color-sound motion picture about dude ranches. Titled "We Dude It," it was available on loan from either Northwest or the Montana Highway Commission. Ranchers came to realize that they had to accept air travel and cooperated with the airlines whenever possible.[52] Dude ranch vacations were featured in brochures published by Frontier, Continental, Braniff, and United Airlines. These items were useful, and dude ranchers' use of them shows that many ranches made the transition to modern forms of advertising successfully. But airlines did not really take the place of railroads; much of the airline literature featured "package deals" with only a few specific ranches included. Airlines had too much other business to concentrate on dude ranches; they never published on a regular basis anything as complete or useful as the railroad dude ranch booklets.[53] The concept of the package deal itself is symbolic of the insistence of the modern tourist for short, rushed, action-packed trips of seven to ten days.

Obviously the transportation changes after World War II permanently altered dude ranching. One of the few modern events in transportation that has helped the ranches has been the energy crisis of the 1970s; that tended to limit itinerant travel while helping destination travel. In other words it forced vacationists to stay put—exactly what dude ranchers desire.[54] The long-range energy situation, however, is quite uncertain, so there is no way to predict how it may affect dude ranches in the coming decades.

Another major problem faced by the dude ranch industry is the loss of ranch land. Dude ranchers were certainly successful in selling their style of vacation to some people, since many guests decided to buy ranches. Paul Van Cleve of the Lazy K Bar Ranch questioned fellow ranchers and estimated that former guests owned more western land than the dude ranchers did. The DRA magazine even published two articles giving details to people interested in buying ranches.[55] The interest in moving to the West increased with the growing affluence of Americans and the constantly improving transportation. Land values, of course, skyrocketed in the 1960s and 1970s; one rancher in the Jackson Hole area spent $150,000 for land and improvements and saw the value (in paper dollars anyway) shoot to $1 million in just a few years. The profit from dude ranching could not approach the income that could be obtained by selling some ranches and investing the money elsewhere. Thus many ranches have disappeared, going into the hands of rich business executives or large corporations. Some ranchers have resisted that apparent road to a life of ease because they find their way of life more interesting and satisfying than anything they could buy; others have been content to stay with the land that seemed to be appreciating more rapidly than anything else. When ranches have been sold, however, it has usually meant the end of dude ranching in one more spot. New owners often have had no desire or need to accept guests; or, if a corporation was involved, any tourist operation planned had to be on a grand or luxurious scale, and an elaborate resort, rather than a dude ranch, was the likely result.[56] There is even a realty company in Denver that specializes in merchandising large ranches to wealthy clients who want to live in the West. Adding to the loss of land is the fact that some children of ranch parents do not want to stay in the ranch business and are willing to accept an attractive offer to sell. Once a dude ranch is sold, it is seldom replaced; the capital required to purchase the land (if a suitable tract can be found), put up buildings, and buy horses and machinery is simply too large for a newcomer to the West to acquire easily. The amount needed would return more dividends if put in a bank or otherwise invested.[57]

In addition to all these problems, dude ranches faced one more that is probably the most frustrating and bewildering of all—the hostility and opposition of the federal government. Some people foresaw these difficulties as far back as 1958; in *The Dude Rancher* a writer noted it was impossible to analyze the future of ranching because farming and ranching had "become a socialized or government controlled operation and there isn't a man alive who can foretell what the government will do."[58] If things were bad then, they certainly deteriorated in the 1960s and 1970s. Some of these problems with the federal government were the same as those faced by other businesses: social security and other taxes constantly increased, workmen's compensation laws became more stringent, and paperwork piled up. One curse that emanated from Washington was the Occupational Safety and Health Act (OSHA), which gave federal inspectors practically unlimited authority to check anywhere for safety violations. Ranch work, especially around horses or machinery, can be dangerous; if the rules and whim of OSHA inspectors had been strictly applied, no ranch could have remained open. Court decisions eventually limited OSHA, but through the 1970s it was a significant problem.[59]

While these rules and others like them were irritating, ranchers faced more serious problems from the National Park Service and National Forest Service—a major concern for ranches in the northern Rockies since most of them bordered national forests or parks.[60] The tradition of friendliness and cooperation between parks and ranches made the changes especially mystifying. Through the years park officials had praised the ranchers for helping to preserve the wilderness and boasted of Yellowstone Park as a drawing card for ranches. Charles Moore was consulted by the Park Service about dude ranching in the Wind River country, and the Park Service hired him in 1952 to survey an area of Teton Park for a potential dude ranch. The Dude Ranchers' Association even urged the state of Montana to sell state-owned land to Glacier Park.[61]

All these past good feelings and relations meant nothing, however, when the Park Service purchased land that was nearby. Some land was acquired in the 1930s but even more after 1950. The largest number of land purchases by Rocky Mountain National Park came in the 1950s; in Glacier and Teton parks the greatest number came in the 1970s, and in all three parks there were numerous purchases from 1950 to 1980. In addition National Park Director Conrad Wirth conceived a ten-year program called Mission 66 in the early 1950s; it was aimed at meeting a projected 60 percent increase in the number of visitors by the fiftieth anniversary of the National Park Service in 1966.[62]

This required an upgrading and expansion of facilities. Park officials began studying the demands of people using the parks. There were generally three types of visitors to the national parks. The first liked nature but not the wilderness; the second liked the parks but stuck to the roads and required entertainment. The third was composed of those who left the roads and walked, hiked, or rode in the wilds and enjoyed the wilderness. The Park Service clearly devoted most of its efforts to the first two groups. Dude ranchers and their guests obviously belonged to the third group and were being ignored as the years went on.[63]

One of the results of this situation was the steady acquisition of ranches that were surrounded by, or adjacent to, national parks. In 1962 Rocky Mountain National Park acquired Stead's Ranch near Estes Park; Stead's included one of the oldest places in the country that had accepted dudes—Sprague's Ranch, which took guests in 1874. In 1964 RMNP took part of McGraw's Ranch in the same area. On the west side of the park it purchased Phantom Valley Ranch at about the same time, Green Mountain Ranch in 1972, and completed its sweep of the Kawuneeche Valley with the acquisition of Holzwarth's Neversummer Ranch in 1974.[64] This last purchase was a particular loss to the public, for this ranch was the last one that had a reasonable access to most scenic areas on the western side of the park.[65]

The Park Service did make an effort at historic preservation at Holzwarth's. It retained the buildings on the west side of the Colorado River and set up a walking tour of the cabins there to allow visitors to see what a tourist facility would have been like in the 1920s. This preservation project seems a bit odd when one realizes that the Park Service auctioned off and had removed the magnificent three-story log lodge that dated to 1929, as well as the other log buildings on the Holzwarth Ranch. The Park Service has never explained why it is worthwhile to reconstruct a 1920s spot complete with enthusiastic young people baking sourdough bread while destroying a ranch that offered people a chance to experience the wilderness. Instead of trips that included the historic sites of the Mica Mine, Dutchtown, or the Wolverine Mine, tourists could follow a well-worn path and hear a "canned" talk about the "good old days."[66]

As already noted, the same sequence of events occurred in Jackson Hole. An area supporting twenty-five to thirty dude ranches soon had fifteen or sixteen, with most of those on a lease or concession basis from the government. One observer there noted that the Park Service probably would have destroyed every building in the valley if it could have acquired the land. Of course, some of the owners negotiated profitable arrangements; they received substantial sums of money and/or got a lifetime lease to allow them to remain on the property. They could continue to enjoy the beautiful scenery, but the public was in a different position.[67] As the government garnered even more land in Jackson Hole, the land that was left became even more valuable. Prices for visitors rose on the few ranches left so the average visitor was faced with a high-priced vacation or a rushed and crowded view of the Tetons and surrounding area. The Park Service has preserved the Tetons but has made it difficult for all but the rich to enjoy an extended, peaceful visit to the area. But the rich elite, who can be guests at the Rockefellers' private resort or who can afford the high prices of the ranches still operating under the sufferance and control of the Park Service, can boast that they "saved" Jackson Hole for the "people"—that is, themselves.

The loss of ranches does not finish the story; the National Park Service has gradually adopted a policy restricting or even eliminating horseback riding in the parks. It is difficult to imagine anything more natural, historic, or traditional than horseback riding as a means of transportation in the West, and especially in the mountainous country where the parks were formed. The desirability and even the necessity of using horses for transportation was long recognized by earlier enthusiasts of the national parks as well as by park officials. Robert Sterling Yard noted that a "well-trained mountain horse" was available to carry visitors over the trails in the high country of the national parks.[68] Park officials had for years gone out of their way to emphasize that they welcomed dude ranch parties on horseback. Superintendent Roger Toll called these horseback trips "the very best" type of travel through Yellowstone and wanted more of them. A 157-mile horseback-riding trail was opened in Yellowstone and named after pioneer rancher Howard Eaton.[69] In 1939 Secretary of the Interior Harold L. Ickes even suggested that hotels, roads, and automobiles be barred from any new parks while foot and horse trails would be maintained. Perhaps the best indication of this once-friendly attitude was a letter from Newton Drury, director of the National Park Service, to Charles Moore. Drury admitted that he was sorry that automobiles had ever come into Old Faithful Basin and other national parks. Horseback and pack trips were the real way to see the national parks, and more people should see them that way.[70]

But publicity for the parks continued, the droves of visitors increased, and by the 1960s and 1970s the horseback rider was under attack. Ranchers had helped get land under federal control, fought the fires that threatened the forests and animals, and explained to people for decades how to preserve the wild areas, but they were now being attacked by groups and individuals who seemed to know nothing of the past. In answer to pressure from these groups, especially backpackers in the 1970s, the Park Service restricted horse use in the parks; and many trails were closed on the grounds that horses damaged the environment too much. These restrictions became so annoying that some dude ranchers avoided riding in the parks when they could ride in national forests or on other land.[71] The problems were so bad that in 1973 the Dude Ranchers' Association felt compelled to petition the federal government not to abolish the use of horses:

> Whereas, there are many beautiful and unspoiled areas in the
> Rocky Mountain West which can be reached only by horseback,
> and
> Whereas, horses have been used almost exclusively in the early
> settlement and travel of the west that they are a distinct part of
> the Americana scene,
> Now, be it resolved that the Dude Ranchers' Association go on
> record in support of the use of horses in our National Parks,
> Forests and all federally owned lands.[72]

The fact that such a resolution was even necessary is an indication of some very strange twists in federal policies. The idea that these restrictions somehow preserve the environment from irreversible damage is questionable, to say the least. While horse usage of trails does indeed move dirt around, this does not mean that there is permanent damage done; minimal trail maintenance could easily alleviate any problems that developed. In addition, hiking has the same kind of effect; a few hikers wearing heavy boots can move as much or more dirt around as any shod horse. There are two other important facts that are usually overlooked or simply unknown in the debate about horse usage of the land. It is much easier for horseback riders to bring out cans or any other debris because they have saddlebags or packs in which to carry this material. A second factor is that horseback riders have been able to get to, and enjoy, scenic areas in a shorter period of time than hikers or backpackers. Thus the latter groups use an area twice as long or more than do horsemen. It seems clear that hostility to horse use of the parks is not based on detailed, scientific studies designed to protect and preserve the environment, but instead is in response to intense, well-organized campaigns by pressure groups. The simple fact is that hikers, backpackers, and others opposed to horses are more numerous and/or better organized than horseback riders at ranches and stables.

What is even more perplexing is the stated attitude of some park officials, who deny their antihorse attitude even as they spell it out. The superintendent of Rocky Mountain National Park stated that "horses have access to nearly all major high-country areas" while listing numerous trails throughout the park that are completely closed to horse use. These trails include all but one of the high-country trails west of Trail Ridge Road on the west side of that park. This clearly eliminates rides to Skeleton Gulch, Dutchtown, Lake of the Clouds, and Green Knoll and apparently those to Blue Lake, Ruby Lake, Parika Pass, Parika Lake, Baker Pass, and the west side of the Neversummer Mountains. The same superintendent also states that *"the riding of a horse within the Park should be considered as a means of seeing the Park rather than an end in itself"* (emphasis in original).[73]

And yet the list of closed trails and the restrictions that make use of the park so onerous prevent the public from seeing the most remote and beautiful sections. Meanwhile, concessions inside the park offer short rides that seem to be the very type of riding the superintendent deplores.[74] Those outside liveries allowed to use the trails are automatically restricted by distance or by regulations so that they seldom, if ever, can offer rides into the remote and scenic spots. This point, of course, is not intended as criticism of the concessions or liveries; they have no choice but to follow park rules or lose their "privileges."

It is sad and strange, to say the least, when horsemen who have long enjoyed the parks are made to feel like criminals when they wish to journey into the beautiful, isolated areas. One expert horseman and enthusiastic naturalist is Frank Wright, who has taken perhaps 30,000 people on rides in Rocky Mountain National Park. On a week-long trip through the park in the early 1970s Wright was not surprised to see that areas he had once traveled bore no scars from those thousands of riders of past years. No mountainsides had been laid bare and no permanent damage had been done. Like most dedicated outdoorsmen Wright is ardently concerned with protection of the environment; he knows that ecology is important in a world of smog, jet noise, pollution, and general cluttering of recreational areas.[75] But that doesn't mean everything done under the banner of ecology is worthwhile; not everyone who screams "ecology" knows what is really going on or actually understands how to protect the environment.

Dude ranchers have had mixed relations with other federal agencies although none seems to have caused them as much trouble as the Park Service. Ranchers and the Forest Service have generally gotten along better since the Forest Service has been more sympathetic to recreational use of national forests by many different groups as part of its overall multiple-use system. But sometimes ranchers have even had trouble with forest officials. The building of roads in the forests has remained a matter of disagreement among different people; some want to retain the primitive nature of the forests while others demand better access to them.[76] In addition, there has been a trend to restrict commercial use of the forests (i.e., use by ranchers and outfitters) while not restricting private individuals. The irony, of course, is that many of the public (i.e., private individuals) would be able to use the forests only in conjunction with dude ranchers or outfitters that could supply them with horses. One Wyoming rancher was even faced with the possibility of paying a fee every day just to collect his mail, since his mail box was on Forest Service land. In Colorado, forest officials have succumbed to pressure from hikers and closed some of the trails in the Indian Peaks country to horseback riders.[77]

In Montana the Van Cleve family has had a series of conflicts with the National Forest Service. When these hardy ranchers got tired of federal officials dictating where they could camp, they bought a huge mountain in the Crazy Mountain chain. In Colorado the massive water project that included Granby Reservoir had its detrimental effects. The enormous lake created by the dam there destroyed the feed for the game so the elk and deer disappeared. It also covered the old Lehman Ranch, dating to the 1890s. The bodies of the members of the Lehman family had to be exhumed and reburied in Grand Lake cemetery; the long arm of the government even reached the dead.[78]

In all of these conflicts, especially those with park officials, it is pertinent to note again the peculiar irony of the situations. The National Park Service was founded so the natural beauty of certain areas would be preserved and could be enjoyed by the public. And many park officials, both past and present, have sincerely tried to fulfill this purpose. But Park Service policies have worked in a contrary manner; these policies were geared to winning the support of the public in the early days and then to supplying roads and facilities that could cater to the visitors. The park publicity was so successful that automobile visitors have threatened in the last two decades to overrun the parks. The crowded conditions of the national parks were the very things many visitors were trying to avoid. Beginning in the late 1960s, another grim element was added to the problem of crowds—serious crime. Both federal and state park rangers have become policemen to combat thievery and violent crime on a grand scale.[79]

While these problems grow, the federal officials continue their programs that eliminate or restrict dude and guest ranches. Ranches were founded to furnish the very type of vacation and attitude that fit the purpose of the national parks—to keep as much of the land as possible in its natural state and to offer people the opportunity to spend some time seeing it and understanding the environment.[80] It seems obvious that a person who spends a whole week or a month at the home of ranchers will gradually acquire a greater appreciation of the land and respect for it than will the fast-moving tourist who can drive to the edge of a beautiful sight or a fragile ecosystem and be gone ten minutes later. The traveler who has had to work to get to a remote spot (i.e., the horseback rider) has a different attitude from the casual auto tourist who assumes a road can be built to every mountain lake or stream that he might want to see. This is not really the fault of the casual tourists; they do not even know what they are missing. They are victims of federal policy decisions just as the dude rancher and his guests are. The latter two at least know what they have lost since they once were able to ride where they wished; the casual tourists are not even aware of the problem.

ELEVEN

The Dude Ranch IS

The Dude Ranch IS. Its meaning is defined in modern dictionaries. The quotation marks have been chiseled off. It has a being and a future. Ask anyone who has been to a dude ranch and his face lights up to tell you he has experienced the ultimate in recreation, vacation, and life.

—L. L. Newton, Minutes of the Fifth Annual
Dude Ranchers' Meeting, 177.

Dude ranching is declining in significance in most states, but the industry retains a stronghold in the northern Rockies. A few dude and guest ranches seem destined to remain in the Southwest but most of those appear to be on the road (or already at the end of the road) to becoming resorts with a western flavor. A few others may remain scattered across the plains states and in the scenic areas of the Northwest. Wyoming, Montana, and Colorado have once again become the core of dude and guest ranching, so it is worthwhile to examine a few in each state to see how they have weathered the changing times and conditions.

In Colorado the Bar Lazy J (Buckhorn Lodge) is probably the oldest continuously operating guest ranch in the state. Located along the Colorado River in Middle Park, it has changed owners a number of times in its seven decades of operation. James Ferguson and Edgar Messiter ran it from 1912 to 1917, and, after Ferguson's death, Mr. and Mrs. Messiter operated it until 1945. Because they felt they were getting too old to continue in the business, they decided to sell it in 1945 to some people they knew, Mr. and Mrs. Hugh Neece. The Neeces continued to operate it as a guest ranch and, for a few years after the war, they added beef and dairy cattle, chickens, and a garden to supply fresh food for the guests. Most of their visitors came from Chicago, where the Neeces did most of their advertising, from New York City, and from Kansas City. The Neeces never made much money on the ranch but stayed because they enjoyed the life.[1] Finally, Mr. Neece's other business interests in Texas took up so much time that he and Mrs. Neece were forced to sell the ranch to Rudy and Mabel Menghini in 1952. The Menghinis could see the growing competition from nearby motels and lodges; they met this competition by enlarging a cocktail lounge and heated swimming pool on the ranch and by modernizing the guests' living units. Fishing remained the ranch's key activity, although horseback riding was also a frequent diversion. In 1968 the Menghinis sold the Bar Lazy J to Chuck and Phyl Broady, who have operated it ever since. The ranch emphasizes its modern cabins, special activities for children, and a swimming pool. Fishing and horseback riding are still featured but it is clear that current guests take an interest in many other activities.[2] The Bar Lazy J is unusual since it has changed hands several times but remains a guest ranch. Its location on a main Colorado road has altered it from a once-remote ranch to one that is easily accessible, and this location has been a major factor in convincing its owners to add innovations to make it competitive with other recreational facilities.

A very different story emerges about Devil's Thumb Ranch near Fraser, Colorado. Unlike the Bar Lazy J, it sits far off the main highway along a dirt road. The ranch was begun by the Yager family in 1937; in 1941 a ranch lodge was built and brothers George, Don, and Louis raised and sold cattle and hay and accepted guests. With over 900 acres of land and forty-two horses, the remote ranch was a haven for urbanites seeking an escape from noise and crowds. The ranch featured a strenuous twenty-eight-mile ride from the valley, up 3,000 feet in elevation, to the rim of the Continental Divide, past the unusual 200-foot spire from which the ranch got its name. Devil's Thumb Ranch operated for over thirty years as a combination working-dude ranch; rising land values finally led the Yagers to sell their beautiful property in 1973.[3] Devil's Thumb ceased operating as a dude ranch for a while but soon reappeared as a combination ski center and guest ranch. It features cross-country skiing and offers transportation to nearby Winter Park for downhill skiing. Horseback riding has been reduced considerably and the ranch schedules only two two-hour rides per day. While Devil's Thumb is still a guest ranch, it also serves as a high-altitude training center and the Rocky Mountain training site for the U.S. ski team; dude ranching has clearly taken a back seat to other interests there.[4]

Holzwarth's Neversummer Ranch, north of Grand Lake, Colorado, went through a different evolution. Operating since 1919, it was first a fishing lodge and ranch but developed primarily into a horseback-riding ranch with few peers. Even though it was located next to the heavily traveled Trail Ridge Road, the Holzwarth family never succumbed to the pressures to change it into a resort. The Holzwarths offered pack trips every summer and scheduled at least three all-day rides per week as soon as melting snow left the trails open. Holzwarth guests and wranglers often didn't wait for the melt as they cleared the trails themselves if late snows blocked their favorite rides. The ranch raised hay and some of its own horses but mainly catered to its guests; it had no bar, swimming pool, or television, and little organized entertainment beyond Sunday afternoon games on horseback in a small arena. Above all, however, there were horseback rides through Rocky Mountain National Park and the Neversummer Mountains; it was a unique ranch since it allowed competent guests to ride alone. This gave them the freedom to roam as they wished to, unhindered by schedules of any kind.[5]

Holzwarth's Ranch finally succumbed to the constant pressure exerted by the National Park Service and its open checkbook. The Neversummer Ranch was virtually surrounded by federal land and the park officials decided it had to go. Aided by the Nature Conservancy, the NPS purchased Holzwarth's Neversummer Ranch in 1974 for over $1.5 million.[6] Most of the buildings were dismantled; an era of fifty-four years of public use and enjoyment of Rocky Mountain National Park had ended.

In Wyoming, Holm Lodge, which was apparently the first ranch to be totally dependent on the dude business, still operates west of Cody, near the eastern entrance of Yellowstone Park. It has, however, gone through numerous changes of ownership and one period of inactivity, and has been known by two names—Holm Lodge and Crossed Sabres Ranch. It was originally a stagecoach stop for visitors to Yellowstone Park operated by Tex Holm beginning in 1898; in 1903 he had tents set up and a lodge erected for the guests who stayed there. This lodge was destroyed by fire in 1906, but a new one was built the following year and remains in use to this day.[7] In 1914 he turned this lodge over to Billy Howell, one of his employees, who operated it as a dude ranch. Howell later took on a partner, Mary Shawver, and they operated Holm Lodge successfully and built it into one of the most famous dude ranches in the West. Both Billy Howell and Mary Shawver became very active members of the Dude Ranchers' Association, he in game management and she in home management.

They sold the lodge in 1947 to a group of Californians headed by C. Desmond;

these men intended to operate it as a private hunting lodge, but it was located on national forest land and the forest officials would not permit it to be used that way. The place was closed to the public for twelve years and fell into disrepair. The Forest Service threatened to level it unless it was reopened to the public, so Desmond sold it to Jess Phyllis Spragg in 1963.[8] They fixed it up and reopened it in 1964, running it again as a dude ranch and tourist lodge for five years. In 1969 they sold it to Dode Hershey, who continued its operation as a dude ranch, offering horseback riding, fishing, hunting, hiking, and other activities. In 1974 Don and Sandra Gerrits bought it from Hershey and his partners, the Reiders. The Gerrits's daughter and son-in-law, Rich and Donna Marta, managed Crossed Sabres and soon became its owners. By 1982 the ranch had been sold again, this time to Fred and Alvie Norris. Still a member of the Dude Ranchers' Association, Crossed Sabres Ranch has gone through many owners, just as the Bar Lazy J in Colorado did, and continues to operate as one of the oldest dude ranches in the country.[9]

Southwest of Cody, the Valley Ranch also continues to function, but it has gone through fewer changes in ownership. I. H. Larom and Win Brooks began the ranch operation in 1915; Larom married Irma Dew in 1920 and bought out Brooks's interest a few years later. Larom operated the Valley Ranch School for several years, but the most important activity over the years was the summer dude operation; the Laroms entertained thousands of guests from the East before and after the school functioned. Larry Larom was the first president of the Dude Ranchers' Association and truly shaped that organization's development since he remained president for eighteen years. Although Larry Larom suffered from a number of serious and painful diseases in his later years, he was reluctant to sell the Valley Ranch to anyone who did not share his concern for protection of the environment. The Laroms were finally able to sell it to someone they knew, Dr. Oakleigh Thorne II, in 1969. Dr. Thorne had been coming to the ranch since 1947, knew the area well, and was the founder and president of Thorne Ecological Institute, which carried out programs in outdoor education. Dr. Thorne was particularly anxious to preserve the rustic character of the Valley Ranch since he had seen the drastic changes that development had brought to Long Island, where he was reared, and to Boulder, Colorado, where he lived in the 1950s and 1960s. Thus the Laroms could feel confident that the ranch would be run in the same fashion as it had for over a half century, and they retained the right to continue living at the ranch that had been their home for many years.[10]

West of the Valley Ranch in Jackson Hole country is Turner's Triangle X Ranch, still operated by the same family after about fifty years as a dude ranch. John S. Turner went to Jackson Hole to vacation before moving there in the

1920s. He bought land there in 1925 and tried to start a potato farm; when this failed the Turners began raising cattle on their ranch. Fishermen and elk hunters frequently visited the area so the Turners built some cabins for them while continuing their cattle operation. John S. Turner then sold his land to the Rockefeller interests and leased it back for two years. His son, John C. Turner, leased the land again in the 1930s and ran Triangle X as a boys' ranch for a while before converting it into a ranch for families. After World War II the dude ranch part of the Triangle X became quite popular. John C. Turner was very active in advertising in magazines, in using travel services and clubs, and in following up leads for prospective guests. He prepared lists of guests from each state which he included as references when responding to new inquiries.

This aggressiveness proved very successful; eventually, his three sons, Harold, John, and Don, took over the Triangle X Ranch and have continued to operate it to the present. They offer horseback riding, float trips, and pack trips and also take out hunting groups.[11]

In the Sheridan-Buffalo area of Wyoming the number of dude ranches has declined, but some of the older ones still operate. One of these is the HF Bar Ranch, which has been in the Horton family since the first decade of the twentieth century. The demand for accommodations came from friends and the HF Bar was accepting guests by 1915. Located northwest of Buffalo, this large ranch of 15,000 acres is at an elevation of 5,300 feet, adjacent to the Bighorn National Forest. For a time the Hortons also managed Paradise Ranch for those guests who liked a vacation at a higher elevation (7,500 feet); the HF Bar still operates a mountain camp, fifteen miles from the main ranch in the Big Horn mountains.[12]

Of course, Eatons' Ranch still functions in the Sheridan area, and no story of dude ranching would be complete without mentioning its continued operation. The ranch is located about eight miles by dirt and gravel roads from the small town of Dayton at the site chosen by Howard, Alden, and Willis in 1903–4. Howard Hall, a recreation building, contains numerous animals heads recalling the hunting expeditions of Howard Eaton; there is also a framed letter from Theodore Roosevelt that mentions his long friendship with Howard Eaton. The white barn is still used, and the guests' horses are roped by horsemen in the corral just as they have been for many years.[13] The third and fourth generations of the Eaton family now operate the ranch, and the fifth generation is growing up there. Some families have sent five generations of guests to Eatons, and one woman came to the ranch for her fifty-fourth consecutive summer in 1978.[14]

Since the Eaton brothers accepted their first paying guest in 1882 in North Dakota, Eatons' Ranch is now celebrating one hundred years of dude ranching. That is a noteworthy event when one really considers it. How many frontier businesses of 1881 still operate the same way they did then and with the same family still in control?

In Montana, too, several of the older ranches are still functioning. Elkhorn Ranch, just a few miles from the northwestern corner of Yellowstone Park, has remained in the Miller family and still provides the traditional dude ranch vacation. Ernest and Grace Miller started the dude ranch in 1922, and he was one of the prime movers in the founding of the Dude Ranchers' Association. He died in 1949 but Grace remained active in the DRA through the 1970s and still lives in Montana. Their daughter and son-in-law, Barbara and Ronald Hymas, operate the Elkhorn in Montana; it offers horseback riding, pack mule trips, visits to Yellowstone Park, fishing, and shooting. Mr. and Mrs. Robert Miller, son and daughter-in-law of Ernest and Grace, operate the Elkhorn Ranch in Arizona; activities include desert and mountain riding, working cattle, swimming, and visits to nearby scenic spots.[15]

Another Montana ranch that began accepting guests in 1922 was the Lazy K Bar near Melville. The Paul Van Cleve family has owned the ranch since the 1880s with the fourth generation now involved in its operation. Paul II, known as Scrumper, was one of the charter members of the DRA; he was elected president in 1948 and served in that office for two years. His son, Paul III, nicknamed Spike, was elected president in 1972 and also served for two years; Spike was also the author of one of the most recent and interesting books written about dude ranching. Spike and Barbara's children, Paul IV (Tack), Michele, Carole, and Barbie, have all been active in running the Lazy K Bar, and Tack was elected president of the Dude Ranchers' Association for 1981. The Lazy K Bar produces its own meat and dairy items and breeds its own horses; there are few scheduled activities as guests take part in the regular ranch work.[16] The slump in cattle prices in the early 1920s that prompted the Van Cleves to accept dudes was a problem to ranchers at the time but the result has been a boon to dudes for six decades.

Another Montana ranch, the Ox Yoke, south of Livingston, has not survived the changes over the years. Charlie and Peg Murphy started the Ox Yoke dude ranch in 1929 along Bear Creek near the small town of Emigrant. Their son Jim took over the ranch in 1946 and operated it successfully while also raising Hereford, Angus, and Shorthorn cattle. In 1958 he married Gayle McCracken, a guest from Huntington, West Virginia, and they continued it as a working dude ranch for about twenty more years. In 1977, however, they sold the guest part of the ranch to the Black Otter Guide Service. The name Ox Yoke was retained for one season but Black Otter became the permanent name; the new owners operated more as outfitters and guides for pack trips, hunting expeditions, and mountain camps. Even though Murphy's Ox Yoke Ranch ceased to operate, the buildings and land still serve as the base for people riding out to enjoy the wilderness.[17]

Despite the problems and difficulties that some of these ranches have had, the institution of dude ranching is by no means dead. Its pioneering phase was over long ago, covering the period from the 1880s to the 1920s; in those years it introduced the West as a scenic area to the easterner, generating interest that drew needed capital westward. Thousands of people visited the West, and hundreds of ambitious ones stayed as permanent citizens.[18]

But in the 1970s and 1980s dude ranches certainly have not been the prime movers in drawing people or money to the West. One of the recent developments that may bode well for dude ranching is the growth of interest in the environment. The push to "save the West" could be closely tied to dude ranchers since they have been in the forefront of this idea for eight decades or more.[19] And yet there is little awareness of this fact on the part of the various environmental groups. Some people have even criticized ranchers for allegedly trying to monopolize national parks and forests.[20] This criticism hardly seems appropriate since dude ranchers were in favorable locations near the parks and forests because they were far-sighted enough to choose desirable land. Most did it long before the recent environmental "movement" began; they saw the new use of the land as recreational terrain and picked prime sites. Maybe the true dude ranches—those that have not sold out to giant corporations or become gaudy resorts—now have a different role to perform. Those featuring outdoor activities, plain food, and friendly hospitality can give the modern, rushing tourist a deeper appreciation of the West. Some ranches have decided to add backpacking to their activities to appeal to a new generation of people concerned with enjoying and preserving the wilderness.[21]

Certainly there still are people trying to enjoy the outdoor, western life. Outfitting for pack trips has grown in popularity, and these trips were long the strongholds of dude ranchers. Indeed, outfitters are, to some degree, an integral part of the history of dude ranching. Many of them continue the traditions of the wilderness vacation for which ranches were once known. Outfitters and dude ranchers are really branches off the same tree of western development.[22] The newly awakened desire among many Americans to participate instead of being mere spectators is made to order for traditional dude ranches. "Canned" ranch vacations from Sunday to Saturday with a specific activity scheduled for each day won't satisfy this feeling, but ranches that let guests join in ranch work or plan their own activities could. Because the dude has always been a producer of his own entertainment to a degree, this aspect of ranch life might be reemphasized or retained to make the ranch vacation much more as it once was—active and participatory.[23]

There have been signs of a growing interest in rural life in general, and rural vacations have increased somewhat in the last decade or so. William Wolfe started a vacation guide for farms and ranches in 1949; he was successful in matching the public up with farms and ranches and his book eventually developed into the popular *Farm Ranch and Countryside Guide*. It lists many types of rural vacations, including dude ranches, and is widely known and sold throughout the United States.[24] And there has been some formal training offered for people who want to supply these demands for outdoor vacations. In the 1970s Central Wyoming College at Riverton offered a six-week course on packing and guiding in the summer on a ranch near Dubois. Another group, Wilderness Guides and Packers School at Jackson, offered thirty-day courses, both basic and advanced, to teach guiding, packing, horsemanship, handling firearms, use and maintenance of camp equipment, and other pertinent skills for the packer, guide, or dude rancher.[25]

The demand for such outdoor programs in Wyoming is not surprising since many people in this state have appreciated the historic and economic importance of dude ranching. Wyoming officials have continually published descriptive brochures that listed dude ranches and have one of the most complete lists that exist for any state. In 1981 the Historic Preservation Office of the Wyoming Recreation Commission even launched a program to try to enroll some of the most significant Wyoming dude ranches on the National Register of Historic Places. At least some dude ranches in Wyoming may be recognized for their historic importance.[26]

The two principal dude ranch organizations are still functioning, the Dude Ranchers' Association founded in 1926, and the Colorado Dude and Guest Ranch Association, founded in 1933. The DRA has remained rather broad in its objectives with conservation and game activities important in its operation. But it has tried to remain relatively rigid in its membership policy in trying to protect the concept of the dude ranch. Its members require advance reservations with deposits and do not cater to transient trade; they offer the American Plan with rates on a weekly basis. They do not have bars, do not use billboards for advertising, and must offer horseback riding.[27] The DRA has declined somewhat in membership and has had other problems in the last decade. In 1972 its board of directors agreed to cease publication of its forty-year-old magazine, *The Dude Rancher,* and to replace it with *West: The Official Publication of The Dude Ranchers' Association.* This project, however, was soon abandoned, and *The Dude Rancher* was resumed until 1977 when printing and mailing costs forced its suspension.

A small newsletter, *Nickers,* was published instead, but the magazine reappeared in 1979, to be published less frequently than its former quarterly basis. By 1981 Peggy Schaffer, who had edited the magazine for years and who had served as executive secretary, took charge of getting *The Dude Rancher* out twice each year.[28] Even in the midst of its troubles, however, the DRA celebrated its fiftieth anniversary, and in 1981 it had fifty-three active member ranches in seven states.

The Colorado Dude and Guest Ranch Association has operated somewhat differently from the DRA, although the two organizations have cooperated with each other. The CD & GRA has not published a magazine, and few of its records have been made public; it has regularly published a list of its members with descriptions and rates of the ranches and has aggressively distributed these by the hundreds of thousands through state agencies, travel bureaus, and twenty airlines. The CD & GRA also produced a twenty-eight-minute color-sound movie, "Ranch Country U.S.A." Twenty-five copies have been circulated for years and shown to millions of viewers; the film features various activities that people enjoy on Colorado ranches: scenery, watching big game, branding and corral activities, cookouts, fishing, horseback riding, and so on.[29] Overall the CD & GRA has been the more aggressive of the two organizations, oriented to the general public and using all available types of tourist advertising. It requires that members use the word *ranch* in their names and that they foster and promote "western atmosphere." They also must solicit weekly or longer visits, have at least 50 percent of their business on the American Plan, and offer a resident, supervised horse program. In 1981 the CD & GRA had forty-three active members; seven of these were also members of the DRA.[30]

What then of the future of dude ranching? The number of dude ranches has certainly declined from the days when there was one in every canyon on the eastern slope of the Big Horn Mountains.[31] There is, however, no accurate count of dude ranches and there never has been. In 1973 one author claimed there were 1,800 in the western U.S., while another author in the same year claimed there were 1,500 vacation farms and ranches combined scattered across the entire United States.[32] Obviously any numerical estimate is very difficult to make because many facilities that are something else have been listed as dude ranches. Such listings are frustrating but they still point to the lingering success of early ranchers in publicizing their dude ranch vacations and name.

State bureaus and agencies, meanwhile, have admitted that they don't really know how important dude ranches are or have been to the economy or the development of the state.[33] The DRA itself has constantly had difficulties getting information from ranchers so its officials could compile statistics on ranch importance. Some dude ranchers have even questioned whether their business is profitable. Certainly satisfactions other than making money have kept many ranchers in the business.[34]

But the lure of running dude ranches still exists. In 1960 Robert Foster left his career as a Los Angeles businessman and moved to Colorado, where he began operating the Lost Valley Ranch near Sedalia. He was still running it in 1981.[35] The Gordon family has operated Tarryall River Ranch near Lake George, Colorado, for eighteen years; they had to close it temporarily in 1981 to keep up with a booming safari business in Africa, but they hope to keep it operating as it has in the past. Mr. and Mrs. Roy Chambers started taking dudes at their cattle ranch, the Flying V in Jackson Hole, in 1966. They have managed to combine the two businesses of raising cattle and accommodating guests just as the original dude ranches did.[36]

The future of dude ranching is, of course, unknown. But from this study it seems clear that dude ranchers face three major problems: the hostility of the federal government, especially the National Park Service; the general desire of vacationers for short, rushed trips; and the failure of dude ranchers to define their industry and make clear the type of vacation they offer.

Alleviation of the first problem would require a virtual revolution in the thinking of National Park Service officials. One way this could be accomplished is by an intense lobbying effort. Dude ranchers are not numerous enough to form a substantial pressure group by themselves; however, they might be able to enlist the help of their guests and other groups who believe that people should be able to use the national parks freely and that the parks should not grow indefinitely.[37] But dude ranchers have not shown the ability to unite and concentrate on leading such a lobbying effort.

Another way to change Park Service policy would be to alter the views of Congress and/or the president. It is interesting that suggestions made in 1981 by Secretary of the Interior James Watt were greeted by vociferous opposition. He was attacked for the relatively mild suggestion that the fees collected by the NPS be used for maintenance and upkeep rather than to buy more land. In view of this uproar, it seems unlikely that any changes will come in Park Service policy without vigorous support of such change by the president. Realistically, there is nothing in sight to indicate any softening of the hostile attitude that park officials show toward dude ranchers and others who wish to ride horses in the parks. It thus seems likely that there will be no horseback use in any national parks; this will, of course, be a tremendous loss to the general public as well as to those ranches located close to the national parks.

As for the preference of most people for short, rushed vacations, many dude ranchers have adapted to the one or two week stays that tourists demand. Many ranchers have also decided to add whatever activities are necessary to please their guests, so numerous ranches now feature swimming pools, counselors for children, and so on. Some have a completely planned program with specific activities arranged for each day of the week; each week is a unit of vacation and is like every other week of the season. This may well be the easiest and most convenient way for ranchers to operate, but such rigid scheduling certainly differs from the original concept of a relaxed vacation on a ranch with varied, un-scheduled activities. Modern ranchers could try to show their guests the appeal of the more relaxed, unplanned vacation and reemphasize horseback riding, fishing, hiking, and similar activities that are available when wanted. Indeed some dude ranches still function in this way and offer these activities; however, they appear to be the exception in the trend toward regimentation and planning.

The third problem—the lack of a clear definition—is probably the strangest difficulty that dude ranchers face. Despite the many years that dude ranches have existed, there has never been complete agreement about just what they were. The Dude Ranchers' Association has generally done the most to try to define the industry and to preserve its integrity; but even the DRA has had difficulty in formulating an adequate definition. In 1951, for instance, the president of the DRA, Dave Branger, stated he didn't know what dude ranching was even though his family had been in the business for forty years. Charles Moore, the organization's second president, also admitted that the definition of a dude ranch was rather vague.[38] At times the DRA has emphasized that a dude ranch was a real, working stock ranch that took guests; yet from its earliest days, the DRA accepted as members mountain ranches that raised no stock (other than horses for riding) and catered strictly to their guests.

At times the ranchers have also insisted that a dude ranch was the year-round home of the owners. This has generally been true, but some ranches in the northern states were in a climate so cold that it was impractical for the owners to remain through the harshest winter weather. Another consistent theme has been that dude ranches do not cater to transient trade and accept guests only by reservation for a minimum stay. This certainly has distinguished them from motels and roadside lodges over the decades although there are surely many resorts that have similar policies. And the DRA, which has tried hard in recent years to be selective in the type of members it has accepted, has admitted many different types of facilities in its fifty-five-year history. It has had hot springs, hotels, hunters and guides, lodges, camps, and at least one stable in its orga-nization. This breadth of membership reemphasizes the fact that dude ranching was the pioneer in accommodating travelers and tourists in many parts of the West. But it has also made it difficult for them to define their uniqueness, especially as times have changed the nature of travel and the type of vacationer who visits the Rocky Mountain West.

Dude ranchers have also insisted their ranches were not resorts, and this book has followed this distinction. Yet, by a curious twist, the word has been used by dude ranchers themselves. Eatons' Custer Trail Ranch near Medora, North Dakota is generally considered the first dude ranch in the country. It is interesting, therefore, to note that in their early brochures the Eaton brothers called their ranch a "summer resort" and "an Ideal Summer Resort In the Far West." The building containing the living facilities for guests was even called a hotel in one brochure.[39] Of course, one could argue that in those early days the Eatons were simply using words that would be familiar to easterners so they would understand what accommodations were available in the West. This argument is certainly a valid one.

And yet the Dude Ranchers' Association recently adopted three categories for its members: working dude ranch, dude ranch, and resort dude ranch. These terms have not been clearly defined but have been given only these general descriptions: at a working dude ranch "riding is primarily emphasized"; at a dude ranch "riding is emphasized"; and at a resort dude ranch "riding is available."[40] Thus the confusion continues about just what a dude ranch is.

It should be noted that this confusion occurs even in the DRA which has worked hardest to clarify the nature of its industry. One can imagine how much more difficulty has arisen among other groups that have not been as rigid in their membership policies or among the many facilities that have never joined an organization but that have used the phrase *dude ranch* or *guest ranch.*

Another interesting aspect of this problem of definition is that a few ranches that take guests have emphasized that they are real working ranches, not dude ranches. This is a strange twist, indeed, as some ranchers try to escape unwanted connotations of the phrase that was invented to describe ranches that accepted guests. It is also ironic since dude ranching clearly grew out of the hospitality of stock ranchers who accepted guests into their homes.

Whether dude ranching as an industry can solve or overcome these problems is not clear. Perhaps the working stock ranch that takes a few guests will eventually emerge as a separate vacation facility with a new name. It is possible that many current dude ranches will become resorts that are a little different because they do not accept transient trade and do emphasize horseback riding. Of course, some dude ranches are, and always have been, working stock ranches so they may need no redefinition or change of emphasis. Another strong possibility is that outfitters will absorb much of the dude ranch business. This has already occurred to some degree since people specializing in pack trips have begun to appeal to those who formerly sought dude ranch vacations. While early ranches offered frequent pack trips and some still do, many have abandoned them as they have added other facilities and emphasized less strenuous activities. To some vacationers the outfitter thus offers a way to get to the wilderness—a function dude ranches once fulfilled.

Obviously the above list of possibilities is merely suggestive and not definitive; dude ranching could go in many different directions in the decades ahead.

From the 1880s to 1920 dude ranching was relatively unknown and catered to a few people. Ironically, in the 1980s it is again relatively unknown in comparison to the myriad of vacation facilities in the West. But whatever the fate of specific ranches and whether the two current dude ranch organizations prosper or not, the importance of dude ranching is well established. The early dude ranchers were true pioneers; they opened the West, although not in the same way as the mountain men, or miners, or soldiers. But they did see the land in a new way, with a clear vision. They saw that the West had beauty in its wildness; it needed protection from thoughtless use and careless misuse. Treated properly by people who knew and loved the land, it could serve many purposes. It could bring joy and understanding to those who would stop and look and become part of it.

Appendix

The following lists are adapted from Lawrence B. Smith, *Dude Ranches and Ponies* (New York: Coward-McCann, 1936), 265–88. All are listed under the general heading of dude ranches although some are obviously other types of facilities for travelers. Some ranches are listed several times since they were served by different railroads and were also members of the Dude Ranchers' Association. Railroads often listed ranches by different cities and even different states depending on the station the railroad served that was closest to each ranch. The DRA generally listed the city that was closest to the ranch so this designation is used when available. When more than one ranch name and/or city are mentioned, the additional name(s) are noted in Column 4, followed by the number of the list where this alternate appears.

The list numbers refer to the following lists as described by Smith.

1. Active members of the Dude Ranchers' Association as of April 15, 1934.

2. Ranches reached by the Northern Pacific Railroad—northern Wyoming and Montana.

3. Ranches reached by the Chicago, Burlington & Quincy Railroad, the Buffalo Bill Country, and the Big Horn Country, Wyoming.

4. Ranches reached by the Union Pacific Railroad—the Rocky Mountain West.

5. Ranches reached by the Great Northern Railway—Montana and the Northwest.

6. Dude ranches reached by the Santa Fe Railroad (May 1, 1935), New Mexico, Arizona, Colorado, California.

7. Guest ranches reached by the Southern Pacific Railroad.

8. Guest ranches reached by the Rock Island Railroad.

After eliminating identifiable duplicates, the number of all places listed is:

Montana	114
Wyoming	95
Arizona	65
New Mexico	26
Colorado	25
Idaho	14
California	6
Nevada	4
Texas	3
Oregon	3
Canada	1
	356

This list is not definitive, but it is the earliest and most comprehensive list the author has located. In some cases one individual or group owned more than one of the ranches listed. But they are listed separately since the railroads or DRA listed them that way.

MONTANA   114

Lists	Ranch	City	Other Names/Cities
25	Alhambra Hot Springs	Helena	Alhambra #5
125	Allan Ranch	Augusta	Helena #2
12	Alpine Lodge	Alpine	
5	Arps Ranch	Augusta	
5	Baker Guest Ranch	Choteau	
2	Bar Lazy D A Ranch	Livingston	
5	Bar M Z Ranch	Libby	
1	Beartooth Ranch	Dean	Columbus #2
2	Binko Ranch	Missoula	
123	Bones Brothers Ranch	Birney	Forsyth #2
5	Bosworth Cabins	Swan Lake	
2	Boulder Hot Springs	Helena	
2	Bower's Ranch	Norris	
2	Brannin Ranch	Big Timber	
5	Broken Arrow Ranch	Glacier Park	
2	Camp Beartooth	Red Lodge	
2	Camp Lincoln	Helena	
2	Camp Mason	Helena	
123	Camp Sawtooth	Red Lodge	
3	Camp Senia	Red Lodge	
25	Camp Tuffit	Polson	Proctor #5
2	Campfire Inn	Norris	
2	Chico Hot Springs	Emigrant	
25	Circle 8 Ranch	Helena	Choteau #5
12	Circle W Ranch	Ovando	Missoula #2
12	Clyde Hurst	Contact	Clydehurst-on-the-Boulder, Big Timber #2
25	Covington Lodge	Polson	Swan Lake #5
2	Crescent Lazy H Ranch	Gardiner	
124	Cross Quarter Circle Ranch	West Yellowstone	
5	Curley Dunlap Dude Ranch	Lewiston	
12	Deep Canyon Ranch	Choteau	Helena #2
12	Diamond J Ranch	Norris	Bozeman #2
12	Donald Cattle Co.	Melville	Big Timber #2
12	Dot S. Dot Ranch	Melville	Big Timber #2
124	Double Arrow Ranch	Greenough	Missoula #2
2	Double Diamond Ranch	Gardiner	
124	E Bar L Ranch	Greenough	Missoula #2
124	Elkhorn Ranch	Bozeman	

MONTANA   continued

Lists	Ranch	City	Other Names/Cities
12	Elkhorn Springs Lodge	Polaris	Elkhorn Hot Springs Hotel, Dillon #2
5	Fender's Ranch	Augusta	
5	Fish Lake Resort	Stryker	
125	Flathead Recreation Ranch	Big Fork	Flathead Ranch #5, Flathead Recreation Lodge, Polson #2
2	Forest Meadow Camp	Plains	
124	Forsythe Range	Bozeman	Forsythe Range, Inc. #4
12	Four K Ranch	Dean	Columbus #2
2	Gallatin Way Ranch	Bozeman	
5	Glacier Bay Lake Resort	Somers	
5	Gleason Ranch	Choteau	
2	Gordon Ranch	Missoula	
2	Grayling Inn	Bozeman	
2	Gros Ventre Ranch	Gardiner	
124	Haggin Y/P Ranch	Anaconda	Haggin Dude Ranch, Anaconda #4, Haggin Ranch, Butte #2
5	Happy's Inn	Libby	
5	Hard Trigger Ranch	Glacier Park	
2	Harris Inn	Norris	
124	H Bar 9 Ranch	West Yellowstone	
1	Herford Wellington Ranch	Limestone	
25	Hiawatha Lodge	Polson	Dayton #5
2	Holland Lake Lodge	Missoula	
2	Hot Springs	Plains	
2	Hutchins' Ranch	Norris	
5	Jennings Ranch	Glacier Park	
2	Karst's Dude Ranch	Bozeman	
2	Keewaydin Rocky Mountain	Missoula and Drummond	
5	Kintla Guest Ranch	Trail Creek	
12	Kratz Ranch	Absarokee	Columbus #2
124	Laird's Recreation Lodge	Seeley Lake P.O.	Captain Laird's Recreation Lodge, Missoula #2

MONTANA   continued

Lists	Ranch	City	Other Names/Cities
25	Laron's Lodge	Polson	Larson Lodge, Big Fork #5
12	Lazy K Bar Ranch	Big Timber	
123	L-T Ranch	Cooke City	Nordquist's L Bar T, Gardiner #2, L-T Ranch, Crandell, Wyoming #3
2	Lolo Hot Springs	Missoula	
2	Lone Wolf Ranch	Billings	
2	Matterhorn Camp	Polson	
2	McLeod Hot Springs	Big Timber	
5	Meadow Mountain Ranch	Marion	
2	Mill Creek Ranch	Livingston	
2	Mission Range Ranch	Ravalli	
5	M Lazy V Ranch	Marion	
2	Old Kaintuck Camp	Big Timber	
12	OTO Ranch	Dude Ranch	Corwin Springs #2
124	Ox Yoke Ranch	Emigrant	Livingston #2
123	Quater Circle U Ranch	Birney	Forsythe #2
2	Rainbow Ranch	Bozeman	
3	Red Rim Ranch	Wyola	
5	Retiro Cabins	Belton	
23	Richel Lodge	Red Lodge	
12	Rimrocks Ranch	Lodge Grass	Sheridan, Wyo. #2
2	Rising Sun Ranches	Bozeman	
2	Rocking Arrow Ranch	Bozeman	
5	Rocky Bar O Ranch	Big Fork	
3	Rosebud X4 Ranch	Kirby	
5	Scenic Rest Camp	Big Arm	
2	Seven Bar 9	Helena	
1245	Seven Up Ranch	Lincoln	Helena #2
2	Seventy Acres	Big Timber	
2	Sharp's Ranch	Missoula	
2	Shaw's Camps	Gardiner	
5	Shining Mountain Camp	Somers	
2	Sixty Three Ranch	Livingston	
2	Sleeping Child Springs	Hamilton	
12	Snowy Range Ranch	Livingston	
5	Spotted Bear Camp	Big Fork	
2	Sprague Ranch	Norris	
5	Stecker Ranch	Augusta	

MONTANA   continued

Lists	Ranch	City	Other Names/Cities
5	Sunrise Ranch	Kalispell	
5	Swift Creek Ranch	R-1 Whitefish	
2	Swinging H Ranch	Columbus	
2	Tamaracks	Missoula	
12	T O Bar Ranch	Roscoe	Red Lodge #2
2	Triangle Seven Ranch	Livingston	
5	Two Medicine Ranch	Glacier Park	
2	White's Dude Ranch	Ravallia	
2	Wightman-Lawton Ranch	Bozeman	
2	X Bar A	Big Timber	

Breakdown of Montana Ranches by Area

25	Northwest Montana—Glacier Park area/Flathead Lake/Libby/Trail Creek/Stryker/Polson/Marion/Kalispell/Whitefish/Big Fork/Somers/Swan Lake/Big Arm/Belton
22	Missoula/Helena/Greenough/Ravalli/Lincoln/Ovando/Seeley Lake/Plains
15	Bozeman/Norris
12	Gardiner/Corwin Springs/Emigrant/Livingston
11	Red Lodge/Columbus/Dean/Absarokee/Roscoe/Cooke City/Billings
9	Big Timber/Contact/Melville
7	Augusta/Choteau
4	Birney/Lodge Grass/Wyola
2	West Yellowstone
2	Hamilton/Anaconda
1	Polaris (near Dillon)
1	Lewiston
1	Rosebud
1	Limestone
1	Alpine

WYOMING   95

Lists	Ranch	City	Other Names/Cities
14	A Bar A Ranch	Encampment	
2	Absaroka Lodge	Cody	
123	Aldrich Lodge	Ishawooa	
4	Aspen Ridge Ranch	Kelly P.O.	
123	A 2 Z Ranch	Valley	
124	Bar B C Ranch	Moose	Gardiner, Mont. #2
4	Bar B C J-O (Juniors Outfit)	Moose	
23	Bar M C Ranch	Ranchester	Dayton #3
12	Bar P Quarter Circle	Shell	Greybull #2
3	Big Horn Lodge	Ten Sleep	
123	Blackwater Lodge	Cody	
3	Bobcat Ranch	Ishawooa	
14	Boyer Ranch	Savery	Boyer YL Ranch #4
4	Brooklyn Lodge	Centennial	
3	Camp Big Horn (for boys)	Big Horn	
1	Camp Red Cloud	Story	
3	Camp Wigwam	Shell	
4	Castle Rock Ranch	Jackson	
23	Circle H	Cody	
124	C M Ranch	Dubois	Bonneville #2
4	C P Bar Ranch	Cora	
3	Crescent H Bar Camp (for girls)	Buffalo	
14	Crescent Lazy H Ranch	Wilson	
4	D C Bar Ranch	Kendall	
4	Diamond Double L Outfit	Moose P.O.	
12	Diamond G Ranch	Dubois	Bonneville #2
12	Diamond Tail Ranch	Greybull	
123	Double Dee Ranch	Sunshine	Cody #2
14	Double Diamond Ranch	Jackson	Moose #4
123	Eaton Brothers Ranch	Wolf	Sheridan #2
123	Elephant Head Lodge	Cody	
4	Flying A Ranch	Daniel	
4	Flying V Ranch	Moose	
23	Four Bear Ranch	Cody	
1	Gannett Peak Ranches	Cora	
23	Gros Ventre Ranch	Kelly	
1234	H F Bar Ranch	Buffalo	Clearmont #2

WYOMING   continued

Lists	Ranch	City	Other Names/Cities
123	Hillman Ranch	Big Horn	Sheridan #2, Hilman Ranch #2 and #3
1234	Holm Lodge	Cody	
12	Hot Foot Ranch	Duncan	Cody #2
2	Hunter's Peak Ranch	Cody	
23	IXL Ranch	Sheridan	Dayton #3
124	Jackson Lake Lodge	Moran	Gardiner, Mont. #2
1	J O Ranch	Moose	
1	Monte Jones (Big Game Hunter)	Cody	
123	Klondike Ranch	Buffalo	Brookside, Dayton #3
12	Lazy Bar F Ranch	Valley	Cody #2
23	Lazy Bar H	Cody	Wapiti #3
4	Leek's Camps	Jackson	
4	Libby Lodge	Centennial	
3	Log Cabin Ranch	Pointer	
4	L U Bar Ranch	Dwyer	
3	L V Bar Ranch	Wapiti	
23	Majo Ranch	Cody	
3	Meadow Lark	Ten Sleep	
4	Medicine Bow Lodge	Saratoga	
4	Moose Head Ranch	Jackson Hole	
23	Morris Ranch	Cody	
3	Mountain Home Ranch	Parkman	
4	One-Bar-Eleven Ranch	Encampment	
123	Pahaska Tepee	Cody	
1234	Paradise Ranch	Buffalo	
12	Pass Creek Ranch	Parkman	Sheridan #2
3	The Pines	Buffalo	
23	Piney Inn and Ranch	Sheridan	Story #3
2	Pitchfork Ranch	Cody	
3	R Bar Ranch	Birney	
3	Red Cliff Ranch	Buffalo	
23	Richard Ranch	Cody	
12	Riddle Ranch	Pointer	Cody #2
23	Rimrock Ranch	Cody	
4	Sky Meadows	Encampment	

WYOMING   continued

Lists	Ranch	City	Other Names/Cities
123	Spear O Wigwam	Big Horn	Spear Mountain Camp #3, Sheridan #2
3	Spear X Ranch	Arvada	
23	Staples Resort	Sheridan	Staples Ranch, Story #3
14	STS Ranch	Moose	
1234	Sunlight Ranch	Pointer	Cody #2 and #4
1	TAT Ranch	Kearney	
1234	T Cross Ranch	Dubois	Bonneville #2
123	Tepee Lodge	Big Horn	Canon Trail Ranch, Wyola, Mont. #3, Sheridan #2
4	Teton Lodge	Moran	
124	Two N Ranch	Dubois	Bonneville #2
2	Two X Ranch	Sheridan	
3	Triangle A Ranch	Sheridan	
4	Triangle F Lodge	Triangle F P.O.	
2	Triangle X	Cody	
4	Triangle X Ranch	Jackson Hole (Grovont P.O.)	
2	U X U Ranch	Cody	
1234	Valley Ranch	Valley	Cody #2
3	Van's Lodge	Worland	
124	White Grass Ranch	Moose	Gardiner, Mont. #2
23	Wigwam	Worland	The Wigwam #3
4	Y-Cross Ranch	Horse Creek	
2	Z Cross	Cody	

Breakdown of Wyoming Ranches by Area

29	Cody (Ishawooa, Wapiti, Pointer, Sunshine, Duncan, Valley)
17	Jackson (Moose, Kelly, Wilson, Moran, Grovont)
17	Sheridan (Ranchester, Big Horn, Story, Parkman, Wolf, Kearney, Arvada)
7	Medicine Bow National Forest (Encampment, Centennial, Savery, Saratoga)
6	Buffalo
4	Dubois
4	Worland/Ten Sleep
3	Shell/Greybull
3	Cora/Daniel
1	Dwyer (eastern Wyoming, north of Wheatland)
1	Horse Creek (northeast of Laramie)
1	Kendall
1	Birney
1	Triangle F

ARIZONA   65

Lists	Ranch	City	Other Names/Cities
8	Adolee House	Scottsdale	
8	Apache Guest Ranch	Dragoon	
6	Arrowood Ranch	Skull Valley	
8	Aztec Lodge Ranch	via Globe	
678	Bar F X Guest Ranch	Wickenburg	Bar F X Ranch #7 and #8
78	Bar O Ranch	Tombstone	
67	Bar 37 Ranch	Prescott (Camp Wood Route)	Bar Thirty-Seven Ranch #7
6	Beaver Creek Ranch	Rimrock	
8	Catalina Vista Ranch	Tucson	
8	C Bar Ranch	Dragoon	
678	C 4 Ranch	Wickenburg	C-4 Ranch #8, C-4 Guest Ranch #7
678	Champie Ranch	Hot Springs	
78	Circle "Z" Ranch	Patagonia	Circle Z Ranch #8
67	Cross Triangle Ranch	Prescott	
8	Diamond C Ranch	Elgin	
6	El Rancho Grande	Mesa	
78	Faraway Ranch	Dos Cabezas	Dos Cabezos #8
78	Flying V Ranch	Tucson	
6	Foxboro Ranches	Flagstaff	
7	Fresnal Ranch School	Tucson	
78	Garden of Allah Guest Ranch	Wickenburg	Garden of Allah Ranch #8
8	Glover Ranch	Tucson	
78	Hacienda de La Osa	Tucson	Hacienda de La Osa Ranch #8
7	Hacienda los Encinos	Sonoita	
8	Harding Guest Ranch	Tucson	
8	Hatchet	Mesa	
78	Hayden Guest Ranch	Tempe	
67	H W Ranch	Chino Valley	H. W. Ranch #7
67	Jokake Inn	Phoenix	Scottsdale #7
678	Kay-el-Bar	Wickenburg	Kay-el-Bar Ranch #7 and #8
8	Las Moras Ranch	Tucson	
6	Lazy R C Ranch	Wickenburg	
6	Los Arroyos Inn	Scottsdale	
6	M- Bar- V Ranch	Flagstaff	
678	Monte Vista Ranch	Wickenburg	

ARIZONA   continued

Lists	Ranch	City	Other Names/Cities
6	Natural Bridge Ranch	Payson	
6	Oak Creek Lodge	Flagstaff	
78	Old Homestead Ranch	Phoenix	
8	Outlook Ranch	Elgin	
67	Paradise Canyon Ranch	Marble Canyon	
6	Phantom Ranch	Grand Canyon	
678	Pima Estate Guest Ranch	Laveen	Pima Estate Ranch #7 and #8
67	Quarter Circle v-Bar Ranch	Mayer	
8	Rancho del Vaquero	Mesa	
78	Rancho Linda Vista	Oracle	
8	Rancho Santa Cruz	Tubac	
678	Remuda Ranch	Wickenburg	Remuda Guest Ranch #7
16	Rimrock Ranch	Rimrock	
1678	Sahuro Lake Ranch	Mesa	
78	Seventy-Six Ranch	Bonita	
78	Sierra Linda Ranch	Portal	
8	Silver Bell Ranch	Tucson	
6	Soda Springs Ranch	Rimrock	
7	Spur Cross Ranch	Cave Creek	
78	Tanque Verde Ranch	Tucson	
6	Thunder Bird Ranch	Chinle	
6	Timberline Ranch (for girls)	Vernon (via Holbrook)	
6	T. P. Ranch	Hot Springs	
67	Triangle H. C. Ranch	Camp Wood	
78	Triangle T Ranch	Dragoon	
7	Vah-Ki Inn	Coolidge	
8	Wanada Lodge	Phoenix	
67	The Wigwam (guest inn and bungalows)	Litchfield Park	The Wigwam #7
78	Y–Lightning Ranch	Hereford	

Breakdown of Arizona Ranches by Area

23	Southeastern Arizona, Tucson area—10, East of Tucson—8 (Bonita, Tombstone, Dragoon, Hereford, Portal, Dos Cabezas), North of Nogales—5 (Elgin, Tubac, Patagonia, Sonoita)
13	Phoenix area
10	Prescott area
7	Wickenburg area
3	Flagstaff
2	Globe/Coolidge
2	Hot Springs
1	Marble Canyon
1	Grand Canyon
1	Poyson
1	Holbrook
1	Chinle

NEW MEXICO   26

Lists	Ranch	City	Other Names/Cities
6	Bishop's Lodge	Santa Fe	
678	Bonnell Ranch	Glencoe	
6	Brush Ranch (formerly Irvins-on-Pecos)	Tererro	
6	Cimarroncita Ranch Camp (for girls)	Ute Park	
78	C. X. Ranch	Elk	
678	Double-S-Ranch	Cliff	
6	El Porvenir	El Porvenir	
6	Forked Lightning Ranch	Rowe	
6	Frijoles Canyon Ranch	Santa Fe	
6	Kickapoo Kamp (for girls)	Gascon	
6	Kit Carson Camp (for boys)	Tres Piedras	El Rancho Del Vallecito
6	Jay-C-Bar Ranch	Rociada	
78	Ladder Ranch	Hillsboro	
6	Lobo Ranch	Cuba	
67	Lone Pine Ranch	Glencoe	
6	Los Pinos	Cowles	
6	Mountain View Ranch	Tererro	
6	Piñon Lodge	Crystal	
6	Rancho de Dias Alegres	Las Vegas	
6	Rancho del Monte	Santa Fe	
6	Rancho de Tres Ritos	Taos via Vadito	
6	Tent Rock Ranch, Inc.	Pena Blanca	
78	T. V. Bar Ranch	Gila	T V Bar Ranch #8
6	Valley Ranch	Valley Ranch	
6	V. R. Ranch	Cuba	
6	X-T Ranch	Carlsbad	

Breakdown of New Mexico Ranches by Area

14	Near Taos, Santa Fe, or Las Vegas
3	West of Roswell
3	Near Silver City
2	Tererro
1	Carlsbad
1	Crystal
1	Rociada
1	Valley Ranch

COLORADO   25

Lists	Ranch	City	Other Names/Cities
4	Bar 1 L Ranch (boys and girls)	Tabernash	
1	Buckhorn Lodge	Parshall	
4	Camp Chief Ouray (boys)	Denver	[Granby]
4	Cheley Camps (boys and girls)	Estes Park	
4	Double M Ranch	Boulder	
4	Hacienda del Monte Ranch	Redwing	
6	Hu Ranch	Bayfield	
4	Hudler Riding Camp (for girls)	near Granby	
4	K A Rose Resort	Granby	
4	L X Bar Ranches	Hayden	
4	Phantom Valley Ranch	Grand Lake	
4	Ralston Creek Ranch (for boys)	Golden	
4	Rugh Ranch	Greeley	
14	Saddle Pockets Ranch	Battle Creek	Saddle Pocket #4
4	S Bar L Ranch	Ward	
4	S L W Home Ranch	Greeley	
4	Smillie's F Slash Ranch	Granby	
4	Stead Guest Ranch	Estes Park	
4	Stony Point Lodge (for boys)	Boulder	
6	Teelawuket Ranch	Bayfield	
4	Touzalin Ranch	Colorado Springs	
4	Trail's End Ranch	Fort Collins	
4	Tom Tucker Ranch	Nederland	
46	Valley View Ranch	Westcliffe	
4	Wind River Ranch	Estes Park	

Breakdown of Colorado Ranches by Area

7	Granby/Grand Lake area
4	Boulder area
3	Estes Park
3	Greeley/Fort Collins
2	Bayfield (near Durango)
1	Hayden (near Steamboat Springs)
1	Golden
1	Colorado Springs
1	Westcliffe
1	Redwing
1	Battle Creek

IDAHO   14

Lists	Ranch	City	Other Names/Cities
4	Alturas Lake Resort	Hailey	
4	Big Springs Inn	Guild P.O.	
4	Bower's Ranch	Lake P.O.	
4	Boyle's Ranch	Loon Creek (Stanley P.O.)	
4	Four S Hereford Ranch	Soda Springs	
4	Gameland Sporting Ranches	Yellow Pine	
1	Hideout Lodge	Clayton	
4	Idaho Rocky Mountain Club	Stanley	
4	Ketchums Camp and Hotel	Ketchum	
4	Mack's Inn and Tourist Cabins	Mack's Inn P.O.	
2	Red River Hot Springs	Grangeville	
4	Robinson Bar Ranch	Mackay	
4	Rocking N F Ranch	Ketchum	
4	V Bar V Ranch	Victor	

Breakdown of Idaho Ranches by Area

7	Sun Valley/Sawtooth National Recreation Area
3	Eastern Idaho (western entrance Yellowstone National Park)
1	Yellow Pine (northeast of Boise)
1	Grangeville (southeast of Lewiston)
1	Guild
1	Lake

OTHER STATES

Lists	Ranch	City	Other Names/Cities
TEXAS—3			
17	Gallagher Ranch	San Antonio	
7	Haley Ranch	Alpine	
7	Mitre Peak Ranch	Mitre Peak Park	
OREGON—3			
4	Diamond-and-A-Half Ranch	Hereford	
4	Horse Ranch	Union	
14	M J G Ranch	Joseph	
CANADA—1			
1	Half Diamond S Ranch	Skookumchuck, B.C.	
CALIFORNIA—6			
678	Deep Well Guest Ranch	Palm Springs	Deep Well Ranch #8
4	Glenn Ranch	Glen Ranch	
4	North Verde Ranch	Victorville	
1467	Pierson's Dude Ranch	Delpiedra	Pierson Dude Ranch #6 and #7
7	San Clemente Ranch	Monterey	
678	Smoke Tree Ranch	Palm Springs	
NEVADA—4			
7	Lone Star Guest Ranch House	Reno	
7	Monte Cristo Ranch	Reno	
7	Pyramid Lake Ranch	Sutcliff	
7	T H Ranch	Sutcliff	

Notes

Chapter 1

1. Ingolf K. Vogeler, "Farm and Ranch Vacationing in the United States" (Ph.D. diss., University of Minnesota), iii, 15; Joseph P. Sullivan, "A Description and Analysis of the Dude Ranching Industry in Montana" (Master's thesis, University of Montana, 1971), 1.

2. Outdoor Recreation Resources Review Commission, *Outdoor Recreation for America: A Report to the President and Congress* (Washington, D.C.: Government Printing Office, 1962), 49–50; see esp. 5–6 and 93–94 for the government's role.

3. Charles G. Roundy, "The Origins and Early Development of Dude Ranching in Wyoming," *Annals of Wyoming*, vol. 45, no. 1 (Spring 1973), 13 n. 37.

4. Jerome L. Rodnitzky, "Recapturing the West: The Dude Ranch in American Life,"*Arizona and the West,* vol. 10 (Summer 1968), 111–26. Roundy, "Origins,"

5–25. Charles G. Roundy, "Toward a Golden Anniversary History of the Dude Rancher's Association," speech given November 16, 1972, at the Forty-seventh Annual DRA Meeting in Cheyenne, Box 1, CGR WHRC UW.

5. Frank B. Norris, "The Southern Arizona Guest Ranch as a Symbol of the West" (Master's thesis, University of Arizona, 1976); n. 1 above, Vogeler and Sullivan.

6. Mary R. Rinehart, *Nomad's Land* (New York: George H. Doran Co., 1926), 179–80. Definitions and their sources are discussed further in Chapter 3.

7. David J. Saylor, *Jackson Hole, Wyoming: In the Shadow of the Tetons* (Norman: University of Oklahoma Press, 1970), 209; Neil Morgan, "Hey Dude!" *Western's World: The Magazine of Western Airlines,* vol. 4, no. 3 (June–July 1973), 16.

8. "Dude Ranches Excluded from Unemployment Compensation Contributions in Wyoming," *The Dude Rancher,* vol. 7, no. 1 (January 1939), 2.

9. Roundy, "Origins," 7; Sullivan, "Dude Ranching Industry" (thesis), 9; Dorothea Park-Lewis, "Dude-Ling," *House Beautiful,* vol. 81, no. 4 (April 1939), 127.

10. Daniel J. Boorstin, *The Image: A Guide to Pseudo-Events in America* (New York: Harper & Row, 1964), 84–86; Paul Fussell, "The Stationary Tourist," *Harper's,* vol. 258, no. 1547 (April 1979), 31–33. The distinction is applied to dudes and dude ranches in: Rodnitzky, "Recapturing the West," 125; Hal G. Evarts, "Dude Wranglers," *Saturday Evening Post,* vol. 192 (May 1, 1920), 32; Mary R. Rinehart, "The Sleeping Giant," *Ladies Home Journal,* vol. 28 (May 1921), 21.

11. Peter J. Schmitt, *Back to Nature: The Arcadian Myth in Urban America* (New York: Oxford University Press, 1969), 171–73; Struthers Burt, *The Diary of a Dude-Wrangler* (New York: Charles Scribner's Sons, 1924), 49, 113.

12. Mary R. Rinehart, "Summer Comes to the Ranch," *Saturday Evening Post,* vol. 198, no. 1 (July 4, 1925), 72.

13. There is some evidence that dude ranches were also partly responsible for beginning winter sports activities in the West; e.g., I. H. Larom, "Survey of the Year," *The Dude Rancher,* vol. 6, no. 1 (January 1937), 12.

14. Charles G. Roundy to author, August 30, 1977; *Boston Evening Transcript,* March 26, 1932, Magazine Section, 1; Jesse L. Williams, "Joy-Ranching and Dude-Wrangling," *Collier's,* vol. 51 (August 9, 1913), 23.

15. Courtney R. Cooper, "Dude, Howdy!" *Ladies Home Journal,* vol. 48 (August 1931), 41; DRA Minutes, 1931, 135–41, Pam File, Wyo.S.A. For additional discussion of the importance of women to dude ranching see Chapters 5 and 7.

16. Chapter 8 discusses dude ranching and conservation more fully.

17. DRA Minutes, 1929, 88, Pam File, Wyo.S.A.

18. Earl Pomeroy, *In Search of the Golden West: The Tourist in Western America* (New York: Alfred A. Knopf, 1957), 112–13, 183; Roundy, "Origins," 15.

19. Sullivan, "Dude Ranching Industry" (thesis), 19.

Chapter 2

1. Osborne Russell, *Journal of a Trapper or Nine Years Residence among the Rocky Mountains Between the Years 1834 and 1843*, ed. Aubrey L. Haines (Lincoln: University of Nebraska Press, 1968), 13–14, 60, 118.

2. Le Roy R. Hafen and Ann W. Hafen, eds., *Rufus B. Sage*, 2 vols. (Glendale, Calif.: Arthur H. Clark Co., 1956), 1:13–27. Robert C. Black III, *Island in the Rockies: The History of Grand County, Colorado, to 1930* (Boulder: Pruett Press, 1969), 22–23.

3. Bernard De Voto, *The Year of Decision: 1846* (Boston: Little, Brown, 1943), 54, 65.

4. William F. Cody, "Famous Hunting Parties of the Plains," *The Cosmopolitan*, vol. 17, no. 2 (June 1894), 131–34.

5. Ibid., 136–43.

6. Marshall Sprague, "The Dude from Limerick," *The American West*, vol. 3, no. 4 (Fall 1966), 53–61, 93.

7. Joseph G. Rosa, *They Called Him Wild Bill: The Life and Adventures of James Butler Hickok* (Norman: University of Oklahoma Press, 1974), 246–52, 264–65. Norreys J. O'Conor, "An Irish Sportsman in the Far West," *Arizona Quarterly*, vol. 5, no. 2 (Summer 1949), 114–16.

8. Sprague, "Dude from Limerick," 93.

9. Isabella L. Bird, *A Lady's Life in the Rocky Mountains* (Norman: University of Oklahoma Press, 1960), 104–5. David J. Saylor, *Jackson Hole, Wyoming: In the Shadow of the Tetons* (Norman, University of Oklahoma Press, 1970), 116.

10. Earl Pomeroy, *In Search of the Golden West: The Tourist in Western America* (New York: Alfred A. Knopf, 1957), 74.

11. Bird, *A Lady's Life*, 34–49, 141, 157.

12. Ibid., 73–101, 110–12; 18, 136, 197, 209.

13. Joe B. Frantz and Julian E. Choate, Jr., *The American Cowboy: The Myth and the Reality* (Norman: University of Oklahoma Press, 1968), 148.

14. Owen Wister's Notebook, July–August 1885, 5–6, Biog. MS File, Owen Wister, WHRC UW; Fanny K. Wister, ed., *Owen Wister Out West: His Journals and Letters* (Chicago: University of Chicago Press, 1958), vi–xi, 11, 28.

15. Robert S. Yard, *The Book of the National Parks* (New York: Charles Scribner's Sons, 1919, 1928), 29. There is some dispute about which was the first national park because of different terminology used when the federal government set the land aside.

16. Saylor, *Jackson Hole, Wyoming*, 114–15.

17. Clipping from unidentified newspaper, n.d., n.p., Clippings File, Dude Ranch, Montana, WHRC UW.

18. Pomery, *Golden West*, 78–79. Michael S. Kennedy, ed., *Cowboys and Cattlemen: A Roundup from Montana, The Magazine of Western History* (New York: Hastings House, 1964), 80–81.

19. Lincoln A. Lang, *Ranching with Roosevelt* (Philadelphia: J. B. Lippincott Co., 1926), 13–17, 177; Donald Dresden, *The Marquis de Morès: Emperor of the Bad Lands* (Norman: University of Oklahoma Press, 1970), 25–26. Arthur C. Huidekoper, *My Experience and Investment in the Bad Lands of Dakota and Some of the Men I Met There* (Baltimore: Wirth Brothers, 1947), 24–25.

20. Robert G. Athearn, *Westward the Briton* (Lincoln: University of Nebraska Press, 1969), 46, 62–65; Lewis Atherton, *The Cattle Kings* (Bloomington: Indiana University Press, 1961), 93.

21. For examples of frontier hospitality in a wide variety of places and in different eras, see: Everett Dick, *The Dixie Frontier* (New York: Capricorn, 1964), 324; Orland L. Sims, *Cowpokes, Nesters and So Forth* (Austin: Encino Press, 1970), 119; Gilbert C. Fite, *The Farmer's Frontier, 1865–1900* (New York: Holt, Rinehart & Winston, 1966), 219; Elinor Wilson, *Jim Beckwourth: Black Mountain Man and War Chief of the Crows* (Norman: University of Oklahoma Press, 1972), 117; Frantz and Choate, *American Cowboy*, 64.

22. Robert H. Burns, Andrew S. Gillespie, and Willing G. Richardson, *Wyoming's Pioneer Ranches* (Laramie: Top-of-the-World Press, 1955), 112. Dresden, *Marquis de Morès*, 125.

23. Elizabeth Hayden to author, October 29, 1977.

24. Mary Shawver, *Sincerely, Mary S.* (Casper, Wyo.: Prairie Publishing Co., n.d.), 6–7.

25. Struthers Burt, *The Diary of a Dude-Wrangler* (New York: Charles Scribner's Sons, 1924), 264–65.

26. *Rocky Mountain News*, August 29, 1962, 39, Clippings File, Dude Ranches, DPL.

27. E. C. Abbott, *We Pointed Them North: Recollections of a Cowpuncher* (Norman: University of Oklahoma Press, 1955), 4, 138.

28. Burns, Gillespie, and Richardson, *Wyoming's Pioneer Ranches*, 238, 244–46, 636–37.

29. "The Landed Gentry," n.d., n.p., Clement Stuart Bengough entry; hand-written account by his niece, Evelyn R. Bengough, September 25, 1970; personal property and typed account of his "Personal Property," November 19, 1934; all in Biog. MS File, Clement Stuart Bengough, WHRC UW.

30. Ernest S. Osgood, *The Day of the Cattleman* (Chicago: University of Chicago Press, 1966), 218–22; Harry S. Drago, *The Great Range Wars: Violence on the Grasslands* (New York: Dodd, Mead & Co., 1970), 253–54.

31. F. P. Weaver, "Howard Eaton," Biog. MS File, Howard Eaton, WHRC UW.

32. Huidekoper, *My Experience*, 6, 22–24. Howard Eaton, "Hunting on the Frontier," pt. 1, *In the Open*, vol. 1, no. 9 (May 1912), 6–7, Biog. MS File, Howard Eaton, WHRC UW.

33. Pomeroy, *Golden West*, 95; Lang, *Ranching with Roosevelt*, 102, 114; Dresden, *Marquis de Morès*, 95.

34. Hermann Hagedorn, *Roosevelt in the Bad Lands* (Boston: Houghton Mifflin Co., 1930), 8, 13.

35. Custer Trail Ranch Guest Register, 1883–1903; typed letter on Eatons' Ranch stationery, n.d.; both in MS Collection, Eaton Ranch, WHRC UW.

36. Hagedorn, *Roosevelt*, 109–10.

37. Ibid., 260–61.

38. Weaver, "Howard Eaton," Biog. MS File, Howard Eaton, WHRC UW.

39. Huidekoper, *My Experience*, 5–6, 32–36, 57.

40. Weaver, "Howard Eaton," Biog. MS File, Howard Eaton, WHRC UW.

41. Lang, *Ranching with Roosevelt*, 164–65, 261–63.

42. Roberta Cheney and Clyde Erskine, *Music, Saddles and Flapjacks: Dudes at the OTO Ranch* (Missoula, Mont.: Mountain Press Publishing Co., 1978), 36–37.

43. *Minneapolis Journal*, March 18, 1934, 6.

44. L. W. (Gay) Randall, *Footprints Along the Yellowstone* (San Antonio: Naylor Co., 1961), 28–30, 40, 67; Cheney and Erskine, *Music, Saddles and Flapjacks*, 6–11.

45. Johnnie Holzwarth, interview by Dwight Hamilton and Ferrel Atkins, no. 2 tape, July 16, 1973, HH RMNP. Black, *Island in the Rockies*, 218.

46. *Rocky Mountain News*, April 16, 1896, 6.

47. Accounts of Settlers of Grand County, Colorado, Pioneer Museum, Hot Sulphur Springs, Colorado, n.d., 55–56, 94–99. Nell Pauly, *The Day Before Yesterday* (Apple Valley, Calif.: Apple Valley News, 1972), 104–9.

48. Brochure, n.d., Clippings File, Dude Ranch, Mountain Pass, WHRC UW.

49. William Wells to Prof. Daniel S. Gage, September 2, 1933, MS Collection, M. Struthers Burt, WHRC UW.

50. *Casper Star-Tribune*, April 27, 1968, 14A.

Chapter 3

1. Roberta Cheney and Clyde Erskine, *Music, Saddles and Flapjacks: Dudes at the OTO Ranch* (Missoula, Mont.: Mountain Press Publishing Co., 1978), 14–15, 20. L. W. (Gay) Randall, "The Man Who Put the Dude in Dude Ranching," *Montana*, vol. 10, no. 3 (July 1960), 30–31.

2. Cheney and Erskine, *Music, Saddles and Flapjacks*, 35–37, 59.

3. L. W. (Gay) Randall, *Footprints Along the Yellowstone* (San Antonio: Naylor Co., 1961), 72–73, 77–135.

4. Joseph P. Sullivan, "A Description and Analysis of the Dude Ranching Industry in Montana" (Master's thesis, University of Montana, 1971).

5. F. P. Weaver, "Howard Eaton," 12–15, Biog. MS File, Howard Eaton, WHRC UW.

6. *Sheridan Journal*, May 17, 1929, 1, 7, Vertical Files, Eatons' Ranch, Wyo.S.A. Biog. MS File, Mary Eaton, WHRC UW. Lincoln A. Lang, *Ranching with Roosevelt* (Philadelphia: J. B. Lippincott Co., 1926), 342.

7. *Sheridan Post Enterprise*, May 18, 1930, 12, Clippings File, Dude Ranch, WHRC UW.

8. Eatons' Guest Register, 1904–44, MS Collection, Eaton Ranch, WHRC UW.

9. Brochure, 1904, MS Collection, Eaton Ranch, Document Box 1, "Pamphlets," WHRC UW.

10. *Casper Star-Tribune*, December 22, 1968, 9, Vertical Files, Eatons' Ranch, Wyo.S.A.

11. Document Box 1, "Pamphlets"; Howard Eaton to P.H.L., November 15, 1920; both in MS Collection, Eaton Ranch, WHRC UW.

12. Charles G. Roundy, "The Origins and Early Development of Dude Ranching in Wyoming," *Annals of Wyoming*, vol. 45, no. 1 (Spring 1973), 16. Angela Buell, interview, March 28, 1972, Box 2, CGR WHRC UW.

13. Struthers Burt, "Dude Ranches," *The Outlook: An Illustrated Weekly of Current Life*, vol. 146, no. 4 (May 25, 1927), 112–13.

14. Mary R. Rinehart, *Through Glacier Park: Seeing America First with Howard Eaton* (Boston: Houghton Mifflin Co., 1916), 8–11.

15. Weaver, "Howard Eaton," 15–17, Biog. MS File, Howard Eaton, WHRC

UW. Doris Whithorn, "Wrangling Dudes in Yellowstone," *Frontier Times,* vol. 43, no. 6 (October–November 1969), 19–21.

16. Clippings File, Dude Ranch, IXL, WHRC UW. *Sheridan Post Enterprise,* May 18, 1930, 4, Clippings File, Dude Ranch, WHRC UW.

17. Roundy, "Origins," 17–19.

18. *The Dude Rancher,* vol. 21, no. 3 (July 1952), 8; Crossed Sabres Ranch, Wapiti, Wyoming, brochure, July 1980. Rich Marta and Donna Marta to author, July 11, 1980; *Cody Enterprise,* July 22, 1981, Touring Section, 4.

19. "Through the Year on a Dude Ranch," MS Collection, Marguerite D. Wyman, WHRC UW. Roundy, "Origins," 18. Watson H. Wyman to Gene Gressley, May 3, 1963, Clippings File, Wyoming, Towns, Shell, WHRC UW.

20. *Fort Collins Express,* October 17, 1906, 5, 8.

21. Mrs. Dudley (Betty) Hayden to Charles G. Roundy, n.d., Clippings File, Dude Ranch, Jackson Hole, WHRC UW.

22. Elizabeth Hayden to author, October 29, 1977; Harold Turner, interview, March 1972, Box 2, CGR WHRC UW. Fanny K. Wister, ed., *Owen Wister Out West: His Journals and Letters* (Chicago: University of Chicago Press, 1958), xiv–xvii.

23. *The Dude Rancher,* vol. 23, no. 4 (October 1954), 45, 47. Wendell Wilson, interview, May 20, 1972, Box 2, CGR WHRC UW.

24. Mrs. Dudley (Betty) Hayden to Charles G. Roundy, n.d., Clippings File, Dude Ranch, Jackson Hole, WHRC UW.

25. *Pinedale Roundup,* November 15, 1905, 1. James K. Harrower and Lester Bagley, "The Gros Ventre Lodge," *Wyoming Wild Life,* vol. 16, no. 9 (September 1952), 5–15, Vertical File, Dude Ranches, Wyo.S.A.; *Casper Star-Tribune,* April 27, 1968, 14A.

26. *Denver Times,* June 25, 1899, 17.

27. Lynn Mohn, "Walk with the Pioneers: Kawuneeche Valley Living History Program," brochure, Rocky Mountain Nature Association, Inc., 1976.

28. Mrs. Joyce Maulis to author, July 5, 1979. Rudy Menghini to author, July 4, 1979.

29. Charles C. Moore, "Frontier Notes," December 12, 1967, C. C. Moore, DPL. Idem, Introduction to *Hi, Stranger! The Complete Guide to Dude Ranches,* by Arthur Carhart (Chicago: Ziff-Davis, 1949), vii.

30. "Camping in the Rockies and the Yellowstone Park Summer Camp for Boys," 1907, C. C. Moore, DPL. Mrs. Ernest Miller, "Fiftieth Anniversary," *The Dude Rancher,* vol. 43, no. 1 (Spring 1974), 7.

31. Lists of Boys Camp Records, 1907–16, 1919–23; "Charles Moore, Round-up, Sunday, July 27, 1952"; both in C. C. Moore, DPL.

32. Roundy, "Origins," 10. Anne Chamberlin, "Big Dude Drive in the Crazies," *Saturday Evening Post,* vol. 240, no. 15 (July 29, 1967), 34.

33. *Bozeman Daily Chronicle,* September 28, 1926, 2.

34. Roundy, "Origins," 10.

35. Leon J. B. Dusseau, "Teepee Tours," *The Teepee Book* (March–April–May 1915), 53–88.

36. Jesse L. Williams, "Joy-Ranching and Dude-Wrangling," *Collier's,* vol. 51 (August 9, 1913), 22–23. Struthers Burt, *The Diary of a Dude-Wrangler* (New York: Charles Scribner's Sons, 1924), 49.

37. Jerome L. Rodnitzky, "Recapturing the West: The Dude Ranch in American Life," *Arizona and the West,* vol. 10 (Summer 1968), 122.

38. See, e.g.: Harold Wentworth and Stuart B. Flexner, comps. and eds., *Dictionary of American Slang* (New York: Crowell, 1960), 166; *Webster's New World Dictionary of the American Language,* college ed. (Cleveland and New York: World Publishing, 1962), 448; Lester V. Berrey and Melvin Van Den Bark, *The American Thesaurus of Slang,* 2d ed. (New York: Crowell, 1962), 913; Albert Barrère and Charles G. Leland, comps. and eds., *A Dictionary of Slang, Jargon & Cant,* 2 vols. (Detroit: Gale Research Co., 1967), 1:335.

39. Burt, *Diary of a Dude-Wrangler,* 60. Cheney and Erskine, *Music, Saddles and Flapjacks,* 112.

40. Mary Shawver, *Sincerely, Mary S.* (Casper, Wyo.: Prairie Publishing Co., n.d.), 1. Williams, "Joy-Ranching," 22. Larry Larom, Introduction to *Dude Ranches and Ponies,* by Lawrence B. Smith (New York: Coward-McCann, 1936), xiii, xix.

41. Ramon F. Adams, *Western Words* (Norman: University of Oklahoma Press, 1968), 102, 263, 315.

42. Frank J. Taylor, "Beauts and Saddles," *Collier's,* vol. 98. no. 6 (August 8, 1936), 21, 34. Hal G. Evarts, "Dude Wranglers," *Saturday Evening Post,* vol. 192 (May 1, 1920), 32.

43. Rodnitzky, "Recapturing the West," 112.

44. Williams, "Joy-Ranching," 22–23.

45. "Dude Ranching in Wyoming," *The Dude Rancher,* vol. 23, no. 4 (October 1954), 53. Thomas S. Chamblin, ed., *The Historical Encyclopedia of Colorado,* 2 vols. (Denver?: Colorado Historical Association, 1960?), 1:63–64.

46. Robert S. Yard, *The Book of National Parks* (New York: Charles Scribner's Sons, 1919, 1928), 3–4, 19–20. Earl Pomeroy, *In Search of the Golden West: The Tourist in Western America* (New York: Alfred A. Knopf, 1957), 154.

47. Accounts of Settlers of Grand County, Colorado, n.d., Pioneer Museum, Hot Springs, Colorado, 99.

48. Mary L. Cairns, *Grand Lake: The Pioneers* (Denver: World Press, 1946), 168.

49. Johnnie Holzwarth, interview by Ferrel Atkins, n.d., HH RMNP; Chamblin, *Encyclopedia of Colorado,* 1:688. Letterhead, Holzwarth's Trout Lodge and Ranch, HH RMNP.

50. Johnnie Holzwarth, interview by Ferrel Atkings, tape no. 1, July 16, 1973, HH RMNP.

51. Chamberlin, "Big Dude Drive," 34. Ted Townsend, "Dudes, Mutts & Crackerjacks," *New Republic,* vol. 132, no. 12 (March 21, 1955), 14.

52. *The World,* May 19, 1929, n.p., Clippings File, Dude Ranch, WHRC UW.

53. Mrs. Arch Allen, "The Ox Yoke Story," *Shorthorn World and Farm Magazine,* August 15, 1964, 49–51. "In Memoriam," card from Ox Yoke Ranch, Emigrant, Montana, 1972.

54. *Bozeman Daily Chronicle,* September 26, 1926, 2.

55. "Spending the Vacation on a Ranch," *Literary Digest,* vol. 89 (June 5, 1926), 71.

56. Harold Turner, interview, March 1972, CGR WHRC UW.

57. *Casper Tribune Herald,* July 10, 195?, n.p., C. C. Moore, DPL.

58. Valley Ranch Catalogue, 1925–26, Clippings File, Wyoming, Schools, WHRC UW. "The Round Up," brochure, 1928, Clippings File, Dude Ranch, Valley Ranch, WHRC UW. Charles Donnelly to Frank C. Wright, May 13, 1935, NPRCR, President's File 2001, Letters 1913–67, Old Building, Box 174, Burlington Northern Offices, St. Paul, Minn.

59. Cheney and Erskine, *Music, Saddles and Flapjacks,* 36, 71–73.

60. Ibid., 50, 59–62, 100–101.

61. "Howard Eaton's Horseback Trips," 1919, Clippings File, Dude Ranch, Eatons', WHRC UW. Rinehart, *Through Glacier Park,* 74–76.

62. Burt, "Dude Ranches," 112–13. Eatons' Ranch, brochure, 1941, Clippings File, Dude Ranches Wyoming, DPL.

63. *Sheridan Post,* April 6, 1922; *Pittsburgh Post,* April 16, 1922; both in Biog. MS File, Howard Eaton, WHRC UW.

64. Mary R. Rinehart, *My Story* (New York: Farrar & Rinehart, 1931), 199.

65. Eatons' Ranch, brochure, 1927, 4–6, Clippings File, Dude Ranches Wyoming, DPL. Biog. MS File, Mary Eaton, WHRC UW; Whithorn, "Wrangling Dudes," 22.

66. "Spending the Vacation on a Ranch," *Literary Digest,* vol. 89 (June 5, 1926), 70–71.

Chapter 4

1. Charles C. Moore to Rep. Leslie A. Miller, May 28, 1943, Box 1, Envelope 43, C. C. Moore, DPL. *Bozeman Daily Chrnicle,* September 28, 1926, 1.

2. Arthur H. Carhart, "Dogies and Dudes," *American Forestry,* vol. 29 (August 1923), 476–78. *Denver Times,* September 1, 1900, n.p., Clippings File, Colorado Tourism, DPL.

3. T. A. Larson, *History of Wyoming* (Lincoln: University of Nebraska Press, 1965), 423–24; Charles G. Roundy, "The Origins and Early Development of Dude Ranching in Wyoming," *Annals of Wyoming,* vol. 45, no. 1 (Spring 1973), 23–24.

4. *The World,* May 19, 1929, n.p., Clippings File, Dude Ranch, WHRC UW.

5. Hal G. Evarts, "Dude Wranglers," *Saturday Evening Post,* vol. 192 (May 1, 1920), 32.

6. *Sheridan Post Enterprise,* May 18, 1930, 11, 15. Roberta Cheney and Clyde Erskine, *Music, Saddles and Flapjacks: Dudes at the OTO Ranch* (Missoula, Mont.: Mountain Press Publishing Co., 1978), 35.

7. DRA Minutes, 1929, 61, Pam File, Wyo.S.A.; Mrs. Ernest Miller, "50th Anniversary," *The Dude Rancher,* vol. 43, no. 1 (Spring 1974), 9.

8. DRA Minutes, *The Dude Rancher,* vol. 1, no. 1 (December 1932), 22.

9. *Bozeman Daily Chronicle,* September 26, 1926, 3.

10. Ibid., September 28, 1926, 1; Cheney and Erskine, *Music, Saddles and Flapjacks,* 112; Mrs. Ernest Miller, "50th Anniversary," 7.

11. *Bozeman Daily Chronicle,* September 29, 1926, 1. There is some confusion in this article about the names of Ed Wyman and Dr. Horace Carncross; other information places them at these ranches at this time.

12. Clipping from unidentified newspaper, n.d., Clippings File, Dude Ranch, Montana, WHRC UW.

13. DRA Minutes, 1931, 133, DPL; Mrs. Ernest Miller, "50th Anniversary," 10.

14. DRA Minutes, 1930, 175, Pam File, Wyo.S.A.

15. "Spending the Vacation on a Ranch," *Literary Digest,* vol. 89 (June 5, 1926), 71.

16. *Prescribed Recreation: An Exclusive Feature of All-Year Guest Ranches, Inc.* (Los Angeles: Young & McCallister, 1934?), 1–10, DPL.

17. Ruth Borum, "The Lure of Ranch Life," *Progressive Arizona and the Great Southwest,* vòl. 8 (February, 1929), 22–23; Margaret K. Stewart, "What I've Learned About Ranches," *Progressive Arizona,* vol. 6 (February 1928), 14.

18. Etta G. Young, "The Garden of Allah," *Arizona: The State Magazine,* vol.

3 (June 1913), 4–5; Leb Chapman, "The Story of the Garden of Allah Guest Ranch, Ariz.," *Hoofs and Horns*, vol. 3 (October 1933), 14. For various claimants to the title of first dude ranch in Arizona, see: Philip W. Jones, "And I Learned about Ranching from 'Im," *Progressive Arizona and the Great Southwest*, vol. 8 (March 1929), 24; Joe W. Bloder, "Dude Ranching in Colorado and the West," 41, Documentary Resources, State Historical Society of Colorado; Frank B. Norris, "The Southern Arizona Guest Ranch as a Symbol of the West" (Master's thesis, University of Arizona, 1976), 38 n. 6. Norris has the most information on this subject, although no definitive list of dude ranches exists. Since lists were compiled by various people for different purposes, omission of a ranch does not prove that it was not run as a dude ranch.

19. A. T. Steele, "Lady Boss of Faraway Ranch," *Saturday Evening Post*, vol. 230, no. 37 (March 15, 1958), 134. Dr. Gordon Chappel, National Park Service, interview with author, October 16, 1980, and telephone interview, March 18, 1981. The National Park Service has not yet catalogued and opened for use the records of the Faraway Ranch.

20. Gail I. Gardner to author, August 19, 1974.

21. "Spending the Vacation," *Literary Digest*, 71; Ruth Borum, "Rancho Linda Vista," *Progressive Arizona*, vol. 6 (May 1928), 15–16, 28–29; Lowell J. Arnold, "Dude Ranches of Southern Arizona," *Progressive Arizona*, vol. 1 (September, 1925), 13–15; "Dude Ranches," *Hoofs and Horns*, vol. 1 (November 6, 1931), 8; "Seeing the Guest Ranches," *Tucson*, vol. 8 (January 1935), 10; Lowell J. Arnold, "Dude Ranching," *Progressive Arizona*, vol. 4 (February 1927), 20, 38–39. Josephine D. Corbin, "Beaver Creek Ranch—In the Valley of the Sun," *Progressive Arizona*, vol. 11 (September 1930), 18–20, 27–28; Myrtle S. Peterson, "They Recreate at Beaver Creek," *Progressive Arizona*, vol. 9 (October 1929), 21–23.

22. Cornelius C. Smith, *Tanque Verde: The Story of a Frontier Ranch* (Tucson?: n.p., 1978?), 102–5; copy obtained through courtesy of Dr. Gordon Chappell, National Park Service. Lowell J. Arnold, "Vacationing at the Circle Z," *Progressive Arizona*, vol. 2 (January 1926), 15–16; Manya Winsted, "Arizona's Fabulous Guest Ranches," *Arizona Highways*, vol. 56, no. 11 (November 1980), 2, 11. Margaret K. Stewart, "Vacationing on Y-Lightning," *Progressive Arizona*, vol. 5 (December 1927), 14–15.

23. Charles F. Parker and Jeanne S. Humburg, "Phantom Ranch," *Arizona Highways*, vol. 33, no. 5 (May 1957), 32–33.

24. Leo Weaver, "Life on a 'Dude' Ranch," *Arizona Highways*, vol. 4 (September 1928), 21; Roger Rayburn, "Going Western on a Guest Ranch," *Tucson*, vol. 8 (October 1935), 3–5. "Southern Arizona Guest Ranches," *Tucson*, vol. 3

(February 1930), 6; "Seeing the Guest Ranches," *Tucson,* vol. 8 (January 1935), 20.

25. Lawrence B. Smith, *Dude Ranches and Ponies* (New York: Coward-Mc-Cann, 1936), 282–86; Borum, "Rancho Linda Vista," 15–16, 28–29.

26. "Dude Ranches," *Hoofs and Horns,* 8. Norris, "Southern Arizona Guest Ranch" (thesis), 42; Norris calls the Arizona Dude and Guest Ranchers' Association the first Arizona group.

27. Earl Pomeroy, *In Search of the Golden West: The Tourist in Western America* (New York: Alfred A. Knopf, 1957), 185–88.

28. Basil Woon, *None of the Comforts of Home—But Oh, Those Cowboys!* (Reno: Federated Features, Inc., 1967), 6, 11, 13, 27, 43, 49.

29. Cornelius Vanderbilt, Jr., *Ranches and Ranch Life in America* (New York: Crown Publishers, 1968), 251–53.

30. Jerome L. Rodnitzky, "Recapturing the West: The Dude Ranch in American Life," *Arizona and the West,* vol. 10 (Summer 1968), 116.

31. Arreta L. Watts, "The Increasingly Popular 'Dude' Ranch," *Country Life,* vol. 54 (July 1928), 56.

32. *Boston Evening Transcript,* March 26, 1932, Magazine Section, 1; Rodnitzky, "Recapturing the West," 116.

33. "Spending the Vacation," *Literary Digest,* 71; *The Dude Rancher,* vol. 28, no. 1 (January 1959), 16.

34. Armine Von Tempski, "We Run a Dude-Ranch—in Hawaii!" *Sunset,* vol. 61 (September 1928), 20–23. Gordon von Tempsky to author, July 16, 1979, and telephone interview, April 29, 1981; he is a second cousin of Armine and Lorna. Armine used the spelling "Tempski" in her literary career.

35. Arthur Carhart, *Hi, Stranger! The Complete Guide to Dude Ranches* (Chicago: Ziff-Davis, 1949), 33–34, 36–38. Roundy, "Origins," 21–22.

36. Arthur N. Pack, *The Ghost Ranch Story* (Philadelphia: Board of Christian Education of the United Presbyterian Church in the U.S.A., 1960), 11–12. Lynn Mohn, "Walk with the Pioneers: Kawuneeche Valley Living History Program," brochure, Rocky Mountain Nature Association, Inc., 1976.

37. Angela Buell, interview, March 28, 1972, Box 2, CGR WHRC UW. "Facts, Figures and Fancies," *The Dude Rancher,* vol. 1, no. 1 (December 1932), 4.

38. Joseph P. Sullivan, "A Description and Analysis of the Dude Ranching Industry in Montana" (Master's thesis, University of Montana, 1971), 17. *Sheridan Post Enterprise,* May 18, 1930, 3; Rodnitzky, "Recapturing the West," 115–16; DRA Minutes, 1931, 128, DPL. Rodnitzky's statement that DRA ranchers invested over $6 million in buildings, land, and stock in 1930–32 seems to be

in error. The DRA Minutes indicate that these figures represent the total estimated value of the dude ranchers' property, rather than a massive additional investment.

39. Agnes W. Spring, "Women on a Dude Ranch," *The Western Farm Life 1947 Annual Livestock Review*, 150–51, Clippings File, Dude Ranch, Colorado, WHRC UW. H. Lee Jones, "Everybody's Dudin' It," *New Mexico*, vol. 14, no. 4 (April 1936), 43; Dr. Elizabeth Anderson, interview, March 1972, Box 2, CGR WHRC UW.

40. Robert Venuti, Sr., "Dude Ranching in Colorado," in Thomas S. Chamblin, ed., *The Historical Encyclopedia of Colorado* (Denver?: Colorado Historical Association, 1960?), 1:63. The beginning of the GD & GRA has been put variously between 1924 and 1945. Most evidence supports 1933. For other accounts, see: *Denver Post*, November 14, 1968, Clippings File, Dude Ranches, DPL; Bloder, "Dude Ranching in Colorado and the West," 10, Documentary Resources, State Historical Society of Colorado; Johnnie Holzwarth, interview by Roger J. and Susie Contor, January 1974?, HH RMNP; idem, telephone interview with author, June 4, 1980.

41. "Executive Secretary's Annual Report," *The Dude Rancher*, vol. 1, no. 1 (December 1932), 7.

42. Constitution of the Dude Ranchers' Association, DRA Minutes, 1931, 131, DPL; I. H. Larom, "President's Page," *The Dude Rancher*, vol. 6, no. 7 (July–August 1938), 4. *The Dude Rancher*, vol. 1, no. 1 (December 1932), 19–20.

43. Rodnitzky, "Recapturing the West," 115.

44. I. H. Larom, "President's Page," *The Dude Rancher*, vol. 6, no. 7 (July–August 1938), 25.

45. "'Dude' Ranches," *The Cattleman*, vol. 20, no. 1 (March 1934), 100; Frank J. Taylor, "Beauts and Saddles," *Collier's*, vol. 98, no. 6 (August 8, 1936), 34.

46. Lawrence B. Smith, *Dude Ranches*, 265–88; his appendix lists the ranches by state.

47. "The College of Agriculture," *University of Wyoming Bulletin*, vol. 31, no. 1 (1934–35), 170, WHRC UW. Frederick S. Hultz, *The Course in Recreational Ranching at the University of Wyoming*, 1936?, 3, WHRC UW.

48. "Dude Ranching is Latest Edition," unidentified newspaper, September 6, 1936, n.p., Clippings File, Dude Ranch, WHRC UW.

49. Mrs. Joyce Maulis to author, July 5, 1979.

50. Union Pacific Railroad, "Dude Ranches Out West," ca. 1931, 34–35,

Railroad File, Publicity Brochures, DPL. Mohn, "Walk with the Pioneers"; Johnnie Holzwarth, interview by Ferrel Atkins, ca. 1962–65, HH RMNP.

51. "Charles Moore, Round-up, Sunday, July 27, 1952," p. 4z, C. C. Moore, DPL.

52. Charles Moore to Horace Albright, March 31, 1933, Box 1, Envelope 43, C. C. Moore, DPL.

53. Charles Moore to Sen. Robert D. Carey, February 17, 1933, Box 1, Envelope 43, C. C. Moore, DPL.

54. *Cody Enterprise,* March 19, 1969, IHL BBHC.

55. "Data on Irving H. Larom—Princeton 1913," IHL BBHC.

56. *The Dude Rancher,* vol. 21, no. 3 (July 1952), 8.

57. John Turner? to Mrs. E. D. Carmalt, July 15, 1937, MS Collection, Turner's Triangle X Ranch, Box 17, WHRC UW; Harold Turner, interview, March 1972, Box 2, CGR WHRC UW.

58. Watson H. Wyman to Gene Gressley, May 3, 1963, Clippings File, Wyoming, Towns, Shell, WHRC UW; *The Dude Rancher,* vol. 6, no. 6 (April–May 1938), 17.

59. Clipping from unidentified Sheridan newspaper, February 3, 1927, p. 1?; *Wranglin' Notes,* no. 25 (May 1929); both in Clippings File, Dude Ranch, Eatons', WHRC UW.

60. Mr. and Mrs. Tom Ferguson, interview, March 28, 1972, Box 2, CGR WHRC UW. *The Dude Rancher,* vol. 6, no. 1 (January 1937), 6, 30; Nancy Ferguson to author, May 5, 1981.

61. *Sheridan Post Enterprise* May 18, 1930, 5.

62. Anne Chamberlin, "Big Dude Drive in the Crazies," *Saturday Evening Post,* vol. 240, no. 15 (July 29, 1967), 35.

63. "In Memoriam," card from Ox Yoke Ranch, Emigrant, Montana, 1972.

64. L. W. (Gay) Randall, "The Man Who Put the Dude in Dude Ranching," *Montana,* vol. 10, no. 3 (July 1960), 35, 38.

65. Cheney and Erskine, *Music, Saddles and Flapjacks,* 113–14 and eighth page of photographs after p. 68; *The Dude Rancher,* vol. 6, no. 7 (July–August 1938), 18. Randall, "Man Who Put Dude," 37, 41.

66. Charles H. Cooper to Charles Donnelly, November 10, 1927; memo from A. B. Smith, November 13, 1927; telegram, L. R. Challoner to B. W. Scandrett, October 14, 1929; E. E. Nelson to R. W. Clark, May 5, 1928; J. C. Spracklin to L. R. Challoner, September 17, 1929; J. C. Spracklin to E. E. Nelson, September 28, 1929; E. E. Nelson to J. C. Spracklin, October 3, 1929; all in NPRCR, President's File #2001-1, MHS.

67. *Bozeman Daily Chronicle,* August 3, 1928, 3, and August 26, 1928, 4.

Charles H. Cooper to Charles Donnelly, October 1, 1929, NPRCR, President's File #2001-1, MHS; Union Pacific Railroad, "Dude Ranches Out West," ca. 1931, 49, Railroad File, Publicity Brochures, DPL.

68. Hartley Bell to Ralph Budd, January 10, 1930; C. O. Jenks to Ralph Budd, February 12, 1930; Carl M. Hansen to Ralph Budd, February 13, 1930; Hartley Bell to Ralph Budd, February 19, 1930; Ralph Budd to Carl M. Hansen, February 28, 1930; all in Great Northern Railway Company Records, President's Subject File #13095, MHS. *The Dude Rancher,* vol. 6, no. 1 (January 1937), 12.

69. *Prescribed Recreation,* 11–14, 17–23, DPL. Ann C. Haslanger, *A History of Vermejo Park* (Vermejo Park, N.M.: Vermejo Park, 1980), 8.

Chapter 5

1. Angela Buell, interview, March 28, 1972; Alys Ritterbrown, interview, n.d.; both in Box 2, CGR WHRC UW. *Sheridan Post Enterprise,* August 30, 1925, sec. 4, 1, WHRC UW.

2. Roberta Cheney and Clyde Erskine, *Music, Saddles and Flapjacks: Dudes at the OTO Ranch* (Missoula, Mont.: Mountain Press Publishing Co., 1978), 63 and photo caption fourteen pages after p. 68; L. W. (Gay) Randall, *Footprints Along the Yellowstone* (San Antonio: Naylor Co., 1961), 72–73. A trip east meant a visit anywhere east of the Rocky Mountains, mainly the upper Midwest or the Northeast.

3. *Boston Evening Transcript,* March 26, 1932, Magazine Section, 1. Peggy Schaffer, interview, March 30, 1972; Dr. Elizabeth Anderson, interview, March 1972; Mrs. Donald Siggins, interview, March 31, 1972; all in Box 2, CGR WHRC UW. Frank A. Tinker, "Puttin' Up the Dudes," *Westways,* vol. 65, no. 11 (November 1973), 54; idem, "Whatever Happened to Dude Ranches?" *Catholic Digest,* vol. 38, no. 9 (July 1974), 104–5.

4. *Cody Enterprise,* March 19, 1969, 1, IHL BBHC; Valley Ranch Catalogue, 1925–26, Clippings File, Wyoming, Schools, WHRC UW; M. M. Goodsill to J. F. Berry, March 27, 1956, NPRCR, President's File 2001, Letters 1913–67, Old Building, Box 174, Burlington Northern Offices, St. Paul, Minn.

5. DRA Minutes, 1930, 29 Pam File, Wyo.S.A.; DRA Minutes, 1931, 47, DPL. Mildred A. Martin, *The Martins of Gunbarrel* (Caldwell, Idaho: Caxton, 1959), 218.

6. Johnnie Holzwarth, interview by Ferrel Atkins, n.d., HH RMNP; *Denver Post,* Empire Magazine, December 1, 1974, 73.

7. DRA Minutes, 1929, 99, Pam File, Wyo.S.A. Chapters 6 and 7 also treat

the appeal of dude ranches and their management. *Bozeman Daily Chronicle,* September 28, 1926, 2.

8. DRA Minutes, 1931, 53–54, DPL.

9. For the importance of repeat business, see, e.g.: Ingolf K. Vogeler, "Farm and Ranch Vacationing in the United States" (Ph.D. diss., University of Minnesota, 1973), 112; Anne Chamberlin, "Big Dude Drive in the Crazies," *Saturday Evening Post,* vol. 240, no. 15 (July 29, 1967), 33; Joseph P. Sullivan, "A Description and Analysis of the Dude Ranching Industry in Montana" (Master's thesis, University of Montana, 1971), 34–35; Mr. and Mrs. Roy Chambers, interview, May 20, 1972, Box 2, CGR WHRC UW.

10. *Bozeman Daily Chronicle,* September 19, 1926, 4. B. O. Johnson to Charles Donnelly, November 15, 1927, NPRCR, President's File 2001-1, MHS.

11. DRA Minutes, 1930, 118–22, Pam File, Wyo.S.A. *The World,* May 19, 1929, n.p., Clippings File, Dude Ranch, WHRC UW. DRA Minutes, 1931, 54–56, DPL.

12. DRA Minutes, 1929, 63–71, Pam File, Wyo.S.A.; L. L. Perrin, "You Profit from the Dude Ranch Advertising," *The Dude Rancher,* vol. 1, no. 1 (December 1932), 8.

13. "Ranch Life in the Buffalo Bill Country," ca. 1927, Clippings File, Dude Ranches, DPL. Dude ranch booklets published by railroads may be found in the MS collections of the DPL, State Historical Society of Colorado, WHRC UW, and Wyo.S.A.

14. Jerome L. Rodnitzky, "Recapturing the West: The Dude Ranch in American Life," *Arizona and the West,* vol. 10 (Summer 1968), 125; Earl Pomeroy, *In Search of the Golden West: The Tourist in Western America* (New York: Alfred A. Knopf, 1957), 89. Burlington ranch booklet, 15, 22, 48, 51, Clippings File, Dude Ranches, DPL.

15. "Montana Dude Ranches," *The Dude Rancher,* vol. 6, no. 7 (July–August 1938), 8–9. DRA Minutes, 1929, 61, 63, 87, Pam File, Wyo.S.A.

16. Arthur N. Pack, *The Ghost Ranch Story* (Philadelphia: Board of Christian Education of the United Presbyterian Church in the U.S.A., 1960), 23. *Boston Post,* April 1, 1934, B-6; NPRCR, President's File #356-218, Box 127, MHS.

17. *The World,* May 19, 1929, n.p., Clippings File, Dude Ranch, WHRC UW.

18. DRA Minutes, 1929, 17, 87–88, Pam File, Wyo.S.A.

19. Edward Burnett, misc. Johnson County WPA Files, no. S-500, p. 4, Wyo.S.A.; *The World,* May 19, 1929, n.p., Clippings File, Dude Ranch, WHRC UW.

20. Mary R. Rinehart, "The Sleeping Giant," *Ladies Home Journal,* vol. 28

(May 1921), 21; DRA Minutes, 1930, 67, Pam File, Wyo.S.A. Robert S. Yard, *The Book of the National Parks* (New York: Charles Scribner's Sons, 1919, 1928), 18–19.

21. DRA Minutes, 1931, 27, 131–34, DPL. DRA Minutes, 1929, 25, 27, 33, 41, Pam File, Wyo.S.A. DRA Minutes, 1930, 43, 93–95, Pam File, Wyo.S.A.; *Sheridan Post Enterprise*, May 18, 1930, 6, 12. The newspaper reverses the second- and third-place winners and misspells Gardner.

22. DRA Minutes, 1929, 25, 41–45, Pam File, Wyo.S.A. *The World*, May 19, 1929, n.p., Clippings File, Dude Ranch, WHRC UW.

23. DRA Minutes, 1930, 99, Pam File, Wyo.S.A.

24. DRA Minutes, 1929, 13, 15, 21, 23, 35, 37, 39, 43, 47, 49, 135, Pam File, Wyo.S.A.

25. Ibid., 15, 17. DRA Minutes, 1930, 21–25, 37, 85, 95–101, 112–15, Pam File, Wyo.S.A.

26. DRA Minutes, 1931, 45–46, DPL. DRA Minutes, 1930, 79, Pam File, Wyo.S.A.

27. DRA Minutes, 1929, 29, 31, Pam File, Wyo.S.A.; DRA Minutes, 1931, 127–28, 131–34, DPL.

28. DRA Minutes, 1930, 45, Pam File, Wyo.S.A.; DRA Minutes, 1931, v–vi, 33–42, 94, DPL.

29. DRA Minutes, 1929, 73, Pam File, Wyo.S.A.

30. DRA Minutes, 1931, 26–27, 29–31, DPL.

31. *Sheridan Post Enterprise*, May 18, 1930, 1–16. DRA Minutes, 1931, 93, 119–20, DPL. *The Dude Rancher*, vol. 4, no. 1 (November 1934), 28. A. E. Oakes to J. C. Turner, April 11, 1939, MS Collection, Turner's Triangle X Ranch, Box 17, WHRC UW; Peter Vischer, "Ranching Is All Right!" *Horse and Horseman*, vol. 21, no. 5 (April 1939), 24–25, 34–36; "Ranch Directory," *Horse and Horseman*, vol. 21, no. 5 (April 1939), 12–15, vol. 21, no. 6 (May 1939), 13–15, and vol. 22, no. 1 (June 1939), 13–15.

32. See various issues of *The Dude Rancher* for details.

33. Johnnie Holzwarth, interview with author, July 16, 1974.

34. DRA Minutes, 1930, [3], 125–28, Pam File, Wyo.S.A.

35. DRA Minutes, 1929, 47, 49, 51, Pam File, Wyo.S.A.

36. Ibid., 41, 43, 77, 79.

37. DRA Minutes, 1930, 85, 110–11, Pam File, Wyo.S.A. Convention sites appear in the *Minute Books* and issues of *The Dude Rancher*. DRA Minutes, 1931, 123–28, DPL.

38. For samples of other types of advertising, see: *Outlook*, vol. 145, no. 15 (April 13, 1927), 476; "The Blue Book of Western Dude Ranches," 1949, Clip-

pings File, Dude Ranches, DPL; and numerous letters in MS Collection, Turner's Triangle X Ranch, WHRC UW.

39. Jesse L. Williams, "Joy-Ranching and Dude-Wrangling," *Collier's,* vol. 51 (August 9, 1913), 23.

40. Leon J. B. Dusseau, "Teepee Tours," *The Teepee Book,* Ranch Resort Number (March–April–May 1915), 51–88.

41. Hal G. Evarts, "Dude Wranglers," *Saturday Evening Post,* vol. 192 (May 1, 1920), 32, 34, 181–82.

42. "A Lady on a Dude Ranch," *Literary Digest,* vol. 85 (June 27, 1925), 48, 50.

43. Ross Santee, *The Bar X Golf Course* (Flagstaff: Northland Press, 1971; originally pub. 1933), esp. 28, 45, 88–89.

44. Steve Strang, *Dude Rancher: A Story of Modern Ranching* (New York: Dodd, Mead & Co., 1941), esp. 7, 19–26, 34–35, 84–90, 136, 174–92, 266, 269.

45. Lawrence B. Smith, *Dude Ranches and Ponies* (New York: Coward-Mc-Cann, 1936); Arthur Carhart, *Hi, Stranger! The Complete Guide to Dude Ranches* (Chicago: Ziff-Davis, 1949).

46. Struthers Burt, *The Diary of a Dude-Wrangler* (New York: Charles Scribner's Sons, 1924). Lincoln A. Lang, *Ranching with Roosevelt* (Philadelphia: J. B. Lippincott Co., 1926); Hermann Hagedorn, *Roosevelt in the Bad Lands* (Boston: Houghton Mifflin, 1930); Theodore Roosevelt, *Ranch Life and the Hunting Trail* (Ann Arbor: University Microfilms, 1966) are examples.

47. Loraine H. Fielding, *French Heels to Spurs* (New York: Century Co., 1930); DRA Minutes, 1930, 45, 97, 146, Pam File, Wyo.S.A.

48. Mary R. Rinehart, *My Story* (New York: Farrar & Rinehart, 1931), 310.

49. Ibid., 311.

50. Mary R. Rinehart, "What Is a Dude Ranch?" *Harper's Bazaar,* August 1927, 68; idem, "Sleeping Giant," 21. Idem, *Tenting To-Night: A Chronicle of Sport and Adventure in Glacier Park and the Cascade Mountains* (Boston: Houghton Mifflin Co., 1918). Idem, *My Story,* 310–11.

51. Biog. MS File, Mary R. Rinehart, WHRC UW; see also bibliography.

52. Pomeroy, *Golden West,* 153–54. Mary R. Rinehart, "Summer Comes to the Ranch," *Saturday Evening Post,* vol. 198, no. 1 (July 4, 1925), 72.

53. Mary R. Rinehart, "To Wyoming," *Saturday Evening Post,* vol. 199, no. 14 (October 2, 1926), 16–17, 161–62, 165–66, 169; idem, "The Cavvy," *Saturday Evening Post,* vol. 199, no. 13 (September 25, 1926), 6–7, 129–30, 132; idem, "Riding the Circle on Hanging Woman," *Saturday Evening Post,* vol. 198, no. 16 (October 17, 1925), 6–7, 71–72, 74, 79.

54. Idem, "Sleeping Giant"; idem, "What Is a Dude Ranch?"

Chapter 6

1. "Spending the Vacation on a Ranch," *Literary Digest,* vol. 89 (June 5, 1926), 70.

2. Jerome L. Rodnitzky, "Recapturing the West: The Dude Ranch in American Life," *Arizona and the West,* vol. 10 (Summer 1968), 119–21.

3. Roberta Cheney and Clyde Erskine, *Music, Saddles and Flapjacks: Dudes at the OTO Ranch* (Missoula, Mont.: Mountain Press Publishing Co., 1978), 40–42.

4. Warren J. Belasco, *Americans on the Road: From Autocamp to Motel, 1910–1945* (Cambridge: MIT Press, 1979), 47–48, 56–60.

5. Mary R. Rinehart, "What Is a Dude Ranch?" *Harper's Bazaar,* August 1927, 129–30; Marcia Meigs, "Happy Days on a Dude Ranch," *Country Life,* vol. 64 (May 1933), 43–46. Agnes W. Spring, "Women on a Dude Ranch," *The Western Farm Life 1947 Annual Livestock Review,* Clippings File, Dude Ranch, Colorado, WHRC UW.

6. *Boston Evening Transcript,* March 26, 1932, Magazine Section, 1.

7. Jesse L. Williams, "Joy-Ranching and Dude-Wrangling," *Collier's,* vol. 51 (August 9, 1913), 23. "Dressing the Dude," *Vogue,* vol. 87, no. 9 (May 1, 1936), 140–41.

8. Hal G. Evarts, "Dude Wranglers," *Saturday Evening Post,* vol. 192 (May 1, 1920), 32.

9. Struthers Burt, *The Diary of a Dude Wrangler* (New York: Charles Scribner's Sons, 1924), 292–93.

10. Margaret E. Murie, "Dude Ranchers Are Influential People," *The Dude Rancher,* vol. 39, no. 14 (Winter 1970–71), 10–13. Clippings File, Dude Ranch, Double Dee, WHRC UW.

11. Cheney and Erskine, *Music, Saddles and Flapjacks,* 37.

12. Giving a guest a dangerous horse was rare; for a wild example of such an encounter, see Spike Van Cleve, *40 Years' Gatherin's* (Kansas City: Lowell Press, 1977), 279–87.

13. Struthers Burt, "Western Horses and Eastern Riders," *The Dude Rancher,* vol. 17, no. 2 (April 1948), 34–36.

14. Ibid., 8–9, 38–39.

15. *Rocky Mountain News,* July 31, 1977, Now Section, 2–3, 7.

16. Van Cleve, *40 Years',* 218.

17. Leon J. B. Dusseau, "Teepee Tours," *The Teepee Book,* Ranch Resort Number (March–April–May 1915), 79; *Sheridan Post Enterprise,* May 18, 1930, 7.

18. Cal Queal, "Colorado Dude Wrangler," *Mainliner,* vol. 14 (July 1970),

31–32. Rochelle Klein, *City Slickers on a Dude Ranch* (New York: Comet Press Books, 1959), 1–6.

19. Mary R. Rinehart, *The Out Trail* (New York: George H. Doran Co., 1923), 47–49.

20. Johnnie Holzwarth, telephone interview with author, June 4, 1980. The author has taken this ride a half dozen times.

21. *The World*, May 19, 1929, n.p., Clippings File, Dude Ranch, WHRC UW.

22. Evarts, "Dude Wranglers," 181–82.

23. Struthers Burt, *Diary of a Dude Wrangler*, 154–56.

24. *The World*, May 19, 1929, n.p., Clippings File, Dude Ranch, WHRC UW. Fanny K. Wister, ed., *Owen Wister Out West: His Journals and Letters* (Chicago: University of Chicago Press, 1958), xiv–xv, 47–48.

25. Cheney and Erskine, *Music, Saddles and Flapjacks*, 87–90.

26. "Howard Eaton's Horseback Trips," 1919, Clippings File, Dude Ranch, Eatons', WHRC UW. Angela Buell, interview, March 28, 1972, Box 2, CGR WHRC UW. William T. Hornaday, "Howard Eaton, an Easterner Honored by the Far West," *McClure's Magazine*, May 1923, 40–42; clipping from *Pittsburgh Chronicle Telegraph*, July 31, 1928, n.p.; both in Biog. MS File, Howard Eaton, WHRC UW.

27. Mary R. Rinehart, *Tenting To-Night: A Chronicle of Sport and Adventure in Glacier Park and the Cascade Mountains* (Boston: Houghton Mifflin Co., 1918), 7, 11–14, 102–3; idem, *Through Glacier Park: Seeing America First with Howard Eaton* (Boston: Houghton Mifflin Co., 1916), 18–19, 41.

28. Mary R. Rinehart, *My Story* (New York: Farrar & Rinehart, 1931), 200–205, 215–19.

29. Johnnie Holzwarth, telephone interview with author, June 4, 1980; Johnnie Holzwarth to author, June 1, 1972.

30. Neil Morgan, "Hey Dude!" *Western's World: The Magazine of Western Airlines*, vol. 4, no. 3 (June–July 1973), 43.

31. Frank A. Tinker, "Whatever Happened to Dude Ranches?" *Catholic Digest*, vol. 38, no. 9 (July 1974), 103.

32. Rinehart, "What Is a Dude Ranch?" 129. Raymond J. Raddy, "Dude Ranching Is Not All Yippee!" *The Western Horseman*, vol. 17, no. 4 (April 1952), 36. Leta Tompkins, "Dude Horses," *The Western Horseman*, vol. 17, no. 4 (April 1952), 14, 33–34.

33. Ernest Miller, "Dude Ranch Horses," *The Cattleman,* vol. 28 (September 1941), 139, 141.

34. Burt, "Western Horses," 40. Johnnie Holzwarth, telephone interview with author, June 4, 1980.

35. Carol Van Cleve, "The Making and Breaking of Dude Horses," *The Dude Rancher,* vol. 42, no. 2 (Summer 1973), 16–18. Lewis Smith, "The Packer Sees Spots," *Appaloosa News,* vol. 34, no. 8 (August 1977), 42–43.

36. *Boston Evening Transcript,* March 26, 1932, Magazine Section, 1.

37. Mrs. Dudley (Betty) Hayden to Charles G. Roundy, n.d., Clippings File, Dude Ranch, Jackson Hole, WHRC UW. Harold Turner, interview, March 1972, Box 2, CGR WHRC UW; John C. Turner to Allan Morris, April 4, 1935, MS Collection, Turner's Triangle X Ranch, Box 17, WHRC UW.

38. Art Isberg, "A Meeting in the Fall," *The American Hunter,* vol. 2, no. 10 (October 1974), 47.

39. Ingolf K. Vogeler, "Farm and Ranch Vacationing in the United States" (Ph.D. diss., University of Minnesota, 1973), 85–86. Mr. and Mrs. Roy Chambers, interview, May 20, 1972, Box 2, CGR WHRC UW.

40. Bar Lazy J Guest Ranch, Parshall, Colorado, brochure, n.d. Robert C. Black III, *Island in the Rockies: The History of Grand County, Colorado, to 1930* (Boulder: Pruett Press, 1969), 111, 247.

41. Featured, e.g., in literature from Timber Ridge Ranch (Idaho), Devil's Thumb Ranch (Colorado), and Vee Bar Ranch (Wyoming). Henry A. Miles to J. C. Turner, May 13, 1937, MS Collection, Turner's Triangle X Ranch, Box 17, WHRC UW.

42. Van Cleve, *40 Years',* 215–16.

43. William M. Raine, "The Dude Rides Circle," *Sunset,* vol. 60 (April 1928), 56, 58, 60.

44. "Rope Your Own!" *Sunset,* vol. 57 (September 1926), 12–13.

45. Frank Wright to author, January 25, 1976. Johnnie Holzwarth, taped interview, January 19, 1974, HH RMNP.

46. Dr. Elizabeth Anderson, interview, March 1972, Box 2, CGR WHRC UW. For cowboys and wranglers on dude ranches, see Chapter 7.

47. Alys Ritterbrown, interview, n.d., Box 2, CGR WHRC UW. Barbara C. Hooton, *Guestward Ho!* (New York: Vanguard, 1956), 77.

48. Dorothea Park-Lewis, "Dude-Ling," *House Beautiful,* vol. 81, no. 4 (April 1939), 122. Rinehart, "What Is a Dude Ranch?" 130.

49. Frank Wright to author, January 25, 1976.

50. Mr. and Mrs. Tom Ferguson, interview, March 28, 1972, Box 2, CGR WHRC UW.

Chapter 7

1. Oliver La Farge, "They All Ride," *Vogue,* vol. 87, no. 9 (May 1, 1936), 97.

2. Ingolf K. Vogeler, "Farm and Ranch Vacationing in the United States" (Ph.D. diss., University of Minnesota, 1973), 1, 14–15. *Platte County Record,* August 4, 1939, Biog. MS File, Owen Wister, WHRC UW.

3. Mody C. Boatright, "The American Myth Rides the Range," *Southwest Review,* vol. 36, no. 3 (Summer 1951), 157, 163. Frank A. Tinker, "Puttin' Up the Dudes," *Westways,* vol. 65, no. 11 (November 1973), 53. Roberta Cheney and Clyde Erskine, *Music, Saddles and Flapjacks: Dudes at the OTO Ranch* (Missoula, Mont.: Mountain Press Publishing Co., 1978), 42.

4. Mary R. Rinehart, *My Story* (New York: Farrar & Rinehart, 1931), 410. Arthur N. Pack, *The Ghost Ranch Story* (Philadelphia: Board of Christian Education of the United Presbyterian Church in the U.S.A., 1960), 11–12.

5. Gene Hoopes, *Tales of a Dude Wrangler* (San Antonio: Naylor Co., 1963), 16–20, 73–74, 84–104. Idem, *End of the Trail* (San Antonio: Naylor Co., 1959), 2, 5, 29–34, 97–105, 114–15.

6. Caroline Lockhart, *The Dude Wrangler* (Garden City, N.Y.: Doubleday, Page & Co., 1921), 150.

7. Hal G. Evarts, "Dude Wranglers," *Saturday Evening Post,* vol. 192 (May 1, 1920), 32–34, 181.

8. *Minneapolis Journal,* March 18, 1934, 6.

9. *Wyoming State Tribune–Cheyenne State Leader,* December 19, 1936, 2.

10. Ibid.

11. Pete Smythe, *Pete Smythe: Big City Dropout* (Boulder: Pruett Press, 1968), 208.

12. Frank J. Taylor, "Beauts and Saddles," *Collier's,* vol. 98, no. 6 (August 8, 1936), 34.

13. Basil Woon, *None of the Comforts of Home—But Oh, Those Cowboys!* (Reno: Federated Features, Inc., 1967), n.p.

14. Gail I. Gardner to author, August 19, 1974.

15. Gail I. Gardner, *Orejana Bull for Cowboys Only* (Wickenburg, Ariz.: Desert Caballeros, 1950), 12–13.

16. See also: Jim Whilt, "Fate of the Dude Wrangler," *The Western Horseman,* vol. 28 (September 1963), 13.

17. Struthers Burt, *The Diary of a Dude Wrangler* (New York: Charles Scribner's Sons, 1924), 50. *Rocky Mountain News,* February 17, 1929, Magazine Section, 2.

18. Letter, Mrs. Bucky King, Sheridan, Wyoming, to author, November 28, 1982. La Farge, "They All Ride," 97, 138.

19. Evarts, "Dude Wranglers," 34.

20. Ibid.

21. Jerome L. Rodnitzky, "Recapturing the West: The Dude Ranch in American Life," *Arizona and the West*, vol. 10 (Summer 1968), 125.

22. Cornelius Vanderbilt, Jr., *Ranches and Ranch Life in America* (New York: Crown Publishers, 1968), 253–54. *The World*, May 19, 1929, n.p., Clippings File, Dude Ranch, WHRC UW. Grace E. Ray, "Down the Long Pack Trail," *Independent Women*, vol. 20, no. 7 (July 1941), 204.

23. Raymond Schuessler, "Ever Try a Dude Ranch Vacation?" *Better Homes and Gardens*, vol. 31, no. 3 (March 1953), 251. Spike Van Cleve, *40 Years' Gatherin's* (Kansas City: Lowell Press, 1977), 143.

24. Cheney and Erskine, *Music, Saddles and Flapjacks*, 70–71.

25. Anne Chamberlin, "Big Dude Drive in the Crazies," *Saturday Evening Post*, vol. 240, no. 15 (July 29, 1967), 33. White Grass Ranch, Moose, Wyoming, brochure, n.d.

26. Frank J. Taylor, "Ride Trail, Dude, and Grow Young!" *Hearst's International—Cosmopolitan*, August 1932, 54, Clippings File, Dude Ranch, WHRC UW. Raymond J. Raddy, "Dude Ranching Is Not All Yippee!" *The Western Horseman*, vol. 17, no. 8 (April 1952), 38.

27. Clifford P. Westermeier, *Man, Beast, Dust: The Story of Rodeo* (Denver: World Press, Inc., 1947), 353. This idea is very clearly presented in the 1974 film, *The Great American Cowboy*.

28. *Rocky Mountain News*, July 31, 1977, Now Section, 2–3, 7.

29. Frank A. Tinker, "Whatever Happened to Dude Ranches?" *Catholic Digest*, vol. 38, no. 9 (July 1974), 103.

30. Pack, *Ghost Ranch Story*, 29.

31. Mrs. Joyce Maulis to author, March 1, 1978.

32. Smythe, *Pete Smythe*, 221.

33. Cheney and Erskine, *Music, Saddles and Flapjacks*, 104–6.

34. Barbara C. Hooton, *Guestward Ho!* (New York: Vanguard, 1956), 59, 65, 101, 209. Patricia Lauber, *Cowboys and Cattle Ranching* (New York: Crowell, 1973), 121.

35. Mary (Mrs. Ned) Frost, "House Management Department," *The Dude Rancher*, vol. 6, no. 7 (July–August 1938), 5. "Report to National Park Service by Charles Moore," September 1, 1952, Box 2, Envelop 70, C. C. Moore, DPL. John Holzwarth III, interview with author, July 26, 1974.

36. Raddy, "Not All Yippee!" 37–38.

37. Mr. and Mrs. Tom Ferguson, interview, March 28, 1972; Alys Ritter-brown, interview, n.d.; both in Box 2, CGR WHRC UW.

38. "Rope Your Own!" *Sunset,* vol. 57 (September 1926), 14. Rudy Menghini to author, January 30, 1978; Glen Fales, interview, April 1, 1972, Box 2, CGR WHRC UW.

39. Mrs. Donald Siggins, interview, March 31, 1972, Box 2, CGR WHRC UW. Family operation is noted in most dude ranch brochures.

40. *Denver Post,* December 22, 1947, 4.

41. Agnes W. Spring, "Women on a Dude Ranch," *Western Farm Life 1947 Annual Livestock Review,* 14, 150, Clippings File, Dude Ranch, Colorado, WHRC UW. Allen "Ike" Fordyce, interview, March 28, 1972, Box 2, CGR WHRC UW.

42. "I Want to Buy a Ranch . . .," *The Dude Rancher,* vol. 28, no. 2 (Spring 1958), 18–19. Smythe, *Pete Smythe,* 114.

43. Raddy, "Not All Yippee!" 35.

44. Smythe, *Pete Smythe,* 98–99. "Report to National Park Service by Charles Moore," September 15, 1952, Box 2, Envelope 70, C. C. Moore, DPL. "'Dude' Ranches," *The Cattleman,* vol. 20, no. 1 (March 1934), 100.

45. William T. Hornaday, "Howard Eaton, an Easterner Honored by the Far West," *McClure's Magazine,* May 1923, 40, Biog. MS File, Howard Eaton, WHRC UW; Dr. Elizabeth Anderson, interview, March 1972, Box 2, CGR WHRC UW.

46. Hooton, *Guestward Ho!* 72–73. Struthers Burt, "Dude Ranches," *The Outlook: An Illustrated Weekly of Current Life,* vol. 146, no. 4 (May 25, 1927), 113–14.

47. Burt, *Diary of a Dude-Wrangler,* 50–53.

48. Hooton, *Guestward Ho!* 41, 75–76, 152.

49. B. O. Johnson to Charles Donnelly, November 15, 1927), NPRCR, President's File #2001-1, MHS.

50. "The Model Dude Rancher," *The Dude Rancher,* vol. 23, no. 3 (July 1954), 54–55.

51. Smythe, *Pete Smythe,* 230. *Wyoming State Tribune–Cheyenne State Leader,* December 19, 1936, 2.

52. Rex Stratton, "Financing a Dude Ranch Operation," *The Dude Rancher,* vol. 26, no. 1 (January 1957), 14, 20.

53. Angela Buell, interview, March 28, 1972; Fred Garlow, interview, March 31, 1972; both in Box 2, CGR WHRC UW. Mrs. Joyce Maulis to author, March 1, 1978.

54. Dr. Elizabeth Anderson, interview, March 1972, Box 2, CGR WHRC UW.

55. Evarts, "Dude Wranglers," 32, 182. Rodnitzky, "Recapturing the West," 125.

Chapter 8

1. This discussion of conservation relates chiefly to dude ranchers in the southern Rocky Mountains.

2. Howard Eaton, "Hunting on the Frontier," *In The Open,* vol. 1, no. 9 (May 1912), 5–11; ibid., no. 10 (June), 5–11; ibid., no. 11 (July), 5–12; ibid; vol. 3, no. 1 (August), 5–12; all in MS Collection, Eaton Ranch, WHRC UW. William T. Hornaday, "Howard Eaton, an Easterner Honored by the Far West," *McClure's Magazine,* May 1923, Biog. MS File, Howard Eaton, WHRC UW; Mary R. Rinehart, *My Story* (New York: Farrar & Rinehart, 1931), 198.

3. Lincoln A. Lang, *Ranching with Roosevelt* (Philadelphia: J. B. Lippincott Co., 1926), 31–47, 252–53; Arthur C. Huidekoper, *My Experience and Investment in the Bad Lands of Dakota and Some of the Men I Met There* (Baltimore: Wirth Brothers, 1947), 57.

4. F. P. Weaver, "Howard Eaton"; clipping from unidentified newspaper, n.d.; both in Biog. MS File, Howard Eaton, WHRC UW. Theodore Roosevelt to Howard Eaton, October 24, 1902, Document Box 1, MS Collection, Eaton Ranch, WHRC UW.

5. Rinehart, *My Story,* 199; idem, *Nomad's Land* (New York: George H. Doran Co., 1926), 185; clipping from *Billings Daily Journal,* n.d., Biog. MS File, Howard Eaton, WHRC UW. For examples of delivery data, see Corporate Record Book V, p. 272, and Book VI, p. 400, MS Collection, Eaton Ranch, WHRC UW.

6. John F. Reiger, *American Sportsmen and the Origins of Conservation* (New York: Winchester Press, 1975), 117; John F. Reiger to author, January 6, 1981.

7. Clippings from *Pittsburgh Post,* April 16, 1922, and *Sheridan Post,* April 6, 1922, in Biog. MS File, Howard Eaton, WHRC UW. Chapter 3 details Eaton's death.

8. Roberta Cheney and Clyde Erskine, *Music, Saddles and Flapjacks: Dudes at the OTO Ranch* (Missoula, Mont.: Mountain Press Publishing Co., 1978), 36–37. L. W. (Gay) Randall, "The Man Who Put the Dude in Dude Ranching," *Montana,* vol. 10, no. 3 (July 1960), 29–32.

9. L. W. (Gay) Randall, *Footprings Along the Yellowstone* (San Antonio: Naylor Co., 1961), 88, 171. Joe Back, *The Sucker's Teeth* (Denver: Sage Books, 1965), is informative fiction about the slaughter for elk tusks.

10. Randall, "Man Who Put Dude," 39–41; Cheney and Erskine, *Music, Saddles and Flapjacks*, 23–24.

11. Arthur H. Carhart to author, October 27, 1977.

12. Mrs. Ernest Miller, "50th Anniversary," *The Dude Rancher*, vol. 43, no. 1 (Spring 1974), 7. Charles C. Moore to Gov. Lester Hunt, January 18, 1945, Box 1, Envelope 43; "Article by Charles Moore," October 1947, Box 2, Envelope 71; both in C. C. Moore, DPL.

13. Charles Roundy, Notes, Box 2, Tape 10, CGR WHRC UW. Miller, "50th Anniversary," 9. "Data on Irving H. Larom—Princeton 1913," IHL BBHC. Lawrence R. Borne, *Welcome to My West: I. H. Larom: Dude Rancher, Conservationist, Collector* (Cody, Wyo.: Buffalo Bill Historical Center, 1982), 15–19.

14. Harold Ickes, Secretary of the Interior, to I. H. Larom, June 28, 1940; *Cody Enterprise*, March 19, 1969, 1–2; both in IHL BBHC.

15. DRA Minutes, 1931, 25, 75–76, DPL.

16. Rinehart, *Nomad's Land*, 195.

17. Arthur H. Carhart to Charles C. Moore, July 21, 1945, Box 1, Envelope 6, C. C. Moore, DPL. Arthur Carhart, *Hi, Stranger! The Complete Guide to Dude Ranches* (Chicago: Ziff-Davis, 1949). "The Charles Cornell Moore Memorial Collection," C. C. Moore, DPL; Mrs. C. W. Hayes (Moore's daughter) to author, November 5, 1977.

18. *Bozeman Daily Chronicle*, September 28, 1926, 2. Miller, "50th Anniversary," 9. DRA Minutes, 1931, 13, DPL.

19. See, e.g.: DRA Minutes, 1930, 146, Pam File, Wyo.S.A.; DRA Minutes, 1931, 127–28, [135], DPL.

20. DRA Minutes, 1931, iii, DPL.

21. Ibid., 97–98; DRA Minutes, 1941, 186, Box 1, MS Collection, DRA, WHRC UW. I. H. Larom, "President's Page," *The Dude Rancher*, vol. 6, no. 7 (July–August 1938), 4.

22. DRA Minutes, 1946, 5, 152, Box 1, MS Collection, DRA, WHRC UW; Resolution, October 29, 1946, Box 1, Envelope 47, C. C. Moore, DPL. Statement of Charles C. Moore Before Subcommittee on the Public Lands, House of Representatives, April 15, 1947, Box 1, Envelope 47, C. C. Moore, DPL.

23. "Article by Charles C. Moore," April, 1947, 4, 54, Box 2, Envelope 71, C. C. Moore, DPL; DRA Minutes, 1930, 31, 33, Pam File, Wyo.S.A. This information is scattered throughout various DRA Minutes.

24. Jesse L. Williams, "Joy-Ranching and Dude-Wrangling," *Collier's*, vol. 51 (August 9, 1913), 23. *The Dude Rancher*, vol. 1, no. 1 (December 1932), 12.

25. *The World*, May 19, 1929, n.p., Clippings File, Dude Ranch, WHRC UW. DRA Minutes, 1931, 65–66, DPL.

26. DRA Minutes, 1931, 64–65, 84–85, DPL.

27. Charles G. Roundy, "The Origins and Early Development of Dude Ranching in Wyoming," *Annals of Wyoming*, vol. 45, no. 1 (Spring 1973), 24. Earl Pomeroy, *In Search of the Golden West: The Tourist in Western America* (New York: Alfred A. Knopf, 1957), 155–58. DRA Minutes, 1929, 103–7, Pam File, Wyo.S.A.

28. David J. Saylor, *Jackson Hole, Wyoming: In the Shadow of the Tetons* (Norman: University of Oklahoma Press, 1970), 157.

29. Donald C. Swain, *Wilderness Defender: Horace M. Albright and Conservation* (Chicago: University of Chicago Press, 1970), 38–40, 97.

30. U.S. Statutes, 64th Congress, 1st sess., August 25, 1916, Ch. 408, H.R. 15522, p. 535.

31. Swain, *Wilderness Defender*, 53, 89–90, 133–34, 247.

32. *The World*, May 19, 1929, n.p., Clippings File, Dude Ranch, WHRC UW.

33. Swain, *Wilderness Defender*, 42, 45–46, 52; "A Great Loss Is a Great Challenge," *The Living Wilderness*, vol. 10, no. 13 (July 1945), 1.

34. George Lorimer, "Selling Scenery," *Saturday Evening Post*, vol. 192, no. 15 (October 11, 1919), 28.

35. Swain, *Wilderness Defender*, 136; for data on Hough, see *Who Was Who in America*, vol. 1, 1897–1942 (Chicago: Marquis Co., 1943), 591.

36. Swain, *Wilderness Defender*, 170–71, 183, 192, 205, 280, 292, 321. DRA Minutes, 1931, 111, 113, DPL. DRA Minutes, 1929, 102–3, Pam File, Wyo.S.A.

37. *Kemmerer Gazette*, January 22, 1931, Clippings File, Dude Ranch, WHRC UW. The fur trappers and traders who preceded the hunters and ranchers had vanished years before the recreational promotion of Jackson Hole. Thus the hunters and ranchers pioneered the usage that continues today.

38. Dr. Elizabeth Anderson, interview, March 1972, Box 2, CGR WHRC UW.

39. Saylor, *Jackson Hole, Wyoming*, 141, 149–51, 163, 166–69, 174–75, 178, 195, 200–204; Swain, *Wilderness Defender*, 115–16, 129, 161, 165. Roundy, "Origins," 20.

40. Charles Moore to Horace M. Albright, January 18, 1932, Box 1, Envelope 43, C. C. Moore, DPL.

41. Swain, *Wilderness Defender*, 184, 252–53, 261–71, 280–86.

42. Mrs. Dudley (Betty) Hayden to Charles G. Roundy, Clippings File, Dude Ranch, Jackson Hole, WHRC UW. Dr. Elizabeth Anderson, interview, March 1972; Mrs. Albert Nelson, Jr., interview, May 19, 1972; Harold Turner, interview, March 1972; all in Box 2, CGR WHRC UW.

43. Had the federal government not intervened in Jackson Hole, the number

of dude ranch guests and new dude ranches would probably have risen, but the recreation would have been of a different type. Chapter 10 discusses these differences.

44. Saylor, *Jackson Hole, Wyoming,* 209–10.

45. Union Pacific, "Dude Ranch Out West," ca. 1931, Railroad File, Publicity Brochures, DPL.

46. Scott Fogelsong, "Frank Wright: A Man and His Mountains," *Spice of Life Colorado,* vol. 1, no. 4 (July 1974), 34, 69.

47. Frank Wright to author, January 25, 1976; Johnnie Holzwarth, interview with author, July 28, 1974. Grand Junction *Sentinel,* February 23, 1972, 1, Clippings File, Dude Ranches, Colorado, DPL.

48. John Holzwarth III, interview with author, September 24, 1977.

49. *The World,* May 19, 1929, n.p., Clippings File, Dude Ranch, WHRC UW; Roundy, "Origins," 14–15.

50. Philip A. Stewart to author, October 15, 1975.

51. DRA Minutes, 1929, 108–13, Pam File, Wyo.S.A. *Denver Post,* March 14, 1974, 30. Swain, *Wilderness Defender,* 184.

52. Dwight L. Hamilton to author, September 16, 1975.

53. Chester L. Brooks to author, October 21, 1977.

54. National Park Service, Division of Land Acquisition, *Master Deed Listing,* Status of Lands as of March 31, 1981. The acreage that the National Park Service acquired from individuals or ranches is small compared to any park's total acreage. Yet just a few hundred or even a few dozen choice acres sufficed for a successful ranch.

55. Chapter 10 further explores problems between ranchers and federal officials.

56. Charles Roundy to Thomas R. Wise, [June 1973], Box 6; Mrs. Donald Siggins, interview, March 31, 1972, Box 2; Charles Roundy to Tom Bell, April 11, 1972, Box 4; all in CGR WHRC UW. *The Sky-Hi News,* January 9, 1976, 4; Frank Wright to author, January 25, 1976. Dr. Gordon Chappell, telephone interview with author, March 18, 1981; A. T. Steele, "Lady Boss of Faraway Ranch," *Saturday Evening Post,* vol. 230, no. 37 (March 15, 1958), 134.

Chapter 9

1. Fanny K. Wister, ed., *Owen Wister Out West: His Journals and Letters* (Chicago: University of Chicago Press, 1958), 42. The difficulties of travel are shown throughout this book.

2. Isabella L. Bird, *A Lady's Life in the Rocky Mountains* (Norman: University of Oklahoma Press, 1960), 73–82. Wister, *Owen Wister*, xvii.

3. *Boston Evening Transcript*, March 26, 1932, Magazine Section, 1. *The Dude Rancher*, vol. 1, no. 2 (March 1933), 6. L. W. (Gay) Randall, *Footprints Along the Yellowstone* (San Antonio: Naylor Co., 1961), 72–73.

4. Nannie T. Alderson and Helen H. Smith, *A Bride Goes West* (Lincoln: University of Nebraska Press, 1969), 218–19.

5. Mary R. Rinehart, "What Is a Dude Ranch?" *Harper's Bazaar*, August 1927, 128.

6. Mary Shawver, *Sincerely, Mary S.* (Casper, Wyo.: Prairie Publishing Co., n.d.), 18–21. Clipping from *Cody Enterprise*, American Legion Special, [1934], n.p., Clippings File, Dude Ranch, Buffalo Bill Country, WHRC UW.

7. Roberta Cheney and Clyde Erskine, *Music, Saddles and Flapjacks: Dudes at the OTO Ranch* (Missoula, Mont.: Mountain Press Publishing Co., 1978), 59–62, 87–90. "Charles Moore, Round-Up, Sunday, July 27, 1952," p. 3A, C. C. Moore, DPL.

8. Sophie Burden, telephone interview with author, June 8, 1981; the Burdens ran Remuda Guest Ranch in Arizona from 1925 to 1971.

9. DRA Minutes, 1949, 29, MS Collection, DRA, Box 1, WHRC UW. L. W. (Gay) Randall, "The Man Who Put the Dude in Dude Ranching," *Montana*, vol. 10, no. 3 (July 1960), 40.

10. Rinehart, "What Is a Dude Ranch?" 68–69. Peter J. Schmitt, *Back to Nature: The Arcadian Myth in Urban America* (New York: Oxford University Press, 1969), 159–60. Mrs. Ernest Miller, "50th Anniversary," *The Dude Rancher*, vol. 43, no. 1 (Spring 1974), 9.

11. Ingolf K. Vogeler, "Farm and Ranch Vacationing in the United States" (Ph.D. diss., University of Minnesota, 1973), 96; Randall, *Footprints*, 72–75; Rinehart, "Wht Is a Dude Ranch?" 69. Anne Chamberlin, "Big Dude Drive in the Crazies," *Saturday Evening Post*, vol. 240, no. 15 (July 29, 1967), 34.

12. "Dude Ranches in the Big Horn Mountains," 1930?, 9, State Historical Society of Colorado, Documentary Resources, Subject Collections, Recreation, Dude Ranches.

13. Raymond J. Raddy, "Dude Ranching Is Not All Yippee!" *The Western Horseman*, vol. 17, no. 4 (April 1952), 39.

14. *Cody Enterprise*, March 19, 1969, 1, IHL BBHC. Wendell Wilson, interview, May 20, 1972, Box 2, CGR WHRC UW.

15. DRA Minutes, 1930, 101, 123–24, Pam File, Wyo.S.A.; *Boston Post*, April 1, 1934, B-6, NPRCR, President's File #356-218, Box 127, MHS. *Bozeman Daily Chronicle*, August 1, 1928, 1.

16. DRA Minutes, 1929, 65, 67, 69, Pam File, Wyo.S.A.

17. Ibid., 75.

18. Ibid., 69, 71, 73.

19. DRA Minutes, 1930, 6, 115–18, Pam File, Wyo.S.A. DRA Minutes, 1931, 49–53, 63–64, DPL.

20. Union Pacific, "Dude Ranches Out West," 1931, Railroad File, Publicity Brochures, DPL. DRA Minutes, 1931, 57–59, DPL.

21. Johnnie Holzwarth, telephone interview with author, June 4, 1980.

22. "Dude Ranches," 1937?, Clippings File, Dude Ranches, DPL; "Union Pacific R.R. Publishes Interesting Dude Ranch Book," *The Dude Rancher*, vol. 6, no. 7 (July–August 1938), 11.

23. DRA Minutes, 1931, 59–61, DPL; *Bozeman Daily Chronicle*, August 8, 1928, 6. "Montana Dude Ranches," *The Dude Rancher*, vol. 6, no. 7 (July–August 1938), 8–9; DRA Minutes, 1947, 102, MS Collection, DRA, Box 1, WHRC UW. DRA Minutes, 1931, 73, DPL; DRA Minutes, 1940, 32, 73, MS Collection, DRA, Box 1, WHRC UW.

24. Great Northern Railway, "Western Dude Ranch Vacations," brochure, [1947]; Joseph A. Sullivan, "A Description and Analysis of the Dude Ranching Industry in Montana" (Master's thesis, University of Montana, 1971), 18. Henry W. Wack, "Life on a Dude Ranch," *Arts and Decoration*, vol. 35 (May 1931), 59, 92; see also the Appendix. Chicago & North Western Line, "Wyoming Wild West Ranches," pamphlet, Vertical File, Dude Ranches #3, Wyo.S.A.; Chicago & Northwestern Railroad, "Black Hills of South Dakota 1941 All Expense 8-Day Tours," brochure.

25. DRA Minutes, 1929, 39; DRA Minutes, 1930, 43, 95–96; both in Pam File, Wyo.S.A. DRA Minutes, 1931, 43–44, DPL.

26. *The Dude Rancher*, vol. 1, no. 1 (December 1932), 7. DRA Minutes, 1935, 37–40, MS Collection, DRA, Box 1, WHRC UW.

27. *The Dude Rancher*, vol. 6, no. 7 (July–August 1938), 21; *Billings Gazette*, June 18, 1940, n.p., NPRCR, President's File 2001, Letters 1913–67, Old Building, Box 174, Burlington Northern Offices, St. Paul, Minn. *The Dude Rancher*, vol. 6, no. 2 (April 1937), 15–16.

28. Earl Pomeroy, *In Search of the Golden West: The Tourist in Western America* (New York: Alfred A. Knopf, 1957), 125, 127, 147–49.

29. Spike Van Cleve, *40 Years' Gatherin's* (Kansas City: Lowell Press, 1977), 128. Randall, *Footprints*, 49, 51.

30. Robert S. Yard, *The Book of the National Parks* (New York: Charles Scrib-

ner's Sons, 1919, 1928), 209; "The Lure of the Trail Mark," MS Collection, Jacob M. Schwoob, Document Box 2, WHRC UW.

31. DRA Minutes, 1931, 103–4; Mary R. Rinehart, "To Wyoming," *Saturday Evening Post*, vol. 199, no. 14 (October 2, 1926), 16.

32. Lynn Mohn, "Walk with the Pioneers: Kawuneeche Valley Living History Program," Rocky Mountain Nature Association, Inc., 1976.

33. *Bozeman Daily Chronicle*, November 3, 1926, 1, and November 6, 1926, 1. Randall, "Man Who Put Dude," 36.

34. Madeline L. Woods, "'Dudes' and 'Dude' Ranches," *Wyoming Roads*, vol. 2, no. 10 (June 1926), 3–5; Clippings File, Dude Ranch, Wyoming, WHRC UW.

35. Veroa Haines, American Automobile Association, to J. C. Turner, September 3, 1941, MS Collection, Turner's Triangle X Ranch, Box 17, WHRC UW. *The Dude Rancher*, vol. 4, no. 1 (November 1934), 27; Semi-Annual Report of CD & GRA, March 1936, Clippings File, Dude Ranches, DPL; DRA Minutes, 1930, 95–96, Pam File, Wyo.S.A.

36. Woods, "'Dudes' and 'Dude' Ranches," 3, Clippings File, Dude Ranch, Wyoming, WHRC UW.

37. DRA Minutes, 1931, 79–80, DPL. DRA Minutes, 1935, 26–27, MS Collection, DRA, Box 1, WHRC UW.

38. "Data on Irving H. Larom—Princeton 1913," IHL BBHC.

39. Rudy Menghini to author, January 30, 1978; Menghini ran the Bar Lazy J Guest Ranch (Buckhorn Lodge) in Colorado; Mary R. Rinehart, *The Out Trail* (New York: George H. Doran Co., 1923), 119.

40. Miller, "50th Anniversary," 9.

41. DRA Minutes, 1931, 61, DPL.

42. DRA Minutes, 1935, 51, MS Collection, DRA, Box 1, WHRC UW. "More Disadvantages of Roadside Signs Pointed Out by Struthers Burt," *The Dude Rancher*, vol. 6, no. 7 (July–August 1938), 12.

43. DRA Minutes, 1940, 43, MS Collection, DRA, Box 1, WHRC UW; Margaret Steiner, National Trailways Bus System, to Ranch Manager, February 7, 1941, MS Collection, Turner's Triangle X Ranch, Box 17, WHRC UW.

44. Pomeroy, *Golden West*, 65, 130–31. DRA Minutes, 1931, 61, 130, DPL.

45. H. W. Peterson, United Airlines, to Turpin Meadows Lodge, June 8, 1935; M. P. Bickley, United Airlines, to J. C. Turner, March 28, 1939; both in MS Collection, Turner's Triangle X Ranch, Box 17, WHRC UW; DRA Minutes, 1935, 54–55; DRA Minutes, 1940, 41; both in MS Collection, DRA, Box 1, WHRC UW; Semi-Annual Report of the CD & GRA, March 1936, Clippings

File, Dude Ranches, DPL; R. L. Swanson to John Turner, June 29, 1941, MS Collection, Turner's Triangle X Ranch, Box 17, WHRC UW.

46. Walcott Watson to John Turner, June 24, 1940, MS Collection, Turner's Triangle X Ranch, Box 17, WHRC UW; C. E. Denney to C. W. Disbrow, Wild Horse Island Ranch Lodge, June 29, 1940, NPRCR, President's File 2001, Letters 1913–67, Old Building, Box 174, Burlington Northern Offices, St. Paul, Minn.

47. E. W. Foote, American Travel Service, to J. C. Turner, May 2, 1941, MS Collection, Turner's Triangle X Ranch, Box 17, WHRC UW.

48. DRA Minutes, 1941, 33–34, 41–43, MS Collection, DRA, Box 1, WHRC UW.

49. Mohn, "Walk with the Pioneers."

50. DRA Minutes, 1942, 17–18, 35, 38, 10–11, 126–30, MS Collection, DRA, Box 1, WHRC UW.

51. *Rocky Mountain News*, November 28, 1944, n.p., Clippings File, Dude Ranches, DPL.

52. Peggy Schaffer, interview, March 30, 1972, Box 2, CGR WHRC UW.

53. "Summer Suggestions," brochure, 1944, Clippings File, Dude Ranches Wyoming, DPL.

54. Van Cleve, *40 Years'*, 269–77.

55. Mrs. Donald Siggins, interview, March 31, 1972; Harold Turner, interview, March 1972; both in Box 2, CGR WHRC UW. Raddy, "Not All Yippee!" 16. *Rocky Mountain News*, November 2, 1942, n.p., Clippings File, Dude Ranches, DPL.

56. DRA Minutes, 1943, 9, 13, MS Collection, DRA, Box 1, WHRC UW.

57. Angela Buell, interview, March 28, 1972, Box 2, CGR WHRC UW. John Holzwarth III, interview with author, September 24, 1977.

58. Arthur N. Pack, *The Ghost Ranch Story* (Philadelphia: Board of Christian Education of the United Presbyterian Church in the U.S.A., 1960), 41.

59. *The Dude Rancher*, vol. 13, no. 2 (April 1944), 22–23. "Summer Suggestions," brochure, 1944, Clippings File, Dude Ranches Wyoming, DPL.

60. Wendell Wilson, interview, May 20, 1972, Box 2, CGR WHRC UW.

61. C. E. Denney to I. H. Larom, May 29, 1942, NPRCR, President's File 2001, Letters 1913–67, Old Building, Box 174, Burlington Northern Offices, St. Paul, Minn.

62. *Wyoming Tribune*, July 27, 1943, n.p., Clippings File, Dude Ranches, DPL. Leonard J. Arrington, *The Changing Economic Structure of the Mountain West, 1850–1950* (Logan: Utah State University Press, 1963), 22–24.

63. John Holzwarth III, interview with author, September 24, 1977.

Chapter 10

1. DRA Minutes, 1945, 124, MS Collection, DRA, Box 1, WHRC UW.

2. Ingolf K. Vogeler, "Farm and Ranch Vacationing in the United States" (Ph.D. diss., University of Minnesota, 1973), iii; Mrs. Donald Siggins, interview, March 31, 1972, Box 2, CGR WHRC UW.

3. Norreys J. O'Conor, "An Irish Sportsman in the Far West," *Arizona Quarterly*, vol. 5, no. 2 (Summer 1949), 108. Leonard J. Arrington, *The Changing Economic Structure of the Mountain West, 1850–1950* (Logan: Utah State University Press, 1963), 22–24.

4. *Rocky Mountain News*, September 21, 1947, n.p., Clippings File, Dude Ranches, DPL.

5. *Rocky Mountain News*, September 7, 1941, n.p., Clippings File, Colorado Tourism, DPL.

6. Robert S. Yard, *The Book of the National Parks* (New York: Charles Scribner's Sons, 1919, 1928), 94. Salma A. Waters, ed., *Colorado Year Book 1962–1964* (Denver: Colorado State Planning Division, 1965), 607.

7. List of dude and guest ranches in Colorado in 1947, Clippings File, Dude Ranches, DPL. Colorado ranches' replies to questionnaire, 1974; *Denver Post*, August 18, 1948, n.p., Clippings File, Dude Ranches, DPL. Loudon Kelly, "Chickens, Shikars and Dudes," *Colorado Wonderland*, vol. 6, no. 2 (April 1955), 14.

8. Joseph P. Sullivan, "A Description and Analysis of the Dude Ranching Industry in Montana" (Master's thesis, University of Montana, 1971), 20.

9. Les Branch, CD & GRA, to author, November 5, 1978.

10. Vogeler, "Farm and Ranch Vacationing" (Ph.D. diss.), 98–99. *Denver Post*, November 9, 1959, 2.

11. DRA Minutes, 1946, 66–67, MS Collection, DRA, Box 1, WHRC UW.

12. Charles G. Roundy to Prof. Daniel Tyler, August 1, 1972, Box 4, CGR WHRC UW. DRA Minutes, 1949, 17–33; DRA Minutes, 1950, 1–2; DRA Minutes, 1959, 209–10; all in MS Collection, DRA, Boxes 2 and 3, WHRC UW.

13. Manya Winsted, "Arizona's Fabulous Guest Ranches," *Arizona Highways*, vol. 56, no. 11 (November 1980), 2, 11.

14. Thomas Lesure, "Dude Ranching . . . the Western Vacation Few Westerners Ever Take," *Desert Magazine*, vol. 23 (December 1960), 27; Mernice Murphy, "Relax! You're on an Arizona Dude Ranch," *Arizona Highways*, vol. 12 (April 1936), 8–9. Anita Post, "Local Color in the Southwest," *Hoofs and Horns*,

vol. 5 (November 1935), 3; "Why a Dude Ranch Vacation?" *Magazine Tucson,*
vol. 2 (October 1949), 18.

15. "Appointment in the Sun," *Arizona Highways,* vol. 24, no. 9 (September
1948), 16–25; E. A. Stein, "Day on a Guest Ranch," *Arizona Highways,* vol. 22,
no. 9 (September 1947), 12–13. Allen True, telephone interview with author,
June 8, 1981.

16. Ann C. Haslanger, *A History of Vermejo Park* (Vermejo Park, N.M.: Ver-
mejo Park, 1980), 8. Vermejo Park, flyers, June 1981. New Mexico Dept. of
Development, Tourist Division, Santa Fe, "New Mexico Resorts and Guest
Ranches," brochure, 1976; State of New Mexico, Tourism and Travel Division,
Commerce and Industry Dept., Santa Fe, "Guest Ranches and Resorts," brochure,
1979.

17. Cornelius C. Smith, *Tanque Verde: The Story of a Frontier Ranch* (Tucson?:
n.p., 1978?), 149–61.

18. Raymond Schuessler, "Ever Try a Dude Ranch Vacation?" *Better Homes
and Gardens,* vol. 31, no. 3 (March 1953), 248; Dick Spencer III, "Winter Dude
Ranch," *The Western Horseman,* vol. 25, no. 1 (January 1960), 44; Bob Hartman,
telephone interview with author, June 11, 1981.

19. Howard W. Miller, Sr., to author, July 14, 1981; he has operated several
guest ranches in Arizona. Lesure, "Dude Ranching," 26–27; Miriam Feldman,
"The Disappearing Dude Ranch," *Desert Magazine,* vol. 43 (September 1980),
12–14.

20. Ira Frazier, "From Cows to Dudes," *Magazine Tucson,* vol. 5 (October
1952), 19–22. "Monk's Guest Ranch," *Hoofs and Horns,* vol. 5 (December 1935),
6; Murphy, "Relax!" 19.

21. Note the difference between this situation in Arizona and the school that
Larry Larom developed at his Valley Ranch near Cody, Wyo., to offer boys a
longer exposure to ranch life. His Valley School satisfied that desire while preserving its remoteness; see Chapter 3.

22. "Ranch Directory," *Horse and Horseman,* vol. 21, no. 5 (April 1939), 12–
15.

23. Ibid.; Frank B. Norris, "The Southern Arizona Guest Ranch as a Symbol
of the West" (Master's thesis, University of Arizona, 1976), 42. Since most of
these groups were short-lived and apparently left no records, there has been
disagreement about their exact names and dates of existence. Robert Hartman
of Tucson states that ca. 1950 the Southern Arizona DRA was formed with about
thirty members (letter to author, June 22, 1981). It is not clear whether this is
yet another group or a different name for the organization that Norris said began
in the 1940s.

24. Karen Lingo, 'Home, Home on the Dude Ranch," *Southern Living,* vol. 12, no. 5 (May 1977), 101–3; Chamber of Commerce, Bandera, Texas, "Cowboy Capital of the World Bandera Texas Guest Ranches," brochure, [1981]. Leonard Falkner, "The Call of the Old West," *American Magazine,* vol. 160, no. 5 (November 1955), 84–88; *Cincinnati Enquirer,* December 25, 1977, L-10.

25. "Ranch Directory," *Horse and Horseman,* vol. 21, no. 5 (April 1939), 12–15. *New York Times,* March 16, 1947, sec. 2, 14, and October 28, 1963, 16; Nevada Dept. of Economic Development, Carson City, "Guest Ranches," brochure, 1974.

26. DRA Minutes, 1931, 20, DPL; *The Dude Rancher,* vol. 6, no. 4 (October 1937), 10, and vol. 7, no. 1 (January 1939), 31. DRA, "Dude Ranch Vacation directory, members Dude Ranchers' Association, 1981," 3.

27. "Ranch Directory," *Horse and Horseman,* vol. 21, no. 5 (April 1939), 15; Schuessler, "Ever Try," 248. *The Dude Rancher,* vol. 6, no. 8 (October–November 1938), 4.

28. *New York Times,* June 4, 1950, sec. 2, 25; Schuessler, "Ever Try," 246. Washington Chambers of Commerce to author: Ellensburg, July 18, 1974; Wenatchee, July 16, 1974; Cle Elum, July 26, 1974; Okanogan, July 21, 1974; Winthrop, August 15, 1974.

29. Frank A. Tinker, "Puttin' Up the Dudes," *Westways,* vol. 65, no. 11 (November 1973), 54; Utah Travel Council, Salt Lake City, to author, June 17, 1974, and "Utah Package Tours '74," 25–35, brochure. Dept. of Economic Development, Lincoln, Nebraska, "Ranch/Farm Vacations," brochure, 1974. Letters to author: Kansas Dept. of Economic Development, June 12, 1974; North Dakota Business and Industrial Development Dept., June 7, 1974; South Dakota Division of Tourism, June 11, 1974. *Rocky Mountain News,* November 29, 1967, 32.

30. Jerome L. Rodnitzky, "Recapturing the West: The Dude Ranch in American Life," *Arizona and the West,* vol. 10 (Summer 1968), 117. *The Dude Rancher,* vol. 6, no. 2 (April 1937), 24.

31. *New York Times,* March 14, 1943, sec. 2, 12; June 20, 1943, sec. 2, 11; September 7, 1947, sec. 2, 12; June 16, 1946, sec. 2, 12; October 9, 1977, sec. 10, 9, Sheila C. Nilva, "Vacation on a Dude Ranch," *Mademoiselle,* vol. 87 (April 1981), 104, 106, 108, 112–13.

32. Dept. of Commerce, Albany, "Dude Ranches in New York State," brochure, 1963. Wilbur C. Abbott, *New York in the American Revolution* (New York: Charles Scribner's Sons, 1929), 244, 249; Everett T. Tomlinson, *Days and Deeds of '76* (New York: D. Appleton & Co., 1927), 139.

33. *Denver Post,* June 27, 1948, n.p., Clippings File, Dude Ranches, DPL; Jay Dugan, "The Dude Ranch Goes East," 42–46, Clippings File, Dude Ranch,

WHRC UW; *The Dude Rancher,* vol. 18, no. 2 (April 1949), 46; DRA Minutes, 1949, 39–41, 45–47, MS Collection, DRA, Box 2, WHRC UW; Double H Guest Ranch, Brevort, Mich., brochure, n.d.; Double J Resort, Jack and Jill Ranch, Rothbury, Mich., brochure, n.d.

34. *Cincinnati Enquirer,* July 5, 1979, E-8; Loretta Lynn's Dude Ranch, Hurricane Mills, Tenn., brochure, n.d. *Cincinnati Post and Times Star,* February 8, 1975, 12.

35. Neil Morgan, "Hey Dude!" *Western's World: The Magazine of Western Airlines,* vol. 4, no. 3 (June–July 1973), 15. "Dude Ranching A La Francaise," *The Westerners Brand Book,* vol. 10, no. 8 (October 1953), 58; *New York Times,* January 5, 1969, sec. 10, 33.

36. Les Branch, CD & GRA, telephone interview with author, May 20, 1981. Glen Fales, interview, April 1, 1972, Box 2, CGR WHRC UW.

37. Pete Smythe, *Pete Smythe: Big City Dropout* (Boulder: Pruett Press, 1968), 230.

38. *The Dude Rancher,* vol. 20, no. 1 (January 1951), 16, 18. *Denver Post,* August 21, 1977, sec. C, 35. DRA Minutes, 1949, 48–49, MS Collection, DRA, Box 2, WHRC UW.

39. DRA Minutes, 1950, 19, MS Collection, DRA, Box 2, WHRC UW.

40. *Denver Post,* November 12, 1958, 20; November 13, 1958, 25; Joyce Maulis to author, March 1, 1978.

41. Brooke Burnham, "Are Some Dude Ranchers Flying Under False Colors?" *The Dude Rancher,* vol. 22, no. 1 (January 1953), 14; *New York Times,* June 8, 1958, sec. 11, 43.

42. Mr. and Mrs. Tom Ferguson, interview, March 28, 1972, Box 2, CGR WHRC UW; DRA Minutes, 1959, 143, MS Collection, DRA, Box 3, WHRC UW.

43. Diane Murphy, Alaska Division of Tourism, to author, 1975.

44. Frank A. Tinker, "Whatever Happened to Dude Ranches?" *Catholic Digest,* vol. 38, no. 9 (July 1974), 104.

45. Elizabeth Hayden to author, October 29, 1977.

46. *New York Times,* June 24, 1956, sec. 2, 35.

47. Article by Charles C. Moore, October 1947, 4, 56–57, Box 2, Envelope 71, C. C. Moore, DPL. Vogeler, "Farm and Ranch Vacationing" (Ph.D. diss.), 96–97.

48. DRA Minutes, 1945, 106–7, 120–22; DRA Minutes, 1948, 39; both in MS Collection, DRA, Box 1, WHRC UW; M. M. Goodsill to Florence R. Cassill, August 12, 1952, NPRCR, President's File 2001, Letters 1913–67, Old Building, Box 174, Burlington Northern Offices, St. Paul, Minn.

49. DRA Minutes, 1950, 37–38, 40–44, 2–7, MS Collection, DRA, Box 2, WHRC UW. Peggy Schaffer, interview, March 30, 1972, Box 2, CGR WHRC UW; Joyce Maulis to author, March 1, 1978.

50. J. J. Glaze, Union Pacific Railroad, to author, July 11, 1973, and September 7, 1973; note cards, Box 2, CGR WHRC UW.

51. Mr. and Mrs. Tom Ferguson, interview, March 28, 1972, Box 2, CGR WHRC UW. DRA, "Resolutions of The Dude Ranchers' Association Adopted at the Annual Convention," December 1, 1973, res. no. 8; mailed to Associate Members after the meeting.

52. *The Dude Rancher*, vol. 22, no. 4 (October 1953), advertisements, 41, 43. "We Dude It," *The Dude Rancher*, vol. 28, no. 1 (January 1959), 28.

53. Brochures: American Airlines, "Tucson, Arizona Ranch Resort Vacation," 1970–71. United Airlines, "1973 Vacations Colorado." Braniff Airlines, "Texas Ranch Resorts Braniff Style," 1973–74. Frontier Airlines, "Frontierland Dude Ranch Vacations," 1968; "Outdoor Vacation Excitement, '73"; "Fishing Vacation Excitement, '73"; "Sun Country Excitement '73–'74." Continental Airlines, "Colorado '81 Summer."

54. *Denver Post*, August 21, 1977, sec. C, 29.

55. DRA Minutes, 1950, 38, MS Collection, DRA, Box 2, WHRC UW. "I Want to Buy A Ranch . . .," *The Dude Rancher*, vol. 28, no. 2 (Spring 1958), 26–27, and vol. 28, no. 3 (Summer 1958), 34.

56. Interviews: Mr. and Mrs. Roy Chambers, May 20, 1972; Glen Fales, April 1, 1972; Dick Frost, March 31, 1972; Peggy Schaffer, March 30, 1972; all in Box 2, CGR WHRC UW. *Denver Post*, December 12, 1964, 20, Clippings File, Dude Ranches, DPL; *Denver Post*, July 18, 1973, 41, Clippings File, Dude Ranches Colorado, DPL; Robert T. Smith, "The Big Sky Development: A Lesson for the Future," *The American West*, vol. 12, no. 5 (September 1975), 47, 62.

57. Previews, Inc., Denver, Colo., flyer, 1975. Allen "Ike" Fordyce, interview, March 28, 1972, Box 2, CGR WHRC UW.

58. "Want To Buy," *The Dude Rancher* (Spring 1958), 18.

59. Interviews: Peggy Schaffer, March 30, 1972; Alys Ritterbrown, n.d.; Allen "Ike" Fordyce, March 28, 1972; all in Box 2, CGR WHRC UW. DRA, Post Convention Letter from President "Spike" Van Cleve, December 20, 1973. John F. Turner, "Delights and Dilemmas of Dude Ranching," *Wyoming Wildlife*, vol. 36, no. 7 (July 1972), 23.

60. Vogeler, "Farm and Ranch Vacationing" (Ph.D. diss.), 41; Sullivan, "Dude Ranching Industry" (Master's thesis), 22, 29.

61. Harold A. Huber to C. C. Moore, November 18, 1949; Conrad L. Wirth to C. C. Moore, December 19, 1951; C. C. Moore to Conrad L. Wirth, January

15, 1952; U.S. Dept. of the Interior, National Park Service, to C. C. Moore, June 2, 1952, PO #99-796; Conrad L. Wirth to C. C. Moore, June 6, 1952; Report by Charles Moore, September 15, 1952; all in C. C. Moore, DPL. DRA Minutes, 1950, 47, MS Collection, DRA, Box 2, WHRC UW.

62. National Park Service, Division of Land Acquisition, *Master Deed Listing, Status of Lands as of March 31, 1981*. Donald C. Swain, *Wilderness Defender: Horace M. Albright and Conservation* (Chicago: University of Chicago Press, 1970), 292.

63. Peter J. Schmitt, *Back to Nature: The Arcadian Myth in Urban America* (New York: Oxford University Press, 1969), 165–66.

64. Union Pacific Railroad, "Dude Ranches Out West," [1956], 40; *Rocky Mountain News*, August 29, 1962, 39, Clippings File, Dude Ranches, DPL, and March 14, 1974, 52; *Denver Post*, June 4, 1972, 38, Clippings File Dude Ranches Colorado, DPL, and March 14, 1974, 30; McGraw Guest Ranch, Estes Park, Colo., brochure, n.d. Grand Junction *Sentinel*, February 23, 1972, 1, Clippings File, Dude Ranches Colorado, DPL.

65. After the National Park Service purchased Green Mountain and Holzwarth Neversummer ranches, two guest ranches remained. Outside the park at the valley's southern end, they were too far for access to most of the scenic high country.

66. *Estes Park Trail-Gazette*, July 26, 1974, 5; Rocky Mountain National Park, *Walk and Talk Sheet*, July 23–30, 1974, 3, and *Program of Free Activities for Visitors*, July 8–15, 1975, 4, and August 8–15, 1978, 4.

67. Charles Roundy, Notes, Box 2, Tape 10, CGR WHRC UW. Interviews: Dr. Elizabeth Anderson, March, 1972; Mrs. Albert Nelson, Jr., May 19, 1972; Harold Turner, March 1972; all in Box 2, CGR WHRC UW.

68. Yard, *National Parks*, 97–98.

69. DRA Minutes, 1929, 102–3, Pam File, Wyo.S.A. *Pittsburgh Chronicle Telegraph*, July 31, 1923, n.p., Biog. MS File, Howard Eaton, WHRC UW.

70. *The Dude Rancher*, vol. 7, no. 1 (January 1939), 3. Newton B. Drury to C. C. Moore, February 3, 1945, Box 1, Envelope 12, C. C. Moore, DPL.

71. Lloyd Jones, " A Dude Rancher Speaks to Associate Members and To His Guests," *The Dude Rancher*, vol. 42, no. 2 (Summer 1973), 38. Mr. and Mrs. Roy Chambers, interview, May 20, 1972, Box 2, CGR WHRC UW; Frank Wright to author, December, 1977.

72. DRA, "Resolutions of the Dude Ranchers' Association Adopted at the Annual Convention," December 1, 1973, res. no. 3; mailed to Associate Members after the meeting.

73. Chester L. Brooks to author, October 21, 1977.

74. Ibid., December 7, 1977.

75. Frank Wright to author, December, 1977.

76. Charles Roundy to Tom Bell, April 11, 1972, Box 4, CGR WHRC UW.

77. Interviews: Allen "Ike" Fordyce, March 28, 1972; Stanley Siggins, April 1, 1972; both in Box 2, CGR WHRC UW. Gary D. Morgan, Forest Service, to author, August 20, 1979.

78. Ted Townsend, "Dudes, Mutts and Crackerjacks," *New Republic*, vol. 132, no. 12 (March 21, 1955), 14; Anne Chamberlin, "Big Dude Drive in the Crazies," *Saturday Evening Post*, vol. 240, no. 15 (July 29, 1967), 35. Nell Pauly, *The Day Before Yesterday* (Apple Valley, Calif.: Apple Valley News, 1972), 277.

79. Vogeler, "Farm and Ranch Vacationing" (Ph.D. diss.), 122; *Cincinnati Enquirer*, June 28, 1981, G-10, and September 30, 1977, B-5.

80. Pat Dickerman, ed., *Farm Ranch and Countryside Guide* (New York: Farm and Ranch Vacations, Inc., 1974), 15.

Chapter 11

1. Joyce Maulis to author, March 1, 1978, and July 5, 1979; her parents, Hugh and Florence Neece, owned the Bar Lazy J.

2. Rudy Menghini to author, January 30, 1978. Bar Lazy J Guest Ranch, Parshall, Colo., reply to questionnaire, March 21, 1974, and brochure, n.d.

3. Cal Queal, "Colorado Dude Wrangler," *Mainliner*, vol. 14 (July 1970), 31–32. *Denver Post*, October 3, 1973, 86, Clippings File, Livestock Ranches, DPL.

4. Devil's Thumb Ranch, Fraser, Colo., Cross Country Center brochure, 1981, and telephone interview with author, June 8, 1981.

5. Richard L. Field, "Dudes in the Rockies," *Holiday*, vol. 1, no. 5 (July 1946), 23–25. Johnnie Holzwarth, interview with author, July 26, 1974.

6. *Rocky Mountain News*, March 28, 1965, 48. *Denver Post*, March 17, 1974, 43, and December 1, 1974, Magazine Section, 71, 73.

7. *The Dude Rancher*, vol. 21, no. 3 (July 1952), 8. Crossed Sabres Ranch, Wapiti, Wyo., brochure, July 1980.

8. *Denver Post*, December 22, 1947, 4. As noted in Chapter 3, two names were used: Holm Lodge and Crossed Sabres Ranch. The latter name has been in common use since the 1960s.

9. Phyllis Spragg to author, October 20, 1980. Dode Hershey, Crossed Sabres Ranch, Wapiti, Wyo., reply to questionnaire, February 29, 1974. Rich and Donna Marta to author, July 11, 1980, and July 29, 1980; DRA, "Dude Ranch Vacation Directory, 1982," 6–7.

10. *Cody Enterprise*, March 19, 1969, IHL BBHC: details of Larom's health

problems are scattered throughout the Larom Collection. Bonnie Johnsey, Valley Ranch, to author, January 17, 1978; Dr. and Mrs. Oakleigh Thorne II, interview with author, July 21, 1981.

11. Correspondence, Boxes 17–29, and brochures, Box 32, MS Collection, Turner's Triangle X Ranch, WHRC UW. Harold Turner, interview, March 1972, Box 2, CGR WHRC UW.

12. Leon J. B. Dusseau, "Teepee Tours," 82–85, and advertisement, 92; both in *The Teepee Book* (March–April–May 1915); HF Bar Dude Ranch, brochure, ca. 1922, Clippings File, Dude Ranch, HF Bar, WHRC UW. "Ranch Directory," *Horse and Horseman,* vol. 21, no. 5 (April 1939), 14; *Sheridan Journal,* August 30, 1939, 1, Vertical File, Dude Ranches # 3, Wyo.S.A. Wyoming Travel Commission, "Big Wyoming Accommodations," brochure, 1981.

13. Author's observations, July 1981.

14. *New York Times,* July 22, 1970, 83. Anne Chamberlin, "Big Dude Drive in the Crazies," *Saturday Evening Post,* vol. 240, no. 15 (July 29, 1967), 33. Mr. and Mrs. Tom Ferguson, interview, March 28, 1972, Box 2, CGR WHRC UW; Angela Buell to author, December 1, 1976. Esther McWilliams, *Eaton's Ranch* (Wolf, Wyo.: n.p., 1981), 4.

15. Elkhorn Ranch, Gallatin Gateway, Mont., brochure, [1981], 8. DRA, "Dude Ranch Vacation directory, members Dude Ranchers' Association, 1981," brochure, 2, 6.

16. Chamberlin, "Big Dude Drive," 34–35. *The Dude Rancher,* vol. 48, no. 1 (Spring–Summer 1981), 12; Spike Van Cleve to author, August 14, 1981. DRA, "Dude Ranch Vacation directory, members Dude Ranchers' Association, 1981," brochure, 7.

17. Mrs. Arch Allen, "The Ox Yoke Story," *Shorthorn World and Farm Magazine,* August 15, 1964, 49–51. Jim Murphy to author, July 9, 1977. Black Otter Guide Service, Pray, Mont., to author, April 14, 1977; also form letter and brochure, Winter, 1981.

18. Dick Frost, interview, March 31, 1972, Box 2 CGR WHRC UW.

19. Neil Morgan, "Hey Dude!" *Western's World: The Magazine of Western Airlines,* vol. 4, no. 3 (June–July 1973), 43.

20. See, e.g.: Garet Garrett, "How in the West?" *Saturday Evening Post,* vol. 197, no. 2 (November 22, 1924), 78; Stanley Ross, "The Recreational Industry of Colorado" (Master's thesis, University of Colorado, 1954), 90–93. Garrett attacks dude ranches specifically; Ross attacks all private ownership of property in tourist areas.

21. Interviews: Alys Ritterbrown, n.d.; Stanley Siggins, April 1, 1972; both in Box 2, CGR WHRC UW.

22. Thirty Three Bar Ranch, Seeley Lake, Mont., reply to questionnaire, January 25, 1974. Chapter 6 describes pack trips from dude ranches.

23. Joseph P. Sullivan, "A Description and Analysis of the Dude Ranching Industry in Montana" (Master's thesis, University of Montana, 1971), 6–7.

24. "Life Guide," *Life*, vol. 54, no. 17 (April 26, 1963), 12. Pat Dickerman, ed., *Farm Ranch and Countryside Guide* (New York: Farm and Ranch Vacations, Inc., 1974), 12–13; Ingolf K. Vogeler, "Farm and Ranch Vacationing in the United States" (Ph.D. diss., University of Minnesota, 1973), 89.

25. John F. Turner, "Delights and Dilemmas of Dude Ranching," *Wyoming Wildlife*, vol. 36, no. 7 (July 1972), 23; Central Wyoming College, Riverton, Wyo., brochures, ca. 1975. Wilderness Guides and Packers School, Jackson, Wyo., brochures, 1975 and 1977.

26. Randall A. Wagner, Wyoming Travel Commission, to author, July 10, 1974. Sherry L. Smith, Wyoming Recreation Commission, to author, April 8, 1981 and June 16, 1981.

27. Interviews: Glen Fales, April 1972; Peggy Schaffer, March 30, 1972; Mr. and Mrs. Tom Ferguson, March 28, 1972; all in Box 2, CGR WHRC UW; DRA, "Dude Ranch Vacation directory, members Dude Ranchers' Association, 1981," brochure.

28. *The Dude Rancher*, vol. 41, no. 2 (Summer 1972), 1–2. *Nickers: The Dude Ranchers' Association News*, vol. 1 (March 1977). DRA, "Notice from The Dude Ranchers' Association, Granby, Colorado," 1979; Peggy Schaffer, telephone interview with author, May 20, 1981.

29. Les Branch, telephone interview with author, May 20, 1981. "Ranch Country, U.S.A.," Summit Films Production, Vail, Colo., and Jackson Hole, Wyo., n.d.

30. CD & GRA, "Qualifications for Active Membership in the Colorado Dude and Guest Ranch Association," brochure, 1978, and "1981 Colorado Dude Ranches," brochure.

31. Letter from Angela Buell, note cards, Box 2, CGR WHRC UW.

32. Morgan, "Hey Dude!" 14. Vogeler, "Farm and Ranch Vacationing" (Ph.D. diss.), 20.

33. Letters to author: Diane Murphy, Alaska Division of Tourism, 1975; Don Hawkins, Arizona Office of Economic Planning and Development, June 20, 1974; Max Love, Arkansas Dept. of Parks and Tourism, September 3, 1974; Wesley Catlin, California State Library, October 23, 1975; C. R. Goeldner, University of Colorado, Boulder, August 22, 1977; Lloyd D. Howe, Idaho Dept. of Commerce and Development, June 10, 1974; George H. Mathews, Kansas Dept. of Economic Development, June 12, 1974; Lynne Albright, Montana Dept. of

Highways, December 11, 1974; Miss Pat Brown, Nebraska Dept. of Economic Development, September 4, 1974; Mary Myers, New Mexico Dept. of Development, June 12, 1974; Loren L. Stadig, North Dakota Business and Industrial Development Dept., June 7, 1974; Victor Fryer, Oregon State Highway Division, July 31, 1974; Linda Hughes, South Dakota Division of Tourism, June 11, 1974; Ben Holub, Jr., Texas Tourist Development Agency, June 11, 1974; Lou Miller, Bandera, Texas, Chamber of Commerce, June 13, 1974; Tom Brown, Utah Travel Council, June 17, 1974; Gladine L. Loomis, Washington Travel Development Division, June 11, 1974; Randall A. Wagner, Wyoming Travel Commission, June 10, 1974.

34. DRA Minutes, 1949, 49, MS Collection, DRA, Box 2, WHRC UW. Interviews: Angela Buell, March 28, 1972; Mr. and Mrs. Tom Ferguson, March 28, 1972; both in Box 2, CGR WHRC UW.

35. *Sunday Camera's Focus* (Sunday ed. of *Boulder Daily Camera*), August 21, 1977, 23.

36. Mrs. Cotton (JoAn) Gordon, telephone interview with author, June 12, 1981. Mr. and Mrs. Roy Chambers, interview, May 20, 1972, Box 2, CGR WHRC UW.

37. The park uses meant are horseback riding and boating, plus an end of excessive regulation of any travel other than by motorized vehicle.

38. DRA Minutes, 1951, MS Collection, DRA, Box 2, WHRC UW.

39. "Custer Trail Ranch, Medora, N.D.," brochure, ca. 1901–3, 11, 14; "Spend Your Vacation at Eaton's Ranch, Wolf, Sheridan County, Wyoming," brochure, [1904], n.p.; "Custer Trail Ranch Medora North Dakota," brochure, n.d., n.p.; all in MS Collection, Eaton Ranch, Document Box 1, WHRC UW.

40. DRA, "Dude Ranch Vacation directory, members Dude Ranchers' Association, 1981," brochure, inside front cover.

Bibliography

The following bibliography is not an exhaustive list of all items relating to dude ranching. It contains only those items that the author has examined, and that pertain to this study. Brochures from state and city agencies are listed only if they contain specific references to dude ranches.

Since the author's research began, there have been changes in two of the manuscript collections listed. The Western History Research Center at the University of Wyoming, Laramie, is now called the American Heritage Center. The Northern Pacific Railway Company Records examined at the Burlington Northern Offices, St. Paul, Minnesota, are now at the Minnesota Historical Society, St. Paul.

Government Documents

U.S. GOVERNMENT DOCUMENTS

National Park Service, Division of Land Acquisition, *Master Deed Listing*, Status of Lands as of March 31, 1981. Date of run: April 24, 1981.

Outdoor Recreation Resources Review Commission, *Outdoor Recreation for America: A Report to the President and Congress*. Washington, D.C.: Government Printing Office, 1962.

Rocky Mountain National Park, *Walk and Talk Sheet*, East Side, [July 23–30, 1974].

Rocky Mountain National Park, *Program of Free Activities for Visitors*, July 8–15, 1975; August 8–15, 1978.

U.S. *Statutes at Large*, 1st Session, 64th Congress, 1915–16, vol. 39, pt. 1, 535–36.

STUDIES—STATES AND UNIVERSITIES

Beckert, Carl Von E.; Judith L. Oldham; John J. Ryan. *A Profile of the Tourist Market in Colorado—1968*. Denver: Industrial Economics Division, Denver Research Institute, University of Denver, 1969.

Colorado State Business Directory with Colorado Mining Directory and Colorado Live Stock Directory Department. Sixth Annual Volume. Denver: J. A. Blake, Publisher, 1880.

Lund, Richard E. *A Study of Wyoming's Out-of-State Highway Travelers*. Vol. 2. Laramie: University of Wyoming, Division of Business and Economic Research, 1961.

1976 Colorado Travel Industry Year End Report. Boulder: University of Colorado, Business Research Division, Graduate School of Business Administration.

Peters, W. S., and J. S. Wright. *Tourist Travel and Expenditures in Montana*. Prepared for the Montana State Highway Commission, 1958.

Phillips, Clynn, and Dwight M. Blood. *Outdoor Recreation Participation By Out-of-State Visitors in Wyoming*. Part 2 of *Outdoor Recreation in Wyoming*. Laramie: University of Wyoming, Division of Business and Economic Research, March 1969.

Waters, Salma A., ed. *Colorado Year Book 1962–1964*. [Denver]: Colorado State Planning Division, [1965].

"Wyoming's Travel Barometers," *Wyoming Travel Commission*, August, 1971.

Manuscripts

BURLINGTON NORTHERN OFFICES, ST. PAUL, MINNESOTA

Northern Pacific Railway Company Records, "Dude Ranch Pictures Ranch Album Photos."

Northern Pacific Railway Company Records, President's File 2001, Letters 1913–67, Old Building, Box 174.

STATE HISTORICAL SOCIETY OF COLORADO, DENVER

Bloder, Joe W. "Dude Ranching in Colorado and the West," Documentary Resources.

Denver and Rio Grande Archives, Documentary Resources.

Grand Lake, Vertical File, Documentary Resources.

"Recreation Dude Ranches," Subject Collections, Documentary Resources.

DENVER PUBLIC LIBRARY, WESTERN HISTORY DEPARTMENT

Clippings File, "Colorado Tourism," "Dude Ranches," "Dude Ranches Arizona," "Dude Ranches Colorado," "Dude Ranches Montana," "Dude Ranches New Mexico," "Dude Ranches Texas," "Dude Ranches Wyoming," "Livestock Ranches."

Minutes of the Sixth Annual Convention of the Dude Ranchers' Association at Sheridan, Wyoming November 5–6–7, 1931. Casper: S. E. Boyer & Co., n.d.

Enos Abijah Mills Collection.

Charles Cornell Moore Memorial Collection.

Prescribed Recreation: An Exclusive Feature of All-Year Guest Ranches, Inc. Los Angeles: Young & McCallister, 1934?

Railroad File, Publicity Brochures, Union Pacific, "Dude Ranches Out West," [1930s].

Railroad File, Publicity Brochures, Union Pacific, "Dude Ranches Out West," [1931].

MINNESOTA HISTORICAL SOCIETY, ST. PAUL

Great Northern Railway Company Records, President's Subject File #13095.

Northern Pacific Railway Company Records, President's File #356-218, Box 127.

Northern Pacific Railway Company Records, President's File #356-237, Box 127.

Northern Pacific Railway Company Records, President's File #452 I-50, Box 148.

Northern Pacific Railway Company Records, President's File #2001-1.

UNIVERSITY OF WYOMING, WESTERN HISTORY RESEARCH CENTER, LARAMIE

Biographical Manuscript Files: Bengough, Clement Stuart; Eaton, Howard; Eaton, Mary (Mrs. Alden); Rinehart, Mary Roberts; Wister, Owen; Wolcott, Major Frank.

Manuscript Collections: M. Struthers Burt; Dude Ranchers' Association; Eaton Ranch; Olaus J. and Margaret Murie; Charles G. Roundy; Jacob M. Schwoob; Turner's Triangle X Ranch; Owen Wister; Mrs. Marguerite D. Wyman.

Clippings Files: Dude Ranch; Dude Ranch—Aldrich Lodge; Dude Ranch—Arizona; Dude Ranch—Buffalo Bill Country; Dude Ranch—Colorado; Dude Ranch—Double Dee; Dude Ranch—Eatons'; Dude Ranch—Elbud Ranch for Boys; Dude Ranch—Gros Ventre Lodge; Dude Ranch—HF Bar; Dude Ranch—History; Dude Ranch—Holm Lodge; Dude Ranch—HR Ranch Camp; Dude Ranch—IXL; Dude Ranch—Jackson Hole; Dude Ranch—Klondike; Dude Ranch—Medicine Wheel; Dude Ranch—Montana; Dude Ranch—Mountain Pass; Dude Ranch—Open B; Dude Ranch—Two Bars 7; Dude Ranch—Valley Ranch; Dude Ranch—Wyoming; Dude Ranching—University Course; Wyoming—County—Fremont; Wyoming—County—Sublette; Wyoming—Schools; Wyoming—Towns—Shell.

Miscellaneous

"The College of Agriculture." *University of Wyoming Bulletin*, vol. 31, no. 1 (1934–35), 170.

Hultz, Frederick S. *The Course in Recreational Ranching at the University of Wyoming.* Laramie, 1936?

University of Wyoming, Mississippi Valley Committee, Brief Outline for Wyoming Studies and Plans under the Direction of the Mississippi Valley Committee at the University of Wyoming. Exhibit G, "Dude Ranching," by F. S. Hultz.

WYOMING STATE ARCHIVES AND HISTORICAL DEPARTMENT, CHEYENNE

Pam File

Minutes of the Fifth Annual Dude Ranchers' Meeting held at Billings, Montana November 17, 18, 19, 1930. Cheyenne: Pioneer Printing Co., 1931.

Minutes of the Fourth Annual Dude Ranchers' Meeting held at Billings, Montana in the Northern Hotel Tea Room November 18, 19, 20, 1929. Casper: S. E. Boyer & Co., n.d.

Vertical Files
Diamond Guest Ranch
Dude Ranches
Dude Ranches #2
Dude Ranches #3
Eatons' Ranch

WPA Files
Miscellaneous, Johnson County

MISCELLANEOUS
Holzwarth Ranch Data, INT 417, Holzwarth Homestead Cabins, Rocky Mountain National Park, Colorado.
Irving H. (Larry) Larom Manuscript Collection, Buffalo Bill Historical Center, Cody, Wyoming.
Manuscript received from Grace Nutting Miller, Elkhorn Ranch, Tucson, Arizona.
Accounts of Settlers of Grand County, Colorado, Pioneer Museum, Hot Sulphur Springs, Colorado.

Theses and Dissertations

Nash, Roderick William. "Wilderness and the American Mind." Ph.D. dissertation, University of Wisconsin, 1965.
Norris, Frank Blaine. "The Southern Arizona Guest Ranch as a Symbol of the West." Master's thesis, University of Arizona, 1976.
Ross, Stanley, "The Recreational Industry of Colorado." Master's thesis, University of Colorado, 1954.
Sullivan, Joseph P. "A Description and Analysis of the Dude Ranching Industry in Montana." Master's thesis, University of Montana, 1971.
Vogeler, Ingolf Klaus. "Farm and Ranch Vacationing in the United States." Ph.D. dissertation, University of Minnesota, 1973.

Journals and Periodicals

AUTHOR LISTED
Allen, Mrs. Arch. "The Ox Yoke Story." *Shorthorn World and Farm Magazine,* August 15, 1964, 49–51.

Arnold, Lowell J. "Dude Ranches of Southern Arizona." *Progressive Arizona,* vol. 1 (September 1925), 13–16, 38–39.

———. "Dude Ranching." *Progressive Arizona,* vol. 4 (February 1927), 18–20, 38–39.

———. "Vacationing at the Circle Z." *Progressive Arizona,* vol. 2 (January 1926), 15–16.

Babcock, Frederic. "At Home in a Ten Gallon Hat." *Travel,* vol. 69, no. 1 (May 1937), 30–31, 54.

Bartlett, Richard A. "Old Faithful Inn." *The American West,* vol. 16, no. 4 (July–August 1979), 16–17, 59.

Boatright, Mody C. "The American Myth Rides the Range." *Southwest Review,* vol. 36, no. 3 (Summer 1951), 157–63.

Boissevain, Jan. "Visitors Out of Season." *The American West,* vol. 16, no. 4 (July–August 1979), 30–31, 60–61.

Borne, Lawrence R. "The Cowboy and Dude Ranching." *Red River Valley Historical Review,* vol. 2, no. 1 (Spring 1975), 114–33.

———. "Dude Ranches and the Development of the West." *Journal of the West,* vol. 17, no. 3 (July 1978), 83–94.

———. "Dude Ranching In Print." *The Dude Rancher,* vol. 47, no. 1 (Spring 1980), 33–34.

———. "Recreation, Government, and Freedom." *World Research INK,* vol. 1, no. 11 (August 1977), 3.

Borum, Ruth. "The Lure of Ranch Life." *Progressive Arizona and the Great Southwest,* vol. 8 (February 1929), 22–23, 27.

———. "Rancho Linda Vista." *Progressive Arizona,* vol. 6 (May 1928), 15–16, 28–29.

Brandon, C. Watt. "Building a Town on Wyoming's Last Frontier." *Annals of Wyoming,* vol. 22, no. 2 (July 1950), 27–46.

Bruce, George. "Arizona Comes Into Her Heritage." *Yavapai,* vol. 20 (August 1930), 8–9.

Burnham, Brook. "Are Some Dude Ranchers Flying Under False Colors?" *The Dude Rancher,* vol. 22, no. 1 (January 1953), 14.

Burns, Robert H. "The First Dude." *The Westerner,* vol. 8, no. 9 (November 1945), 26–29.

Burt, Struthers. "Dudes on a Thousand Hills." *Rotarian,* vol. 52 (March 1938), 32–35.

———. "Dudes Ranches." *The Outlook: An Illustrated Weekly of Current Life,* vol. 146, no. 4 (May 25, 1927), 112–14.

———. "More Disadvantages of Roadside Signs Pointed Out by Struthers Burt." *The Dude Rancher*, vol. 6, no. 7 (July–August 1938), 12–13, 17.

———. "Western Horses and Eastern Riders." *The Dude Rancher*, vol. 17, no. 2 (April 1948), 8–9, 33–41.

Butterfield, Roger. "How Reno Lives." *Ladies Home Journal*, vol. 66 (November 1949), 205–10, 254–60.

Carhart, Arthur Hawthorne. "Dogies and Dudes." *American Forestry*, vol. 29 (August 1923), 475–78, 511.

Chamberlin, Anne. "Big Dude Drive in the Crazies." *Saturday Evening Post*, vol. 240, no. 15 (July 29, 1967), 32–37.

Chapman, Leb. "The Story of the Garden of Allah Guest Ranch, Ariz." *Hoofs and Horns*, vol. 3 (October 1933), 14.

Clinton, Bruce. "Desert Dude Wrangler." *Desert Magazine*, vol. 12 (January 1949), 5–10.

[Cody, William F.] Buffalo Bill. "Famous Hunting Parties of the Plains." *The Cosmopolitan*, vol. 17, no. 2 (June 1894), 131–43.

Cooper, Courtney Ryley. "Dude, howdy!" *Ladies Home Journal*, vol. 48 (August 1931), 41.

Copeland, Fred. "Dude-Puncher Steve." *Scribner's Magazine*, vol. 69 (February 1921), 343–52. [Fiction]

Corbin, Josephine Delatour. "Beaver Creek Ranch—In the Valley of the Sun." *Progressive Arizona*, vol. 11 (September 1930), 18–20, 27–28.

Culbertson, E. H. "Ranch Vacation for $15." *Country Life*, vol. 10 (June 1906), 158, 160, 160b, 160d.

Davis, Elmer E. "Rancho Manzanito." *Progressive Arizona*, vol. 7 (December 1928), 13–14.

Doering, Thomas R. "A Reexamination of the Relative Importance of Tourism to State Economies." *Journal of Travel Research*, vol. 15, no. 1 (Summer 1976), 13–17.

Dusseau, Leon J. B. "Teepee Tours." *The Teepee Book*, Ranch Resort Number (March–April–May 1915), 51–88.

Eaton, Mrs. Alden (Aunt Mame). "Eatons' Dude Ranch." *Persimmon Hill*, vol. 11, no. 1 (Winter 1981), 46–55.

Evarts, Hal G. "Dude Wranglers." *Saturday Evening Post*, vol. 192 (May 1, 1920), 32–34, 181–82.

Falkner, Leonard. "The Call of the Old West." *American Magazine*, vol. 160, no. 5 (November 1955), 84–88.

Farmer, Charles J. "Trapperman." *The American Hunter*, vol. 2, no. 8 (August 1974), 50–53.

Feldman, Miriam. "The Disappearing Dude Ranch." *Desert Magazine,* vol. 43 (September 1980), 12–14.

Ferguson, Nancy. "Guests and Saddles." *Wyoming Wildlife,* vol. 36, no. 7 (July 1972), 30–33.

Ferril, Thomas Hornsby. "Tourists, Stay Away From My Door." *Harper's Magazine,* vol. 208, no. 1248 (May 1954), 77–81.

Field, Richard L. "Dudes in the Rockies." *Holiday,* vol. 1, no. 5 (July 1946), 22–25.

Foglesong, Scott. "Frank Wright: A Man and His Mountains." *Spice of Life Colorado,* vol. 1, no. 4 (July 1974), 34–35, 68–71.

[Frazier, Ira]. "From Cows to Dudes." *Magazine Tucson,* vol. 5 (October 1952), 19–22.

Frost, Mary (Mrs. Ned). "House Management Department." *The Dude Rancher,* vol. 6, no. 7 (July–August 1938), 5.

Fussell, Paul. "The Stationary Tourist." *Harper's,* vol. 258, no. 1547 (April 1979), 31–38.

Gabbey, A. W. "The Great American Summer Institution: The Dude Ranch." *Rocky Mountain Sportsman,* vol. 1, no. 1 (June 1938), 3–4.

Garrett, Garet. "How in the West?" *Saturday Evening Post,* vol. 197, no. 2 (November 22, 1924), 10–11, 76, 78, 83, 85.

Greig, Howard, and Patty J. Martineau, eds. "Holiday Handbook." *Holiday,* vol. 45, no. 5 (May 1969), 102–3.

Hall, Alice J. "Buffalo Bill and the Enduring West." *National Geographic,* vol. 160, no. 1 (July 1981), 76–103.

Harrower, James K., and Lester Bagley. "The Gros Ventre Lodge." *Wyoming Wild Life,* vol. 16, no. 9 (September 1952), 4–15.

Hart, Albert Bushnell. "See America First." *Outlook,* vol. 114 (December 27, 1916), 933–38.

Heilman, Joan Rattner. "Meet Brand-New Ranchers Jay and Lorena Walker of Montana." *Family Circle,* vol. 82, no. 6 (June 1973), 12, 16, 48–49, 52, 148.

Hook, James W. "Seven Months in Cody, Wyoming 1905–1906." *Annals of Wyoming,* vol. 26, no. 1 (January 1954), 3–24.

Isberg, Art. "A Meeting in the Fall." *The American Hunter,* vol. 2, no. 10 (October 1974), 46–49.

Jones, H. Lee. "Everybody's Dudin' It." *New Mexico,* vol. 14, no. 4 (April 1936), 9–11, 43–44.

Jones, Lloyd. "A Dude Rancher Speaks to Associate Members and To His Guests." *The Dude Rancher,* vol. 42, no. 2 (Summer 1973), 38.

Jones, Philip W. "And I Learned About Ranching from 'Im." *Progressive Arizona and the Great Southwest*, vol. 8 (March 1929), 24–25, 30–31.

Kelly, Loudon. "Chickens, Shikars and Dudes." *Colorado Wonderland*, vol. 6, no. 2 (April 1955), 14.

King, Bucky (Mrs. Wilber Staunton King). "When Hospitality Fostered an Industry." *In Wyoming*, vol. 8, no. 4 (October–November 1975), 23–29.

La Farge, Oliver. "They All Ride." *Vogue*, vol. 87, no. 9 (May 1, 1936), 96–97, 137–38.

Larom, I. H. "President's Page." *The Dude Rancher*, vol. 6, no. 7 (July–August 1938), 4.

———. "Survey of the Year." *The Dude Rancher*, vol. 6, no. 1 (January 1937), 4, 12, 22.

———. "Valley Ranching in Wyoming." *Arts and Decoration Combined with the Spur*, vol. 53, no. 4 (March 1941), 36–37.

Lasher, Albert C. "Arizona's Dude Ranchers Ride a Golden Roundup." *Wall Street Journal*, March 9, 1953, 11.

Lesure, Thomas. "Dude Ranching . . . the Western Vacation Few Westerners Ever Take." *Desert Magazine*, vol. 23 (December 1960), 26–28.

Lingo, Karen. "Home, Home on the Dude Ranch." *Southern Living*, vol. 12, no. 5 (May 1977), 100–103.

Lipp, George A. "Passing of the Western Cattle Ranches." *Overland Monthly*, 2nd series, vol. 63, no. 2 (February 1914), 131–38.

Lofting, Colin. "Mortifying Visit from a Dude Dad." *Life*, vol. 61, no. 14 (September 30, 1966), 128, 130.

Logue, Roscoe. "Dude Ranches: How Derived." *Hoofs and Horns*, vol. 3 (February 1934), 8.

Lorimer, George. "Selling Scenery." *Saturday Evening Post*, vol. 192, no. 15 (October 11, 1919), 28.

[Lutz, W. E.]. "Montana Dude Ranches." *The Dude Rancher*, vol. VI, no. 7 (July–August 1938), 8–9.

McOmie, Margaret. "Flying V Ranch is Ideally Located." *Progressive Arizona*, vol. 9 (October 1929), 25, 28.

Meigs, Marcia. "Happy Days on a Dude Ranch." *Country Life*, vol. 64 (May 1933), 43–46.

Metzger, S. S. "A Day on the Ranch." *Sunset*, vol. 37 (July 1916), 47.

Miller, Ernest. "Dude Ranch Horses." *The Cattleman*, vol. 28 (September 1941), 139, 141.

Miller, Mrs. Ernest. "50th Anniversary." *The Dude Rancher*, vol. 43, no. 1 (Spring 1974), 7–10.

Morgan, Neil. "Hey, Dude!" *Western's World: The Magazine of Western Airlines*, vol. 4, no. 3 (June–July 1973), 14–16, 43.

Murie, Margaret E. "Dude Ranchers Are Influential People." *The Dude Rancher*, vol. 39, no. 4 (Winter 1970–71), 8, 10, 13–15.

Murphy, Mernice. "Relax! You're on an Arizona Dude Ranch." *Arizona Highways*, vol. 12 (April 1936), 8–9, 19.

Nilva, Sheila Cole. "Vacation on a Dude Ranch." *Mademoiselle*, vol. 87 (April 1981), 104, 106, 108, 112–13.

O'Conor, Norreys Jephson. "An Irish Sportsman in the Far West." *Arizona Quarterly*, vol. 5, no. 2 (Summer 1949), 108–18.

Parker, Charles Franklin, and Jeanne S. Humburg. "Phantom Ranch." *Arizona Highways*, vol. 33, no. 5 (May 1957), 32–33.

Park-Lewis, Dorothea. "Dude-Ling." *House Beautiful*, vol. 81, no. 4 (April 1939), 122, 124–25, 127.

Perrin, L. L. "You Profit from the Dude Ranch Advertising." *The Dude Rancher*, vol. 1, no. 1 (December 1932), 8.

Petersen, Leslie. "Wyoming Dude Ranch." *In Wyoming*, vol. 4, no. 2 (Summer 1971), 8–11.

Peterson, Myrtle S. "They Recreate at Beaver Creek." *Progressive Arizona*, vol. 9 (October 1929), 21–23.

Post, Anita. "Local Color in the Southwest." *Hoofs and Horns*, vol. 5 (November 1935), 3, 16.

Queal, Cal. "Colorado Dude Wrangler." *Mainliner*, vol. 14 (July 1970), 31–32, 34.

Raddy, Raymond J. "Dude Ranching Is Not All Yippee!" *The Western Horseman*, vol. 17, no. 4 (April 1952), 16, 35–40.

Randall, L. W. (Gay). "The Man Who Put the Dude in Dude Ranching." *Montana*, vol. 10, no. 3 (July 1960), 29–41.

Raine, William MacLeod. "The Dude Rides Circle." *Sunset*, vol. 60 (April 1928), 16–17, 56, 58, 60.

Ray, Grace E. "Down the Long Pack Trail." *Independent Women*, vol. 20, no. 7 (July 1941), 202–4.

Rayburn, Roger. "Going Western on a Guest Ranch." *Tucson*, vol. 8 (October 1935), 2–5, 15.

Raynock, Jeanne V. "Dude Ranching in Wyoming." *Wyoming Vacationland*, 1956, S1–S4.

Revis, Kathleen. "Colorado by Car and Campfire." *National Geographic*, vol. 106, no. 2 (August 1954), 207–48.

Rinehart, Mary Roberts. "The Cavvy." *Saturday Evening Post*, vol. 199, no. 13 (September 25, 1926), 6–7, 129–30, 132.

———. "Dude Ranch." *Ladies Home Journal*, vol. 48 (June 1931), 124.

———. "Dude West." *Ladies Home Journal*, vol. 46 (April 1929), 14–15.

———. "Riding the Circle on Hanging Woman." *Saturday Evening Post*, vol. 198, no. 16 (October 17, 1925), 6–7, 71–72, 74, 79.

———. "The Sleeping Giant." *Ladies Home Journal*, vol. 28 (May 1921), 21, 80, 83.

———. "Summer Comes to the Ranch." *Saturday Evening Post*, vol. 198, no. 1 (July 4, 1925), 3–4, 66, 71–72.

———. "To Wyoming." *Saturday Evening Post*, vol. 199, no. 14 (October 2, 1926), 16–17, 161–62, 165–66, 169.

———. "What Is a Dude Ranch?" *Harper's Bazaar*, August 1927, 68–69, 128–31.

Roberts, H. Armstrong. "A Day on a Dude Ranch." *Country Life*, vol. 57 (August 1930), 52–53.

Rodnitzky, Jerome L. "Recapturing The West: The Dude Ranch in American Life." *Arizona and the West*, vol. 10 (Summer 1968), 111–26.

Roundy, Charles G. "The Origins and Early Development of Dude Ranching in Wyoming." *Annals of Wyoming*, vol. 45, no. 1 (Spring 1973), 5–25.

Saban, Vera D. "Men Who Challenged the Bighorn." *The American West*, vol. 11, no. 3 (May 1974), 44–47, 62–63.

Schuessler, Raymond. "Ever Try a Dude Ranch Vacation?" *Better Homes and Gardens*, vol. 31, no. 3 (March 1953), 66, 246, 248, 250–51.

Searl, Helen Hulett. "Week-End Cowboys." *Christian Science Monitor Magazine* (West Coast edition), July 12, 1941, 12.

Seitz, Don C. "The Ranch for Recreation: A New Phase of Summer Outdoor Life in America." *Outlook*, vol. 145, no. 15 (April 13, 1927), 480.

Silliman, Lee. "'As Kind and Generous a Host as ever Lived.'" *The American West*, vol. 16, no. 4 (July–August 1979), 18–22.

Smith, Lewis. "The Packer Sees Spots." *Appaloosa News*, vol. 34, no. 8 (August 1977), 42–44.

Smith, Robert T. "The Big Sky Development: A Lesson for the Future." *The American West*, vol. 12, no. 5 (September 1975), 46–47, 62–63.

Spencer, Dick, III. "Winter Dude Ranch." *The Western Horseman*, vol. 25, no. 1 (January 1960), 44–45, 88–89.

Sprague, Marshall. "The Dude from Limerick." *The American West*, vol. 3, no. 4 (Fall 1966), 53–61, 92–94.

Steele, A. T. "Lady Boss of Faraway Ranch." *Saturday Evening Post*, vol. 230, no. 37 (March 15, 1958), 28–29, 132, 134–35.

Steffen, Randy. "Dude Ranches." *The Western Horseman*, vol. 14, no. 5 (May 1949), 20–21.

Stein, E. A. "Day on a Guest Ranch." *Arizona Highways*, vol. 22, no. 9 (September 1947), 12–13.

Stewart, Margaret K. "Vacationing on Y-Lightning." *Progressive Arizona*, vol. 5 (December 1927), 14–15.

———. "What I've Learned About Ranches." *Progressive Arizona*, vol. 6 (February 1928), 14–16, 30.

Stratton, Rex. "Financing a Dude Ranch Operation." *The Dude Rancher*, vol. 26, no. 1 (January 1957), 14, 20, 30, 42.

Taylor, Frank J. "Beauts and Saddles." *Collier's*, vol. 98, no. 6 (August 8, 1936), 21, 34.

———. "Ride Trail, Dude, and Grow Young." *Cosmopolitan*, vol. 85 (August 1932), 54–55, 108, 110.

Taylor, Rosemary. "Dudes and Don'ts: Practical Hints for the Would-be Ranch Guest." *Magazine Tucson*, vol. 5 (November 1952), 36–37.

Thomas, Agnes Ross. "On a Powder River Ranch." *Overland Monthly*, 2nd series, vol. 58, no. 4 (October 1911), 334–41.

Thure, Karen. "The Dude Ranch Originals." *Arizona Highways*, vol. 56, no. 11 (November 1980), 5–6.

Tinker, Frank A. "Puttin' Up the Dudes." *Westways*, vol. 65, no. 11 (November 1973), 52–55.

———. "Whatever Happened to Dude Ranches?" *Catholic Digest*, vol. 38, no. 9 (July 1974), 102–5.

Tompkins, Leta. "Dude Horse." *The Western Horseman*, vol. 17, no. 4 (April 1952), 14, 33–34.

Townsend, Ted. "Dudes, Mutts & Crackjacks." *New Republic*, vol. 132, no. 12 (March 21, 1955), 14–15.

Turner, John F. "Delights and Dilemmas of Dude Ranching." *Wyoming Wildlife*, vol. 36, no. 7 (July 1972), 23.

Van Cleve, Carol. "The Making and Breaking of Dude Horses." *The Dude Rancher*, vol. 42, no. 2 (Summer 1973), 16–18, 27.

Vischer, Peter. "Ranching is All Right!" *Horse and Horseman*, vol. 21, no. 5 (April 1939), 24–25, 34–36.

Von Tempski, Armine. "We Run a Dude-Ranch—in Hawaii!" *Sunset*, vol. 61 (September 1928), 20–23.

Wack, Henry W. "Life on a Dude Ranch." *Arts and Decoration*, vol. 35 (May 1931), 58–59, 92, 94–95.

Watts, Arretta L. "The Increasingly Popular 'Dude' Ranch." *Country Life*, vol. 54 (July 1928), 55–56.

Weaver, Leo. "Life on a 'Dude' Ranch." *Arizona Highways*, vol. 4 (September 1928), 21, 29–30.

Whithorn, Doris. "Wrangling Dudes in Yellowstone." *Frontier Times*, vol. 43, no. 6 (October–November 1969), 18–22.

Whilt, Jim. "Fate of the Dude Wrangler." *The Western Horseman*, vol. 28 (September 1963), 13.

Williams, Jesse Lynch. "Joy-Ranching and Dude Wrangling." *Collier's*, vol. 51 (August 9, 1913), 22–23.

Winsted, Manya. "Arizona's Fabulous Guest Ranches." *Arizona Highways*, vol. 56, no. 11 (November 1980), 2, 8–13.

Wolff, Meyer H. "The Bob Marshall Wilderness Area." *The Living Wilderness*, vol. 6, no. 6 (July 1941), 5–6.

Young, Etta Gifford. "The Garden of Allah." *Arizona: The State Magazine*, vol. 3 (June 1913), 4–5.

Young, Stark. "Dude Ranch." *New Republic*, vol. 52, no. 665 (August 31, 1927), 43–44.

———. "Dude Ranch: I Miss Cissie." *New Republic*, vol. 55, no. 712 (July 25, 1928), 250–51.

———. "Dude Ranch: II Old Eagle." *New Republic*, vol. 55, no. 713 (August 1, 1928), 279–80.

———. "Dude Ranch: III Trail Driver." *New Republic*, vol. 55, no. 714 (August 8, 1928), 307–8.

Zierer, Clifford M. "Tourism and Recreation in the West." *Geographical Review*, vol. 42, no. 3 (July 1952), 462–81.

NO AUTHOR LISTED

In addition to the items listed, the notes refer to unsigned, untitled material in *The Dude Rancher* and *Outlook*.

"Appointment in the Sun." *Arizona Highways*, vol. 24, no. 9 (September 1948), 16–25.

"Compass Pointers: A journalistic dude takes kindly to horse wrangling." *Home and Field*, vol. 44 (March 1934), 82, 84–85.

"Directory, Ranches Resorts Hotels." *Arizona Highways*, vol. 23, no. 9 (September 1947), 30–44.

"Dressing the Dude," *Vogue,* vol. 87, no. 9 (May 1, 1936), 140–41.

"Dude Ranch Courses Now Included." *The Cattleman,* vol. 22, no. 6 (November 1935), 15.

"'Dude' Ranches." *The Cattleman,* vol. 20, no. 1 (March 1934), 100–101.

"Dude Ranches." *Colorful Colorado,* vol. 11, no. 5 (March–April 1976), 46, 48.

"Dude Ranches." *Hoofs and Horns,* vol. 1 (November 6, 1931), 8.

"Dude Ranches Excluded from Unemployment Compensation Contributions in Wyoming." *The Dude Rancher,* vol. 7, no. 1 (January 1939), 2.

"Dude Ranching A La Francaise." *The Westerners Brand Book,* vol. 10, no. 8 (October 1953), 58.

"Dude Ranching in Wyoming." *The Dude Rancher,* vol. 23, no. 4 (October 1954), 53.

"Executive Secretary's Annual Report." *The Dude Rancher,* vol. 1, no. 1 (December 1932), 7, 21–22.

"Facts, Figures and Fancies." *The Dude Rancher,* vol. 1, no. 1 (December 1932), 4.

"A Great Loss Is a Great Challenge." *The Living Wilderness,* vol. 10, no. 13 (July 1945), 1.

"Guest Ranches." *Hoofs and Horns,* vol. 3 (January 1934), 14–15.

"Guest Ranches." *Hoofs and Horns,* vol. 4 (September 1934), 14.

"How To Get on with a Wrangler." *Magazine Tucson,* vol. 4 (October 1951), 14–15.

"I Want To Buy A Ranch. . . ." *The Dude Rancher,* vol. 17, no. 2 (Spring 1958), 18–19, 26–27.

"I Want To Buy A Ranch. . . ." *The Dude Rancher,* vol. 17, no. 3 (Summer 1958), 12, 34–35.

"A Lady on a Dude Ranch." *Literary Digest,* vol. 85 (June 27, 1925), 48, 50.

"Life Goes to a Dude Ranch." *Life,* vol. 6 (June 19, 1939), 78–81.

"Life Guide." *Life,* vol. 54, no. 17 (April 26, 1963), 12.

"Minutes of the Seventh Annual Meeting Dude Ranchers' Association." *The Dude Rancher,* vol. 1, no. 1 (December 1932), 22, 26, 31.

"The Model Dude Rancher." *The Dude Rancher,* vol. 23, no. 3 (July 1954), 54–55.

"Monk's Guest Ranch." *Hoofs and Horns,* vol. 5 (December 1935), 6.

"Montana Dude Ranches." *The Dude Rancher,* vol. 6, no. 7 (July–August 1938), 8–9.

"News of the Ranches and Resorts." *Magazine Tucson,* vol. 4 (October 1951), 16–17, 40.

"Ranch Directory." *Horse and Horseman,* vol. 21, no. 5 (April 1939), 12–15.

"Ranch Directory." *Horse and Horseman,* vol. 21, no. 6 (May 1939), 13–15.

"Ranch Directory." *Horse and Horseman,* vol. 22, no. 1 (June 1939), 13–15.

"Ranch of the Gentlemen on Horseback." *Point West,* vol. 5 (January 1963), 22–26.

"Rope Your Own!" *Sunset,* vol. 57 (September 1926), 12–14.

"Seeing the Guest Ranches." *Tucson,* vol. 8 (January 1935), 10–11, 20.

"Sierra Linda Ranch." *Hoofs and Horns,* vol. 5 (December 1935), 6.

"Southern Arizona Guest Ranches." *Tucson,* vol. 3 (February 1930), 6–7, 9.

"Spending the Vacation on a Ranch." *Literary Digest,* vol. 89 (June 5, 1926), 70–71.

"Sunset Travel Service." *Sunset,* vol. 64 (June 1930), 62, 65–66.

"Sunshine For Sale: Guest Ranches a New Way of Life for City Dwellers." *Magazine Tucson,* vol. 4 (October 1951), 18–19, 40.

"Through Glacier National Park With Howard Eaton." *The American West,* vol. 16, no. 4 (July–August 1979), 23–29.

"Union Pacific R.R. Publishes Interesting Dude Ranch Book." *The Dude Rancher,* vol. 6, no. 7 (July–August 1938), 11.

"We Dude It." *The Dude Rancher,* vol. 28, no. 1 (January 1959), 28.

"What brings them back to Wickenburg? It's horses but mostly it's the ranches." *Sunset,* vol. 160 (February 1979), 68, 70, 72.

"Why a Dude Ranch Vacation?" *Magazine Tucson,* vol. 2 (October 1949), 18–19, 52.

"Wish You Were Here." *Saturday Evening Post,* vol. 210, no. 50 (June 10, 1939), 20, 103–4, 106.

"Wyoming's Dude Ranches: What They Are and Where." *Outing,* vol. 74 (July 1919), 236, 238.

Newspapers

Arizona Daily Star (Tucson)

Bad Lands Cow Boy (Medora, Dakota Territory)

Billings Gazette

Boston Evening Transcript

Boston Post

Boulder Daily Camera

Bozeman Daily Chronicle

Casper Daily Tribune

Casper Star-Tribune

Casper Tribune Herald

Cervi's Rocky Mountain Journal (Denver)
Cheyenne Tribune Eagle
Cincinnati Enquirer
Cincinnati Post and Times Star
Cody Enterprise
Cody, Wyo. (Cody County Chamber of Commerce)
Denver Post
Denver Times
Dubois Dude Wrangler
Estes Park Trail-Gazette
Fort Collins Express
Great Falls Tribune
Kemmerer Gazette
Minneapolis Journal
New York Times
Pinedale Roundup (Wyoming)
Platte County Record-Times (Wheatland, Wyoming)
Pueblo Star-Journal and Sunday Chieftain
Rocky Mountain News (Denver)
Sky-Hi News (Granby, Colorado)
Wyoming Eagle (Cheyenne)
Wyoming State Journal (Lander)
Wyoming State Tribune–Cheyenne State Leader
Wyoming Tribune (Cheyenne)

Books

NONFICTION

Abbott, E. C. *We Pointed Them North: Recollections of a Cowpuncher.* Norman: University of Oklahoma Press, 1955.

Abbott, Wilbur C. *New York in the American Revolution.* New York: Charles Scribner's Sons, 1929.

Adams, Ramon F. *Western Words.* Norman: University of Oklahoma Press, 1968.

Alderson, Nannie T., and Helen Huntington Smith. *A Bride Goes West.* Lincoln: University of Nebraska Press, 1969.

Arrington, Leonard J. *The Changing Economic Structure of the Mountain West, 1850–1950.* Logan: Utah State University Press, 1963.

Athearn, Robert G. *Westward the Briton.* Lincoln: University of Nebraska Press, 1969.

Atherton, Lewis. *The Cattle Kings.* Bloomington: Indiana University Press, 1961.

Back, Joe. *Horses, Hitches and Rocky Trails.* Denver: Sage Books. 1959.

Bard, Floyd C. *Dude Wrangler, Hunter, Line Rider.* Denver: Sage Books, 1964.

Barrère, Albert, and Charles G. Leland, comps. and eds. *A Dictionary of Slang, Jargon & Cant.* 2 vols. Detroit: Gale Research Co., 1967.

Beale, Howard K. *Theodore Roosevelt and the Rise of America to World Power.* New York: Collier, 1962.

Belasco, Warren James. *Americans on the Road: From Autocamp to Motel, 1910–1945.* Cambridge, Mass.: MIT Press, 1979.

Berrey, Lester V., and Melvin Van Den Bark. *The American Thesaurus of Slang.* 2nd ed. New York: Crowell, 1962.

Bird, Isabella L. *A Lady's Life in the Rocky Mountains.* Norman: University of Oklahoma Press, 1960.

Black, Robert C., III. *Island in the Rockies: The History of Grand County, Colorado, to 1930.* Boulder: Pruett Press, 1969.

Boorstin, Daniel J. *The Image: A Guide to Pseudo-Events in America.* New York: Harper & Row, 1964.

Bronson, Edgar Beecher. *Reminiscences of a Ranchman.* Lincoln: University of Nebraska Press, 1972.

Brown, Ralph H. *Historical Geography of the United States.* New York: Harcourt, Brace & World, 1948.

Burns, Robert Homer; Andrew Springs Gillespie; and Willing Gay Richardson. *Wyoming's Pioneer Ranches.* Laramie: Top-Of-The-World Press, 1955.

Burt, Struthers. *The Diary of a Dude-Wrangler.* New York: Charles Scribner's Sons, 1924.

Cairns, Mary Lyons. *Grand Lake: The Pioneers.* Denver: World Press, 1946.

———. *The Olden Days.* Denver: World Press, 1954.

Carhart, Arthur. *Hi, Stranger! The Complete Guide to Dude Ranches.* Introduction by C. C. Moore. Chicago: Ziff-Davis, 1949.

Carney, Otis. *New Lease on Life: The Story of a City Family Who Quit the Rat Race and Moved to a Ranch in Wyoming.* New York: Random House, 1971.

Chamblin, Thomas S., ed. *The Historical Encyclopedia of Colorado.* 2 vols. [Denver?]: Colorado Historical Association, n.d. [1960?].

———, ed. *The Historical Encyclopedia of Wyoming.* 2 vols. Cheyenne: Wyoming Historical Institute, 1970.

Cheney, Roberta, and Clyde Erskine. *Music, Saddles and Flapjacks: Dudes at the OTO Ranch.* Missoula, Mont.: Mountain Press Publishing Co., 1978.

De Voto, Bernard. *The Year of Decision 1846.* Boston: Little, Brown, 1943.

Dick, Everett. *The Dixie Frontier: A Social History of the Southern Frontier from the First Transmontane Beginnings to the Civil War.* New York: Capricorn, 1964.

Dickerman, Pat, ed. *Farm Ranch and Countryside Guide.* New York: Farm and Ranch Vacations, 1974.

Drago, Harry S. *The Great Range Wars: Violence on the Grasslands.* New York: Dodd, Mead & Co., 1970.

Dresden, Donald. *The Marquis de Morès: Emperor of the Bad Lands.* Norman: University of Oklahoma Press, 1970.

Fielding, Loraine Horanday, *French Heels to Spurs.* New York: Century Co., 1930.

Fite, Gilbert C. *The Farmer's Frontier, 1865–1900.* New York: Holt Rinehart & Winston, 1966.

Frantz, Joe B., and Julian E. Choate, Jr. *The American Cowboy: The Myth and the Reality.* Norman: University of Oklahoma Press, 1968.

Grubbs, Amey. *Medium Well to Extremely Rare: An Easterner's Western Dude Ranch.* [Fort Collins, Colo.: Old Army Press], 1980.

Hafen, Le Roy R., and Ann W. Hafen, eds. *Rufus B. Sage: His Letters and Papers 1836–1847 with an annotated reprint of his "Scenes in the Rocky Mountains and in Oregon, California, New Mexico, Texas and the Grand Prairies."* 2 vols. In *The Far West and Rockies Series,* vols. 4 and 5. Glendale, Calif.: Arthur H. Clark Co., 1956.

Hagedorn, Hermann. *Roosevelt in the Bad Lands.* Boston: Houghton Mifflin Co., 1930.

Hooton, Barbara C. *Guestward Ho!* New York: Vanguard, 1956.

Huidekoper, A. C. *My Experience and Investment in The Bad Lands of Dakota and Some of the Men I Met There.* Baltimore: Wirth Brothers, 1947.

Johnson, Virginia. *The Long, Long Trail.* Boston: Houghton Mifflin Co., 1966.

Kennedy, Michael S., ed. *Cowboys and Cattlemen: A Roundup from Montana, The Magazine of Western History.* New York: Hastings House, 1964.

Klein, Rochelle. *City Slickers on a Dude Ranch.* New York: Comet Press Books, 1959.

Lang, Lincoln A. *Ranching with Roosevelt.* Philadelphia: J. B. Lippincott Co., 1926.

Larson, T. A. *History of Wyoming.* Lincoln: University of Nebraska Press, 1965.

Lauber, Patricia. *Cowboys and Cattle Ranching.* New York: Crowell, 1973.

Leakey, John (as told to Nellie Snyder Yost). *The West That Was: From Texas to Montana.* Lincoln: University of Nebraska Press, 1965.

Martin, Mildred A. *The Martins of Gunbarrel.* Caldwell, Idaho: Caxton, 1959.

McCracken, Harold, Richard I. Frost, Leo A. Platteter, and Don Hedgpeth. *The*

West of Buffalo Bill: Frontier Art, Indian Crafts, Memorabilia from the Buffalo Bill Historical Center. New York: Harry N. Abrams, 1974.

Mills, Enos A. *Early Estes Park.* Estes Park, Colo.: Mrs. Enos A. Mills, 1959.

Osgood, Ernest S. *The Day of the Cattleman.* Chicago: University of Chicago Press, 1966.

Pack, Arthur N. *The Ghost Ranch Story.* Philadelphia: Board of Christian Education of the United Presbyterian Church in the U.S.A., 1960.

Pauly, Nell. *The Day Before Yesterday.* Apple Valley, Calif.: Apple Valley News, 1972.

Pomeroy, Earl. *In Search of the Golden West: The Tourist in Western America.* New York: Alfred A. Knopf, 1957.

Pringle, Henry. *Theodore Roosevelt: A Biography.* New York: Harcourt, Brace & Co., 1931.

Randall, L. W. (Gay). *Footprints Along the Yellowstone.* San Antonio: Naylor Co., 1961.

Reiger, John F. *American Sportsmen and the Origins of Conservation.* New York: Winchester Press, 1975.

Riegel, Robert E., and Robert G. Athearn. *America Moves West.* 5th ed. New York: Holt, Rinehart & Winston, 1971.

Rinehart, Mary Roberts. *My Story.* New York: Farrar & Rinehart, 1931.

———. *Nomad's Land.* New York: George H. Doran Co., 1926.

———. *The Out Trail.* New York: George H. Doran Co., 1923.

———. *Tenting To-Night: A Chronicle of Sport and Adventure in Glacier Park and the Cascade Mountains.* Boston: Houghton Mifflin Co., 1918.

———. *Through Glacier Park: Seeing America First with Howard Eaton.* Boston: Houghton Mifflin Co., 1916.

Roosevelt, Theodore. *Ranch Life and the Hunting Trail.* Ann Arbor: University Microfilms, 1966.

Rosa, Joseph G. *They Called Him Wild Bill: The Life and Adventures of James Butler Hickok.* Norman: University of Oklahoma Press, 1974.

Russell, Osborne. *Journal of a Trapper or Nine Years Residence among the Rocky Mountains Between the Years 1834 and 1843.* Edited by Aubrey L. Haines. Lincoln: University of Nebraska Press, 1968.

Saylor, David J. *Jackson Hole, Wyoming: In the Shadow of the Tetons.* Norman: University of Oklahoma Press, 1970.

Schmitt, Peter J. *Back to Nature: The Arcadian Myth in Urban America.* New York: Oxford University Press, 1969.

Shawver, Mary. *Sincerely, Mary S.* Casper, Wyo.: Prairie Publishing Co., n.d.

Sims, Orland L. *Cowpokes, Nesters, and So Forth.* Austin: Encino Press, 1970.

Smith, Clodus R.; Lloyd F. Portain; and James R. Champlin. *Rural Recreation for Profit.* Danville, Ill.: Interstate Printers & Publishers, 1968.

Smith, Cornelius C. *Tanque Verde: The Story of a Frontier Ranch.* [Tucson?]: no publisher, n.d. [1978?].

Smith, Lawrence B. *Dude Ranches and Ponies.* Introduction by Phillip Rollins and Larry Larom. New York: Coward-McCann, 1936.

Smythe, Pete. *Pete Smythe: Big City Dropout.* Boulder: Pruett Press, 1968.

Sonnichsen, C. L. *Cowboys and Cattle Kings: Life on the Range Today.* Norman: University of Oklahoma Press, 1950.

Swain, Donald C. *Wilderness Defender: Horace M. Albright and Conservation.* Chicago: University of Chicago Press, 1970.

Timmons, William. *Twilight on the Range: Recollections of a Latterday Cowboy.* Austin: University of Texas Press, 1962.

Tomlinson, Everett T. *Days and Deeds of '76.* New York: D. Appleton & Co., 1927.

Van Cleve, Spike. *40 Years' Gatherin's.* Kansas City: Lowell Press, 1977.

Vanderbilt, Cornelius, Jr. *Ranches and Ranch Life in America.* New York: Crown Publishers, 1968.

Wentworth, Harold, and Stuart Berg Flexner, comps. and eds. *Dictionary of American Slang.* New York: Crowell, 1960.

Westermeier, Clifford P. *Man, Beast, Dust: The Story of Rodeo.* Denver: World Press, Inc., 1947.

Wheeler, Burton K. with Paul F. Healy. *Yankee from the West: The candid, turbulent life story of the Yankee-born U.S. Senator from Montana.* New York: Octagon Books, 1977.

Wilson, Elinor. *Jim Beckwourth: Black Mountain Man and War Chief of the Crows.* Norman: University of Oklahoma Press, 1972.

Wister, Fanny Kemble, ed. *Owen Wister Out West: His Journals and Letters.* Chicago: University of Chicago Press, 1958.

Woon, Basil. *None of the Comforts of Home—But Oh, Those Cowboys!* Reno: Federated Features, 1967.

Yard, Robert Sterling. *The Book of the National Parks.* New York: Charles Scribner's Sons, 1928. (Originally published 1919.)

Webster's New World Dictionary of the American Language. Cleveland and New York: World Publishing Co., 1962. (College Edition)

Who Was Who in America. Vol. I. 1897–1942. Chicago: Marquis Co., 1943.

FICTION

Back, Joe. *The Sucker's Teeth.* Denver: Sage Books, 1965.

Hoopes, Gene. *End of the Trail.* San Antonio: Naylor Co., 1959.

————. *Tales of a Dude Wrangler.* San Antonio: Naylor Co., 1963.

Larom, Henry V. *Mountain Pony: A Story of the Wyoming Rockies.* New York: Grosset & Dunlap, 1946.

Lockhart, Caroline. *The Dude Wrangler.* Garden City, N.Y.: Doubleday, Page & Co., 1921.

Rinehart, Mary Roberts. *Lost Ecstasy.* New York: George H. Doran Co., 1927.

Santee, Ross. *The Bar X Golf Course.* Flagstaff: Northland Press, 1971. (Originally published 1933.)

Strang, Steve. *Dude Rancher: A Story of Modern Ranching.* New York: Dodd, Mead & Co., 1941.

Taylor, Rosemary. *Bar Nothing Ranch.* New York: McGraw-Hill Book Co., 1947.

Questionnaires

COLORADO RANCHES

Arapaho Valley Ranch	Granby
Bar Lazy J Guest Ranch	Parshall
Bar X Bar Ranch	Crawford
Beavers Guest Ranch	Winter Park
Black Mountain Ranch Resort	McCoy
C Lazy U Ranch	Granby
Colorado Trails Ranch	Durango
Coulter Lake Guest Ranch	Rifle
Deer Valley Ranch	Nathrop
Don K Ranch	Pueblo
Drowsy Water Ranch	Granby
Horseshoe Bend Guest Ranch	Meredith
Idlewild Guest Ranch and Lodge	Winter Park
Lake Mancos Ranch	Mancos
Lane Guest Ranch	Estes Park
Lazy H Ranch	Allenspark
Lost Valley Ranch	Sedalia
Neversummer Ranch	Grand Lake
Peaceful Valley Lodge and Guest Ranch	Lyons
Ragged Mountain Guest Ranch	Somerset
Rawah Ranch	Glendevey

7 W Guest Ranch	Gypsum
Singing River Ranch	Red Wing
Sitzmark Guest Ranch	Winter Park
Snowshoe Guest Ranch	Kremmling
Swiss Village Resort and Guest Ranch	Estes Park
Tumbling River Ranch	Grant
V C Lodge	Lake City

MONTANA RANCHES

Beartooth Ranch	Nye
Boulder River Ranch	McLeod
Cheff Guest Ranch	Charlo
Chief Mountain Guest Ranch	Babb
Circle Eight Ranch	Choteau
Diamond J Ranch	Ennis
Flathead Lake Lodge	Bigfork
G Bar M Ranch	Clyde Park
Lazy AC Ranch	Livingston
Lazy K Bar Ranch	Big Timber
Lion Head Ranch	Big Timber
Ox Yoke Ranch	Emigrant
Parade Rest Ranch	West Yellowstone
Seven Lazy P Guest Ranch	Choteau
63 Ranch	Livingston
Star Meadows Ranch	Whitefish
Thirty Three Bar Ranch	Seeley Lake
Tobacco Root Guest Ranch	Sheridan
White Tail Ranch	Ovando
X Bar A Ranch	McLeod

WYOMING RANCHES

Broken Arrow Ranch	Jackson
C M Ranch	Dubois
Crossed Sabres Ranch	Wapiti
The Boyer Ranch	Savery
Darwin Ranch	Jackson
Eatons' Ranch	Wolf
Fish Creek Ranch	Wilson
Flying L Skytel Ranch	Cody

Flying V Ranch	Kelly
Highland Meadows Ranch	Dubois
Rimrock Ranch	Cody
Seven D Ranch	Cody
Siggins Triangle X Ranch	Cody
Spear-O-Wigwam Ranch	Sheridan
Triangle X Ranch (Turner)	Moose
Valley Ranch	Valley

Interviews

CHARLES G. ROUNDY COLLECTION, BOX 2, WESTERN HISTORY RESEARCH CENTER, UNIVERSITY OF WYOMING

Anderson, Elizabeth, Ed.D. Moose, Wyoming, Tape 11, side 2, [March 1972.]

Buell, Miss Angela. Sheridan, Wyoming. Tape 4, side 1, March 28, 1972.

Chambers, Mr. and Mrs. Roy. Flying V Ranch, Kelly, Wyoming. Tape 15, May 20, 1972.

Duncan, Mrs. John B. (Dorothy). Sheridan, Wyoming. Tape 2, April 14, 1972.

Fales, Glen. Rimrock Dude Ranch, Cody, Wyoming. Tape 9, side 2, April 1, 1972.

Ferguson, Mr. and Mrs. Tom. Eatons' Ranch, Wolf, Wyoming. Tape 3, March 28, 1972.

Fordyce, Allen "Ike." Tepee Lodge, Big Horn, Wyoming. Tape 4, side 2, March 28, 1972.

Frost, Dick. Curator, Buffalo Bill Historical Center, Cody, Wyoming. Tape 6, side 2, and Tape 7, side 1, March 31, 1972.

Garlow, Fred. Cody, Wyoming. Tape 8, March 31, 1972.

Hayden, Mrs. Elizabeth. Jackson, Wyoming. Tape 13, May 19, 1972.

Larom, I. H. Valley Ranch, Valley, Wyoming. Tape 16, side 2, May 21, 1972.

Nelson, Mrs. Albert, Jr. Jackson, Wyoming. Tape 11, side 1, May 19, 1972.

Ritterbrown, Mrs. Alys. Dead Indian Ranch, Cody, Wyoming. Tape 7, side 2, n.d.

Schaffer, Peggy. Executive secretary, Dude Ranchers' Association. Tape 5, March 30, 1972.

Siggins, Mrs. Donald. Triangle X Ranch, Cody, Wyoming. Tape 6, March 31, 1972.

Siggins, Stanley. Triangle X Ranch, Cody, Wyoming. Tape 9, side 1, April 1, 1972.

Turner, Harold. Triangle X Ranch, [Jackson Hole, Wyoming]. Tape 12, [March 1972].

Wilson, Wendell. Teton Valley Ranch, Kelly, Wyoming. Tape 14, side 2, May 20, 1972.

AUTHOR'S INTERVIEWS

Bloder, J. W. Bloder Realty, Loveland, Colorado. July 25, 1973 (telephone).

Branch, Les. Executive director, Colorado Dude and Guest Ranch Association, Evergreen, Colorado. September 9, 1977, and May 20, 1981 (telephone).

Burden, Mrs. Sophie. Wickenburg, Arizona. June 8, 1981 (telephone).

Chappell, Dr. Gordon. Regional historian, National Park Service. October 16, 1980, in Kansas City, Missouri, and March 18, 1981 (San Francisco; telephone).

Devil's Thumb Ranch. Fraser, Colorado. June 8, 1981 (telephone).

Fales, Glen. Rimrock Ranch, Cody, Wyoming. July 22, 1981.

Ferguson, Mrs. Tom. Eatons' Ranch, Wolf, Wyoming. July 22, 1981.

Gant, Rusty. Rancho de los Caballeros, Wickenburg, Arizona. June 8, 1981 (telephone).

Gordon, Mrs. Cotton (JoAn). Tarryall Ranch, Lake George, Colorado. June 12, 1981 (telephone).

Hartman, Bob. Hacienda del Sol, Tucson, Arizona. June 11, 1981 (telephone).

Holzwarth, Johnnie. Neversummer Ranch, Grand Lake, Colorado. August 5, 1971, July 21, 1973, July 26 and 28, 1974, and June 4, 1980 (telephone).

Holzwarth, John, III. Grand Lake, Colorado. July 26, 1974, and September 24, 1977.

Krewson, Cecil. Snowshoe Guest Ranch, Kremmling, Colorado. July 24 and 25, 1979.

Marta, Mrs. Rich (Donna). Crossed Sabres Ranch, Cody, Wyoming. July 22, 1981.

Schaffer, Mrs. Peggy. Executive secretary, Dude Ranchers' Association, Two Bar Seven Ranch, Virginia Dale, Colorado. August 15, 1975, and May 20, 1981 (telephone).

Tempsky, Gordon von. Kahului, Maui, Hawaii. April 29, 1981 (telephone).

Thorne, Dr. and Mrs. Oakleigh, II. Valley Ranch, Valley, Wyoming. July 21, 1981.

True, Allen. White Stallion Ranch, Tucson, Arizona. June 8, 1981 (telephone).

Wright, Frank. Indian Peaks Stables, Granby, Colorado. July 3, 1982.

MISCELLANEOUS INTERVIEWS

Holzwarth, Johnnie. Holzwarth Homestead Cabins, Rocky Mountain National Park, Colorado. Several tapes, 1962–74.

Larom, I. H. By Dr. Harold McCracken, February 28, 1968. Archives, Buffalo Bill Historical Center, Cody, Wyoming.

Letters

STATE AND CITY AGENCIES

Diane Murphy, travel information officer, Alaska Division of Tourism, Juneau, 1975.

Don Hawking, travel development specialist, Office of Economic Planning and Development, Phoenix, Arizona, June 20, 1974.

Max Love, assistant travel director, Department of Parks and Tourism, Little Rock, Arkansas, September 3, 1974.

Wesley Catlin, California State Library, Sacramento, October 23, 1975.

Lloyd D. Howe, executive secretary, Department of Commerce and Development, Boise, Idaho, June 10, 1974.

George H. Mathews, travel director, Kansas Development of Economic Development, Topeka, June 12, 1974.

Lynne Albright, Travel Promotion Unit, Montana Department of Highways, Helena, December 11, 1974.

Miss Pat Brown, Travel and Tourism Division, Department of Economic Development, Lincoln, Nebraska, September 4, 1974.

Mary Myers, resort development representative, State of New Mexico, Department of Development, Santa Fe, June 12, 1974.

Loren L. Stadig, industrial development specialist, Business and Industrial Development Department, Bismarck, North Dakota, June 7, 1974.

Victor B. Fryer, travel information officer, Oregon State Highway Division, Salem, July 31, 1974.

Linda Hughes, Division of Tourism, Pierre, South Dakota, June 11, 1974.

Ben Holub, Jr., Texas Tourist Development Agency, Austin, June 11, 1974.

Lou Miller, secretary, Chamber of Commerce, Bandera, Texas, June 13, 1974.

Debbie Matlock, secretary, Chamber of Commerce, Bandera, Texas, June, 1981.

Tom Brown, publicity director, Utah Travel Council, Salt Lake City, June 17, 1974.

Gladine L. Loomis, information officer, Travel Development Division, Olympia, Washington, June 11, 1974.

Stan Morse, Lake Chelan Chamber of Commerce, Chelan, Washington, July 1974.

Mrs. Viola Deonigi, secretary-manager, Cle Elum Chamber of Commerce, Cle Elum, Washington, July 26, 1974.

Kay Hageman, manager, Chamber of Commerce, Ellensburg, Washington, July 18, 1974.

David C. Finstad, executive vice-president, Kent Chamber of Commerce, Kent, Washington, July 26, 1974.

Fred J. Horner, secretary, Chamber of Commerce, Okanogan, Washington, July 21, 1974.

Joelle Savenko, Visitor Promotion Division, Wenatchee Chamber of Commerce, Wenatchee, Washington, July 16, 1974.

S. A. MacDuff, president, Winthrop Chamber of Commerce, Winthrop, Washington, August 15, 1974.

Randall A. Wagner, assistant director, Wyoming Travel Commission, Cheyenne, June 10, 1974.

Sherry L. Smith, survey historian, Wyoming State Historic Preservation Office, Wyoming Recreation Commission, Cheyenne, April 8, 1981, and June 6, 1981.

MISCELLANEOUS LETTERS

Lloyd C. Ayres, associate dean and director, College of Agriculture, University of Wyoming, Laramie, July 18, 1974.

Ray Barry, reservations manager, Vermejo Park, Raton, New Mexico, June 10, 1981.

Carol Bergstrand, Vee Bar Ranch, Laramie, Wyoming, October 6, 1977.

Black Otter Guide Service, Pray, Montana, April 14, 1977.

Les Branch, executive secretary, Colorado Dude and Guest Ranch Association, Denver, March 1, 1978, and November 5, 1978.

Chuck and Phyl Broady, Bar Lazy J Guest Ranch, Parshall, Colorado, October and December, 1977.

Chester L. Brooks, superintendent, Rocky Mountain National Park and Shadow Mountain National Recreation Area, Estes Park, Colorado, October 21, 1977, December 7, 1977, and February 21, 1978.

Miss Angela Buell, Sedona, Arizona, December 1, 1976.

Bill Burk, vice-president, Public Relations, Athicson, Topeka & Santa Fe Railway, Chicago, Illinois, July 6, 1973.

Arthur H. Carhart, Escondido, California, October 27, 1977.

Dr. Gordon Chappell, regional historian, U.S. Department of the Interior, San Francisco, California, November 4, 1980, and June 10, 1981.

David Delo, Highland Meadow Ranch, Dubois, Wyoming, March 31, 1982.

Clyde S. Erskine, Sun City, Arizona, October 4, 1978.

H. Bob Fawcett, vice-president/manager, Previews, Inc., Denver, Colorado, August 5, 1975.

Nancy Ferguson, Eatons' Ranch, Wolf, Wyoming, May 5, 1981.

Gail I. Gardner, Prescott, Arizona, August 19, 1974, and September 23, 1974.

J. J. Glaze, assistant to general advertising manager, Union Pacific Railroad Company, Omaha, Nebraska, July 11, 1973, and September 7, 1973.

C. R. Goeldner, director, Business Research Division, Graduate School of Business Administration and College of Business, University of Colorado, Boulder, August 22, 1977.

W. D. Groundwater, advertising manager, United Air Lines, Chicago, Illinois, October 5, 1973.

Dwight L. Hamilton, chief park naturalist, Rocky Mountain National Park, Estes Park, Colorado, July 1, 1975, August 5, 1975, August 28, 1975, and September 16, 1975.

Robert Hartman, Hacienda del Sol, Tucson, Arizona, June 22, 1981.

Mrs. Elizabeth Hayden, Jackson, Wyoming, October 29, 1977.

Mrs. C. W. Hayes, Spring Valley, California, November 5, 1977.

Johnnie Holzwarth, Springfield, Colorado, November 10, 1977.

Bonnie Johnsey, office manager, Valley Ranch, Valley, Wyoming, January 17, 1978.

Thomas J. Judge, public relations representative, Chicago & Northwestern Railway, Chicago, Illinois, July 9, 1973.

Michael Kelly, librarian-archivist, Buffalo Bill Historical Center, Cody, Wyoming, May 10, 1981, August 24, 1981, November 13, 1981, January 21, 1982, and January 29, 1982.

Mrs. Bucky King, King Bros. Ranch, Sheridan, Wyoming, November 28, 1982.

Rich and Donna Marta, Crossed Sabres Ranch, Wapiti, Wyoming, July 11, 1980, and July 29, 1980.

Mrs. Joyce Maulis, Broomfield, Colorado, March 1, 1978, and July 5, 1979.

Rudy Menghini, Payson, Arizona, January 30, 1978, and July 4, 1979.

Mrs. Ernest Miller, Elkhorn Ranch, Gallatin Gateway, Montana, May 3, 1973, February 25, 1974, March 17, 1974, May 14, 1974, and June 29, 1977.

Howard W. Miller, Sr., Tucson, Arizona, [July 14, 1981].

Gary D. Morgan, district ranger, Forest Service, Sulphur Ranger District, Hot Sulphur Springs, Colorado, August 20, 1979, and September 27, 1979.

Neil Morgan, *Evening Tribune,* San Diego, California, May 21, 1974.

Jim Murphy, Ox Yoke Ranch, Emigrant, Montana, July 9, 1977; card, "in Memoriam," 1972; Christmas card, December 14, 1978.

Dorothy W. Newton, area manager, Continental Airlines, Denver, Colorado, October 4, 1973.

William G. Phelps, Public Relations Department, Southern Pacific Transportation Company, San Francisco, California, July 6, 1973.

Professor John F. Reiger, Department of History, University of Miami, Coral Gables, Florida, January 6, 1981.

Charles G. Roundy, executive director, Eastern Maine Development District, Bangor, Maine, August 30, 1977.

Mrs. Peggy Schaffer, Dude Ranchers' Association, Tie Siding, Wyoming, August 30, 1971, March 1, 1974, September 12, 1975, and January 5, 1976.

Phyllis M. Spragg, Wapiti, Wyoming, October 20, 1980.

Philip A. Stewart, acting assistant director, U.S. Department of the Interior, National Park Service, Washington, D.C., October 15, 1975.

Mr. L. Tass, Klondike Ranch, Buffalo, Wyoming, [1974].

Spike Van Cleve, Lazy K Bar Ranch, Big Timber, Montana, January 29, 1974, and August 14, 1981.

Gordon von Tempsky, general manager, Haleakala Motors, Kahului, Maui, Hawaii, July 16, 1979.

Frank Wright, Granby, Colorado, January 25, 1976, and December 1977.

Brochures, Flyers, Etc.

STATE AND CITY AGENCIES

"The Outdoor Guide of Alaska," Alaska Division of Tourism, Juneau, 1975.

"1973–1974 Directory of Guest Ranches and Ranch Resorts," Travel Information Section, Office of Economic Planning and Development, Phoenix, Arizona.

"Arizona Guest Ranches," Arizona Office of Tourism, Phoenix, 1981.

"Travel Directory Colorado," Colorado Visitors Bureau, Denver, 1967.

"Colorado Travel Directory," Colorado Visitors Bureau, Denver, 1970–71.

"Idaho Outfitters and Guides Association," Idaho Division of Economic and Community Affairs, Boise, 1981.

"Montana Outfitters and Dude Ranchers' Association," Montana Department of Highways, Travel Promotion Unit, Helena, n.d.

"Dude Ranch Vacation Directory," State of Montana, Department of Highways, Helena, 1981.

"Montana Outfitters and Guides Association," State of Montana, Department of Highways, Helena, 1981.

"Montana. The Original. Vacation & Information Guide," State of Montana, Department of Highways, Helena, 1981.

"Ranch/Farm Vacations," Travel and Tourism, Department of Economic Development, Lincoln, Nebraska, 1974.

"Guest Ranches," Department of Economic Development, Carson City, Nevada, [1974].

"Guests Ranches Mountain Lodges and Resorts in . . . New Mexico," New Mexico Department of Development, Santa Fe, [1971].

"New Mexico Resorts and Guest Ranches," Tourist Division, New Mexico Department of Development, Santa Fe, 1976.

"Guest Ranches and Resorts," State of New Mexico, Tourism and Travel Division, Commerce and Industry Department, Santa Fe, 1979.

"Dude Ranches in New York State," Department of Commerce, Albany, [1963].

"Roughrider Guide to North Dakota," North Dakota State Travel Division, Bismarck, 1974.

"Oregon Guest Ranches," Oregon State Highway Division, Travel Information Section, Salem, n.d.

"South Dakota Vacation Guide," South Dakota Division of Tourism, Pierre, 1974.

"Cowboy Capital of the World Bandera, Texas Guest Ranches," Chamber of Commerce, Bandera, [1981].

"Utah Package Tours '74," Utah Travel Council, Salt Lake City.

"Dude Ranches Resorts Big Wyoming," Wyoming Travel Commission, Cheyenne, 1973–75.

"Big Wyoming Accommodations," Wyoming Travel Commission, Cheyenne, 1981.

RAILROAD BROCHURES

Atchison Topeka & Santa Fe Railway. "Santa Fe News," October 15, 1965.

Chicago & Northwestern Railroad. "Black Hills of South Dakota 1941 All Expense 8-Day Tours."

Great Northern Railway. "Western Dude Ranch Vacations," [1947].

Northern Pacific Railway. "Dude Ranch Vacations," 1962.

Union Pacific Railroad. "Colorado," [1954].

———. "Dude Ranches Out West," [1956].

———. "Dude Ranches Out West," [1959].

AIRLINE BROCHURES

American Airlines. "Tucson, Arizona Ranch Resort Vacation," 1970–71.

Braniff Airlines. "Texas Ranch Resorts Braniff Style," 1973–74.

Consolidated Air Tours. "Big Wyoming Spectacular Wapiti Valley Guest Ranches," 1970.

Continental Airlines. "Colorado Continental Holidays 1969."

———. "Colorado Continental Holidays 1970."

———. "Colorado '81 Summer."

Frontier Airlines. "Fishing Vacation Excitement, '73."

———. "Frontierland Dude Ranch Vacations," n.d.

———. "Outdoor Vacation Excitement, '73."

———. "Sun Country Excitement, '73–74."

United Airlines. "1973 Vacations Colorado."

BROCHURES AND DOCUMENTS, DUDE RANCHERS' ASSOCIATION

"Dude Ranch Vacation directory, members Dude Ranchers' Association, 1981."

"Dude Ranch Vacation Directory 1982, Dude Ranchers' Association."

Letter from Dude Ranchers' Association announcing 1976 Annual Meeting in Bozeman, Montana. Fiftieth Anniversary Convention. November 18–20, 1976.

"A List of Western Ranches Accepting Guests," 1957, Dude Ranchers' Association, Billings, Montana.

Nickers: The Dude Ranchers' Association News, vol. 1 (March 1977).

"Notice from Dude Ranchers' Association," Granby, Colorado, [1979].

Post Convention Letter from President "Spike" Van Cleve, December 20, 1973.

"Ranch Vacations," [1960s], Dude Ranchers' Association, Billings, Montana.

"Resolutions of The Dude Ranchers' Association Adopted at the Annual Convention," December 1, 1973.

BROCHURES AND DOCUMENTS, THE COLORADO DUDE AND
GUEST RANCH ASSOCIATION

"Colorado's 1971 Dude Ranch Vacations."

"Colorado's 1973 Dude Ranch Vacations."

"Colorado's 1974 Dude Ranches."

"Colorado Ranch Vacations, 1876–1976."

"1978 Colorado Dude Ranches."

"1981 Colorado Dude Ranches."

"Qualifications for Active Membership in the Colorado Dude and Guest Ranch Association," [1978].

RANCH BROCHURES AND FLYERS

Arizona

Brave Bull Ranch Resort	Tucson
Cochise Lodge and Guest Ranch	Elfrida
Dancing Apache Guest Ranch	Sedona
Flying E Ranch	Wickenburg
Hacienda del Sol	Tucson
Kohl's Ranch	Payson
Lazy K Bar Guest Ranch	Tucson
Price Canyon Ranch	Douglas
Rancho de la Osa	Sasabe
Rancho de los Caballeros	Wickenburg
Rex Ranch	Amado
Saguaro Lake Ranch Resort	Mesa
South Fork Guest Ranch	Springerville
Sunglow Mission Ranch	Pearce
Wild Horse Ranch Club	Tucson
White Stallion Ranch	Tucson
Wickenburg Inn Tennis and Guest Ranch	Wickenburg

Colorado

Arapaho Valley Ranch	Granby
Aspen Lodge & Guest Ranch	Estes Park
Bar Lazy J Guest Ranch	Parshall
Bar X Bar Ranch	Crawford
Beavers Guest Ranch	Winter Park
Black Mountain Ranch	McCoy
Cherry Creek Guest Ranch	Mancos
C Lazy U Ranch	Granby
Colorado Trails Ranch	Durango
Coulter Lake Guest Ranch	Rifle
Deer Valley Ranch	Nathrop
Devil's Thumb Ranch	Fraser
Don K Ranch	Pueblo
Double JK Ranch	Estes Park
Drowsy Water Ranch	Granby
Elk Mountain Ranch	Evergreen

Focus Ranch	Slater
Futurity Lodge	Nathrop
Hamilton's Rainbow Trout Lodges	Antonito
Harmel's Ranch Resort	Gunnison
Hi Country Stables	Estes Park
The Home Ranch	Clark
Horseshoe Bend Guest Ranch	Meredith
Holzwarth's Neversummer Ranch	Grand Lake
Idlewild Guest Ranch	Winter Park
Indian Head Ranch	Estes Park
Lake Mancos Ranch	Mancos
Lazy H Ranch	Allenspark
Long's Peak Inn and Guest Ranch	Estes Park
Lost Valley Ranch	Sedalia
M-M Lodge	Gould
McGraw Guest Ranch	Estes Park
Paradise Ranch	Woodland Park
Peaceful Valley Lodge and Guest Ranch	Lyons
Powderhorn Guest Ranch	Powderhorn
Rawah Guest Ranch	Glendevey
Ripple Creek Lodge	Meeker
San Juan Ranch	Ridgway
7 W Ranch	Gypsum
Sitzmark Guest Ranch	Winter Park
Snowshoe Guest Ranch	Kremmling
Sombrero Ranch Riding Stables	Grand Lake
"Stupid Charlie" Guest Ranch	Mancos
Sun Valley Guest Ranch	Grand Lake
Swiss Village	Estes Park
Sylvan Dale Ranch	Loveland
Tarryall River Ranch	Lake George
Triple 'B' Ranch	Woodland Park
Tumbling River Ranch	Grant
Vista Verde Guest Ranch	Steamboat Springs
Waunita Hot Springs Ranch	Gunnison
Wilderness Trails Ranch	Bayfield
Winding River Guest Ranch	Grand Lake
Wind River Ranch	Estes Park

Idaho

Garden Valley Ranch	Garden Valley
Perkins Ranch	Ola
Robinson Bar Ranch	Clayton
Timber Ridge Ranch	Harrison

Montana

Black Otter Guide Service	Pray
Boulder River Ranch	McLeod
Canyon Creek Ranch	Melrose
Cheff Ranch	Charlo
Circle Eight Ranch	Choteau
Double Arrow Wilderness Outfitters	Seeley Lake
Elkhorn Ranch	Gallatin Gateway
Flathorn Lake Lodge Quarter Circle LA Dude Ranch	Bigfork
G Bar M Ranch	Livingston
Holland Lake Lodge	Seeley Lake
JJJ Ranch	Augusta
Lakeview Ranch	Lima
Lazy K Bar Ranch	Big Timber
Lion Head Ranch	Big Timber
Lone Mountain Ranch	Big Sky
Montana Sports Ranch	Cordon
Rising Sun Guest Ranch	Emigrant
Rocking J Ranch	Park City
Silver Spur Dude Ranch	Roundup
63 Ranch	Livingston
Stillwater Valley Ranch	Nye
Star Meadows Ranch	Whitefish
Tobacco Root Guest Ranch	Sheridan
White Tail Ranch	Ovando

New Mexico

Bar X Bar Ranch	Pecos
Bear Mountain Guest Ranch	Silver City
Berry Guest Ranch	Raton
Bishop's Lodge	Santa Fe
Bitter Creek Guest Ranch	Red River
Chama Land and Cattle Company	Chama

El Vado Ranch	Tierra Amarilla
Finley's La Junta Guest Ranch	Alto
High Country Lodge	Alto
Inn of the Mountain Gods	Mescalero
Lobo Lodge	Chama
Moreno Ranch	Eagle Nest
Rancho Encantado	Santa Fe
River Ranch	Red River
Singing River Ranch	Questa
Surprise Valley Ranch	Sapello
Tres Lagunas Guest Ranch	Pecos
Vermejo Park	Raton

Oregon

Baker's Bar-M Ranch	Adams
Flying Arrow Resort	Joseph
Flying M Ranch	Yamhill
Red's Wallowa Horse Ranch	Joseph
Rock Springs Guest Ranch	Bend

Texas

Circle R Resort Ranch	Medina
Dixie Dude Ranch	Bandera
Flying L Ranch	Bandera
Lost Valley Resort Ranch	Bandera
Mayan Dude Ranch	Bandera
Montague Ranch Resort	Bandera
Peaceful Valley Ranch	Bandera
Silver Spur Ranch	Bandera
Twin Elm Guest Ranch	Bandera
Whispering Winds Guest Ranch	Bandera

Washington

Bar 41 Ranch	Wilbur
Hidden Valley Guest Ranch	Cle Elum
Sun Mountain Lodge	Winthrop

Wyoming

Bill Cody's Ranch Inn	Cody
Bitterroot Ranch	Dubois
Boulder Lake Ranch	Pinedale

Box K Ranch	Moran
Box R Ranch	Cora
Circle H Ranch	Wapiti
Crossed Sabres Ranch	Wapiti
Darwin Ranch	Jackson
Dead Indian Ranch	Sunlight Basin
Deer Forks Ranch	Douglas
Diamond Guest Ranch	Chugwater
Eatons' Ranch	Wolf
Elephant Head Lodge	Wapiti
Fir Creek Ranch	Moran
Flying Skytel Ranch	Cody
Flying U Ranch	Cora
Flying V Ranch	Kelly
Green River Guest Ranch	Cora
Grizzly Ranch	Cody
Heart Six Ranch	Moran
HF Bar Ranch	Saddlestring
Hidden Valley Ranch	Cody
Highland Meadow Ranch	Dubois
Hunter Peak Ranch	Cody
K Bar Z Ranch	Cody
Lava Creek Ranch	Dubois
Lazy L and B Ranch	Dubois
Lost Creek Ranch	Moose
Medicine Bow Lodge & Guest Ranch	Saratoga
Moore Ranch	Encampment
Moose Head Ranch	Moose
Ram's Horn Guest Ranch	Dubois
Rimrock Dude Ranch	Cody
R Lazy S Ranch	Jackson Hole
Spear-O-Wigwam Ranch	Sheridan
Spotted Horse Ranch	Jackson Hole
Sweetwater Gap Ranch	Rock Springs
Triangle C Ranch	Dubois
Vee Bar Ranch	Laramie
White Grass Ranch	Moose
Wind River Ranch	Dubois

Other States

Scott Valley Dude Ranch	Mountain Home, Arkansas
Double H Guest Ranch	Brevort, Michigan
Double J Resort, Jack and Jill Ranch	Rothbury, Michigan
Loretta Lynn's Dude Ranch	Hurricane Mills, Tennessee
Pack Creek Ranch	Moab, Utah

MISCELLANEOUS BROCHURES

Adventure Guides, Inc., New York, New York.

Central Wyoming College, Riverton, Wyoming.

Guest Ranch Reservation Service, Los Angeles, California.

Mohn, Lynn. "Walk with the Pioneers: Kawuneeche Valley Living History Program." Rocky Mountain Nature Association, Inc., 1976.

Ohio Farm and Rural Vacation Association, Zanesfield, Ohio.

Previews, Incorporated, Denver, Colorado.

Wilderness Guides and Packers School, Jackson, Wyoming.

Miscellaneous Sources

Borne, Lawrence R. *Welcome to My West: I. H. Larom: Dude Rancher, Conservationist, Collector.* Cody, Wyo.: Buffalo Bill Historical Center, 1982.

Foglesong, Scott. "Frank Wright: A Man and His Mountains, A Multi-Image Presentation," n.d.

Gardner, Gail I. *Orejana Bull for Cowboys Only.* Wickenburg, Ariz.: Desert Caballeros, 1950.

Haslanger, Ann C. A *History of Vermejo Park.* Vermejo Park, N.M.: Vermejo Park, 1980.

McWilliams, Esther. *Eaton's Ranch.* Wolf, Wyo.: n.p., 1981.

"Ranch Country, U.S.A." Film produced by Colorado Dude and Guest Ranch Association, Summit Films Production, Vail, Colo., and Jackson Hole, Wyo., n.d.

Index